JEFFERSON COUNTY RURAL LIBRARY DISTRICT

3 3522 00133 0830

W9-BRM-234

JEFFERSON COUNTY LIBRARY
620 Cedar Avenue
Port Hadlock, WA 98339
(360) 385-6544   www.jclibrary.info

DATE DUE

JUN 17 2009	
JUL 28 2009	
MAY 17 2012	
JUN 16 2012	
DEC 22 2012	
APR 25 2016	
JUL 28 2016	
OCT 29	29

DISCARD

DEMCO, INC. 38-2971

THE NATURE COMPANIONS
BACKYARD BIRDING

THE NATURE COMPANIONS
BACKYARD BIRDING

JOHN KADEL BORING, JOSEPH FORSHAW,
ERICA GLASENER, STEVE HOWELL, GLENN KEATOR,
JIM KNOPF, TERENCE LINDSEY, JANE SCOTT,
RICH STALLCUP, SALLY WASOWSKI

CONSULTANT EDITORS
TERENCE LINDSEY
RG TURNER JR

FOG CITY PRESS

598
B AC

Jefferson County Library
P.O. Box 990/620 Cedar Ave.
Port Hadlock, WA 98339
(360) 385-6544
www.jclibrary.info

Published by Fog City Press
814 Montgomery Street
San Francisco, CA 94133 USA

Copyright © 2002 Weldon Owen Pty Ltd

CHIEF EXECUTIVE OFFICER: John Owen
PRESIDENT: Terry Newell
PUBLISHER: Lynn Humphries
MANAGING EDITOR: Janine Flew
ART DIRECTOR: Kylie Mulquin
EDITORIAL COORDINATOR: Tracey Gibson
PRODUCTION MANAGER: Martha Malic-Chavez
BUSINESS MANAGER: Emily Jahn
VICE PRESIDENT INTERNATIONAL SALES: Stuart Laurence

PROJECT EDITORS: Scott Forbes, Julia Cain, Dawn Titmus
COPY EDITORS: Glenda Downing, Gillian Hewitt
EDITORIAL ASSITANTS: Greg Hassall, Vesna Radojcic
PROJECT ART DIRECTOR: Hilda Mendham
PROJECT DESIGNERS: Stephanie Cannon, Gabrielle Tydd
PICTURE RESEARCH: Connie Komack, Pictures & Words, Rockport,
Massachusetts; Terence Lindsey; Gillian Manning

All rights reserved. Unauthorized reproduction,
in any manner, is prohibited.
A catalog record for this book is available from
the Library of Congress, Washington, D.C.

ISBN 1 876778 90 3

Color reproduction by Colourscan Co Pte Ltd
Printed by Kyodo Printing Co (S'pore) Pte Ltd
Printed in Singapore

10 9 8 7 6 5 4

A Weldon Owen Production

Nature—wild nature—dwells in gardens just as she dwells in the tangled woods, in the deeps of the sea, and on the heights of the mountains; and the wilder the garden, the more you will see of her there.

Adventures in Green Places,
HERBERT RAVENEL SASS (1884–1958), American nature writer

CONTENTS

INTRODUCTION

In an age of environmental crisis, people tend to lose sight of the fact that not everything we do to the land is bad for the plants, animals, and birds with which we share it. Most of us automatically assume that the best we can do in nature is the least: to leave the land alone. Yet, as many a gardener has observed, it is possible to make changes in the land that actually contribute to its ecological health—that add to the abundance and diversity of life in a place.

Natural gardening is the name of a method, and a rapidly growing movement, that aims to enhance the ecological well-being of the places where we live, and which we share with birds. This can mean many things: overthrowing the tyranny of the American lawn in your front-yard; planting a wildflower meadow; digging a pond; creating nesting boxes; providing flora that will attract the local fauna; or restoring native plants to a place from which they've vanished. Your garden can become a sanctuary.

Why do we care so much for birds? Of all the creatures in the world, birds share our perceptual space the most. They sing and call at frequencies most of us can hear, and they display colors and behaviors that we can easily see and enjoy. Thus, we are able to identify with birds and share in their lives to a greater extent than we can with most of the other creatures with which we share our planet.

Backyard Birding is your guide to the world of birds that surrounds us in our own gardens. Read it through at least once for an excellent introduction to the delightful and complementary pastimes of gardening and birding. Refer to it again and again to learn more about what you observe outdoors, and the wildlife that surrounds you.

In a world that seems so very puzzling is it any wonder birds have such appeal? Birds are, perhaps, the most eloquent expression of reality.

ROGER TORY PETERSON (b. 1908),
American ornithologist

CHAPTER ONE

UNDERSTANDING BIRDS

THE WORLD *of* BIRDS

Step out of your door, almost anywhere in the world, and,

within minutes, you will see birds of one kind or another.

Dark-eyed
Junco

Birds are among the most mobile of all animals. There are other animals that roam widely, but birds alone can, at least in principle, go anywhere they please on the earth's surface.

Although most numerous in marshes, woodlands, and rainforests, birds inhabit the most inhospitable of deserts, and have been seen within a few miles of both poles. Some never stray from home in their entire lives, but others can, and frequently do, span entire oceans or continents, sometimes in a single flight.

There are about 9,300 species of birds in the world, and they range from the tiny Bee Hummingbird, which weighs little more than a dime, to the imposing Ostrich, which stands taller than a man and weighs over 300 pounds (136 kg). Among these species can be found almost any color of the rainbow. These colors may be arranged in the dazzling patterns found in breeding peacocks or in the astonishingly effective camouflage of birds such as the Tawny Frogmouth, which evades predators by imitating a dead tree stump.

Some birds hover on the brink of extinction; on the other hand, there are far more domestic chickens on earth than humans.

Golden-plovers, taking off with a load of fuel almost equal to their own weight, fly nonstop from Alaska to Hawaii and back each year, while Peregrine Falcons reach speeds approaching 200 miles (320 km) per hour as they dive upon their winged prey. In contrast to these masters of the air, there are a few birds —the Ostrich, for example— that cannot fly at all.

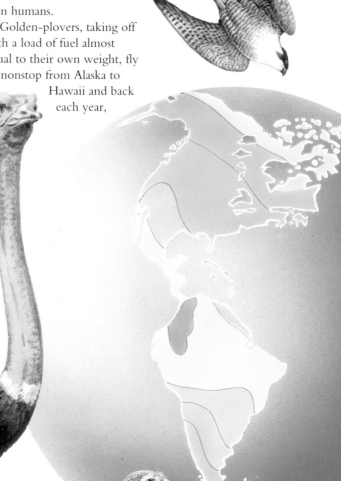

Peregrine
Falcon

Ostrich

Tawny
Frogmouth

Anna's Hummingbird

Resplendent
Quetzal

Gray-headed
Albatross

The maps on these pages show how species
density varies around the world. Tropical
rainforests have most species, polar icecaps
least. Note that most mainly temperate areas,
such as North America, Europe, and Australia,
have roughly similar numbers of species.

☐ 50 or less species   ☐ 500–1,000 species
☐ 50–250 species   ☐ 1,000–1,500 species
☐ 250–500 species   ☐ over 1,500 species

Peacock

Cockerel

BIRDS, REAL *and* IMAGINARY

From the Phoenix rising from the ashes to the sacred Garuda, king of the birds,

from the dove of peace to the bluebird of happiness, birds real and imaginary

have featured prominently in the human imagination.

THE ROC *One of the oldest and most widespread bird myths concerns this giant bird that feeds on elephants. In this scene from* The Arabian Nights *(left), merchants pull a roc chick from its egg.*

It is, perhaps, not surprising that birds, being among the most easily observed of all animals, have captured the human imagination. Their attributes and habits have proved a rich source of inspiration to us since prehistoric times.

Bird song, for example, has inspired some of the finest poetry in the English language, and for centuries the power of flight was the envy of humankind.

Throughout history, birds have been used to symbolize particular qualities and states: the wise owl, the dove of peace, the bluebird of happiness, and so on. And deep in our past lurk myths and legends about birds, some of uncertain origin.

CLASSICAL MYTHS

One of the most enduring of bird myths is that of the Phoenix. This legendary bird was well known to Greek and Roman scholars more than 2,000 years ago, and elements of its story can be traced to the ancient Egyptians, several thousand years earlier.

In most legends, the Phoenix is a bird of great beauty that lives for 500 or 600 years in the Arabian desert. It then burns itself to ashes on a funeral pyre, from which it emerges with renewed youth.

Through the Dark Ages, this story was commonly used as a metaphor for the resurrection of Christ, and there are many references to the Phoenix in literature. The Phoenix is still referred to

today, to symbolize a new structure or idea arising from the ruins or ashes of its predecessor.

Another story of uncertain origin is the Greek myth of the halcyon. This bird, often associated with the kingfisher, floated its nest on the open sea. Aeolus, god of the winds, decreed that all storms must cease while the halcyon's young were reared. This fable gave rise to the expression "halcyon days", which is used to describe any interlude of peace and serenity.

Now I will believe…

that in Arabia,

There is one tree, the

phoenix' throne,

one phoenix, At this

time reigning there.

The Tempest,
WILLIAM SHAKESPEARE (1564–1616),
English playwright

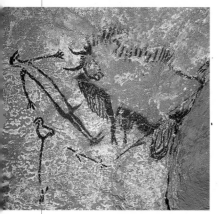

BIRD-MAN *One of the earliest images of a bird—dating from over 15,000 years ago—is to be found in the Lascaux caves in France. It depicts a bison, a bird, and what seems to be a bird-headed human.*

SYMBOL OF POWER

Few birds have impressed humankind as much as the eagle. Its powerful flight was noted in The Song of Solomon, and an eagle was the emblem of the Babylonian god Ashur. An eagle adorned the scepter of Zeus, supreme god of the ancient Greeks.

In Hindu mythology, it was an eagle that brought to humankind the sacred drink soma, and in the old Norse sagas, Odin, king of the Gods, often took the form of an eagle. The warbonnets of American Plains Indians were dressed only with eagle feathers. The double-headed eagle was a common Byzantine motif, and eagles were adopted as imperial symbols by a number of nations, including Austria, Germany, Poland, and Russia.

Today an eagle occurs on the Mexican coat of arms and is the national symbol of the United States of America.

EASTERN LEGENDS

Myths involving birds of supernatural proportions are common around the world. One of the most monstrous of all birds, real or imaginary, is Garuda, sacred to the Hindu god Vishnu, preserver of the world. King of birds and herald of storms, Garuda is a huge winged monster that feeds on snakes. Its image can be seen wherever the Hindu religion has spread, and has been adopted as the symbol of Indonesia's national airline.

The roc, or rukh, entered Western folklore from a fifteenth-century collection of Arabian tales called *The Arabian Nights*. The central character, Sinbad the Sailor, is wrecked on an island in the Indian Ocean, where he encounters a bird so enormous that it feeds its young on elephants.

An almost identical story is found in ancient Chinese literature, and the bird was even mentioned by Marco Polo, who recorded that a roc's feather was presented to the Mongul ruler Genghis Khan.

AMERICAN MYTHS

Most of the native peoples of North and South America have myths of monstrous birds. The Thunderbird, for example, is an eagle-like bird so huge that lightning flashes when it blinks and

MYTHICAL BIRDS *The Hindu god Garuda (top); and the Thunderbird of Native American legend (right), depicted as part of a totem pole.*

SELF-SACRIFICE *A pelican feeding its young on its own blood, in a woodcut from Ulisse Aldrovandi's Ornithologiae (1559–1603).*

Ornithologiæ. Lib. X I X.   47
Pelicanus Pictorum & vulgi.

thunder rolls at the slightest movement of its wings. This fabulous bird is known to the Athapascans, Inuit, and Hopi among others. According to the Tlingit tribe, of the Pacific Northwest, it carries a lake of water in the hollow of its back that, spilling out as it flies, produces torrents of rain.

MYTHICAL QUALITIES

Alongside stories of imaginary birds, legends relating to real birds have been common too.

In ancient China, the pheasant was regarded as a symbol of harmony and heaven's favor. The "love-pheasant" was, in fact, one of the four chief supernatural creatures of Chinese mythology, ranking equally with the tortoise, the unicorn, and the dragon.

In medieval Europe, it was widely believed that the pelican fed its young on its own blood, and the bird became a common symbol of Christian piety.

Today, among Aboriginal people in Australia, the Willie-wagtail, a small song-bird, is widely regarded as a tattler. It is said to hang around the mens' councils picking up secrets that it then carries to the women.

In many countries in Europe, the wood-pecker is believed to call up rain.

THE ORIGINS *of* BIRDS

Contrasting markedly with our comprehensive knowledge of living birds is our tentative, piecemeal understanding of their origins.

Birds are poorly represented in fossil deposits for a variety of reasons. Bird bones are fragile and many are hollow, so they are easily broken and fragmented. In addition, few landbirds die where their remains can be buried in waterlaid sediments, the richest source of fossils. It also seems likely that many ancient birds, like birds today, were preyed upon by carnivorous animals.

IMAGES IN STONE *Both nature and humankind have created images of birds in stone. This Egyptian carving (left) dates from the eighth century.*

It has been estimated that between the time of *Archaeopteryx*, the earliest known bird, and the present, between 1.5 million and 2 million species of bird have existed. Of these, we have specimen evidence for the existence of fewer than 12,000 species!

"FEATHERED DINOSAURS"

The exact origins of birds are still uncertain, but it has long been thought that they evolved from reptiles. One popular theory links birds to a specific subgroup of dinosaurs called theropods, which were common approximately 200 million years ago.

THE EARLIEST KNOWN BIRD

In the Jurassic cycad forests of Europe, about 150 million years ago, a group of dinosaurs was browsing on plants along the shoreline of a Bavarian lake, while in the taller vegetation strange bird-like creatures were clambering among the branches and fluttering from tree to tree. Perhaps in a frantic effort to escape capture by an arboreal predator, one of these creatures lost its balance and fell into shallow waters at the lake's edge, where it drowned and sank into sedimentary silt.

Some time in the first part of the nineteenth century, a worker in a quarry near Solnhofen, in Bavaria, Germany, found a fossilized feather. Then, in 1861, in the same quarry, the incomplete fossilized skeleton of the bird-like creature was found. German paleontologist Hermann von Meyer examined these remains and made a formal description of them, naming this earliest known fossil bird *Archaeopteryx lithographica*.

FOSSILS *(above) have provided us with a fairly clear idea of what Archaeopteryx must have looked like (above right).*

Archaeopteryx provided what is still the most important evidence of the link between birds and dinosaurs. *Archaeopteryx* was certainly a bird, as it clearly possessed feathers and a U-shaped "wishbone", but it also had prominent reptilian characteristics, including teeth and clawed digits on the forewing.

About the size of a crow, *Archaeopteryx* was a predator, and probably caught insects or small vertebrates, such as lizards. Recently, there has been much debate about its flight capabilities, and whether it was terrestrial or arboreal in its habits. Some authors claim that it would have been a weak flier, while others argue that it would have been capable of sustained flight.

HESPERORNIS, *a flightless fish-eating bird, first appeared over 100 million years ago during the Cretaceous period. Many present-day waterbirds, including the pelican (below right), have their origins in this era of prehistory.*

An important piece of evidence for this link is a U-shaped furcula or "wishbone" found both in birds and in some theropods. In birds, this feature plays an important role in flight. In the dinosaurs it probably evolved as a support for the short forelimbs that they used for catching prey.

CRETACEOUS BIRDS

Though only slightly younger than *Archaeopteryx*, birds of the early Cretaceous period (about 130 million years ago) were much more like modern birds. Most were undoubtedly strong fliers.

Probably the most famous of the many Cretaceous fossil birds are *Hesperornis* and *Ichthyornis* from North America. Both are notable in that they possessed teeth, a primitive condition prominent in *Archaeopteryx* and its theropod ancestors. *Hesperornis* was a flightless, fish-eating, diving-bird, whereas *Ichthyornis* was a strong flier.

THE PLEISTOCENE EPOCH

Fossils of the Pleistocene epoch (2 million to 10,000 years ago) include many species that are alive today, as well as numerous species that are now extinct.

A rich source of these fossils are the Rancho La Brea tarpits in California. These have yielded specimens of birds like the *Teratornis*, which used its 12½-foot (3.8-m) wingspan to soar across the skies of North America.

MODERN BIRDS

Present-day birds really are not so "modern", since most of the species we know today have been around for thousands of years. Indeed, about 11,500 species probably occurred during the Pleistocene—approximately 1,500 more species than exist today. Bird species probably reached a peak from 250,000 to 500,000 years ago, and have been in gradual decline ever since.

In times prehistoric, 'tis easily proved… That birds and not gods were the rulers of men.

The Birds,
ARISTOPHANES (c. 448–380 BC),
Greek dramatist

TERATORNIS *Many fossils of this large, vulture-like predator that lived in western North America in the Pleistocene epoch have been found in the Rancho La Brea tarpits in California.*

NAMING *the* BIRDS

The spectacular diversity of birds is a delight, but it presents us with the challenge of establishing which birds are related and how best to classify them.

The science of classifying living things is called taxonomy. Early taxonomists based their classifications of birds almost entirely on external appearances, in the way that a child might organize building blocks according to size, shape, and color. These methods frequently resulted in birds that were not related being linked and some that were related being kept apart.

Advances in scientific procedures have led to new techniques being applied to determining alliances between kinds of bird, and the systems of classification have become increasingly sophisticated. Taxonomy now draws on a synthesis of data from many fields of biology, including paleontology, ecology, physiology, behavior, and DNA and protein analysis.

SYMBOLS AS NAMES *The ancient Egyptians used several birds in their system of hieroglyphics. The falcon (left), for example, represented the god Horus, personal god of the ruling pharaoh.*

THE SPECIES CONCEPT

The keystone of modern taxonomy (and the focus of bird identification) is the species. A species is defined as a population whose members do not freely interbreed with members of other neighboring populations (although this is sometimes difficult to establish one way or the other).

Within a species, there are often groups or populations which differ in minor ways, such as in size or plumage coloration. These interbreeding groups are recognized as subspecies or races. Populations separated by geographical barriers (such as mountain ranges and oceans) are also known as isolates.

HIGHER CATEGORIES

All birds are related to some extent and the practice and procedures of taxonomy operate to establish different levels of relationship. Above species level, related species are grouped into genera, related genera are grouped into families, and related families into orders. Some intermediate categories are used by taxonomists to express fine distinctions, but these need not concern the beginning birder.

Together, birds form a class, Aves, and, along with other classes of backboned animals, this class is part of the Subphylum Vertebrata (the vertebrates) and the Animal Kingdom.

WHAT'S IN A NAME?

Most animal species have a common name—the English name in English-speaking countries—and a scientific name. The latter consists of two main elements: the genus and the specific name. Where there are subspecies, the subspecies name is sometimes included as a third element.

The scientific name is latinized and highlighted in a different type (normally italic). Only the generic name is capitalized.

FAMILY TIES *The close relationship between the three bluebird species—Mountain Bluebird (left), Eastern Bluebird (above right), and Western Bluebird (far left) is described taxonomically by their inclusion in the genus Sialis. The American Robin (opposite), on the other hand, is obviously related, yet not closely enough to share the same genus. It belongs to the genus Turdus. Both genera are members of the family Turdidae.*

CAROLUS LINNAEUS

The system of biological nomenclature used today was devised by the Swedish botanist, Carolus Linnaeus (1707–78).

Linnaeus was born in South Rashult in Sweden. From an early age, he loved plants, and this led him to a career in botany. In the course of his studies, he became aware that every organism needed to have a unique scientific name that could be used and understood by people of all nationalities. He therefore developed a system using Latin names, Latin being the language used by scholars throughout Europe at the time. This system, still referred to today as the Linnaean system, was presented to the scientific community in the *Systema Naturae*, published in 1735.

In 1741, Linnaeus was appointed to the chair of medicine at Uppsala University, but in the following year he exchanged this for the chair of botany. In 1761, he was granted a patent of nobility, becoming

Carl von Linné. During his lifetime, Linnaeus published more than 180 works. It was in editions of the *Systema Naturae* that many species of birds were first formally named.

The purpose of scientific names is to provide an internationally recognizable system of classification. A single species' common name may vary between languages and countries, but its scientific name will always be the same. Conversely, one or more birds may have the same common name in different countries but not be related at all. For example, we often talk about "robins" in America, but the "robins" of the UK and Australia are quite different birds. Use of the scientific name eliminates any confusion.

THE CODE OF LIVING THINGS

A computer simulation of the structure of DNA (below), showing its intricate double-spiral structure.

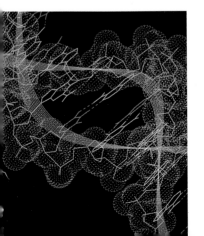

DNA CLASSIFICATION
Recent work in the field of biochemical research, especially analyses of DNA (deoxyribonucleic acid)—the essential genetic material— has proved a powerful tool in clarifying the relationships of birds.

Pioneered by Charles Sibley and Jon Ahlquist at Yale University, this research started out using protein material from blood and egg-white for analysis. It has now reached the point where the scientists are able to examine the DNA itself and measure relatedness in an extraordinarily precise manner.

Some fascinating results have emerged from these studies, and Sibley and Ahlquist's findings have allowed researchers to resolve a number of long-standing uncertainties in the field of taxonomy.

CLASSIFYING THE ROBIN

The purposes of taxonomy are twofold: to assign a unique name to each species and to place it within a structure of relationships. The American Robin, for example, is classified in the following way:

- Class Aves
- Order Passeriformes
- Family Turdidae
- Genus *Turdus*
- Species *migratorius*

Subspecies may also be named. Robins breeding in Texas, for example, are identified as *Turdus migratorius achrusterus*.

BIRD ANATOMY

Despite their external diversity, birds are remarkably uniform

in basic structure. This similarity results chiefly

from adaptations associated with flight.

Birds are the only living things with feathers. Also, they are vertebrates, which means that, just like reptiles, amphibians, fish, and mammals (including ourselves), they have a jointed internal skeleton with two forelimbs and two hindlimbs; the brain is encased in a strong bony container (the skull); and the main nerve route in the body is carried down the center of the back inside a flexible column of bones (the spine).

If you compare the skeleton, muscle, and organ systems of a bird with those of a human, you will find many points of similarity. Broadly speaking, the same basic elements—eyes, ears, skull, ribs, lungs, heart, and so on— are found in corresponding places in both and serve comparable functions.

SKELETAL SYSTEM

Almost all of the differences between human and bird skeletons are the result of profound modifications in birds to enable sustained flight. The sternum, or breastbone, for example, lies in the same relative position and serves the same basic function as the sternum in our own bodies. However, in birds it is much bigger in relative terms and bears,

skull

radius

furcula (half of "wishbone")

carpometacarpus

synsacrum

pygostyle

femur

ulna (attachment of secondaries)

keel of sternum

tibiotarsus

tarsus

HOLLOW BONES *Many of the larger bones in a bird's skeleton are thin-walled and hollow, to minimize weight, but intricately braced and strutted inside, to maximize strength.*

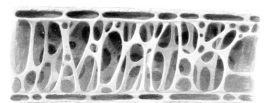

FORMED FOR FLIGHT *A Northern Harrier (top left) soars through the open skies. The skeleton of a bird (above) could be described as a typical vertebrate skeleton that has undergone significant modification to support powered flight.*

projecting at right angles, the most obvious and distinctive of avian skeletal structures: a large flat keel (called the carina). This serves as a point of attachment for the huge pectoral muscles used to flap the wings.

Another unique feature of the avian skeleton is that in many birds the collarbones have fused to form a rigid brace for the wings: the furcula or "wishbone".

ORGAN SYSTEMS

The organ systems, too, are comparable to those of other vertebrates but are heavily modified to service the needs of powered flight. In particular, they support a far higher metabolism than that of most other animals. The large size of a bird's heart is an indication of this.

Birds have a highly specialized and remarkably efficient respiratory system. A multitude of empty spaces (called pulmonary sacs or air sacs) extend throughout the body, in

NEVER OUT OF BREATH *The net result of a bird's sophisticated respiratory system (below) is that air flows through the bird's lungs, rather than in-and-out as in humans and other animals.*

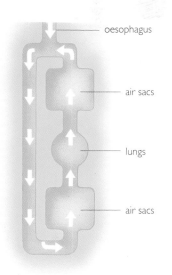

— oesophagus

— air sacs

— lungs

— air sacs

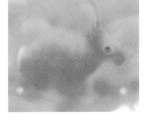

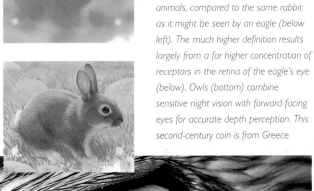

KEEN EYESIGHT *An image of a rabbit (left), as it might be seen by most animals, compared to the same rabbit as it might be seen by an eagle (below left). The much higher definition results largely from a far higher concentration of receptors in the retina of the eagle's eye (below). Owls (bottom) combine sensitive night vision with forward-facing eyes for accurate depth perception. This second-century coin is from Greece.*

many birds extending even into the hollow bones. Air flows through this system of interconnected sacs almost like blood in the circulatory system. The lungs are located so that air flows through them, not in-and-out as in other vertebrates. Oxygen transfer to the blood is therefore a continuous process, taking place during both inhalation and exhalation. This system is so efficient that, paradoxically, birds get by with much smaller lungs than other vertebrates.

SENSORY SYSTEMS

Birds have poor powers of smell but acute hearing, and their eyes are among the most sophisticated sensory organs in the animal kingdom.

The eye of a large eagle, for example, is approximately the same size as a human eye, but has a far greater density of sensory elements (rods and cones) in the retina (the rear inner surface of the eye on which the image is formed).

A unique feature of birds' eyes is the pecten, a highly vascularized structure that emerges from the retina. Despite numerous studies, its function is still unclear, but it is believed to play a role in improving the supply of oxygen and nutrients to the light-sensitive cells of the retina.

My heart in hiding

Stirred for a bird, —the

achieve of, the

mastery of

the thing!

GERARD MANLEY HOPKINS
(1844–1889), English poet

FEATHERS *and* PLUMAGE

Feathers define birds and are unique to birds—no other animal has feathers. The feather itself is a complex product of a bird's skin, and its structure is one of nature's great wonders.

One of the marvels of animal engineering, the feather is light, flexible, and strong. Feathers play a critical part in controlling a bird's internal temperature, and an obviously crucial role in flight.

MATERIAL AND DESIGN

The material from which the feather is built is keratin, the same substance that makes up our hair and fingernails. Along the length of the central stalk (rachis) of a feather, structures called barbs emerge in parallel and on one plane, in an arrangement

COLOR *Feathers come in all colors, from the sober shades of sparrows to the vibrant hues of the the American Flamingo (above) and the male Altamira Oriole (below).*

reminiscent of a plastic comb. Each barb in turn carries even smaller structures called barbules, arranged in the same manner along its length. The whole assembly is held together by a myriad of tiny hooks on the barbules which lock onto the barbules of the neighboring barb.

A bird spends part of each day making minor repairs to tears in its feathers (preening). Most repairs involve reattaching the hooks, rather like reclosing Velcro strips. The bird does this by nibbling along the barbs of each feather to bring the "Velcro" in contact again.

BARBS AND BARBULES *This electron microscope photograph (below) shows a barb and the barbules arranged along its sides. Each barbule bears tiny hooks (left) that lock the whole structure together.*

HOW A FEATHER GROWS *Each feather grows from a structure in a bird's skin roughly comparable to a hair follicle in humans. First, the old feather falls away. As a new one grows, it starts to look like a plastic drinking straw. Within this tube, or sheath, the feather itself develops, its barbs and barbules crammed in a tight-packed spiral. After some time, the tip of the sheath splits, allowing the feather to unfold, fan-like, into its final shape.*

sheath

barbs

central stalk (rachis)

PLUMAGE

The mass of feathers on a bird's body constitutes its plumage. In most birds, feathers tend to clump in distinct tracts, known as pterylae (the spaces between the tracts are apterylae). As a general rule, birds' color patterns are built of these units—which is why it is valuable to know the details of a bird's surface "geography". Bird identification is simpler and more reliable if you can express pattern in terms of feather tracts.

Birds have many different kinds of feathers, but most of them are either contour feathers or flight feathers. Contour feathers are those that cover the body itself and

are basically there to keep the bird warm. The flight feathers are those directly involved in the business of flying. These are considerably longer, stiffer, and less curved than contour feathers, and are aerodynamically shaped.

Other types of feathers include down feathers, which form a soft underlayer that further insulates the bird. Some birds also have specialized feathers called powderdown. These break down into a waxy powder that the bird spreads throughout its plumage during preening.

TYPES OF FEATHER *Most contour or body feathers (above left) are small, blunt and fluffy, whereas flight feathers (top and above) are larger, longer, stiffer, and more smoothly shaped.*

The total number of feathers on a bird varies widely, though it correlates, roughly, with body size. A typical hummingbird has about 1,000 feathers, whereas a swan has more than 20 times as many. Plumage represents a substantial proportion of a bird's total body weight. The frigatebird, for example, is outweighed by its own feathers. The feathers of a typical songbird are about one-third its body weight.

PLUMAGE FEATURES *Knowing the names of the different tracts of feathers will make identification simpler.*

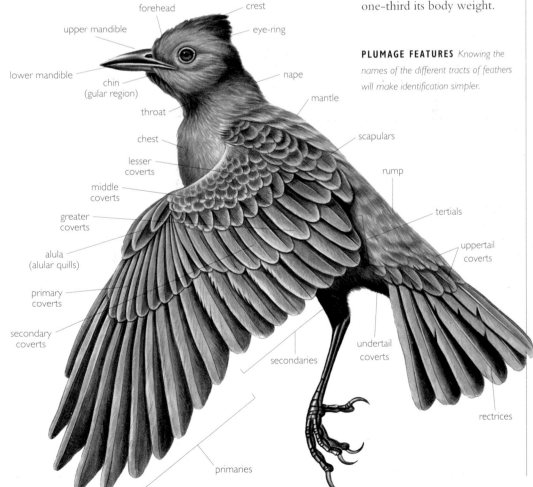

forehead

crest

upper mandible

eye-ring

lower mandible

nape

chin
(gular region)

mantle

throat

scapulars

chest

rump

lesser
coverts

middle
coverts

tertials

greater
coverts

alula
(alular quills)

uppertail
coverts

primary
coverts

secondary
coverts

undertail
coverts

secondaries

rectrices

primaries

PLUMAGE CYCLES

As a bird matures, so its plumage changes. In addition, plumage varies from season to season in many species and will, at least once a year, be completely replaced in a process known as molt.

Despite preening and constant care, the marvelously intricate structure of the feather inevitably wears out. All adult birds molt their feathers at least once a year, and if you carefully study the birds you see around you, you will learn to recognize the frayed, ragged appearance of feathers that are nearing the end of their useful life.

Molting is one of the most intricate things a bird does in its annual life cycle. Two distinct processes are involved. The first step is when the old, worn feather is dropped, or shed. The second is when a new feather grows in its place. When each feather has been shed and replaced, then the molt can be said to be complete. This, however, is an abstraction that often does not happen: incomplete, overlapping, and arrested molts are quite common.

TIMING

Molt requires that a bird find and process enough protein to rebuild around one-third of its body weight, so it is not surprising that a bird in heavy molt often seems listless and unwell. But far from being random and ad hoc, molt is controlled by strong evolutionary forces that have established an optimum time and duration.

Generally, molt occurs at the time of least stress on the bird. Many songbirds, for instance, molt in late summer, when the hard work of breeding is done but the weather is still warm and food still plentiful. This is why the woods in late summer often seem so quiet, when compared with the exuberant choruses of spring.

INTRICACIES OF MOLT

Molt of the flight feathers is the most highly organized part of the process. Some species, for example, begin by dropping the outermost primary on each side (to retain balance in the air) and

CARE AND WEAR *All birds spend a substantial amount of time preening (above left), but at least once a year they replace their feathers during molt. The feathers on the back of this young Ring-billed Gull (below) are fresh, but its wing feathers are badly worn and frayed, yet to be molted.*

wait until the replacement feathers are about one-third grown before shedding the next outermost, and so on. Others always start with the innermost primary and work outward. Yet other species begin in the middle and work outward on both sides. Most ducks shed all their wing feathers at once, and remain flightless for two or three weeks while the replacement feathers grow.

DURATION

Molt may be overlapped, extended, incomplete, or interrupted, so it is almost impossible to generalize about the time it takes. Furthermore, the process is strongly influenced by the season, and the age and general health of

THERMAL UNDERWEAR *A Pine Grosbeak fluffs up its contour plumage to keep out winter cold.*

YEAR-ROUND CAMOUFLAGE *In Willow Ptarmigan, molt changes the bird's appearance so that its camouflage is effective in winter (below) and throughout the rest of the year (left).*

the bird. On the whole, a songbird takes around three weeks to complete its molt.

IDENTIFICATION AND MOLT

A basic understanding of the molting process can be very useful in birding. As color and pattern are very strongly influenced by feather wear, and of course completely changed by molt, you may often find that the bird you are looking at through your binoculars looks quite different from its picture in your field guide.

This is often the case, for example, with migratory shorebirds. In a process known as arrested molt, they replace their flight feathers quickly after nesting, then put the rest of the molt on hold until they have completed their migration. As a result, they spend much of the year in a plumage that is neither "breeding" nor "non-breeding", but somewhere in between.

PLUMAGE SEQUENCES

When a bird first hatches from the egg, it may be nearly naked, as in a typical songbird, or covered in down, like a baby chicken or a duckling. In either case, development of the ability to fly is generally the point at which the young bird reaches independence.

The juvenile plumage of a bird is defined as the first plumage state in which true contour feathers are present, but for most practical purposes it can be viewed as the first set of feathers with which flight is possible. Any subsequent plumages (there may be several) between the juvenile plumage and full sexual maturity are referred to as immature plumages.

In most birds, first breeding marks the point at which an adult cycle of plumages is attained, which will then continue throughout life. In many American birds, this involves a continuous cycle of two alternating plumages: winter and summer, or breeding and non-breeding.

Not all birds breed in summer, however, and some birds court and form pair bonds in their "breeding" plumage but molt out of it before they actually breed. These terms are therefore not always precise. Many specialists evade such difficulties by referring to the winter or non-breeding plumage as the "basic" plumage, and any other plumage states (such as breeding) as "first alternate", "second alternate", and so on.

DRESSED TO IMPRESS *In birds such as the Wood Duck, molt alternates a dull winter plumage with a bold breeding plumage (left).*

FLIGHT

*The size and shape of a bird's wing can tell you
a great deal about its lifestyle and feeding requirements.*

I n the same way that aircraft are designed with
different wing shapes
according to their function,
so evolution has ensured
that the forms of birds' wings
exactly suit their lifestyle.

In both birds and aircraft,
lift, thrust, and maneuverability all depend on the form
of the wing and tail, and these
properties are related in such
a manner that improvement
in any one can generally
be achieved only by some
sacrifice of performance in
the other two.

HUMMINGBIRDS *achieve the ultimate in avian maneuverability: they can fly in any
direction without needing to turn in that direction first. All other birds, such as this
Eastern Bluebird (above left), are limited to flying forwards.*

IN CONTROL *Just as a pilot uses
flaps on the wings of an aircraft (top)
to control its speed, so a bird employs
certain wing feathers to do the same.
Here, a gull uses its alulas to slow itself
down during descent.*

EFFICIENCY AND FORM

The most significant feature
in relation to flight is of
course the wing shape.
Generally, a long, narrow
wing is more efficient than a
short, blunt wing—for purely
aerodynamic, non-biological
reasons that are well understood by aircraft designers. So
birds that spend much time
in the air, such as swallows,
swifts, and migratory shorebirds such as Golden-Plovers,
have long, narrow wings that
provide maximum efficiency.

But, for a bird, flapping
long wings is harder work
than flapping short ones.

Many ground-dwelling birds,
such as quail and partridges,
need flight for little more
than escape from predators.
What matters for these
birds is rapid acceleration;
efficiency is less significant
because their flights are
generally of short duration.
The best possible configuration is therefore a short,
blunt wing.

Tail shapes also have
a bearing on flight performance and vary for similar
reasons. A short tail is
aerodynamically efficient
but a long tail can improve
maneuverability.

WATERFOWL *fly fast in a direct line, flapping their wings at a steady rate to maintain speed.*

VULTURES *use rising air currents to propel them in an upward spiral.*

WOODPECKERS *alternately flap their wings to gain speed and glide to conserve energy.*

MODES OF FLIGHT

This close relationship between lifestyle and wing and tail configuration is manifest in most birds.

Like fighter aircraft, falcons have narrow, backswept wings that provide a high level of performance in open skies. Some other raptors, such as accipiters, operate in more cluttered environments, such as woodlands, and rely heavily on surprise. They have broad wings and long tails, offering maximum agility and acceleration.

Large birds of prey, such as vultures and eagles, ride thermals all day to conserve energy. They therefore have little need to flap their wings, which consequently tend to be long and broad, providing maximum lift.

Hummingbirds, on the other hand, flap their wings at an incredible rate that requires a high expenditure of energy. Their wings have more in common with helicopter rotor blades than with conventional aircraft wings, and they share many of the same flight characteristics,

DREAMS OF FLIGHT *From the legend of Icarus (right) to Leonardo's designs for flying machines (below right) and more recent visions of "bird-men" (below left), the idea of flight has captured the imagination of humans through the centuries.*

especially in the sacrifice of speed and range in return for a significant gain in precision. Like helicopters, hummingbirds can hover in midair, or fly backwards or forwards with almost equal ease.

O that I had wings like a dove, for then I would fly away and be at rest.

Psalms, 55: 6

LEONARDO AND THE DREAM OF FLIGHT

The quest for flight is one of humankind's oldest passions. From the fable of Daedalus and Icarus, through the tower jumpers of medieval times and the "bird-men" of later centuries, history is filled with accounts of people building wings and leaping from hillsides and towers, in the vain effort to fly like a bird.

Among the most noted of early bird-men was the Italian Renaissance artist and engineer, Leonardo da Vinci (1452–1519), whose theories and designs formed the basis and stimulant for actual flight, generations later.

The fundamental idea that Leonardo followed was that human flight could be achieved by studying and imitating bird flight. Based on this, he evolved a series of machines with flapping wings, called ornithopters. "Write of swimming in the water and you will have the flight of the bird through the air" he wrote. His fecund imagination also generated the first designs for a parachute and a helicopter.

Leonardo's obsession with flight is reflected in his notebooks, which were filled with sketches of bird flight and flying machines. The most famous of these works, *Sul volo degli uccelli* (On the Flight of Birds), was published in Florence in 1505.

HABITATS *and* NICHES

The bird species that have survived the process of evolution are those that have most effectively exploited a niche within a specific habitat.

To a certain extent, we are all familiar with the concept of habitat in relation to birds. We normally associate ducks, for example, with wetland areas, and gulls with seashores. But a bird's habitat is more than just a place: it is a complex web of relationships between the bird species that occupy it, the vegetation, the climate, the food supply, and predators.

Birds are versatile animals and have come to occupy almost all habitats from frozen wastelands to deserts, and from swamps to dense forests.

ECOLOGICAL NICHES

Bird species have specialized to such an extent in order to survive that not only do they favor a particular habitat but also a specific slot, or ecological niche, within that habitat. This niche is often associated with the means of gathering food.

Let's take as an example a group of insect eaters that may be found together in American woodlands. Among them, Rufous-sided Towhees spend much time on the forest floor, where they search for prey in the leaf litter. In the understory, Carolina Wrens flit from shrub to shrub in search of insects. Brown Creepers climb tree trunks extracting insects from the bark, while Hairy Woodpeckers peck repeatedly at the trunks to get at wood-boring insects. From their perches under the canopy, Acadian Flycatchers dart out to seize flying insects. High in the canopy, Yellow-throated Warblers creep methodically along the branches in search of prey, while Chimney Swifts pursue flying insects in the air above.

All these birds occupy the same habitat and share the same basic diet (insects). They differ, however, in the equipment and the techniques they use to obtain their food. These differences define each bird's position—its niche—within its community.

HABITAT PREFERENCES *The subtle distinction between habitat and niche becomes most evident in highly specialized birds, such as the Roseate Spoonbill (above right) and the Brown Creeper (right). Both inhabit very different environments, and both exploit their habitats in very particular ways.*

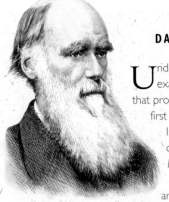

DARWIN'S FINCHES

Undoubtedly the most famous example of niche adaptation is that provided by a group of finches first discovered in the Galapagos Islands by Charles Darwin (left) during his voyage on the HMS *Beagle* in 1835.

All the finches on the islands are descended from one species—a seed-eating ground finch. Some of the finches have taken up typical seed-eating niches, but others have evolved in quite different ways to take advantage of the niches that were originally available to them in the absence of other land birds.

One species has developed a longer bill for feeding on cactus flowers and fruits as well as seeds. Other tree-dwelling finches have adapted to feeding on fruits, seeds, and insects. Another species—the Warbler Finch—has adopted the habits of a warbler and gleans insects from foliage.

The Woodpecker Finch, on the other hand, has learned to use a twig or cactus spine to dislodge insects from beneath bark or from cracks in rotten wood. Perhaps the most remarkable of all these finches, however, is the Sharp-billed Finch, which pecks at the bases of wing and tail feathers of molting seabirds and then drinks the oozing blood!

FOOD THAT FITS THE BILL

Bill shape often betrays diet more obviously than any other feature. If you guess from its bill shape that whatever the avocet (below, top) feeds on, it must be very small and agile, you would be right—it eats tiny shrimps living in shallow water. Similarly, finches (upper center) have deep, short conical bills for crushing the husks of seeds; eagles (lower center) have hooked bills that are ideal for tearing flesh; and herons (bottom) have bills that resemble spears in function as well as shape.

MORPHOLOGICAL ADAPTATIONS

Of all the characteristics that relate to a bird's niche and how it obtains its food, the most obvious are the sizes and shapes of the bill and feet. Indeed, the shape of a bird's bill and feet can tell you a good deal about what and how it eats.

Returning to the insect-eating birds of our American woodlands, we can link physical characteristics to foraging strategies. The Rufous-sided Towhee has large, strong feet, ideal for kicking leaves aside to reveal insects. The fine, pointed bill of the Carolina Wren is suited to gleaning insects from underbrush foliage.

Both the Brown Creeper and the Hairy Woodpecker have short legs with long claws adapted for grasping the surface of tree trunks, and stiffened tail feathers that serve as props, but their bills reflect different ways of capturing their prey. The straight, stout bill of the woodpecker is used for hammering the trunk to remove bark, whereas the fine, downward-curving bill of the creeper serves to probe beneath the bark or into fissures.

Long, pointed wings enable the Chimney Swift to stay aloft most of the day, and its short, triangular bill with a broad gape is ideal for capturing and swallowing flying insects.

In the introduction to each habitat in the Habitat Bird-finder section of this book (p. 134), you will find further illustrations of the way birds interrelate with their environment.

LIFE CYCLE

Once it reaches adulthood, a bird follows

an annual cycle of events for the rest of its life.

After fledging and leaving its parent's territory, a typical young bird begins a nomadic period that may last several years. If the bird is a male, he probably will not be able to establish a territory (and therefore breed) for some time because most suitable territories will already be occupied by resident males that he has little chance of ousting. He therefore can only slip inconspicuously from one territory to another, always risking hostility from the occupier.

Mortality is generally high during this period. But if the bird can survive long enough, sooner or later he may stumble upon a territory that has been recently vacated by its occupier. He can then establish the territory as his own, attract a mate, and begin his own breeding cycle.

THE ANNUAL CYCLE OF THE YELLOW WARBLER
The chart on these pages shows the annual cycle of a Yellow Warbler (see also p. 190) that winters in Costa Rica and breeds in the northeastern United States. This chart is obviously a generalization, even for this species, but it is fairly typical of most North American songbirds. Further information on each phase of this cycle is provided elsewhere in this chapter.

LEAVE COSTA RICA
Warblers migrate by night, covering around 120 miles (200 km) each day.

ARRIVE AT BREEDING GROUND
Timing is critical during spring migration. Fish-eating birds, for example, cannot arrive until lakes and rivers are clear of ice.

DEPART BREEDING GROUND
Timing is less significant in fall than in spring. In fall, departure and travel therefore tend to be spread over a broader time frame.

MOLT *This may last up to two weeks. It precedes migration in most landbirds, but in many other birds may be delayed until after migration.*

ESCORT YOUNG, YOUNG DEPART
Having left the nest, juveniles remain with the adults for only a few days before dispersing (right).

SING, ATTRACT MATE *Small songbirds often begin breeding in their first spring, but larger birds often take longer to reach sexual maturity: some albatrosses, for example, may not breed until their seventh year. Small migratory songbirds form their pair bonds on arrival at their breeding grounds, but many larger birds, such as wildfowl, mate at their wintering grounds then migrate north together.*

BUILD NEST *The forms of nests seem to have a bearing on mortality rates. Song Sparrows, for example, build open nests, and successfully raise to fledging only about 41% of total eggs laid, whereas cavity-nesting birds like the House Wren may raise about 79%.*

FEED YOUNG *Typically, this is when male birds get more involved in the process, foraging and supplying food to the hungry young (below).*

MAY

LAY EGGS, INCUBATE EGGS *Among most birds, average breeding success (that is, the number of young raised to independence against the number of eggs laid) tends to rise slightly after the first year or two, showing that learning and experience often play a part in the nesting cycle.*

JUNE

NOV | DEC

RETURN TO COSTA RICA *Losses during migration are frequently very heavy, particularly among young birds and during water-crossings. However, average life expectancy tends to stabilize after the first successful crossing.*

THE TIMING *of the above events will vary among Yellow Warblers according to where in North America the birds breed and how long they spend there. The duration of each phase, however, is relatively consistent. For example, the following timescales will hold true for most Yellow Warblers:*

Nest construction	4–5 days
Egg laying *(clutch size: 3–6 eggs)*	5–7 days
Incubation	11 days
Fledging *(from hatching to departure of young)*	9–12 days

Photographs, clockwise from the top of page 32: female Yellow Warbler incubating eggs; juvenile bird shortly after leaving nest; collecting nest-building materials; male Yellow Warbler bathing.

LIFE EXPECTANCY *As mortality is high in the first months (75% in some cases), figures for average life expectancy are low. As indicated below, larger birds tend to live longer.*

YEARS 0 5 10 15 20 25 30 35

Yellow Warbler
Song Sparrow
American Robin
Blue Jay
Herring Gull
Canada Goose

Average
Maximum

33

DISPLAYS

Like humans, and unlike most other animals, birds respond strongly to visual signs. Much of their communication therefore involves displays, and these convey a wide range of messages.

In the course of evolution, certain actions by birds have come to have a communicative function. Song, of course, is one such action but most other communication between birds is visual and often involves plumage displays.

PLUMAGE AS DISPLAY

Plumage patterns and colors are among birds' most appealing features, and we rely strongly on them for field identification. Among the birds themselves, plumage plays a significant role in communication. When Dark-eyed Juncos fly up, for example, they flash their white outer tail feathers. This says "follow me" to other birds in the flock.

A wide variety of birds have developed plumage colors and patterns that send messages at

COURTSHIP DISPLAYS *Displays in sexual contexts often involve plumage features. One of the most remarkable of these features is the male peacock's tail, portrayed here in a Roman mosaic from Ravenna in Italy.*

certain times of the year. The most common manifestation of this is the colorful breeding plumage that many acquire each spring, often extending to elaborate features that may be used in specific displays. Such features take a variety of forms and usually occur on the most visible parts of the body, especially the head, neck and breast, upper wings, or tail. For example, they may be specialized feathers. Male egrets develop elaborate and colorful plumes, and male hummingbirds have iridescent gorgets and crowns that change color as they move. Possibly the most spectacular feather display of all is the fanning of raised upper tail-coverts by a male peacock.

In some cases the combination of color and pattern is particularly important. The male Wood Duck, for example, has glossy, brightly colored plumage with a sleek

TERRITORIAL DISPLAYS *A Red-winged Blackbird uses song to announce its territory. In many other birds, displays may be visual rather than vocal or they may use a combination of both.*

crest or hood. This crest can be depressed tightly against its neck and spread to one side to accentuate its appearance.

More bizarre features have evolved, purely for display, in other species. For example, the neck feathers of some grouse and prairie-chickens can be erected during courtship to reveal large, inflated air sacs with brightly colored skin.

DISPLAY BEHAVIOR

Displays are not confined to the appearance of the bird. While they may be given in conjunction with plumage displays, they can also take other forms.

The male Peacock performs as he fans his extraordinary tail. Breeding egrets posture to show themselves to best effect. If you watch male Wood Ducks in the breeding season, you may note that they always parade past the female in the same posture and at the same angle, showing only their best side!

Sometimes the behavioral component in the display dominates. Displays by raptors, for example, are almost entirely behavioral, and usually involve some kind of demonstration of aerial agility or power.

A number of other birds also give display flights, including hummingbirds,

SEXUAL DISPLAYS *In the breeding season, male Sage Grouse (top) indulge in elaborate displays that are essentially one-way. Other displays may be mutual, male and female performing them together. Examples include the "rushing" displays of Western Grebes (above), the "greeting" ceremony of Northern Gannets (right), and the dancing displays of Sandhill Cranes (above right).*

woodcock, snipe, and larks. These flights are often accompanied by singing.

THE FUNCTIONS OF DISPLAY

Most displays, particularly the more elaborate ones, are sexual—they are designed to attract potential mates—and the male bird generally takes the initiative. Males therefore have more colorful plumage and perform most of the display routines (though there are exceptions).

There are various other types of display, such as actions of greeting, threat, and submission, and some birds, such as the Killdeer, use displays to distract predators.

35

SONGS *and* CALLS

Down through the ages, humankind has delighted in the charm of birdsong, but only recently have we acquired the technology to find out what these songs and calls signify.

The joyous sound of birdsong is not only a source of pleasure and inspiration, it is also a valuable aid to field identification, and many birders rely on songs and calls to name more reclusive species in the field.

HOW BIRDS SING

In birds, as opposed to mammals, the larynx lacks vocal cords. Instead, vocalization is produced by the syrinx, a specialized organ found only in birds that is situated at the base of the windpipe or trachea. The syrinx is remarkably sophisticated, having two chambers which the bird can use simultaneously to produce extremely complex sounds.

CALLS

Vocalizations are commonly divided into calls and songs. These terms are useful, but they are difficult to define precisely. Generally, songs are used in sexual contexts and calls are used for all other types of vocal communication.

There are calls covering most aspects of social behavior, including threat, alarm, flight, begging, and so on, and some species have calls that have specialized functions. Cave-dwelling swifts, for example, emit a series of echolocating clicks when flying in the dark.

Although calls are relatively short and simple, there is evidence that they transmit information about the identity of the calling bird.

SONGS

Generally, the male does the singing (but there are exceptions) and the songs function as either territorial announcements or as sexual attractants.

Although each species has a distinctive song, some birds incorporate mimicry of other species in their repertoires. Sometimes a song includes contributions from two individuals, usually a mated pair. This is known as duetting and, at times, the co-ordination between the two singers is remarkable.

Experiments show that while some birds are born with their songs, others learn them from their parents. As with human languages, local dialects occur, with certain characteristics of songs in one population differing from those in other populations. Some first-year males sing a

RACHEL CARSON

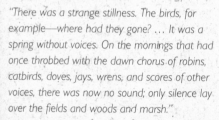

"There was a strange stillness. The birds, for example—where had they gone? … It was a spring without voices. On the mornings that had once throbbed with the dawn chorus of robins, catbirds, doves, jays, wrens, and scores of other voices, there was now no sound; only silence lay over the fields and woods and marsh."

So wrote Rachel Carson (1907–64) in her historic book *Silent Spring*, published in 1962, which alerted the public to the disastrous consequences of the uncontrolled use of chemical pesticides.

A lifelong birder, Carson conjured images of a countryside without birdsong— a frightening picture of nature in deathly silence. Even people who generally pay little attention to conservation issues are concerned at the thought of losing the concertos and symphonies of nature that emanate from gardens and parklands as winter gives way to spring.

In her warnings, Rachel Carson confirmed birdsong as a precious part of our natural world.

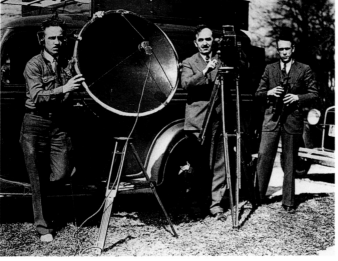

SOUNDING OUT THE BIRDS *Most bird sounds are vocal, as in the songs of the Yellow-headed Blackbird (above) and the Eastern Meadowlark (far left). Exceptions include the Ruffed Grouse (top), which uses wingbeats to produce a sound like distant thunder. Scientific study of bird sounds was made possible by the work of Dr Arthur Allen (left, in the center) and his associates. Today a common research tool is the sonogram (inset, above left). This one portrays the call of a Common Loon.*

little differently from adult birds, and different songs may be sung as the breeding season progresses.

Overall, the complexity of vocalizations varies widely. There are, however, a few birds, such as the stork, that never vocalize at all.

OTHER BIRD SOUNDS

Sounds other than songs and calls are also created by birds in a number of ways.

Some species produce loud, distinctive sounds by diving at high speed so that air passes rapidly through stiffened or modified wing and tail feathers. Others, including most grouse and prairie-chickens, use air sacs on the neck to produce loud booming sounds.

SCIENTIFIC STUDY

Only relatively recently have we been able to study bird vocalization scientifically.

The first ever recording of a bird was made by Ludwig Koch in Germany in 1889, and Sylvester Judd, a biologist, was the first person to achieve this in America, in 1898. But it was not until 1932 that scientists at Cornell University, led by Arthur Allen, perfected the techniques and equipment required to successfully record birdsong in the field.

This pioneering work allowed scientists and students of ornithology to study and compare the songs of different species. The subsequent evolution of technology has enabled ornithologists to not

only record bird songs and calls but also modify them electronically and play them back to birds in order to study how they react. Scientists are also able to reproduce bird sounds in graphic form as sonograms: charts that plot frequency, or "pitch", (vertical scale) against time (horizontal scale).

Among the artistic hierarchy, birds are probably the greatest musicians to inhabit our planet.

OLIVIER MESSIAEN (1908–92), French composer. Messiaen's music was strongly influenced by birdsong.

TERRITORY *and* PAIR FORMATION

Whether it be a large tract of land or a few inches of a branch for roosting, the quality of a bird's territory plays a crucial role in its breeding success.

For a bird, a desirable territory is an area that provides all that it requires in the way of food, shelter, and a nesting site, either for its general survival or for breeding. All territories are defended, usually against other birds of the same species, but also—particularly where there is a valuable food resource or nesting site at stake—against other species.

TYPES OF TERRITORIES

Those territories that provide all the necessary resources will be occupied by a pair of birds throughout the breeding season, or even throughout their entire lives. Other territories may be used for particular purposes, notably roosting and feeding.

Most territories are well-defined areas, with only minor boundary changes taking place from time to time, but birds may also defend additional territories—a foraging resource such as a berry bush, for example—that are outside their main territory.

Colonial nesters, such as seabirds, herons, egrets, and swallows, nest close to each other, and each pair will defend the immediate surrounds of the nest out to a distance at which pecking contact can be made with neighbors. Food may be gathered at a shared foraging site, such as in the sea or at a nearby swamp, or pairs may occupy and defend separate feeding territories.

Sizes of feeding territories usually depend upon the amount of food available. Nectar feeders, for example, require a certain number of flowers to produce sufficient nectar to meet the energy

SOUL MATES *The souls of the Pharoah Ani and his wife depicted as birds (left), from The Theban Book of the Dead, c. 1250 BC.*

requirements of each bird or pair of birds, and that number of flowers may be scattered over a wide area or found on a single bush.

TERRITORIES AND COURTSHIP

A variety of resources, the most obvious one being food, attracts females to territories held by males for breeding or specifically for courtship and mating. If a resource is scarce or unevenly distributed, then males with better-quality territories are likely to attract a greater number of females. For example, male humming-birds that defend the best

THE TERRITORY OF A SONGBIRD

nest site

* Saplings for roosting
* Tall trees for song perches
* Trees for foraging
* Brush for nest-building materials

BIRD TERRITORIES *may encompass only a single resource, such as the individual nest sites in this colony of gannets (right), or all the resources needed to sustain a breeding attempt, as in this diagram of a typical songbird territory (left). The highlighted area in the diagram indicates the extent of the territory, and the key indicates the uses of the resources within the territory.*

COURTSHIP *sometimes involves the transfer of a "gift" from one partner to the other, as in the "weed-swapping" display of Western Grebes (left) and the courtship feeding of Arctic Terns (below).*

nectar supplies attract the most females. Female Lark Buntings are more attracted to territories with shaded nest sites, for prolonged exposure to the sun often results in the death of nestlings.

Other types of territories play a part in courtship. For example, males of polygynous species (such as Sage Grouse) congregate at communal display areas, known as leks, where they compete for patches of ground. Males that win control of central territories are the ones that attract the most females.

FORMING A BOND

Generally, when a female first appears in a male's territory she is greeted as an intruder, but in response to submissive behavior on her part the male stops being aggressive and begins courting her. This may involve intricate social ceremonies. Courtship feeding, for example, is widespread. Not only is this a means of winning the female, but it also reflects her need for a high level of nutrition to support her through the demanding process of breeding and incubation.

PAIR BONDS

Some birds bond for life; some form new partnerships each breeding season; and some do not form pairs at all, the male mating with a number of females and taking no part in the rearing of the young.

Most songbirds form a pair bond for breeding, and the relationship may be resumed in subsequent breeding seasons. However, this may have more to do with convenience—the birds tend to return to the same area after migration and are thus likely to find the same partner again—than with any strong bond with a particular mate.

MARGARET MORSE NICE

One of the most influential studies of territorial birds was carried out in the 1930s by the renowned ornithologist Margaret Morse Nice (1883–1974). For eight years she observed a population of Song Sparrows living in an area at the back of her home near Columbus, Ohio. With painstaking attention to detail, she charted 39 acres (16 hectares), producing maps showing the location and movements of each bird.

Each spring, new maps had to be made almost every day to keep track of new arrivals. The resident sparrows were all trapped, weighed, and fitted with legbands for identification. Like many skilled birders, Nice was also able to recognize each individual bird by its song. One male bird was observed for over seven years as he established and defended his territory, attracted a mate, and reared successive broods.

Nice's pioneering work is widely regarded as one of the most significant contributions to our understanding of bird populations and their territories.

NESTS *and* EGGS

Most birds create a nest of one kind or another in preparation for the physically demanding process of egg-laying, incubation, and raising a brood.

As soon as a breeding pair has formed, work will begin on building a nest. This will serve as a cradle for the eggs and a temporary home for the developing chicks. Selection of the nest site and building the nest may be undertaken by the female alone or in co-operation with her mate.

Most nests are built for a single attempt at breeding. A few birds use nests at other times of the year for sleeping or shelter, but these dormitory nests are rarely used for raising young.

DIVERSITY OF NESTS

We usually think of nests as being constructed from twigs, leaves, and grass stems placed in a tree or bush. However, birds use an extraordinary range of techniques to create a wide variety of structures.

Some species, such as Ospreys and Bald Eagles, reuse their nests, each year adding new material to their platforms of sticks so that the structures grow larger and larger. Other birds reuse the nests of other species. Great Horned Owls, for example, often use old hawk nests, and many cavity-nesting birds use abandoned woodpecker holes.

EGG-LAYING AND EGGS

The batch of eggs laid in a single breeding attempt is known as a clutch and may take up to a week to lay. A complete clutch may comprise only a single egg, as in some seabirds and vultures, or up to a dozen or more in the case of quail, pheasants, and waterfowl. Some species will relay if their first nesting attempt fails, even if they normally produce only one clutch a season.

Many birds, especially the smaller songbirds, habitually lay two or more clutches a season, and these renestings can sometimes be so rapid that the male will still be feeding young from the first nesting while his mate is laying eggs in a second nest.

EGG COLOR

Most brightly colored eggs are laid where their owners can recognize them by daylight. Where their brightness would stand out from the surroundings, the eggs tend to be laid in deep nests or ones well hidden by foliage. Eggs laid in

A NEW LIFE *Using the tip of its bill to first puncture the tough inner membrane and smash a small opening in the hard outer shell, a baby bird struggles to free itself. This hatching process may last up to a day.*

CRADLES FOR THE YOUNG *Nest materials and structures vary widely, from virtually none, as with this Black Skimmer nest (below right), to the intricate cobweb structures of humming-birds (above), and the mud-brick homes of certain swallows (below).*

open nests, particularly on or near the ground, are usually colored and patterned so that they blend in with their immediate surroundings. Eggs that are laid in hollows or burrows are generally white or near-white.

INCUBATION

In the breeding season, most female birds (and some males that share incubation) have brood patches. These bare patches of skin on the belly permit a more efficient transfer of heat from the bird's body to the eggs.

Incubation is hard work, and the incubating bird may have to double its thermal output. The period of incubation varies from a couple of weeks in smaller birds to over eight weeks in gannets, vultures, and eagles.

CARE OF THE YOUNG

The term altricial is used to describe chicks that are born blind and helpless. Chicks that hatch with their eyes open, are covered with down feathers, and are capable of leaving the nest shortly after emerging from the eggs are described as precocial. (Some chicks, however, have both altricial and precocial characteristics.)

During their development in the nest, altricial chicks are fed and cared for by the parents. This nestling period will last from an average of eight to twelve days for some small songbirds to more than a month for large woodpeckers and about five months for the California Condor.

Precocial chicks vary in their level of dependence on the parents. Some remain in the nest for a few days after hatching. After leaving the

KONRAD LORENZ AND IMPRINTING

For centuries, people have adopted ducklings, goslings, and other types of domesticated fowl as pets, giving little thought as to why the birds accepted them as foster parents. Only in 1935 was the process fully explained by the Viennese zoologist and ethologist, Konrad Lorenz (1903–89).

Lorenz had been interested in this question since childhood when he had adopted goslings as pets and found that he could get them to follow him as if he were their mother. In later experiments he was able to establish that there is a critical period immediately after the chick has hatched from the egg during which the first image that it sees will be imprinted in its mind and henceforth regarded as its parent.

Lorenz's work on this and other aspects of bird behavior provided ornithologists with a remarkable insight into the socialization of birds. He was awarded the Nobel Prize for physiology in 1973.

CHICK TYPES *Two broad groups can be distinguished among newly hatched birds. Altricial chicks (below) are naked, blind, and helpless. Precocial chicks (left) are alert, mobile, and covered in fluffy down.*

nest, chicks of certain species (grebe and rail, for example) are fed by the parents, whereas others, such as young gamebirds, are merely shown food by the parents. Other newly hatched birds may follow their parents, but find their own food, as do ducklings and young waders.

BROOD PARASITES

Some species have developed techniques to bypass the tasks of incubating and caring for their offspring. The most widespread are the brood parasites, which lay their eggs in the nests of other birds, leaving these eggs to be hatched and the chicks to be reared by the unwitting foster parents. In America, cowbirds are the best known brood parasites.

MIGRATION

In North America the flux of bird migration is greater than anywhere else, and the arrivals and departures of birds are major signs of seasonal change.

Some sedentary birds remain in the same geographical area throughout their lives. However, nearly half the world's birds divide their year between two main localities and undertake annual migrations.

Most migrations result from seasonal fluctuations in the availability of a particular food. In temperate countries, there tends to be more food around in summer and fall than in winter and spring. Winter weather causes a reduction in the amount of food available and shorter days mean there is less time to gather it.

This situation is pronounced at higher latitudes in North America, where the availability of food declines dramatically in winter, particularly in deciduous forest. The only insect eaters that can remain in such areas are a few wood-peckers and nuthatches that are able to extract prey from the trunks of leafless trees.

While most birds travel alone, some migrate in flocks of one or more species. The benefits of traveling in flocks include greater protection against predation (particularly for daytime travelers), and, for younger migrants, in some cases at least (geese and cranes, for example), being guided by more experienced birds.

Some migrants travel by day, while many others journey by night. Typical day migrants include most waterfowl, the Chimney Swift, the Barn Swallow, and the American Robin. Night migrants include almost all warblers, vireos, grosbeaks, and buntings; many fly-catchers; and most sparrows.

ON THE WING *Many birds, such as cranes (top), travel mainly overland, but some of the most dramatic migrations involve ocean crossings by birds, such as shorebirds (above), that cannot land on water and must therefore complete their journey in a single flight. Migration studies have been greatly aided by the use of radar (top left), which can be used to track flocks of migrating birds.*

THE MYSTERY OF MIGRATION

For centuries, the annual disappearance of bird species perplexed humankind. Many primitive peoples considered the departure and return of birds to be a divine manifestation and there are many myths associated with migratory birds. Aristotle and his contemporaries proposed scientific theories to explain the disappearance of some species, suggesting, for example, that swallows (right) overwintered in burrows in the ground. Not surprisingly, many people believed that the birds that disappeared went into hibernation. As late as the sixteenth century, there was a theory that swallows formed tight balls under the surfaces of ponds, where they passed the winter.

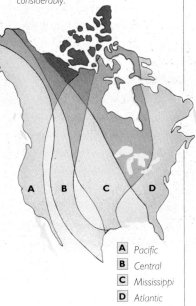

MIGRATION ROUTES *Migrating birds traverse almost every part of North America. However, the flow (particularly of waterfowl) is heaviest along four main corridors: the Pacific, Mississippi, Central, and Atlantic flyways (below). At their northern end, these flyways overlap considerably.*

A *Pacific*
B *Central*
C *Mississippi*
D *Atlantic*

NAVIGATION

Migratory birds are natural navigators with remarkable homing capabilities. In June 1952, a Manx Shearwater was taken from its burrow on Skokholm Island, off the coast of Wales, tagged with a leg band, and taken across the Atlantic to Boston. Here it was released, some 3,100 miles (5,000 km) from home. It was found safe in its burrow on Skokholm Island 12½ days later.

It is thought that most birds navigate by sight, using the sun to guide them during the day and the stars to lead them at night. Birds also have a built-in "chronometer", or innate time sense, that tells them when it is time to depart, how long the journey will take, and so on. But while these senses and abilities are present from birth, migrants also learn from experience, becoming familiar with territories and flyways.

Is it by thy wisdom that the

hawk soareth and stretcheth

her wings towards the south?

Book of Job, 39: 26

They also learn to follow certain air and sea currents, to use changes in temperature as guides, and to watch the passage flights of other birds.

STRATEGIES

Migration strategies vary widely. Most songbirds, for example, break their journey into short hops of 200 miles (320 km) or so and they may delay their journey in the event of severe or overcast weather. Large groups of birds often find themselves waiting together in one place for weather more conducive to traveling. Consequently, songbirds often migrate in waves, and the arrival of such a wave can be an incredible sight.

Other birds undertake epic nonstop journeys. The greatest globetrotter in terms of distance covered each year is the Arctic Tern. Terns that breed in Arctic and North Atlantic regions overwinter on the edge of Antarctica at the opposite side of the globe. From North America, the Barn Swallow makes annual journeys of up to 7,000 miles (11,300 km). The American Golden-Plover also makes nonstop transoceanic flights of thousands of miles from the

Atlantic coast of Canada to northeastern South America. This amazing journey is also made by one small landbird, the Blackpoll Warbler.

IRRUPTIONS

Not all movements of birds involve migration. Non-seasonal movements, mainly brought about by regular or irregular changes in food supplies, can result in a species appearing in areas well outside its normal range. Such movements are known as irruptions.

The Snowy Owl, for example, visits the United States from the American Arctic only when there is a drastic decline in the number of lemmings, its chief prey.

I sat in my sunny doorway from sunrise till noon, rapt in revery, amidst the pines and hickories and sumachs, in undisturbed solitude, while birds sang around or flitted noiselessly through the house.

Walden, HENRY DAVID THOREAU (1817–62), American writer and naturalist

CHAPTER TWO
BIRDING *at* HOME

BACKYARD BIRDING

Whether you live in a downtown apartment with a shared backyard or a country cottage with an extensive garden, birding can begin at home.

Through the centuries, people have delighted in observing the activities of the birds frequenting the land around their homes. Their beauty has always been a source of joy and wonder, and at times a consolation.

Providing food, water, and nesting sites for birds in your yard will significantly increase opportunities for observing them. It will also help many species that in recent years have struggled to find suitable nesting and foraging habitats.

Once they have discovered your yard, many birds will keep coming back. Resident species, such as Song Sparrows and House Finches, may build their whole life cycle around a particular feeder station. Some migratory birds too, such as White-crowned Sparrows and Purple Finches, will return to spend winter in the same yard year after year.

FAST FOOD *Carefully presented food will attract many birds, especially in winter when smaller species often find it difficult to gather enough food by day to see them through the long nights.*

SETTING UP A FEEDER STATION

Birds have a number of basic requirements. They need food, water, protection from predators, and somewhere to nest. All these needs can be catered for in an average garden, even in urban areas.

For your feeder station to be as effective as possible it's important that you choose appropriate foods, present them in the right way, and make sure your visitors are well protected.

To further assist local birds and increase opportunities for observing bird behavior, you may also decide to put up a

HENRY DAVID THOREAU

Some of the most interesting accounts of backyard birding can be found in *Walden* or *Life in the Woods*, written by the nineteenth-century essayist and philosopher, Henry David Thoreau. This series of 18 essays explores the relationship between humans and nature and features numerous, detailed notes on the activities of the birds found in and around Thoreau's wooded garden.

Rejecting the constraints and conformity of a commercial society, in 1845 Thoreau retreated to the woods to conduct an experiment in basic living. For two years, he lived in a cabin, which he had built on the shores of Walden Pond near Concord in Massachusetts. Here he spent many hours contemplating the wonders of nature. With little human contact during these years, the woodland birds became his constant companions and he devoted much of his writing to observations of their behavior.

In birds, he discovered kindred spirits, and he marveled at the simplicity and freedom of their lives. The experience at Walden gave rise to a lifelong fascination with birds and ultimately shaped Thoreau's philosophy on nature.

BIRD GARDENS *Since antiquity, birds have been seen as a necessary adjunct to any fine garden, as shown in this mural from Pompeii.*

nestbox or two. And, if you have the space, cultivating trees and other plants will help turn your yard into a veritable wildlife refuge.

There is sufficient guidance in the following pages to get you started with backyard birding, but always try to learn from the birds themselves. Each area of the country has its own species, every species has different requirements, and individual birds will act in different ways. Creating the perfect environment for local birds will involve trial and error. Don't become discouraged. The rewards for both bird and birder are great.

OBSERVING BIRDS IN THE YARD

Backyard birding can provide you with a rich insight into the life cycle of birds.

OPERATION FEEDERWATCH

One way of putting your backyard birding experience to good use is to become involved in Operation FeederWatch. This is run by the Laboratory of Ornithology at Cornell University. From November to March, participants all over North America record the species that visit their feeders each week.

This information is then collated at Cornell and provides scientists with a measure of the fluctuations in species populations around North America.

Right: Northern Cardinal

Birds generally follow a regular routine. They do the same things—feeding, preening, bathing—at the same time, and for the same length of time, each day. Even if you only attract a few common species, being able to watch them at different times of the day, for as long as you want is a great way to learn more about them.

Watching birds in the yard will also help you hone your identification skills. In the field, most songbirds move quickly and keep their distance from humans. Difficult to see, they are even harder to name. Feeders and nestboxes bring the birds to the observer, and if the birds feel well protected, they will become confident enough to spend long periods close to buildings and people. This makes it far easier for you to identify them and learn more about them by consulting field guides like our Habitat Birdfinder (p. 134).

BIRD FOOD BASICS

Knowing something about the eating habits of birds in the wild will help you choose the right foods for the species you wish to attract to your yard.

In its natural habitat, each bird occupies a niche in the food chain based on the type of food it eats and the way it obtains this food.

Among seed eaters, sparrows, towhees, and juncos normally feed on the ground, scavenging seeds that have fallen or been blown there. House and Purple Finches, goldfinches, siskins, and Black-headed and Rose-breasted Grosbeaks harvest seeds from docks and thistles, and catkins from birch and alder trees. Crossbills and Evening Grosbeaks work seeds from pine, fir, and spruce cones.

HULLED SUNFLOWER SEEDS *Enjoyed by most seed eaters and some insectivores, such as chickadees*

The natural forage for warblers, vireos, titmice, chickadees, creepers, kinglets, wrens, and most woodpeckers is insects and spiders and their eggs. Thrushes like robins, waxwings, bluebirds, and solitaires are fruit eaters that depend on the fruit of native plants like elderberry, raspberry, madrone, and toyon, though all of these species also eat flying and terrestrial insects and even mollusks and slugs. Hummingbirds also eat insects but feed mainly on nectar from flowers.

Birds will be attracted to feeding stations because they offer food in concentrated doses and require little expenditure of energy. To attract a range of species, you need to supply a range of the above foods, or their nearest equivalents.

BLACK-OIL SUNFLOWER SEEDS
Expensive, but highly nutritious and popular with most birds—the best all-round seed

I value my garden more for being full of blackbirds than of cherries, and very frankly give them fruit for their songs.

JOSEPH ADDISON (1672–1719), English writer

HIDDEN DANGERS

Be wary of the dangers lurking in some foods you may think suitable for birds.

What may be considered low-level pesticides by farmers using them on human food can turn out to be poisonous for small wildlife. All seeds and fruit left out for birds should thus be purchased from suppliers of pesticide-free produce.

Sticky stuff like peanut butter can be a danger as it clogs the nostrils of messy eaters like chickadees and Yellow-rumped Warblers. Serve this and other butters sparingly, or mix them into suet cakes (see p. 49).

STRIPED SUNFLOWER SEEDS *The next best thing to the more costly black-oil sunflower seeds*

Kitchen scraps will attract birds, but it is questionable as to whether these are good for them, and scraps give you little control over which species you attract. It is better to select foods that correspond to birds' natural preferences. That means seeds for seed eaters; suet for insect eaters; fruit for fruit eaters; and sugar water for hummingbirds.

The foods illustrated here are among the most effective and widely available.

SHELLED PEANUTS
Favored by jays, titmice, and some woodpeckers

THISTLE SEED *The best way to attract goldfinches and siskins*

WHITE PROSO MILLET
A favorite with finches and sparrows

FRUIT *Treats for fruit eaters include raspberries, grapes, and bananas, and dried fruit such as raisins.*

MILO (SORGHUM) *Commercial seed mixes with a strong orange color probably have too high a level of milo. Such mixes are unpalatable to most birds and should therefore be avoided.*

SUET *Ideal food for chickadees, nuthatches, and woodpeckers. Ready-made suet cakes that fit suet feeders are available. Suet is primarily a cold-weather food. In warm weather, it can melt and transfer to a bird's feathers, causing loss of insulation and flight form, and possibly loss of feathers.*

ICK SCRATCH
e, cracked corn is inexpensive and will be ten by most sparrows. Quail and doves love it.

MAKING SUET CAKES

There are a number of advantages in making your own suet cakes. First of all, it's a fun activity that even the children can become involved in (under close supervision of course!). Secondly, it means you can control exactly what is going into your "cakes" and add extra ingredients to increase the variety of birds that will feed on them. And finally, making your own cakes adds a personal touch to what you offer your feathered friends.

Rendering suet can be done on a stovetop or in a microwave. Suet is available in large chunks from butchers and supermarkets. Usually it is free but some outlets may charge a small fee.

Cut the suet block into one-inch (2.5-cm) squares (or ask the butcher to do it) and heat, stirring occasionally, until it has melted. Drain off the liquid into a container. Discard any crispy chunks or leave them out in your garden for nocturnal mammals. Repeat the process until you have 2 quarts (2.5 l) of liquid.

Then stir in a pound (500 g) of chunky peanut butter and a couple of cups of corn meal or flour. These dry materials will help keep your suet cakes from melting in the sun or during a hot spell. Also add some raisins or other dried fruit. It is better not to add seeds as these will entice jays and sparrows, which will crowd out the insectivores that the suet is intended for.

You can use the warm suet mixture for log or cone feeders (see p. 51). Otherwise spoon the mixture into pie tins (½–¾" [1–2 cm] deep) and refrigerate. When firm, cut it into chunks that will fit your suet holder, serve some immediately, and freeze the rest for future use.

BIRDFEEDERS

*Most birds will come to a handful of food thrown
onto the ground, but birdfeeders offer the birds protection and comfort,
and give the birder a clearer view of the bird.*

Birdfeeders offer a number of advantages over ground feeding. They let you choose where you view the birds, and at the same time keep your yard tidier by holding all the food in one place. They also allow you some degree of control over which species you attract. You can use a variety of foods and feeders if you want to draw in as many birds as possible, or you can select from a wide range of specialized feeders in order to target individual species.

Some species—many sparrows, for example—like to feed on the ground, but most prefer feeders because they simulate their natural foraging conditions. For finches, tube feeders are just like the stalks of thistle they feed on. To hummingbirds, a well-maintained feeder is a wonderful, perpetual flower. Other birds find feeders attractive because they allow them to feed at a safe distance from predators (see p. 52).

The following types of feeders are the best known and most effective. Each is available in a variety of styles.

Platform feeders These simple wooden platforms with raised sides are suitable for all types of food, will hold large quantities, and are easy to clean. A canopy to keep the seeds dry and shelter the birds, and a mesh base to allow water to drain away are desirable features. Platforms are good for attracting feeding flocks and larger birds.

Hopper feeders These can be hung up or mounted on a pole. Look for models with even-flow seed distributors that ration seeds—thus avoiding the need for frequent refilling—and a canopy.

Tube feeders The best of these have dividers below each portal so that only one section at a time is emptied and you can fill each compartment with a different type of seed.

Tube feeders are usually hung but can also be pole-mounted. Often they feature a tray under the bottom portal to catch any seeds that are spilled.

Some tube feeders are made specifically to hold thistle seeds.

Bowl feeders These normally consist of a clear plastic bowl and an adjustable dome that will keep out larger, more aggressive birds and squirrels. They are easy to clean and hold a considerable amount of seeds. Most have perches for small birds.

Tube feed

PLATFORM FEEDERS *hold large quantities of food and will accommodate larger birds such as jays and doves. They also allow whole flocks, like these Evening Grosbeaks, to feed together in one place.*

FEEDING HUMMINGBIRDS

Hummingbirds are among nature's most wonderful creations, and by far the best way to see them is at a feeder in your yard.

Hummingbirds feed on insects and nectar. They are particularly attracted to bright red flowers but will also visit artificial feeders filled with a sugar water solution. They are fearless little birds and will happily feed close to buildings.

Feeders and Food

Most hummingbird feeders are made of plastic, and have a main reservoir linked to a number of outlets. They are often red, as this color attracts hummers. Some ready-made sugar solutions contain red food coloring for the same reason, but this should not be used as it may be harmful.

To make your own "nectar", put 4 cups of water in a pan with 1 cup of granulated white sugar. (Hummingbirds will not eat brown sugar. Nor should you use honey as it can transmit a fungal infection.) Stir while heating almost to the boil, then cool. Any excess can be stored in the refrigerator for several weeks.

Begin by offering small amounts of fluid. It may take time to attract birds, and the mixture will go off and lose its appeal if it remains in the feeder for any length of time.

Maintenance of Feeders

Change the fluid and clean the feeders every week, even if no birds are in attendance. Use bottle brushes, Q-tips, pipe-cleaners, and hot water. To remove black slime from the main reservoir, half fill it with water and drop in a 10 inch (25 cm) bathtub chain or some sand. Shake and swirl the feeder until clean.

Sometimes a single bird will claim your feeder as its own and chase other birds away. To discourage such behavior, hang a second feeder in another area or hang two or three spaced out along a clothesline. The bully will soon tire of trying to keep other birds away from all the feeders.

Preparing for Winter

In colder parts of the country in particular, hummingbirds should be weaned off their food before migration. To do this, weaken the solution to 5 or 6 parts water to 1 part sugar. If a freeze occurs, bring the feeders in at night, but remember to put them back out at first light, as hummers must be able to feed throughout daylight hours.

SUET *can be presented in any number of ways.*

Window feeders These clear plastic seed feeders can be attached to your window by means of suction cups, bringing the birds as close to you as possible. To prevent nervous birds flushing every time there is movement inside your house, install one-way glass or hang see-through curtains.

Suet feeders Suet can be presented in a ready-made feeder (a variety of models is available), or in a simple net or mesh bag hung from a line or a tree. Another type of suet feeder can be made by drilling ½ to 1 inch (1 to 2.5 cm) holes in a log or a wooden stump and plugging them with homemade suet, or by dipping a pine cone in warm suet.

Hopper feeder

SUGAR WATER *is an acceptable substitute for the nectar that hummingbirds normally feed on. It should be presented in feeders like this.*

TAKING CARE of YOUR GUESTS

While feeders offer birds a concentrated supply of food, they also expose them to a number of risks. A responsible feeder steward makes sure that these risks are minimized.

Like having children or buying a puppy, beginning a bird feeding station requires commitment. Try to have fresh food available at all times (or at least at regular intervals). Birds can tolerate some change in food availability but try to be consistent, especially in cold weather.

Some birds become partly or wholly dependent on a particular feeding station. If their supply of food suddenly stops or is erratic, it can leave them in a precarious position, particularly in winter when millions of feeder visitors move from northerly nesting grounds to temperate winter locations. If you have to be away, make sure you get someone to take your place as feeder steward.

Make sure that all food is fresh and clean. Check suet occasionally to make sure that it is not rotting and change the hummingbird sugar water each week. Scrub containers and thoroughly dry those which will contain dry food like seeds or nuts. Wet seeds are not as nutritious and are likely to be rejected.

PLACEMENT OF FEEDERS

Of course, you will want to place your feeders where you can see them, but bear in mind that the placement of feeders can also affect the well-being of the birds.

Particularly in cold areas, try to place feeders in sheltered parts of your yard where there is a reasonable amount of sun. This will help the birds stay warm and keep the seeds dry.

Coming to the same spot every day makes birds vulnerable to attacks from predators. Careful placement of your feeders can minimize these risks. Most ground-feeding birds like to be near shrubbery so that they can take cover as soon as they perceive a threat. Low platform feeders and ground-feeding areas should therefore be within reach of cover but not so near that predators can creep up on the birds unawares.

Other seed eaters that take flight when disturbed, such as goldfinches, Purple and House finches, and siskins, will only feed in comfort from elevated structures that provide them with a good view of their surroundings. Hopper feeders and tube feeders should therefore be at least 3 feet (1 m) off the ground.

Insect eaters dislike flying through wide open spaces and will feel safer coming to suet feeders on or close to trees.

WINTER FEEDING *Birds often become dependent on winter feeders, bringing responsibilities as well as rewards for their human carers.*

DETERRING PREDATORS

You may need to take certain steps to protect your visitors from a range of predators.

Cats are the most common threat to birds that visit yards. If a cat enters your refuge, you should chase it away. Squirting cats with water may keep them away and of course a dog—particularly a small one that barks a lot—

PREDATORS WITH PURR *Finding effective ways of discouraging feline hunters is a challenging aspect of backyard bird-feeding.*

can be effective. You may have to talk to cat-owning neighbors and ask them to keep their pets away. The Humane Society may be able to help you deal with intruders that no-one claims.

Hawks—usually Cooper's, Sharp-shinned, or American Kestrels—can be a problem too. Birdfeeders provide them with a concentrated source of prey.

While it may be painful to watch a hawk take a finch or a junco, these native birds are protected by law and need nourishment as much as your local goldfinches. Remember that the hawk is going to get its meals somewhere. If it happens to be at your feeder it can be a spectacular sight to witness, and a reminder that birds face a constant struggle for survival.

If, however, you find the prospect of one of your visitors being taken too distressing, try scaring the hawk away by making a loud noise when it appears. If that does not work, consider downgrading the amount of food offered so that the abundance of prey is thereby reduced.

SQUIRRELS

Squirrels are cute and fun to watch, but where they occur (mainly in the east) even one can terrorize the entire bird population of a backyard.

Keeping them away from feeders and nestboxes is an eternal problem as squirrels are remarkably adept at overcoming obstacles and outwitting all attempts to thwart their activities.

In particular, platform and suet feeders that aren't protected are constantly in danger of being ambushed. Squirrel-proof feeders, special squirrel baffles (impassable cones that attach to the pole

or post supporting feeders and nestboxes), and unclimbable poles are all available.

One diplomatic solution is to give your squirrel its own feeding station, positioned well away from the birdfeeders, and stocked with favorites like cracked corn, corn-on-the-cob, pine nuts, walnuts, and whole peanuts. In exchange, it should keep its distance from the birds. The drawback is that when the squirrel realizes what a good deal this is, it is likely to return with its friends and family!

WINDOW KILLS

Estimates suggest that over 100 million songbirds are killed each year as a result of collisions with windows. In descending order of frequency, the species most often involved are: Pine Siskin, American Goldfinch, Dark-eyed Junco, Northern Cardinal, Mourning Dove, and House Finch.

Most strikes happen during panic flights caused by the appearance of a predator. The birds are either confused by the reflection or decide that what they see through the window would be a good place to lie low for a while until the danger has passed.

To reduce the chance of birds colliding with your windows, consider placing some attractive and prominent decals on windows that are near feeders, or hang nylon netting in front of them.

NESTBOXES

Attracting birds to nest in your yard will help species that are struggling to find suitable nesting sites, and give you an insight into the fascinating events that take place during breeding.

Whether it be as a result of habitat destruction or competition with introduced species, many birds have trouble finding places to nest. One way to help birds in this predicament and entice more species to your yard is to provide nestboxes.

CHOOSING A NESTBOX
Three main types of nestbox are available.

A basic shelf suits birds like robins that, in the wild, place their mud-based, grass-cupped nests in the fork of a tree or on a stout limb.

An enclosed box is favored by most species. Preferred dimensions vary (see the table below) but the basic shape is the same. Some birds, such as chickadees and nuthatches, like to pause before entering the nest and therefore prefer boxes that have a front porch perch. Others—wrens and woodpeckers, for example— dive directly into the nest.

Large condominium-style birdhouses suit birds that nest colonially, particularly Purple Martins.

SITING A NESTBOX
Finding the right spot for a nestbox is to some extent a matter of trial and error. Generally, it should be hung at least 6 feet (2 m) off the ground in a sheltered and secluded part of your yard. Try to find a place that will receive enough sunshine to keep the box dry but not so much that the birds will suffer from the heat. Give some thought to protecting the box from predators (see p. 53).

Open-shelf boxes should be placed on the trunk of a tree, and will be all the more attractive to the birds if overhanging leaves provide extra cover.

To discourage House Sparrows, hang nestboxes away from buildings—their favored habitat. If introduced species like starlings or House Sparrows do take up residence and you do not welcome them, you can evict them at the nestbuilding stage without causing them any great harm.

TYPES OF NESTBOXES *Open shelf (above left); enclosed box (above and top left); martin house (below left)*

SPECIES PREFERENCES

Species	Entrance hole	Floor	Depth	Height of hole above floor	Height above ground or water
House Wren	1⅛"	4" × 4"	6–10"	4–7"	4–10'
Chickadees	1⅛"	4" × 4"	8–10"	6–8"	4–15'
Titmice	1¼"	4" × 4"	8–10"	6–8"	5–15'
Bluebirds	1½"	5" × 5"	8"	6"	3–6'
House Finch	2"	5½" × 5½"	6–7"	4–5"	5–7'
Robin	open sides	6" × 8"	6–8"	open sides	5–20'
Purple Martin	2¼"	6" × 6"	6"	1"	10–20'
Downy Woodpecker	1¼"	4" × 4"	7–10"	5–8"	5–15'
Hairy Woodpecker	1½"	6" × 6"	12–14"	8–12"	12–20'
Flickers	2½"	7" × 7"	16–20"	14–18"	6–30'

BUILDING A BASIC NESTBOX

Anyone who can saw, turn screws, drill, and hammer nails can build a basic nestbox. If the end result is less than perfect, don't worry—the birds won't notice!

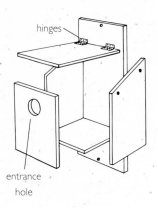

hinges

entrance hole

First of all, decide what kind of birds you want to attract and refer to the chart opposite for the appropriate dimensions.

Use insect and rot resistant wood like cedar or pine from ½ to 1 inch (1 to 2.5 cm) thick. Cut the wood to the required lengths. Drill ventilation and drainage holes, and partly screw in the hinges.

Use galvanized box nails to hammer the pieces together as shown in the diagram (left) and screw in the hinge to the top.

Be sure any rough areas are sanded smooth—especially the entrance hole. Do not use

chemical finishes or paint. Leave the wood untreated. Weathering and aging will give the birdbox a natural look.

Attach the back-board firmly to your chosen tree or post.

Put nestboxes out only when you know your preferred species will be looking for a nesting site (see The Habitat Birdfinder). Don't be discouraged if your nestbox isn't occupied straight away. Try moving it, and carefully consider the needs of the species you are targeting. If birds do take up residence, do not approach the nest as this may cause the birds to abandon it or direct predators to the nest.

Leave the nestbox in place until the nesting season is over, as many pairs will try to raise two or even three broods a season, or another species might move in. Once the season is over, however, take the nestbox down and clean it for the next year.

OBSERVING NESTING

The presence of a single bird or a pair near a nestbox may be the first sign of future occupancy. After a few hours

or days of inspection of the area and the box, one or both parents may start lining the box with sticks, and grasses. Most hole-nesters build a cup-shaped nest in the cavity.

Things will then slow down and you may only see the male bringing food to the incubating female. Once the eggs have hatched, the female will reappear and both parents will make trips to find food for the chicks, increasing in frequency as the chicks grow.

Often, after entering the box with food, the adult will leave with a white ball in its beak. This is a fecal sac containing nestling feces. To keep the nest clean, clear of parasites, and free from smells that may attract predators, the adult will dispose of the sac well away from the nest.

After fledging, some family groups will remain in the yard, so you can observe parent birds caring for their young.

HOUSE WRENS (above) are not too fussy about design and are easily lured to any nesting opportunity. Nestboxes have helped the Eastern Bluebird (above right) cope with competition from introduced species for nesting sites.

PLANNING *a* GARDEN *for* BIRDS

Creating a haven for birds can entail more than providing feeders and nestboxes. A little extra effort can turn your garden into an attractive wildlife habitat.

Exactly how you plan your birding garden will, of course, depend on what kind of yard you have and your geographical location. There are, however, three elements that are crucial in attracting birds: cover, in the form of trees and shrubs; food, in the form of native plants; and water for the birds to drink and bathe in.

COVER
Dense vegetation will attract birds as it is likely to provide shelter, nesting sites, and protection from predators. Coniferous trees and denser deciduous species will attract many species.

Cover should include both live and dead vegetation. Planting a dead tree or hanging up some attractive leafless branch can add stark beauty to the garden and provide perches for birds.

In most areas, trees will be the main features in a garden, but remember that many seed-eating birds live near or on the ground and will therefore prefer brush piles, bushes, and flowers.

PLANTS AS FOOD
Food in the form of native plants should be the mainstay of a bird's diet, and, as far as possible, the food you place in feeders should only supplement natural forage.

Most coniferous trees are attractive to insects and these, in turn, provide food for many birds. Fruit-bearing trees and berry-bearing shrubs

The chickadee and the nuthatch are more inspiring society than statesmen and philosophers.

A Winter Walk,
HENRY DAVID THOREAU (1817–62),
American writer and naturalist

provide food for mockingbirds, robins, and waxwings.

Use only native plants in your garden. Native deciduous trees like maples, alders, some oaks, and dogwood provide much better general forage for birds than do exotics. Birds tend to avoid non-native species like acacias because they fail to attract native insects.

PLANTING FOR BIRDS

Plant	Provides	Favored by
Shrubs and Vines		
Elderberry (*Sambucus*)	Fruit, insects, shelter	Warblers, vireos, robins, Hermit Thrush
Honeysuckle (*Lonicera*)	Flowers, insects	Warblers, wrens, hummingbirds
Blackberry/raspberry (*Rubus*)	Fruit, dense cover, insects	Wrens, thrushes, sparrows, thrashers
Gooseberry/currant (*Ribes*)	Fruit, nectar	Kinglets, thrushes, hummingbirds
Trees		
Oak (*Quercus*)*	Acorns, insects, cover	Titmice, chickadees, woodpeckers
Pine (*Pinus*)*	Nuts, insects, cover	Crossbills, creepers, woodpeckers
Maple (*Acer*)*	Seeds, insects	Finches, warblers, vireos, tanagers
Plum/cherry (*Prunus*)*	Fruit, insects, nectar	Warblers, thrushes, orioles, sapsuckers
Mulberry (*Morus*)*	Fruit, insects, cover	Warblers, woodpeckers, thrushes, grosbeaks

* Make sure you use the right species for your area.

Eucalyptus trees can even be dangerous, as native birds have not evolved the subtle adaptations required to forage from this source. Many short-beaked nectar feeders, such as Yellow-rumped Warblers and Ruby-crowned Kinglets, have trouble removing the pitch of eucalypts from their bills and may even suffocate as a result.

Try to avoid using pesticides. These may have little effect on humans, but they can be extremely harmful to birds.

BIRDBATHS AND PONDS

Water is an important factor in attracting birds to your garden. On larger properties, a pond may attract ducks, geese, herons, and even some migrating shorebirds in late summer and fall.

In more restricted areas, a small pond with a recirculating stream will bring migrant tanagers, orioles, warblers, and vireos, as well as the resident jays, towhees,

A GARDEN HAVEN *for birds involves water, food, shelter, and safety from predators. A mixture of carefully chosen ornamental shrubs can fill several of these roles.*

MAIN ATTRACTIONS *A homemade birdbath like this one (above) will be almost irresistible to small birds. Feeders (left) are all the more attractive if positioned close to cover.*

and thrashers to bathe and drink. Overhanging branches and thick cover nearby will keep them coming back.

Birdbaths are an attractive addition to almost any backyard. Those which recirculate

MAKING A BIRDBATH

A simple birdbath can be made out of almost anything that is non-toxic and can hold shallow water. To accommodate several birds at one time, a surface diameter of at least 20 inches (50 cm) is best. Nearly any garbage can lid will do and the dark-colored plastic ones are best.

Place the lid on the ground or on a solid foundation above ground level. To avoid puncturing it with nails, use rocks or branches to weigh the lid down. If placed in the water, these objects will be used as perches by the birds.

Since birds find moving water particularly attractive, something like a dripping garden hose supported above the edge of the bath on a forked stake will be very effective. Overflow can easily be channeled so that it irrigates nearby plants. You can even create a waterfall effect by placing another lid at a lower level below the first and increasing the water supply. However, it may then be necessary to recycle the water.

dripping water are much more appealing to birds than those with still water.

Many commercial ponds, pond and stream liners, recirculating pumps, pond and bath heaters, and even waterfalls are available, but it can be much more fun to design and build your own.

Through intimate association with the living things around us, we reach out beyond the narrow human sphere into the larger natural world …

ALEXANDER FRANK SKUTCH (b. 1904),
American naturalist

CHAPTER THREE
CREATING *a* NATURAL GARDEN

GARDENING *with* NATURE

A natural garden is a place that is attractive and welcoming for both people and wildlife.

Beauty, discovery, wonder, and joy—the possibilities that lie in a backyard, a frontyard, a sideyard, or even a schoolyard cannot be underestimated. Gardening with nature is an approach that opens up innumerable opportunities and creates myriad possibilities. It can turn a disappointing site into a delightful experience, involve food production and wildlife, and even an appreciation of other cultures. Gardening with nature is a means of connecting people and their environment. It's about working with the natural climate—the sun and the shade, the soils and the topography—and the local wildlife. It is a wonder-filled way to make the very most of any location.

By contrast, most modern American landscapes are models of like-minded conformity, and are built upon a heritage of dominating nature rather than learning from it and enjoying working with it. The destruction of the native vegetation has left a society with little contact with the natural environment. Widespread loss of habitat has put many native species, both flora and fauna, at risk of extinction. The use of toxic chemicals has resulted in serious degradation of land, water, and atmosphere.

CHANGING ATTITUDES

As we advance into the twenty-first century, new attitudes about stewarding our land have begun to take hold throughout North America. The organic gardening movement has grown steadily; now, even organically grown farm produce has achieved mass-market recognition. Increasingly, home gardeners are searching out nontoxic methods of pest control, and taking the time to learn about the benefits of composting. There is a resurgence of interest in regional designs built upon natural models.

THE NATURAL MODEL

A garden is, by its nature, artificial, yet it contains natural elements. To use nature as the model for the garden is to recognize the incredible fit that native plants, and animals, have to the land. Gardens based on

A NEEDLEPOINT DEPICTION *(top) of early European settlers enjoying their natural surroundings. Plant vibrant perennials, such as daisies and yarrows (right), to bring your garden to life.*

SHRUBS PROVIDE *food and protection (above) for garden visitors such as the colorful northern cardinal. It is rewarding to work with nature (left) and create a beautiful natural garden.*

such a model are kinder to the environment and less wasteful of precious resources. They are easier to maintain, because native plants are generally well suited to the local conditions and may be more resistant to pests and diseases. Knowledge of the native flora gives insights into the appropriateness of plants introduced from other areas.

Plantings to attract wildlife can provide homes for birds, mammals, reptiles, and amphibians, as well as bees, butterflies, and other species of beneficial insect. Gardens that are planted with seasonal change in mind can be more visually interesting and varied throughout the year for the gardener and more appealing for desirable wildlife, while discouraging wildlife problems.

The quest to put ourselves at ease with the natural world

LOW-MAINTENANCE, *natural desert gardens (right) offer much to wildlife, from edible cactus fruits to palo verde trees for shade and nesting materials.*

is constant. Searching for the essence of original, natural landscapes is a relevant and rewarding part of this quest. *Backyard Birding* is about this satisfying search for natural landscapes and the fascinating world of wildlife that can be observed in the natural garden. The emphasis throughout the book is on planting to attract wildlife, particularly birds, as a way to open vistas into the natural world around us.

JUST THE START

Backyard Birding should not be the only book you own on gardening to attract birds and other wildlife; as an introduction to the subject, it is designed to focus on the

principles more than the practice of natural gardening. Many other books will present more completely the process of designing an attractive and functional garden, while others discuss in detail the day-to-day cultural practices necessary for planting and maintaining a garden. Still others offer a more detailed compendium of plants suitable for growing in each region of the country.

Backyard Birding is an invitation to see that gardening can offer the most rewards when it is done in concert with nature, rather than in competition with it. Gardens are best when they are designed and created with inspiration from nature, rather than by radically altering nature. And, no matter the size of the garden, gardening with nature is fun, beautiful, relevant, and wonder-filled.

THE NATURE *of* PLANTS

Plants set the stage in a natural garden, weather changes the scenes,

wildlife form the cast, and people are the interactive audience.

Plants, in their glorious variety, form the basis of gardening. From the daintiest mosses to towering trees, they all serve wildlife in some manner. Bark, twigs, leaves, flowers, fruits, and seeds provide nourishment; cavities and branches form nesting sites; and foliage provides valuable cover from predators and harsh weather. Even plants that appear inhospitable to humans can, in fact, offer shelter. Gila woodpeckers, for example, raise their broods in the fleshy trunks of the huge saguaro cactus (*Carnegiea gigantea*) of the Desert Southwest. These nesting sites protect them from the harsh extremes of the desert climate, and the thorns deter predators.

THE PLANT KINGDOM

The world of plants is broadly divided into vascular and non-vascular plants. The more advanced vascular plants have specialized water- and food-conducting tissues. These enable the plants to grow in a greater range of forms and become much larger—and, therefore, are of greater value to gardeners—than those that are nonvascular (such as algae, lichens, and mosses).

Vascular plants reproduce either by spores (the ferns and their allies) or by seeds. Plants in both groups make valuable garden plants, and are classified scientifically by the structure of their reproductive parts. The oldest seed-bearing plants are called the gymnosperms; though the name means "naked seed", seeds of these plants are usually held in woody or fleshy cones. The best-known gymnosperms are the cone-bearing pines and firs, and the fleshy-fruited ginkgo, juniper, and yews. The angiosperms, or flowering plants, form the largest and most diverse group in the plant kingdom, with more than 250,000 species, ranging from grasses to trees, and cacti to waterlilies. Flowering plants produce seeds enclosed in fleshy, papery, or woody fruits to protect the fragile seed and to allow it to disperse away from the parent plant.

Herbaceous plants sometimes die to the ground in freezing weather or in drought, and have stems that are usually green and soft-tissued. Woody plants develop permanent

GARDEN VARIETY *Plant your garden with a range of annuals, perennials, evergreens, and deciduous plants (below and right) to create different habitats and for an ever-changing garden scene throughout the year.*

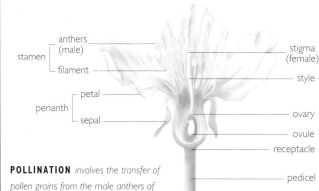

stamen — anthers (male) / filament

perianth — petal / sepal

stigma (female)

style

pistil

ovary

ovule

receptacle

pedicel

POLLINATION *involves the transfer of pollen grains from the male anthers of one flower to the female stigma of another of the same species, resulting in fertilization of the eggs (ovules) in the ovary and the production of seeds.*

SOME PLANTS RELY ON THE *wind to disperse their seed (left). Encasing seeds in tasty fruits, such as berries (above) and nuts, is a strategy that depends on animals, especially birds, for dispersal.*

stems, or trunks, of cellulose tissue toughened with lignin.

POLLINATION PLOYS

Plants, like animals, depend upon the uniting of males and females to produce offspring. To circumvent their inability to move around, plants have developed an array of strategies to ensure pollination. The gymnosperms, grasses, and many forest trees rely upon the wind, releasing great masses of pollen to increase

the chances for some to actually land on female flowers of the same species.

Many plants, however, use their flowers to attract visiting animals to do the job. Bright colors, fragrance, patterns, or shapes that mimic sexual partners entice creatures such as hummingbirds, butterflies, and bees to move pollen from male to female flower parts. The reward for the visitor is nourishing pollen, nectar, or flower tissue.

SEED DISPERSAL

For a plant to reproduce successfully, some of its seeds must fall on fertile ground, germinate, and in time, reproduce. Ideally, the seeds will land where they will not compete with the parent plant for water, sunlight, and nutrients. Seeds are dispersed in a variety of ways, including being carried by wind and animals. Some seeds cling to passing creatures, such as the burdock seeds that inspired the invention of Velcro.

LIFE CYCLES

In horticulture, grasses and herbaceous garden flowers can be grouped according to their life cycle. Annuals germinate, flower, produce seed, and die all in one growing season. Biennials germinate the first season, then flower, produce seed, and die in the second season. Perennials have an indefinite life span. They are generally slower to develop than annuals, but flower and set seed year after year.

Trees, shrubs, and vines are also perennials, but their soft, young stems quickly become tough and woody, forming trunks covered with protective bark. These woody perennials are either deciduous or evergreen. Deciduous plants cope with environmental stress (such as cold winters or extreme heat) by losing their leaves, a new set appearing when conditions improve. Evergreen trees and shrubs have tough, needle-like, or leathery, leaves that remain on the plants through stressful periods.

63

PLANT NAMES

Scientific names assist in identifying those plants that have more than one common name.

THE DISTINCTIVE LEAF *shape and fruit (acorn) of* Quercus macrocarpa *(left) identify the plant as belonging to the genus* Quercus *(oaks).*

Most of us are familiar with the common names of plants. Unfortunately, these can present us with a few problems. Some names refer to quite different plants: in Britain, for example, *Hypericum calycinum*, a low groundcover, is known as rose-of-Sharon, while in the United States, the same common name applies to *Hibiscus syriacus*, a large shrub. Other plants have numerous common names, and, just to add to the confusion, still others have no common name at all.

SCIENTIFIC NAMES

Clearly, there was a need for an orderly way to name plants. To address this requirement, Carl Linnaeus, the eighteenth-century Swedish botanist, developed a scientific classification system. His system gives each plant a botanical name of two words (a "binomial"), in Latin or Greek. The first word is the plant's genus, which associates it with a group of similar plants; the second, its species name, identifies the plant more precisely. For example, oaks form the genus *Quercus*, with over 400 species that vary in size and form, but share the characteristic of fruits called acorns. When we are referring to a specific tree within the genus, we add its species name, as in *Quercus alba*, the white oak.

Plant families are larger groupings of genera (the plural of genus) that have similar characteristics of flower and fruit. The oaks are grouped with the beeches (*Fagus*) and chestnuts (*Castanea*) into the Fagaceae, the beech or oak family. There are six genera in this family, and more than 600 species, but they all have more-or-less pendant, catkin-like flowers that are wind-pollinated, and fruits that are nut-like and enclosed in a tough shell.

A plant's botanical name generally tells us something about it, such as the person who discovered it, where it grows naturally, what it looks like, and so on. Many plants

THE FAMILY TREE *for the Bignonia family illustrates the relationships of genera, species, variety, and cultivars.*

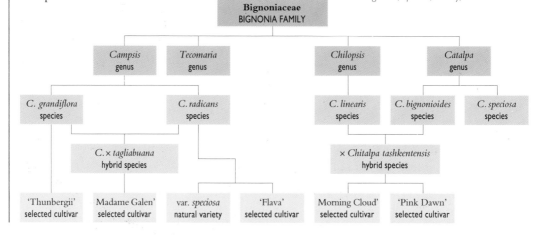

Bignoniaceae BIGNONIA FAMILY			
Campsis genus	*Tecomaria* genus	*Chilopsis* genus	*Catalpa* genus
C. grandiflora species	*C. radicans* species	*C. linearis* species	*C. bignonioides* species / *C. speciosa* species
C. × *tagliabuana* hybrid species		× *Chitalpa tashkentensis* hybrid species	
'Thunbergii' selected cultivar / Madame Galen' selected cultivar	var. *speciosa* natural variety / 'Flava' selected cultivar	Morning Cloud' selected cultivar / 'Pink Dawn' selected cultivar	

carry the names of famous botanists. Linnaeus named the genus *Magnolia* after the seventeenth-century French botanist, Pierre Magnol, whose idea it was to group related species into a single genus.

Some names refer to the geographical or ecological origin of the plant, as in *Aesculus californica*, a buckeye from California, or *Nyssa sylvatica*, the sour gum of the eastern forests (*sylvatica* means "of the forest"). Other names describe the physical characteristics of a plant. *Salvia azurea* (blue sage) has blue flowers, *Viguiera multiflora* (showy goldeneye) has many flowers, and *Parthenocissus quinquefolia* (Virginia creeper) has leaves divided into five leaflets. *Carnegiea gigantea* (saguaro) is a large cactus.

ADDITIONAL DIVISIONS

Subspecific names (subspecies, variety, and form) are on occasion given by botanists to plants that display naturally

occurring variations from the typical character of a species. *Salvia azurea* var. *grandiflora* is a blue sage with larger flowers than normal.

Hybrid plants are the result of natural or artificial crosses between different species (and occasionally genera) and are identified by a multiplication sign. For example, the trumpet creeper (*Campsis radicans*) of North America has been crossed with an Asian cousin (*Campsis grandiflora*) to produce the hybrid species known as

Campsis × tagliabuana. This species displays characteristics of both parents.

Many of our most common garden plants are cultivars (*cultivated varieties*) that have been selected, developed, and propagated by nurseries for their outstanding appearance, size, or vigor. Some cultivars have been found in the wild, while others may be the result of selecting the very best from a group of seedlings in a nursery. They are noted by the use of single quotation marks. *Campsis × tagliabuana* 'Madame Galen', is a selected form of that hybrid species.

THE NATURAL VARIETY Viola papilionacea *var.* priceana *is now known as* Viola sororia *(above). California poppy (*Eschsholzia californica*) (above left) takes its common name from its native region. Common names of plants can be delightfully inventive, such as the romantically named love-in-a-mist (*Nigella damascena*) (below).*

WEATHER WISDOM

The wise gardener has a good idea of what to expect from the climate and plans a garden that will make the most of prevailing conditions.

All aspects of the climate influence the growth of plants: temperature, precipitation, humidity, wind, and sunlight. Native plants are found growing naturally where soil and climatic conditions are most suitable for them; those that are naturally widespread are likely to be more tolerant of a range of conditions. Plants that are introduced have preferences for climate and soil, as well, but will often adapt readily to a variety of conditions. To understand how best to use both native and exotic plants, you must study their needs and determine if your conditions are suitable for their good growth.

EXTREMES OF WEATHER *such as frequent high rainfall and storm activity (below) must be taken into account when designing your natural garden.*

HARDINESS ZONES

A plant's ability to endure harsh conditions is known as its hardiness; although soil, water, sunlight, and humidity may affect a plant's hardiness, the most important factor—and the most quantifiable—is temperature. The gardener will therefore want to know what extremes of temperature a given plant can be expected to survive. To this end, the United States Department of Agriculture (USDA) has prepared a Plant Hardiness Zone Map that divides the United States and Canada into 11 zones, the lower numbers representing the colder zones based on *average minimum winter temperatures*. Plant references, including those in The Backyard Habitat, beginning on p. 304, usually provide the zone numbers for each plant to indicate the areas in which it can reasonably be expected to survive.

THE USDA PLANT HARDINESS ZONE MAP *(right) divides the USA and Canada into 11 zones, from zone 1 (below -50ºF) to zone 11 (above 40ºF). Hardy evergreen trees and shrubs (far right) are suited to areas of extreme cold.*

The USDA map is a good starting point for selecting plants for your garden, but average winter temperatures give only part of the story. Often the timing of cold weather is the constraining factor; an early freeze in fall may kill plants that are still settling in for the cold winter even though they could survive much colder temperatures in midwinter Likewise, a spring freeze can seriously harm plants which have already started their seasonal growth; native plants are often better programmed to wait until after the last chance of frost to begin their season's growth.

The plants that thrive in winter low temperatures are very much dependent upon cool winter weather to give them a dormancy or rest. In the mildest regions of the country, the same plants may suffer from the lack of winter chill. Conversely, those plants accustomed to a cool summer, will suffer if the summer temperatures are too high.

The USDA map is most effective in the eastern two-thirds of the continent, where there are few mountains to influence the movement of

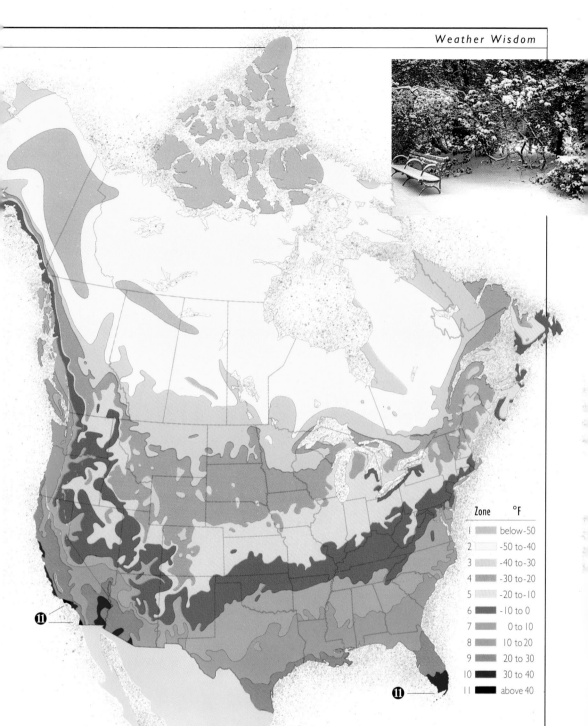

Zone	°F
1	below -50
2	-50 to -40
3	-40 to -30
4	-30 to -20
5	-20 to -10
6	-10 to 0
7	0 to 10
8	10 to 20
9	20 to 30
10	30 to 40
11	above 40

cold air masses. In the western regions, the north–south mountain ranges have a profound impact on the climate, with the proximity to the moderating influence of the ocean among the most important factors.

WESTERN CLIMATE ZONES

Recognizing that winter low temperatures are only one factor in considering a plant's climatic suitability, the editors of the *Sunset Western Garden Book* have mapped out a much more detailed set of climate zones for the West. This system divides the region from east of the Rocky Mountains to the Pacific coast into 24 climate zones using six key factors: *latitude* (distance from the equator affects sun angle, day length, and season length); *altitude* (elevation above sea level affects intensity of the sun, night temperatures, and season length); *proximity to the Pacific Ocean* (affects humidity, temperature, rain and wind patterns); *influence of the continental air mass* (affects rainfall and seasonal temperature extremes); *mountains and hills* (influences the movement of oceanic and continental air masses); and the *local terrain* (mostly affects winter temperatures). Indicator plants have been used to define what is likely to succeed in each of these zones. Similar maps are being researched for other regions of the country, but are not yet ready for publication.

MAINTAINING *the* GARDEN NATURALLY

Time needs to be set aside on a regular basis to provide for the care of your plants.

Maintaining a garden naturally means understanding the natural processes that keep any community of native plants healthy and growing, and adapting them for your own maintenance program. Make certain that the plants you select are appropriate for the environment in which you will be planting them. Observe their growth patterns and learn what you can expect from each at different seasons. Study how nature provides moisture and essential nutrients, and attends to pest and disease problems. Bear in mind that some form of succession will occur naturally if you do not exert a little energy at least toward maintaining the community you have planted.

A HEALTHY SOIL ENVIRONMENT

Nature maintains a healthy soil environment by recycling old leaves, twigs, flowers, and fruits into a layer of organic mulch, which *reduces* evaporation from the soil, erosion by wind and water, and compaction from foot traffic; *moderates* temperature fluctuations in the soil; *hinders* the sprouting of weed seeds; and *releases* nutrients back into the soil as

earthworms and other organisms decompose the organic matter. Mulch also provides habitat for insects and other ground-feeding organisms. Recycle your own garden trimmings into a deep mulch around your plants; use home shredding machines to chop tough, woody branches. Avoid burying the leaves of perennials and annuals with mulch, and keep the mulch

Nature knows how to produce the greatest efforts with the most limited means.

HEINRICH HEINE
(1797–1856), German poet

PRUNING PLANTS *(left) is an essential part of garden maintenance to increase flowering or fruiting. A layer of mulch, made from leaves and newspapers (below), encourages the growth of healthy vegetables and flowers such as* Viola rotundifolia *(right).*

away from direct contact with the trunks of trees and shrubs, particularly in the arid West. In desert regions, a mulch of small pebbles will mimic the coarse sand layer that tops most desert soils.

Many of our native plants do better without excessively fertile soils. If soil tests dictate the addition of fertilizers, provide them in the form of organic products that usually offer a range of trace minerals

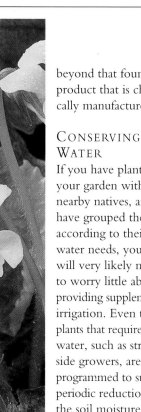

beyond that found in product that is chemically manufactured.

CONSERVING WATER

If you have planted your garden with nearby natives, and have grouped them according to their water needs, you will very likely need to worry little about providing supplemental irrigation. Even those plants that require extra water, such as stream-side growers, are programmed to survive periodic reductions in the soil moisture level, and will spring back when the rains come again.

Admittedly, most of us want our plants to thrive, not just survive under our care. An irrigation system may prove necessary to get new plants established, and for an occasional boost of water once established. For many, hose-end sprinklers will be sufficient; for others, a complete underground system may be needed, but avoid total dependence upon an automated system. Take time to observe your plants and their water needs; most plants will begin to show signs of water stress long before they dry out completely, giving you plenty of time to provide the necessary moisture. Look for sprinkler heads that release low-volume streams of relatively large droplets; you will then reduce the loss to evaporation, and will avoid eroding the soil's surface. Irrigate in the early morning

WEEDING *(top)* **AND WATERING** *(above) are important in maintaining a healthy garden environment. Most natives, however, require little extra water beyond the natural rainfall.*

to avoid evaporation by the sun and loss due to winds, and to avoid damp, disease-prone leaves in the evening. Water deeply, but infrequently, even during the establishment period, to encourage deep rooting that will allow plants to survive water shortages easily. Water plants that are widely spaced with a drip, or trickle, system of tiny emitters that slowly release measured quantities of water where it can soak down directly into the root zone of each plant.

PRUNING TO SHAPE AND CONTROL

Prune plants to remove any dead, damaged, disfiguring, weak, diseased, or crowded stems or branches; to increase the flowering or fruiting; to direct the growth or shape of a plant; and, lastly,

to control the size of a plant. Select plants that will stay within the space you have allocated for them on your planting plan. When shaping is called for, avoid shearing into dense, unnatural shapes that block the entry of birds and other wildlife. Always prune to enhance the natural shape of your plants. You can also control the growth of part of your garden to maintain it at a particular successional stage.

Nature, in her blind search for life, has filled every possible cranny of the Earth with some sort of fantastic creature.

JOSEPH WOOD KRUTCH (1893–1970),
American critic and naturalist

CHAPTER FOUR

GARDENING *to* ATTRACT WILDLIFE

CREATING *the* WILDLIFE GARDEN

*Our curiosity about the natural world
and a sense of kinship with other living creatures
create a desire to observe wildlife at close range.*

For many gardeners, attracting a variety of animals into the garden is one of the major goals of their efforts. Gaily colored birds and butterflies flitting about the backyard are a popular focus of interest, but the possibilities include less obvious creatures, such as a spider curled up in a flower or a shy lizard making a fleeting visit to the water's edge— such creatures play their own, important roles in a balanced garden community.

Success in drawing wildlife into the garden lies in understanding and providing for its needs: food, water, shelter, and nesting sites. At the same time, integrating habitat with amenities for people—space for relaxation, entertainment, and recreation—enables you to enjoy the sights and sounds of garden wildlife.

ASSESSING YOUR GARDEN'S POTENTIAL

It's useful to begin with a plan, both in the mind's eye and on paper. Initially, it's helpful to view your garden as a unique combination of assets and limitations, reflecting its location, existing site conditions, and the potential aspects that could be targeted for improvement.

BRIGHTLY COLORED BUTTERFLIES

such as this gulf fritillary are a popular visitor to wildlife gardens. If you want to attract butterflies to the garden, resist the urge to combat problem insects with inorganic pesticides: they are likely to kill the innocent along with the guilty.

Since regional climate varies so dramatically, and since some animals occur only in certain parts of the continent, the geographical location of your garden will determine the wildlife you might realistically hope to attract and which plants are likely to thrive. Refer to The Backyard Habitat, starting on p. 304, for some direction on the particular animals and adaptability of specific plants that are a feature of your region. More detailed and comprehensive information can be found in other books on North American wildlife and plants.

TARGETING DESIRABLES AND UNDESIRABLES

Start to create a list of the animals you wish to attract, and note their habitat needs and behaviors. You should also consider those animals you might want to discourage, such as raccoons or deer. Be sure to consider the concerns of neighbors, who might resent efforts to support certain animals they consider to be a nuisance.

Avoid sentimentality when you discover that a cherished garden animal is preyed upon by another. Whether it's a snake that eats toads or a bird that eats bees, recognize the valid role that predation plays at all levels in the garden, as in the wild, and take pride in fostering a balanced community of animals and plants.

GARDEN HABITATS *Providing cover near amenities such as ponds (above) will enhance their attractiveness. A garden linked to woodland habitat (right) will attract forest-dwelling species.*

Take a look at which plant species grow best in your neighborhood and in nearby wild habitat to help you decide what to plant to attract your favorite wildlife species.

Assess your garden's current performance in providing habitat essentials. By identifying those plants currently favored by wildlife, you can decide which plants to repeat and which ones deserve to be phased out or relocated.

THE GARDEN AS HAVEN

To survive, animals must contend with predators, the elements, and competition from other animals for food. Wildlife-sensitive design creates patches of animal-friendly habitat—secure space for breeding, resting, drinking, bathing, and feeding.

Plants constitute the most important element in meeting the varied needs of wildlife. Trees, hedges, and shrubs moderate wind, sun, and evaporation to create different garden microclimates. Branches and foliage provide shelter, cover, and nesting space. Plants are the main source of food in the garden, and animals have evolved feeding habits to take advantage of plant pollen, sap, nectar, leaves, flowers, buds, seeds, fruits, nuts, and even the wood fiber itself. In some cases, the plants support small insects that more conspicuous wildlife, such as dragonflies and warblers, require in their diet.

CREATING
HABITAT NICHES

Generally, the more wildlife habitats, or niches, you create, the more wildlife species will be attracted. Be sure to establish sufficient habitats to satisfy the basic needs of the animals you want to attract; this may vary from a pool the size of a washbasin for certain small frogs, to acres of critical habitat for mammals.

… a taste for the beautiful

is most cultivated out

of doors, …

HENRY DAVID THOREAU
(1817–62), American essayist,
poet, naturalist, and philosopher

IN YOUR NEIGHBORHOOD

The real rewards of natural gardening come from learning the details of what matters to local wildlife.

Each region, and location within a region, has plants with value for native wildlife species. Native plants usually are the most attractive plants for wildlife, but they don't always reign supreme. Some introduced plants can be highly popular with local wildlife. For example, the Russian olive (*Elaeagnus angustifolia*), in the Denver, Colorado, area, seems to be a favorite of nearly every raccoon, bird, squirrel, and deer. But such plants may constrain wildlife diversity, or may be invasive in the garden.

CONSIDERING THE SITE

Each site comprises its own unique combination of assets and limitations, and even in the middle of large urban areas, some of the best wildlife dramas occur. An established, self-seeding core of plants is the most welcome asset a garden might have to offer. A grove of trees nearing maturity provides considerable habitat value that even extends to its declining years, when hollow trunks provide nest cavities. Brush piles, naturally decaying leaf litter, and other organic materials enrich soils and create feeding and shelter opportunities for many kinds of different wildlife.

Physical features on the site can be equally important: a natural water feature, such as a pond, stream, or seep, is very valuable, providing water for drinking, and habitat for specialized wetland species of plants and animals. Moderate slopes and varied terrain help to divide the garden into different habitat zones.

Physical extremes can limit a garden's potential. A very small size obviously limits the ability to create habitat variety, but even a well-stocked window box draws a host of visitors. Soils that are very sandy or slow-draining limit the plants that can be grown without a program of soil amendment. The best type of soil is a combination of sand, silt, and clay, called loam. Dense soil also directly limits the ability of burrowing animals to create homes, though this defect can be useful in deterring problem animals, such as gophers and woodchucks.

Neighborhood factors can also diminish a garden's

CREATING SUCCESSFUL WILDLIFE HABITAT

- Plant to suit the natural topography: low points are suited to moisture-loving plants or water features; a high, sloping bank is ideal for dry rockeries.
- Shield the garden from winds, especially cold, winter ones.
- Introduce food plants favored by animals you have specifically targeted.
- Strive for diverse plantings, but avoid a hodgepodge of unique or isolated specimens.
- Coordinate habitat with water use: lush, irrigated habitat close to the house; drier farther away.
- Locate some food plants and feeders in the more secluded corners of the property to attract the shyer, ground-dwelling animals.
- Don't use inorganic pesticides: they will unbalance the predator–prey relationships natural gardening helps to foster.
- Arrange plantings of shrubs to lead shy wildlife closer to the house and patio for convenient viewing.
- Supplement food plants with feeding stations; boost nesting opportunities with nestboxes.

EVERGREENS *such as Engelmann's spruce (Picea engelmannii) (top) will provide food in the form of cones for birds and small mammals. The fruits of some plants are highly appealing to many birds. This American robin (left) is feeding on whole cherries (Prunus spp.).*

FLOWERING PLANTS
Increasing the number of flowering plants in the garden (right) will attract many more wildlife species, particularly pollinators, such as this hummingbird moth (below).

potential. Isolation from sources of wildlife immigration is a serious concern, though less so in the case of particularly mobile animals such as birds. A background of heavy urban noise constrains animals dependent on vocal communication, and will deter the more wary roaming mammals, in particular, from entering the site. Berms, walls, and other strategically placed structures can help to alleviate noise pollution.

POLLINATION AND OTHER PARTNERSHIPS

The relationships between local animals and plants are a fascinating part of planning a wildlife garden, and you can organize your planting schemes to encourage such partnerships to occur in the garden. Cooperative relationships, such as hummingbird

pollination, in which all participants benefit, is one kind of partnership, but there are also natural predator–prey relationships in which the system, not the individual, benefits. For example, ladybugs and their larvae will devour the black aphids that appear on plants such as big sagebrush (*Artemisia tridentata*) in spring.

The absence of pesticides allows insect pollination to take place unimpeded. In the case of the more open, bowl-like flowers, a variety of insects cooperates with the flowers in exchange for pollen

CERTAIN PLANTS *will act like magnets to local bees and butterflies. The blue ceanothus 'Julia Phelps' seen growing here (above) will be highly attractive in the West Coast region.*

or nectar. Flowers such as the penstemons are more selective: their corolla is easily penetrated only by the long tongues of hummingbirds. Conversely, roses offer pollen alone, appealing to bees, in particular, and hummingbirds not at all. Pollination partnerships can be amazingly precise, as in the case of certain yucca species that are pollinated solely by the yucca moth.

75

FOOD, WATER, *and* SHELTER

*By deliberately focusing on the various habitat essentials,
you can make the most of any garden's wildlife potential.*

Plants, of course, provide the main source of food in the garden, whether in the form of foliage, sap, nectar, pollen, seeds, berries and soft fruit, or nuts. Aim to have food available from plantings and feeders every month of the year: this will attract a diverse range of wildlife species, and birds and mammals will learn where to go when the going gets tough. In severe winter, birds' survival may depend on the day-to-day availability of extra food.

THE BARE ESSENTIALS *Many songbirds, such as Purple finches (top), appreciate a source of calcium, which can be provided by crushed eggshells. Probably the best-known North American bird, the American Robin is sure to visit a cooling birdbath (below).*

FEED THE BIRDS

Installing a birdfeeder will boost your garden's capacity to support songbirds. Situate it in a visible location, a minimum of 4½ feet (1.4 m) above ground, within 20 feet (6 m) of dense evergreens where the birds can readily find cover. While feeders that provide food on an open platform are more quickly noticed by birds, a sloping roof is advisable to keep food dry and fungus-free.

Seed mixes can be customized to suit the birds in your locality, but they usually include red and white proso millet, sunflower seeds and kernels, and peanut kernels. Include a small amount of grit in the mix, such as sand, to aid in the digestion of seeds.

Kitchen scraps are an asset to garden birds. Suet and other solid animal fats provide an energy-rich resource, but should be offered only when temperatures are under

70 degrees Fahrenheit (21°C), lest they go rancid. Many birds appreciate crumbs, crusts, raw dough, cooked potato, and dried-up cheese; even spaghetti, coconut, and fruit jelly are consumed. Fresh fruit, such as orange slices and grapes, are often popular during summer, when birds may find seed mixes less enticing.

THE FOUNTAIN OF LIFE

A water source is crucial to attract wildlife to the garden. It doesn't have to be large and elaborate— even a small birdbath or a rain barrel is an economical way to introduce a water feature into the garden. Ponds can serve as a visual focus, and you can create a cool and tranquil haven for people and animals with a well-planned pond area. Since the sound of running water is particularly alluring to birds, consider installing a simple water-drip device or fountain in conjunction with a small pool. Amphibians, such as frogs and toads, will also be attracted to a garden pond, along with colorful dragonflies and other pond insects (see By the Pond on pp. 96–7).

WILDFLOWERS AND GRASSES
*allowed to grow freely in the garden will
not only provide food for insects and
birds, but will also offer cover and nesting
sites for birds and small mammals.*

plant may serve multiple purposes for the same or different species. Significant shelter can also be offered in the form of nestboxes, butterfly shelters, and bat boxes.

A scarcity of nesting sites often limits the number of birds and mammals residing and raising young in the garden. Provide boxes for cavity-nesting bird species, such as bluebirds, and shelves for those accustomed to less enclosed nest sites, such as barn swallows. In general, nest sites that are nestled up against concealing vegetation on two or three sides will win wider acceptance.

Fill the feeders regularly, keep the birdbath full, and plan a garden to provide a continuous supply of flowers, foliage, and seeds, and the local cast of wildlife characters will reward you with a garden full of daily drama. (See pp. 50–1 for additional detailed information on types of feeders and advice on feeding hummingbirds.)

Birdbaths serve birds' drinking and bathing needs. Gently sloping sides are essential to allow easy entry, and the maximum depth should be no greater than 3 inches (8 cm), with rock to serve as a perch. The perils from hunting house cats argues in favor of an elevated location, at least 3 feet (1 m) off the ground and 15 feet (4.5 m) away from dense, camouflaging vegetation.

NESTING SITES AND SHELTER

Plants provide two other essentials of habitat for the garden's inhabitants: first, opportunities for nesting, both in terms of nest material and safe locations for building; and second, shelter from predators and severe weather. For instance, a single, large, evergreen tree or shrub on a cold, windy day is invaluable to wildlife. Furthermore, a given

HOMES FOR THE BIRDS: BUILDING A NESTBOX

Different bird species prefer different-sized entry holes (refer to a good birding guide for details). Other key attributes to ensure success include a sloping roof with 3-inch (8 cm) eaves in front to prevent rain from collecting inside, four ⅜-inch (1 cm) drain holes on the bottom, and several ventilation holes near the top. The top should be screwed or hinged for easy opening and cleaning between occupancies.

Use exterior-grade plywood, 6-inch (15 cm) floorboards, or seasoned rough-grade lumber for a more rustic appearance. Alternatively, a hollowed-out piece of tree trunk suits certain species, such as chickadees. Use rust-proof nails; you may wish to paint the exterior in semi-solid stain, but don't apply any preservative inside. Unobtrusive colors are best: a light gray, tan, or brown. Mount nestboxes atop a post, or attach them to a pole or tree trunk.

PROTECTION *and* DIVERSITY

Animals may at first venture into your garden in search of food, water, and shelter, but they will stay only if they feel secure.

Protection from predators and environmental dangers is vital if you wish to witness such aspects of animal behavior as courting rituals and rearing young.

Cats lying in wait at feeders, at favorite hummingbird flowers, or at birdbaths is a common concern. One of the

THE WOOD DUCK'S *preference for cavities (top) allows it to breed in areas without groundcover. This summer garden (below) combines retreats for both people and wildlife.*

easiest strategies to circumvent predatory cats is to provide open space near these attractions so that the birds can see the threat. Chicken wire spread on the ground in early spring can deter cats from lying in a garden waiting for birds. The garden herb rue (*Ruta* spp.) planted in the problem area may also be effective in discouraging a troublesome cat.

Window-bashing by birds may need some ingenuity to prevent. Streamers hanging from eaves sometimes helps, and hawk silhouettes on the glass may work well, but you will have to move them around now and then.

Closing curtains is an obvious method to help deter birds hurling themselves into glass.

GARDEN DANGERS

Environmental danger also comes in the form of herbicides and pesticides. If you want butterflies in the garden, you must be ready to live with some caterpillars. A smattering of caterpillar-chewed leaves is testament to a balanced community in your garden; handpick the worst offenders into a jar of soapy water. Even the so-called environmentally friendly bacterial insecticide BT (*Bacillus thuringiensis*) can kill too many butterfly cater-

HABITAT DIVERSITY

Deliberately providing a wide range of blooming times, seed types, and foliage is a good strategy for attracting the greatest number of wildlife species. Diversity in the garden can be created simply by arranging the landscape into different watering zones. In general, the greater the diversity, the greater the array of wildlife that will be attracted. Vertical diversity is another way to look at the landscape. Low-growing, mid-height, and overhead plantings will be of more interest to wildlife than a landscape composed only of lawn and a few shade trees.

pillars. Likewise, the botanical insecticide pyrethrin can be highly destructive to praying mantises and butterflies. Tolerating less-than-perfect leaves and very carefully targeting only very troublesome insects are essential to successful wildlife gardening.

THE EDGE EFFECT

The location of various elements is very important. If a birdfeeder doesn't attract birds in one location, try another spot. It's not always easy to tell why a feeder might be successful in one place and not in another. The same type of nestbox located at different levels above the ground, even on the same tree, might attract different birds. Birdbaths and feeders in morning sun are much more likely to be popular than those in shady, dark morning locations. After a long winter night, the birds appreciate the warmth of the sun.

When planting areas are arranged according to the patterns found in nature, valuable edge habitat is created where two different habitats meet. Landscape edges offer many opportunities to reduce maintenance and improve the garden's appearance, and create interesting wildlife watching opportunities. In this transitional zone, you have the chance to see animals that prefer each of the two habitats alone, as well as others that require aspects of both habitats. For example, secretive animals, such as quail, dwell in dense shrubbery, but if provided with an adjoining area of low groundcover, will occasionally venture out to feed in the more exposed habitat.

SOME SPECIES of *plant and wildlife prefer the transitional zone between two habitats (top), and maximizing edge habitat in the garden is a good strategy. Despite their sometimes small size, salamanders (above) are often abundant on the woodland floor, where there is ample, moist leaf litter. The red squirrel (right) is the smallest tree squirrel in its range. It nests in hollow or fallen trees, or in holes in the ground.*

TREES *in the* NATURAL GARDEN

The symmetry, grandeur, and soaring stature of trees

provide the garden with its visual framework.

As well as being pleasing to the eye, trees function as prodigious factories: from solar energy, water, and soil nutrients, they manufacture the leaves, buds, sap, wood fiber, roots, berries, and nuts that serve the nutritional needs of the animal kingdom in a myriad of ways. Many trees support caterpillars and other insects that attract insect-eating birds.

The structure of trees provides multiple opportunities for refuge and nesting: at different levels above the ground, concealed inside masses of foliage, secluded on hard-to-reach outer branches, nestled in crotches, and buried inside cavities. Birds such as orioles and Black-headed grosbeaks are likely to nest in the uppermost parts of tall trees, while cavity nesters use the lower levels. Even with just a few trees growing in the garden, you can emulate the patterns found in natural forests: high canopy, sub-canopy of lower branches and smaller trees, as well as woodland edge habitat.

Deciduous trees offer variety through the seasons. With careful selection, they can provide spring flowering, summer foliage and shade, fall color, and interesting winter branching—a changing visual treat throughout the year.

LIFE CYCLE OF A TREE

Habitat value evolves through the tree's life cycle of growth and decay. For example, a thriving, green fir tree is home to needle-eating caterpillars that are food for a family of warblers; these birds also nest in a dense cluster of its foliage. Fallen cones lure nut-gathering chipmunks. In its declining years, that same tree, laden with wood-eating insects, will provide food for a woodpecker. Elsewhere on the tree, the woodpecker excavates a hole to serve as a protected nest-site. As the tree dies and hollows out to become a snag, it provides refuge to small birds escaping the elements and a home for a family of raccoons. In its final years, the snag supports an enveloping, climbing vine that bears a heavy crop of fruit, lasting well after the warm-weather insects have disappeared.

To enjoy the benefits of a snag, allow old trees to stay in the garden, pruning only to avoid danger from falling branches. When branches do fall, let them decay in place or move them to a more suitable spot in the garden, where, in the process of becoming soil-enriching humus, they support fungi nibbled on by rodents and ferns that lure ground-nesting birds.

TREES TO ATTRACT WILDLIFE

Common name	Scientific name	Mature height	Attraction
serviceberries and shadbush	*Amelanchier* spp.	20–30 feet (6–9 m)	berries
dogwoods	*Cornus* spp.	20–35 feet (6–10.5 m)	fruits
hawthorns	*Crataegus* spp.	15–35 feet (4.5–10.5 m)	berries/cover
hollies	*Ilex* spp.	15–40 feet (4.5–12 m)	berries/cover
cherry, plum	*Prunus* spp.	15–40 feet (4.5–12 m)	soft fruits
mountain ashes	*Sorbus* spp.	20–30 feet (6–9 m)	berries
birches	*Betula* spp.	30–90 feet (9–27.5 m)	buds/seeds
oaks	*Quercus* spp.	40–125 feet (12–38 m)	nuts/cover
junipers and cedars	*Juniperus* spp.	10–50 feet (3–15 m)	cones/cover
pines	*Pinus* spp.	10–80 feet (3–24 m)	cones/cover
Douglas fir	*Pseudotsuga menziesii*	50–150 feet (15–45.5 m)	cones/cover

TREE PLANTINGS

When planting for the future, favor robust native species whose mature size suits the scale of your garden; avoid, for example, species that would ultimately enshroud the entire garden in midday shade. Nurture a variety of trees, selected according to the wildlife you wish to attract and realistic time expectations. For example, planting oaks for a bountiful acorn crop, requires a decade or more of patience, while some smaller trees will more quickly bear flowers and fruit.

Careful placement of trees is essential to the long-term success of the garden. In general, it is wise to plant trees toward the periphery to blend with adjacent habitat, to provide privacy, and to create convenient viewing angles from house and patio. If an existing tree is poorly placed— for example, shading an area you wish to develop as a sunny border—consider converting a liability into an asset by leaving the lower trunk to decay as a snag. Since mature trees are a precious resource, replaceable only over great time, try to design your garden around them.

Apart from their inherent habitat value in the garden, the ability of trees to diminish harsh winds and scorching sunlight renders them attractive to people and wildlife alike. Depending on their foliage density, and on their placement within the garden, trees can create a variety of shady exposures in the landscape, from deep, consistent shade on the north side of dense evergreens, to bright sun and dappled shade beneath the airier deciduous species. Since shaded woodland is one of the last places to dry out, apportioning a part of the garden to a low-lying forest glade offers a cool, moist retreat for wildlife during dry spells or drought.

A WILDLIFE APARTMENT BLOCK

Even an aged or dead tree can provide food and cover for a multitude of wildlife in the natural garden. Visitors might include, from top to bottom, a Red-shafted Flicker and its young; a gray squirrel; a Screech Owl; shelf fungi (a tasty treat for chipmunks and other rodents); and a marbled salamander, which will spend most of its life underground or secluded in rotted tree roots.

SHRUBS *in the* NATURAL GARDEN

Shrubs, like trees, provide a wide array of benefits for the gardener and wildlife alike.

While trees provide dramatic vertical layering within the garden, shrubs are the primary way the gardener can diversify the garden horizontally. They also provide food and cover for wildlife at a smaller scale, often down to ground level and closer to human dwellings and outdoor living space. Among shrubs are found some of the most fecund flower- and berry-producing plants, and some deciduous shrubs—such as highbush cranberry (*Viburnum trilobum*) and smooth sumac (*Rhus glabra*)—display the most brilliant fall color.

ALL KINDS OF COVER

Apart from their aesthetic role, shrubs also provide cover for shy animals. Remember that cover valuable to animals may defy conventions of what some consider a properly groomed suburban garden. For example, some gardeners may find a dense thicket of thorny shrubs, such as brambles (*Rubus* spp.), untidy and scratchy, but it will be very welcome to certain birds and reclusive mammals.

Just as trees create shady microclimates, shrubs provide the cover required by some smaller, shade-loving plants. In natural plant communities, these beneficiaries include young trees conditioned to grow up in cover provided by

NATIVE FRUIT-BEARING SHRUBS

- bearberries, manzanitas (*Arctostaphylos*) spp.
- chokeberries (*Aronia* spp.)
- barberries (*Berberis* spp.)
- salal (*Gaultheria shallon*)
- toyon (*Heteromeles arbutifolia*)
- junipers (*Juniperus* spp.)
- mahonias (*Mahonia* spp.)
- wax myrtles (*Myrica* spp.)
- chokecherry (*Prunus virginiana*)
- coffeeberries (*Rhamnus* spp.)
- currants, gooseberries (*Ribes* spp.)
- roses (*Rosa* spp.)
- raspberries, blackberries, brambles (*Rubus* spp.)
- elderberries (*Sambucus* spp.)
- snowberries (*Symphoricarpos* spp.)
- blueberries, huckleberries (*Vaccinium* spp.)
- viburnums, arrowwoods (*Viburnum* spp.)

WHEN DENSE AND TWIGGY,
shrubs are well suited to blending fences and buildings into the landscape (above and above right) to achieve a softened, seamless appearance. When pruning shrubs, take care not to shear off long-lasting berries and flower buds that promise a future food supply for birds (left, top, and right). The shrubs shown here, clockwise from above, are staghorn sumac (Rhus typhina), western azalea (Rhododendron occidentale), bear-berry (Arctostaphylos uva-ursi), blue elderberry (Sambucus mexicana), and pink fairyduster (Calliandra eriophylla).

shrubs, which, as a part of the process of plant succession, they will eventually replace. Utilize shrubs to nurture seedling trees in the garden, and either allow them to ascend and eventually take over, or intervene by removing the trees that grow beyond a desired height to maintain a complex, robust thicket of shrubs and saplings.

THE MANY VIRTUES OF HEDGEROWS

More so than trees, shrubs accept pruning to direct and contain their growth, and can be planted in dense congregations. Shrubs planted as hedges, or hedgerows, are an excellent means for interweaving several species of shrub into a narrow area to create a unified, vertical face of diverse, wildlife-friendly plants. You can customize the hedgerow to provide a nearly continuous progression of nutritious fruit and seed through all four seasons.

In garden design, hedgerows can function as dividers between gardens or sections within the garden. When at least 6 feet (1.8 m) high, they can help to screen the garden from strong winds. Depending on their orientation, they can provide different sun exposures; for example, in gardens with a

... let your garden be a wild place.

HERBERT RAVENEL SASS
(1884–1958), American nature writer and author

hedgerow established along a western boundary running approximately north to south, the east-facing exposure is favored by wildlife inclined to warm up in the morning sun—such as flying insects and the birds that pursue them. A curving hedgerow meandering through the garden offers the advantage of a variety of different sun exposures.

83

THE VALUE
of VINES

*Vines offer a wealth of food and cover for wildlife, and
can create a dramatic flush of color in season.*

The distinguishing value of vines lies in their flexible and often vigorous growth habits, by which they adapt to fill in shallow or narrow spaces, both horizontally and vertically. They can climb dramatically, and provide height and lush enclosure, as a background or a focal point to the garden. Despite their vigor, they are dependent upon structures and other plants for the physical support to climb.

METHODS OF CLIMBING

Curling, coiling, clasping, clinging, hooking, twining, and rambling—vines climb by many means. Some species cling firmly to wood or stone; others ascend by twining or clasping with tendrils around trelliswork or wire supports. A few, such as climbing roses, merely recline on a vertical feature and will benefit from being tied into place.

Twining vines climb by spiraling around a support; such vines include hardy kiwi (*Actinidia arguta*), pipe vines (*Aristolochia* spp.), American bittersweet (*Celastrus scandens*), honeysuckles (*Lonicera* spp.), Chinese wisteria (*Wisteria sinensis*), and Japanese wisteria (*W. floribunda*).

Some vines, such as grapes (*Vitis* spp.), climb by means of tendrils, which grow outward from the main stem and move in a circular motion until they make contact with a support. Tendrils will not coil around a horizontal support. Some tendril-climbing vines, such as Virginia creeper (*Parthenocissus quinquefolia*), have disk-like, adhesive holdfasts at the tips of the tendrils. In addition to ordinary tendrils, leaf stems, branches, and even flowers can serve as tendrils. Clematis vines (*Clematis* spp.), for example, wrap their leaf stems around supports.

Scrambling vines, such as blackberries (*Rubus* spp.), use thorns to hook themselves onto supports; while rooting vines, such as English ivy (*Hedera helix*), develop aerial rootlets to cling to supports.

VIRGINIA CREEPER (Parthenocissus quinquefolia) *(top) will grow both as a groundcover and a vine. Many shrubs can be trained as espaliers, flat against the wall, such as this flowering quince (Chaenomeles spp.) (above). Rambling and climbing roses (left) can be used to form a pretty garden hedge.*

two or three species together to create a tapestry-like wall of contrasting textures.

WILDLIFE VALUE

Vines provide food for wildlife, in the form of fruit, nectar, pollen, and leaves; as well as some shelter from predators and the elements. Vines can just as easily ascend shrubs, tree trunks, snags, and hedges, where they reinforce the leafy, twiggy habitat desired by nesting birds.

GROUNDCOVERS

Groundcovers help hold the soil in place, and if carefully selected, they can greatly reduce watering, fertilizing, and other maintenance tasks. They also provide cover for small creatures such as toads and salamanders, and for ground-dwelling birds such as the golden crowned sparrow. A few vines will grow well as groundcovers; for example, Virginia creeper and trumpet honeysuckle (*Lonicera sempervirens*). Other good groundcovers include grasses such as buffalograss (*Buchloe dactyloides*); evergreen shrubs such as bearberry (*Arctostaphylos uva-ursi*), junipers (*Juniperus* spp.), and creeping mahonia (*Mahonia repens*); and herbaceous garden flowers such as daylilies (*Hemerocallis* spp.).

DESIGNING FOR VINES

In garden design, vines complement architecture, softening sharp lines and angles and helping structures to blend into the landscape. Use them to disguise ordinary fences, walls, and trelliswork, and to dress up expanses of dark metalwork. In small gardens where there is not enough space for a hedge, vines provide privacy with a blanket of vegetation. Vines will divide the garden neatly into different areas, or simply provide shade. Versatile, deciduous vines trained atop a pergola filter the hot sun.

Vines such as Virginia creeper add a flare of fall color to gray tree bark and dark-needled conifers. Try growing

WILD GINGER (*Asarum caudatum*) (above) is an excellent groundcover for moist soil in shaded woodland gardens. Red passion flower (*Passiflora coccinea*) (left) and California pipevine (*Aristolochia californica*) (below) have unusual flowers.

VINES FOR FALL COLOR

- trumpet creeper (*Campsis radicans*)
- clematis (*Clematis spp.*)
- Virginia creeper (*Parthenocissus quinquefolia*)
- *greenbriers (*Smilax* spp.)
- trumpet honeysuckle (*Lonicera sempervirens*)
- *wild grape (*Vitis* spp.)

NON-NATIVE VINES WITH WILDLIFE HABITAT VALUE

- bougainvilleas (*Bougainvillea spp.*)
- common hop (*Humulus lupulus*)
- morning-glories, moonflowers (*Ipomoea* spp.)
- *Boston ivy (*Parthenocissus tricuspidata*)
- *passion flower (*Passiflora* spp.)
- jasmine (*Jasminum* spp.)
- *climbing roses (*Rosa* cvrs)
- potato vine (*Solanum jasminoides*)

*All vines provide cover for wildlife; these vines offer fruit.

HERBACEOUS GARDEN FLOWERS

Much of what gardeners find appealing in the form,

color, and scent of flowers evolved to lure pollinators.

Herbaceous flowers are justly renowned for their prolific flowering, which simultaneously pleases the eye of the gardener and, via bountiful pollen and nectar, satisfies the food needs of butterflies, hummingbirds, and bees. Encompassing great natural and cultivated variety, these plants deliver character and vivid color even to small areas in a short period of time. Many species and cultivars serve equally well as pocket plantings, in containers, or in large, formal borders, yielding their beauty and benefits at close quarters, by paths and patios, or dispersed in casual meadows for romantic drifts of seasonal color. They are available in a range of heights and forms—from petite and single-blossomed plants to tall, impressive spikes—and there are attributes to suit any taste. Refer to The Backyard Habitat, starting on p. 304, for more details.

FLOWERS TO LURE POLLINATORS

Flowers dependent on animals for pollination must advertise the availability of their food resource—nectar and/or the protein-rich pollen itself. Bright colors help blossoms to stand out and gain the attention of pollinators. Glossy, satiny, or velvety textures also enhance a flower's attractiveness. Sometimes, special markings, such as the speckled throat of the foxglove blossom (*Digitalis* spp.), help pollinators to zero in on their sugary target and bring them into contact with sticky pollen once they've settled on the landing strip. Occasionally, this advertisement is invisible to people: in certain cinquefoils of the genus *Potentilla*, an ultraviolet-light-reflecting center provides a target for honeybees, who cannot detect color but can see the patterns in such flowers.

The key to attracting and enjoying consistent attendance by butterflies, hummingbirds, and insects is a garden that features a sequence of flowers. Early-spring bulbs will lure the earliest bees, while a little later, the first perennial will

bloom to welcome arriving hummingbirds. From late spring to the peak of plant growth and blooming time in midsummer, herbaceous plants join forces with flowering woody plants to serve pollinators during their season of fervent feeding and procreation. By fall and until decisive frost, blooming annuals and perennials play a critical role in providing food for lingering butterflies, beetles, and bees. By late fall and into the winter, these late bloomers pay out further

TRY NOT TO USE your perennial border or meadow as a cutting garden, since you risk denying pollinators, such as the queen butterfly (top), the full benefit of this resource. Irises (left) are usually pollinated by bees, although hummingbirds rob the nectar without achieving pollination.

PLANT WILDFLOWERS *for a splash of color in the garden (left and above) that's accessible not only to pollinators and other wildlife but also to people. Deadheading encourages some annuals to bloom repeatedly.*

dividends in the way of seed for finches and other birds. In mild winter climates, annuals planted in fall provide floral color even when the sun is low in the sky.

North American pollinators readily accept cultivars and comparable flowers—such as daisies and roses—originating from other continents, as well as native ones. In the natural garden, however, gardeners can play a role in increasing the populations of wildflower species that are disappearing in the face of human encroachment on habitat. Since wildflowers are frequently fussier than tried-and-true commercial cultivars, the key to success in growing them lies in matching a selection of wildflowers to the climate, soil, and conditions in your garden. At the same time, consider the needs of fauna in and surrounding your garden.

PLANTING FLOWERS

Whenever possible, plant those wildflower species and varieties native to your region. They are very likely better adapted to your climate, and reduce the possibility that cross-pollination by hummingbirds or bees, who may frequent wild areas as well as your garden, will dilute the uniqueness and integrity of this local stock. If your garden adjoins a wild area, refrain from planting aggressive non-natives, which might seed into and compromise the existing native plant community.

FLOWER FAMILIES TO ATTRACT WILDLIFE

The following is a listing of genera, by family, that contain wildlife-pleasing species.

- Asteraceae, sunflowers (*Aster, Helianthus, Gaillardia, Chrysanthemum, Coreopsis, Liatris, Rudbeckia, Solidago*)
- Lamiaceae, mints (*Lavandula, Mentha, Monarda, Salvia, Rosmarinus*)
- Scrophulariaceae, figworts (*Penstemon, Antirrhinum, Digitalis, Mimulus*)
- Cruciferae, crucifers (*Lobularia, Matthiola*)
- Leguminosae, peas (*Lupinus*)
- Lobeliaceae, lobelias (*Lobelia*)
- Violaceae, violets (*Viola*)
- Verbenaceae, verbenas (*Verbena*)
- Onagraceae, evening primroses (*Clarkia, Oenothera, Zauschneria*)
- Papaveraceae, poppies (*Eschscholzia, Papaver*)
- Polygonaceae, buckwheats (*Eriogonum, Polygonum*)
- Ranunculaceae, buttercups (*Anemone, Aquilegia, Delphinium, Ranunculus*)

GRASSES *and* WEEDS *in the* NATURAL GARDEN

Free-growing grasses do not demand the same intensive maintenance as mowed turf grasses, and offer far greater variety.

Ornamental and native grasses, along with grass-like sedges and rushes, comprise the key element in the creation of meadows and prairie-like habitats. They also serve well at the edges of streams and ponds and as a patchy, informal groundcover.

The fine, delicate textures of grass leaves, flowers, and seed heads, waving to the tempo of the wind, are a welcome contrast to the boldness and solidity of other herbaceous and woody plants. Their subtle, modulated colors include creamy and silvery variegation and shades of purple, bronze, orange, and red, especially in fall and winter. While many are low-growing, others become impressive upright or arching specimens. Some, such as giant wild rye (*Elymus condensatus*), are tall enough to serve as windbreaks.

Sod-forming grasses, such as Kentucky bluegrass (*Poa pratensis*) and buffalograss (*Buchloe dactyloides*), spread either by above- or below-ground runners, and are generally found in moist sites. Bunchgrasses don't spread, but form clumps and are generally more common in dry locations. Many native and introduced bunchgrasses are popular ornamental plants for gardens, such as blue grama (*Bouteloua gracilis*), Indian grass (*Sorghastrum nutans*), Indian rice grass (*Oryzopsis hymenoides*), little and big bluestem (*Schizachyrium scoparium and Andropogon gerardii*), and sideoats grama (*Bouteloua curtipendula*). (Refer also to The Backyard Habitat, starting on p. 304, for details about grasses for your region.)

ORNAMENTAL GRASSES *such as these* Miscanthus *cultivars (above) provide variety in form and color in the garden. Plant grasses with wildflowers to re-create natural habitat for wildlife (above right and right).*

THE BENEFITS OF GRASSES AND WEEDS

The deep, fibrous roots of grasses help to forestall erosion by anchoring soil, and most are well adapted to poor soil conditions. Most native grasses are resilient in the face of foliage-browsing insects and mammals, provided their numbers are moderate. Many tolerate dry, exposed conditions, while others thrive in damp, shady situations.

So-called "weeds"—those tough, hard-to-eradicate herbaceous plants with modest appeal as garden specimens—produce crops of seeds with substantial food value for wildlife, especially birds. Weeds are easily tolerated when merged with grasses and showy wildflowers, though you may choose to omit the nutritious but allergy-inducing ragweed (*Ambrosia* spp.). Compose your meadow to suit your taste, the local character of your site, and the specific wildlife you aspire to attract by devising your own customized planting plan, as opposed to relying on the widely available field-in-a-can seed assortments. Be sure to avoid planting two invasive perennial grasses, Bermuda grass (*Cynodon dactylon*) and quack grass (*Agropyron repens*), lest they proliferate to the exclusion of other useful attractive species. And take care to contain these aggressive grasses: pampas grass (*Cortaderia* spp.), common reed (*Phragmites australis*), and ribbon grass (*Phalaris arundinacea* var. *picta*).

GRASS MEADOWS AND WILDLIFE

What appears to be a graceful, flower-studded plain, rippling in the breeze, is actually a complex habitat of densely ordered plants, with vertical definition and a range of wildlife habitat opportunities, or niches. A forest in itself, a botanically diverse meadow supports a multitude of beetles, bugs, flying insects, and spiders. Reptiles such as the eastern box turtle hunt for earthworms, beetles, caterpillars, and berries in damp meadows, and even some amphibians take advantage of a grassland's abundant summertime food. Naturally, many insect-eating birds are drawn to grassy habitat to feed and raise their young.

NON-INVASIVE GRASSES AND WEEDS FOR THE NATURAL GARDEN

Grasses *denotes non-natives*
- bluestems, beardgrass (*Andropogon* spp.)
- gramas (*Bouteloua* spp.)
- reed grasses (*Calamagrostis* spp. & cvrs)
- hairgrasses (*Deschampsia* spp. & cvrs)
- wild rye, Pacific dune grass (*Elymus* spp.)
- plume grasses (*Erianthus* spp.)
- fescues (*Festuca* spp. & cvrs)
- *blue oat grass (*Helictotrichon sempervirens*)
- *silver grasses, maiden grass (*Miscanthus* spp. & cvrs)
- muhly grasses, deer grasses (*Muhlenbergia* spp.)
- switch grass, deer tongue grass (*Panicum* spp.)

- little bluestem (*Schizachyrium scoparium*)
- Indian grass (*Sorghastrum nutans*)
- dropseeds (*Sporobolus* spp.)
- feather grasses, needle grasses (*Stipa* spp.)
- gamma grasses (*Tripsicum* spp.)

Weeds
- turkey mullein (*Eremocarpus setigerus*)
- red-stemmed filaree (*Erodium cicutarium*)
- bush clovers (*Lespedeza* spp.)
- common tarweed (*Madia elegans*)
- pokeweed (*Phytolacca americana*)

PLANTS *for the* BACKYARD POND

A water source, especially running water, is the key to luring birds and mammals to the garden.

Watery habitats in natural ecosystems are vitally important. The sudden splash of a frog, the darting of a fish-eating bird, the flash of a dragonfly: water appeals strongly to wildlife, which will congregate by ponds and streams for drinking, feeding, and bathing. In the case of amphibians, a clean, watery environment is necessary for reproduction as well.

THE CENTERPIECE OF THE GARDEN

Ponds are well suited to serve as the centerpiece of a garden: their shimmering, sky-reflecting surface opens up a busy landscape and they complement all variety of plant forms.

In addition to the soothing sound of water, a pond will moderate the extremes of heat through surface evaporation, and create a microclimatic

Nights of watching … will let us into some secrets about the ponds and fields that the sun … will never know.

DALLAS LORE SHARP (1870–1929), American author, naturalist, and educator

effect enhanced by the flow of air over the pool—like in an oasis. The sound of running water can also be used to buffer the harsh sounds of urban life, such as vehicular traffic.

Depth is important: frogs prefer depths between 6 and 24 inches (15 and 60 cm), along with sloping walls that permit adults to exit; while waterbirds favor ponds with an average depth of about 18 inches (45 cm).

To reap the full benefit of a garden pond, gardeners must plan carefully and provide a clean source of water. Pollution from septic tanks and excess fertilizer from farmyards and gardens interfere with the natural chemistry of a body of water. Pesticide residues, swimming-pool chlorine, and petroleum-tainted runoff from highways all have the potential to poison aquatic life.

POND ZONES AND PLANTS

Different plants are suited to different zones in the pond: for example, submerged plants such as water milfoil (*Myriophyllum* spp.); floating plants, such as water fern (*Azolla* spp.) and duckweed (*Lemna* spp.); emergent plants, with their roots on the bottom, such as waterlilies; and plants for the pond margin, such as cattails (*Typha* spp.), pickerel weed (*Pontederia cordata*), and sedges (*Carex* spp.).

If waterfowl are a priority, it's best to grow some resilient native plants that particularly suit their tastes; these include pondweed (*Potamogeton* spp.), wild celery (*Vallisneria americana*), and wild rice (*Zizania aquatica*)

If waterfowl are not present, you can grow interesting foliage plants such as arrow-

GARDEN PONDS *A natural stream running through a garden is worth treasuring and enhancing, but the stiller water of a pond (above and right) supports a more diverse array of water plants and provides a greater variety of niches for wildlife.*

POND PLANTS such as waterlilies (left and bottom) introduce oxygen into the water as a natural result of their photosynthesis. Plants can also serve as floating platforms for frogs (below).

head (*Sagittaria* spp.) and the native waterlilies. The latter are of particular value, not only for their showy flowers and long bloom season, but also for the variety of habitats they offer the smaller pond-dwelling animals. Buds and blossoms provide convenient perches for dragonflies; their bold, floating leaves form sunny platforms for frogs. Beneath the surface, some very small pond animals, such as rotifers, hydra, and insect larvae, attach to their stems. These wide-leafed plants also benefit wildlife by partially shading the pond water, preventing overheating during intense summer sunshine, and by providing seclusion for fishes, tadpoles, and salamanders. Prime possibilities include the yellow pond lily (*Nuphar advena*) and the fragrant waterlily (*Nymphaea odorata*).

As well as introducing oxygen into the water, water-lilies achieve two other important goals: excess carbon dioxide is removed and the sun's energy is utilized to construct the plant tissue that feeds wildlife. Plants of particular merit in aerating the pond include the bladderwort (*Utricularia vulgaris*), water milfoil, water pennywort (*Hydrocotyle* spp.), and water shield (*Brasenia schreberi*).

GETTING THE MOST FROM YOUR POND

- Emulate nature by positioning the pond in lush vegetation.
- Ensure the pond is not entirely visible from any one vantage point, to create an air of mystery and to invite discovery.
- Situate the pond in a low point in the landscape, where water would naturally collect.
- Choose plants such as yellow flag (*Iris pseudacorus*), which will provide a contrasting vertical line in its growth habit.
- Lush foliage hanging over or creeping up to the water will soften hard corners or edges. Good pond-edge plants include wild iris (*Iris versicolor*), marsh marigold (*Caltha palustris*), and spike rush (*Eleocharis montevidensis*).
- To create harmony in the garden, use stones to edge the pond only if they are present elsewhere in the garden.
- Don't allow bare concrete or exposed plastic liner to show, or cover them with ground-hugging plants such as marsh marigold (*Caltha palustris*) or one of the sedges (*Carex* spp.).

... all those little fiddles in the grass, all those cricket pipes, those delicate flutes, are they not lovely beyond words when heard in midsummer on a moonlight night?

HENRY BESTON (1888–1968),
American writer and editor

FROM TREETOP *to* BURROW

Natural gardening at its best provides welcome habitat for a diverse community of wild creatures.

Gardeners attuned to the well-oiled machinery of natural ecosystems can design plantings that are not simply an amenity for people. They can compose habitat essentials for birds and mammals, even amphibians, reptiles, and insects, to create a garden that both satisfies the eye and attracts and supports these animals.

In the flush moments of early-morning feeding, during migrations, or as night-loving animals emerge at dusk, the natural garden may resemble a busy stage-set, as characterful as a Dickens novel, humming with the pulse and spontaneity of the wild. In this thriving sanctuary, far removed from the manicured yard adorned with picture-perfect, exotic flowers, you may be witness to behaviors as poignant as the feeding of young, as absorbing as a fierce dispute over territory, or as dramatic as predators stalking and capturing their prey.

BARN SWALLOWS *(top) are swift and graceful flyers. Black-eyed Susans* (Rudbeckia hirta), *(right) provide a good source of nectar for honeybees and butterflies.*

PLANNING YOUR SITE

A garden comprising a variety of plant life provides a mosaic of opportunities—called niches by ecologists—for different species of wildlife. Throughout the year, hundreds of insect species and scores of bird species will frequent the garden planned for *diversity*. Of key importance here are the food resources offered by trees, shrubs, and herbaceous plants. Nesting sites and shelter from the elements and predators are of equal importance. For example, a Tree Swallow may be drawn to a backyard to feed upon a wealth of flying insects over a pond and patch of meadow, but will reside in the garden only if a suitable hollow tree or nesting box is available.

All nature wears one universal grin.

HENRY FIELDING (1707–54), English writer.

Many small mammals require secluded recesses or grassy cover to escape predators, such as the hungry hawk or owl. In some cases, an animal's needs vary through its life cycle: in many butterflies, the caterpillars depend on particular foliage, while the adults prefer the nectar of certain flowers. And don't neglect water: it's a magnet for all types of creature, particularly where it's scarce, as in the desert and during frozen northern winters.

PLANTING TIPS TO ATTRACT WILDLIFE

• Plan the garden around a backbone of native and non-invasive adapted plants. Re-creating the attractive qualities of healthy plant communities—such as species diversity, toughness, and the provision of reliable resources—gives you the best chance of meeting the specific needs of native fauna in the backyard habitat.
• Take care to preserve tall trees, since they yield the most dividends in the way of food, cover, and habitat complexity. In their absence, think long-term and plant a grove for the future to restore some of the forest sacrificed to human needs.
• If your yard is too small for substantial trees, create vertical niches with vines. Plant two or three different species together to make a tapestry of habitat.
• Plant for a seasonal sequence of flowering and fruiting to provide wildlife with food sources throughout the year.

You can learn much from natural ecosystems when designing your garden for wildlife. Establishing a vertical layering of vegetation, from low groundcover to high canopy, like that found in nature, can be as important as plant variety. By graduating garden plants from short ones in the foreground to progressively taller ones farther away, you'll optimize your viewing opportunities in all the different layers.

Horizontal habitat diversity is also important. Different habitats will attract different species, of course, and edges, where different habitats converge, attract still others. The transition between forest and shrubbery, the zone straddling meadow and thicket —each of these harbors more species than isolated patches of any one habitat alone, because they can satisfy a greater variety of animal needs. For example, certain flycatchers favor high, exposed perches at the forest edge where they can hunt insects that fly over a meadow. Both habitats are required—one for the food, one for the perch—

for this species to prosper along with strictly woodland and meadow bird species.

Keep in mind that a garden both layered vertically and diversified horizontally must be organized in a natural way to be effective. For example, a stream winding through a variety of low, leafy plantings is more attractive to many animals than one that flows within an open expanse of patio or lawn. One reason for this is that many animals are as concerned as we are with personal safety. A handsome but shy woodland bird that feels secure bathing in a stream enclosed by shrubbery beneath oak trees would not feel the same security about venturing into the more exposed, and hence, more dangerous, mid-lawn waterway.

A GARDEN *planned for diversity (top) creates different microhabitats and a variety of niches for wildlife. The monarch (above right) is one of the best-known and most widespread of North American butterflies, while the Olympic marmot (right) is found only in the Olympic Mountains of Washington.*

95

BY *the* POND

A garden pond or stream will do more to attract wild creatures than any other single improvement.

Beyond its aesthetic value, water is essential to life. A variety of insects and birds finds food in or around water, and virtually all creatures, including some otherwise secretive birds and mammals, are drawn to ponds and streams to drink.

WATER LOVERS

Amphibians are among the easiest water-loving animals to oblige. Certain frogs can prosper and breed in very small pools—the size of a large kitchen sink will suffice.

Details of the life cycle vary with the species, but breeding customarily

THE PACIFIC TREE FROG (below) is *less arboreal than many of its relatives, and can be found in low shrublands and damp meadows. Dragonflies (below right) are beneficial predators that devour huge numbers of mosquitoes.*

commences when males vocalize on spring nights to attract females, forming loud choruses on occasion. After mating, females lay fertilized eggs in water; the eggs stay submerged in a mass, sometimes attached to vegetation. Tadpoles hatch from the eggs, and capture insect larvae and other aquatic life. They typically spend several months underwater, gradually transforming themselves into four-legged adults lacking tails. Strong hind legs power energetic leaps either in pursuit of prey or to avoid predators, while webbed feet enhance their prowess as swimmers.

If your new garden pond has not yet attracted any migrating frogs, you can establish a population by transferring a small number of eggs from nearby natural ponds. Many species abound in the rainier eastern and central parts of North America, including the pickerel frog, the green frog,

AFTER WINTERING *in warmer climes, Canada geese return each year in spring to their ancestral breeding grounds.*

the northern and southern cricket frog, and the spring peeper, well known for its reedy, nighttime chorus. The red-legged frog may show up in West Coast water gardens, along with the especially musical Pacific tree frog.

Toads, too, lay eggs in water, but the tadpoles develop much more rapidly, and even a temporary pool in a depression will suffice. Adult toads lead largely terrestrial lives, preferring damp, shady recesses in the garden and by the house. Like all amphibians, they need some contact with moisture to prevent drying out. Toads have neck glands that secrete a poison to deter would-be predators.

WARM, SPRINGTIME RAIN *will often see the spotted salamander (right) emerge to breed in woodland ponds. The iridescent colors of male Wood Ducks (below right) are a visual delight on woodland ponds and streams.*

A toad's typical diet includes major garden pests, such as cutworms, armyworms, slugs, and snails, as well as the beneficial earthworm.

The Woodhouse's toad, found in the central United States, adapts well to gardens. Primarily a nocturnal insect hunter, it snaps at flying bugs attracted to house lights. During the day, it rests hidden in vegetation or retreats into its burrow. The spadefoot toads, of which there are several North American species, lack the poison glands of the true toads, but excel at accelerated breeding: a new generation emerges from short-lived puddles in less than two weeks.

FEATHERED POND DWELLERS

Potential avian visitors to larger ponds include some avid vegetarians, including the Canada Goose, the American Coot, and various ducks. The widespread Mallard is the duck most likely to visit your pond; it will dabble at the surface or browse succulent underwater plants, occasionally taking fish and frog eggs and aquatic insects as well.

POND INSECTS

Well-aerated water makes it possible for animals that absorb oxygen from the water to breathe and thrive. These include animals with gills (fish, tadpoles, and salamander larvae) and a multitude of aquatic insects that breathe through their skin. Among the most common insect larvae that use this oxygen are the dragonfly nymphs. After feeding voraciously on the larvae of mosquitoes and other pond dwellers, they emerge as agile, fast-flying adults. Patrolling ponds and streams for adult mosquitoes, midges, and flies, they have been clocked at speeds up to 60 mph (100 kph). The female lays eggs on floating leaves and moist rocks.

Other predator insects operate at the very surface of the water itself. Water striders glide across almost every pond or stream, relying on the surface tension of the water for support. Like the land-dwelling spiders they superficially resemble (they are actually related to the plant-sucking bugs), water striders sense the vibrations of any small, hapless insect caught on the surface and scoot over to give a paralyzing kiss.

Groups of small, black, oval whirligig beetles, swimming in smooth arcs about the surface, are another common sight. They send out a series of ripples, and by "reading" the tiny wave reflections with their sensitive antennae, they detect and home in on struggling insects.

Backswimmers suspend themselves upside down at an angle just below the surface. They dart up quickly to prey, using their long back legs as oars. Farther down, in the murkier depths, lurks the giant water bug, a formidable hunter of tadpoles and young salamanders.

HUMMINGBIRDS

*Tiny, delicate hummingbirds are the only birds
on Earth that have the ability to fly backward.*

ENERGY AND SPEED IN A SMALL PACKAGE

As they gather the sugary fuel, in the form of nectar, to meet their high energy demands, hummingbirds astonish us with their deliberate speed, visiting many flowers in quick succession, each for a fleeting moment. In fact, they can't keep up this breakneck pace constantly, and like all animals, they need to rest. So it's not unusual to find them perching quietly for five to 15 minutes; during these pauses, energy needs drop to a sixth of that required when flying. While taking these breaks, they slowly digest nectar stored in their small crop, a pouch-like receptacle inside their throat.

*Everything about a
hummingbird is
a superlative.*

TOM COLAZO
(20th century), American naturalist.

At night, when they cannot feed, their metabolic rate can drop even further to conserve energy. Their heart slows from 1,200 to 50 beats per minute and their body temperature cools as they enter a state of torpor. This energy-saving strategy is particularly useful during spells of cold or inclement weather, such as during the birds' spring and fall migration periods, when nectar-rich flowers are scarce.

Hummingbirds are the smallest of birds, delicately proportioned, with very slender bills and sweeping, narrow-tipped wings. At the same time, they are the fastest and most energetic birds to visit the garden, fierce in their defense of territory and ethereal in their courtship displays. Capable of nearly instantaneous changes in direction and speed, hummingbirds hover in midair with superlative ease. Their ability to fly backward allows them to back out of deep, tubular flowers. This incomparable agility suits their specialized role as nectar feeders, for which they have no serious rivals among the other birds of North America.

ANNA'S HUMMINGBIRD *(top),
depicted here by John James Audubon,
is a resident of California, while the
ruby-throated hummingbird (right),
shown here at the nest, is the only
species found in the East.*

RED FLOWERS *are particularly attractive to all hummingbirds, including the white-eared hummingbird (right).*

Body fat is important as fuel for long migrations. Before their travels between North America and their winter haunts in Central America, Ruby-throated Humming-birds feed feverishly on flower nectar to add 50 percent to their weight in the form of fat. Such energy stores are altogether necessary if these tiny birds are to accomplish their 600-mile (1,000 km) crossing of the Gulf of Mexico.

HUMMINGBIRD FLOWERS

The flowers that provide hummingbirds with their energy receive the benefit of cross-pollination by these highly mobile feathered visitors. Some flowers specialize in attracting hummingbirds as pollinators, increasing the likelihood that their pollen will be carried to other plants of the same species.

Typical hummingbird flowers have deep, tubular corollas, requiring the long bills, protruding tongues, and artful hovering approach of these birds to reach their nectar-rich centers, and rendering them inaccessible to most flying insects, such as bees. Hummingbirds are drawn to red, in particular, but not exclusively. Other favored colors in approximate descending order of preference are orange, yellow, pink, and purple. Nearly any intense color will gain the attention of hummingbirds, and once they discover a recurrent source of nectar, they will remember it and will revisit flowers displaying that signal hue.

THE AERIAL FEATS OF A SMALL BIRD

The aerial feats of humming-birds are carried out so smoothly as to appear effortless, while, in fact, these maneuvers cost highly in energy. Relative to their small size—many are no more than 3½ inches (9 cm) long—they consume nearly three times the calories of other garden birds on a busy summer day. The impressive flight muscles amount to about 30 percent of a hummingbird's body weight, which is proportionally larger than that of any other bird. This uniquely well-developed musculature provides a powerful *upstroke* as well as the customary downstroke that powers the flight of other birds.

The key to the aerial versatility of hummingbirds lies in their ability to rotate their powerful wings rapidly and in a number of different ways at the shoulder joints, an unparalleled innovation in the engineering of bird flight. The illustrations on the right show the three basic flight modes. Normal forward flight (Figs 1 and 2) is made possible by the up-and-down wing strokes that provide forward momentum and lift, at the rate of 80 beats per second. To hover in midair (Fig. 3), the wing tips move through a horizontal figure-of-eight at the rate of 55 beats per second. To back away from a flower (Fig. 4), the wings rotate in a circle above and to the rear of the bird at 61 beats per second, providing some reverse momentum in addition to lift.

The tail serves as a rudder, enabling sudden stops and changes in direction, and the audible whir of their wings produces the humming for which these birds are named. Males execute spectacular, deep dives and U-shaped swoops, which they often finish by hovering and flashing the jewel-like throat patch (gorget) in front of a prospective mate.

❶

❷

❸

❹

PLANTS TO ATTRACT HUMMINGBIRDS

To encourage long-term residency by hummingbirds, design your garden to include suitable nectar-bearing plants that flower through the different seasons.

Common name	Scientific name	Type	Flowering time
glossy abelia	Abelia × grandiflora	shrub	summer–fall
California buckeye	Aesculus californica	tree	spring
red buckeye	Aesculus pavia	shrub	spring
mosquito plant	Agastache cana	perennial	summer–fall
century plant	Agave spp.	shrubs	summer
columbine	Aquilegia spp.	perennials	spring–summer
trumpet creeper	Campsis radicans	vine	summer
flowering quince	Chaenomeles japonica	shrub	spring
desert willow	Chilopsis linearis	tree	summer
ocotillo	Fouquieria splendens	shrub	spring
fuchsia	Fuchsia magellanica & hybrids	shrubs	summer–fall
daylilies	Hemerocallis hybrids	perennials	summer
red yucca	Hesperaloe parviflora	shrub	spring–fall
coralbells	Heuchera sanguinea	perennial	summer
desert lavender	Hyptis emoryi	shrub	spring
scarlet gilia	Ipomopsis aggregata	biennial	summer
irises	Iris spp. & cvrs	bulbs, perennials	spring–summer
chuparosa	Justicia californica	shrub	fall–winter
lilies	Lilium spp.	bulbs	summer
cardinal flower	Lobelia cardinalis	perennial	summer
honeysuckles	Lonicera spp.	vines, shrubs	spring–summer
lupines	Lupinus spp.	annuals, perennials	spring–summer
bluebells	Mertensia virginica	perennial	spring
scarlet monkeyflower	Mimulus cardinalis	perennial	summer
four o'clocks	Mirabilis spp.	perennials	summer
bee balm, bergamot	Monarda spp.	perennials	summer–fall
flowering tobacco	Nicotiana alata	annual	summer–fall
garden geraniums	Pelargonium spp. & cvrs	perennials, shrubs	summer
penstemons	Penstemon spp.	perennials	summer
summer phlox	Phlox paniculata	perennial	summer
flowering currants	Ribes spp.	shrubs	spring
sages	Salvia spp.	perennials, shrubs	spring–fall
figworts	Scrophularia spp.	perennials	summer
scarlet hedge nettle	Stachys coccinea	perennial	summer–fall
cape honeysuckle	Tecomaria capensis	vine, shrub	fall–winter
California fuchsia	Zauschneria spp.	perennials	fall–winter

HUMMINGBIRD FEATHERS

Hummingbirds dazzle the eye not only with the deftness of their flight but also with the shimmering beauty of their plumage. So gem-like are the feathers of the male birds that Europeans used their plumage to make jewelry, and Mesoamerican cultures used it in ritual adornment. Shown here, from left to right, are feathers from Anna's, Blue-throated, Costa's and Black-chinned hummingbirds.

THE COSTA'S *hummingbird (left) breeds in the Southwest. The pan-shaped feeder (above) features an ant moat at the top that prevents ants reaching the feeder's sugar solution.*

SUGARY SUPPLEMENTS

Gardeners may attract hummingbirds more reliably and in greater numbers by maintaining one or more feeders filled with sugar water. Feeders complement flowers by providing a dependable source of energy when natural nectar becomes scarce, as may happen during unseasonable cool, cloudy weather or simply during lulls in garden blooming. The recommended recipe for this nectar substitute is a maximum of one part sugar to four parts distilled water, boiled briefly to kill off any bacteria. More concentrated solutions may cause liver damage in hummingbirds over the long term. Anything weaker than a one to eight solution (11 percent) is unlikely to satisfy their energy needs. Red dye in the water is unnecessary, though something brightly colored, such as a red ribbon

or the red plastic collars that surround the tubes on some feeders, will help to grab the attention of hummingbirds in your neighborhood. Never use honey because it some-times harbors a fungus that is deadly to hummingbirds.

Replace the feeder solution and clean the sugar water receptacle and tubes on a regular basis—at least once a week is recommended. Any black mold that appears can be cleaned out using vinegar; avoid using soaps or deter-gents, which could leave a harmful residue.

Other birds, especially orioles and house finches, will occasionally visit humming-bird feeders with perches.

THE BROAD-TAILED HUMMINGBIRD *(left) is a resident of the Rockies, while the Rufous Hummingbird (right), depicted here by John James Audubon, can be found in the Pacific Northwest.*

Wasps and bees are also drawn to sugar-water feeders. When their number rises to the point where they intimidate the hummingbirds, cover the end of the feeding tube with a plastic mesh protector that prevents bees from directly sipping the solution; placing the feeder in shade will also deter these and other insects. Hummingbirds seek out a cool perch on occasion. (For more information, see p.51.)

INSECT-EATING BIRDS

*Many bird species readily adapt to our gardens
and hold the greatest immediate appeal for gardeners.*

With their mantle of feathers, birds share the human emphasis on colorful visual display, and their song is often melodious to human ears. They are an interesting spectacle: not too small and given to a warm-blooded liveliness in their feeding and social behavior. Indeed, they not infrequently raise their young right before our eyes. Many bird species will quite willingly gravitate to our yards for food when we offer it. Furthermore, it is exceedingly easy to design planting schemes that satisfy both their needs and our aesthetic goals.

An attentive gardener could easily record a dozen species of bird in a garden designed for habitat diversity. A core group will comprise year-round garden residents.

INSECTS AND MIXED DIETS

To attract the greatest variety of birdlife, you must take into account the critical insect component of the avian diet. Chicks need protein in their diet to develop from fragile hatchlings to robust flyers, an accelerated process that takes only a matter of weeks. So most songbirds raise their young during the flush months of summer, when insect populations, the nutritional answer to their needs, are surging. This is the time of year that the gardener is most likely to encounter birds as consumers of insects and other invertebrates. In the other seasons, fruit and seeds are likely to figure more significantly in bird diets. Even in winter, however, some species still focus primarily on insects (especially eggs and pupae).

PLANTS THAT ARE HOST TO INSECTS

Many plants that develop seeds and fruits in summer and fall host a rich array of insects when the plants are blooming and leafing out in spring. Densely vegetated meadows and borders composed of herbaceous plants are a rich, buggy environment during their bloom season, visited by many insect-eating birds. Flowers of all kinds attract a host of six-legged pollinators and pollen eaters, which become the prey of birds such as flycatchers, bluebirds, and others. The supple, young foliage of some common native trees, such as oaks and willows, is initially free of insect-repelling tannins, and, along with the flowering cat-kins, supports an abundance of spring caterpillars. Large numbers of migrating song-birds, particularly warblers, vireos, and tanagers, feed on this springtime bounty as they pause on the way north to their breeding grounds. The bark of trees of all sizes and types is home to insects, spiders, and pupae, which birds such as nuthatches, chickadees, and the Brown Creeper frequently seek out while a part of mixed feeding flocks.

THE TUFTED TITMOUSE *(top) uses its small, short bill to pick off tiny insects from branches and bark. This female Indigo Bunting (left) is feeding her chicks the protein they need in the form of juicy, green caterpillars.*

THE SCARLET TANAGER *(above) has a slightly hooked bill to snare large prey, while the pileated woodpecker, (right), recognizable by its red crest, excavates deeply in tree bark for insects.*

CATCHING INSECTS

Insect-eating birds have strong, yet nimble feet that are variously adapted to perching on the slenderest of twigs, hanging upside down, walking up trees, or hopping across the ground. The bills of insect-eating birds are suited to seizing crawling and flying insects, picking away at tiny bugs and cocoons, pounding into trees, or crushing hard-shelled beetles and other specialized tasks.

The most common method of insect-eating birds is to glean plant-eating insects directly off foliage, stems, and flowers. Warblers, vireos, and tanagers adopt this approach, with various species focusing on different levels and types of vegetation. Using their slender bills, warblers hunt leaf-loving creatures at a speedy pace, hovering and flitting in pursuit of caterpillars and other small prey items. By comparison, vireos and tanagers have marginally heavier bills, slightly hooked to snare larger prey,

which they stalk in a more deliberate fashion. Catching flying insects on the wing is the preferred method of the agile flycatchers, whose bills are more gaping and whose long, narrow wings enable deft midair turns.

Woodpeckers excavate for prey in decaying trees, using their sharp, powerful bills and extensile tongues, with their feet firmly anchored to the trunk or branch. They sometimes plumb the ground for ants and visit feeders.

Yet other species operate at ground level, walking, hopping, or scuffling

while they search through leaf litter for crawling insects and other invertebrates. The excellent vision of songbirds serves not only to detect elusive prey, but also to keep a watchful eye out for predators, whether they be gliding hawks or terrestrial mammals.

BLACK-CAPPED *chickadees (far right) nest in tree cavities and will accept nestboxes. Bullock's orioles (right) feed on insects and fruit alike during their spring and fall migrations.*

BIRDS *that* EAT FRUIT *and* SEED

The fruit and seed of many plants are often deliberately conspicuous and alluring to birds.

When birds pursue prey such as insects and other invertebrates, they frequently must contend with elusive, moving targets and concealed quarry. Fruit and seed are much more easy prey. Plants trade the transport of their viable seed to new locations in exchange for providing food (carbohydrate, fat, protein, and vitamins) to birds, as well as to some accommodating mammals—a mutually satisfactory arrangement. In this way, fruit- and seed-

SOME MEMBERS *of the pheasant family, such as the Gambel's Quail (below) of the Southwest, visit gardens in search of fruit and seed. Typical of most sparrows, the Dark-eyed Junco (below right) uses its stout bill to crush seed and fruit, and sometimes, insects.*

eating birds play a direct role both in the dispersal of seed far from parent plants and in the spread of many plant species to new locations and environments.

WAYS PLANTS CAN DISPERSE SEED

Plants have evolved various strategies to accomplish this vital goal of seed dispersal. Brightly colored fruits with agreeably pulpy, nutritious flesh initially attract birds. After the birds have had their fill, they frequently discard the pits if they are large and hard to crack open. The bird sometimes drops the pits only after it has flown to a new perch, transferring the seed within to a new location. The smaller seed of some fruiting plants, such as the barberries (*Berberis* spp.), will withstand bird digestion intact and is transported for as long as that process takes. The successful fruit trees belonging to the *Prunus* genus—apricots and cherries—have bitter, even poisonous seed that discourages the bird from eating after it has consumed the tasty flesh of the fruit.

Birds, the free tenants of

land, air, and ocean,

Their forms all symmetry,

their motions grace.

JAMES MONTGOMERY
(1771–1864), British poet

Employing another clever strategy, the seed inside the fruit of the mistletoes is so disagreeably sticky that birds, after sating their appetites, often rub the seed off their bills onto tree bark, exactly where this parasitic plant prefers to grow.

Many species of plant do not coat their seed in an inviting rich fruit wrapping, but suffer some of it to be broken open and eaten, relying on the minority that is scattered or misplaced by foraging seed eaters, such as sparrows and squirrels, to perpetuate their line. The seed heads of certain plants, such as *Impatiens*, burst open when birds start to peck them, propelling some seed a few feet away. In other plants, the seed simply shakes free when the birds alight, so that some escape being eaten. In watery environments, seed blows down to rest at the muddy water's edge and then travels

THE PURPLE FINCH (right) eats primarily seeds from grasses and herbaceous plants. The Seed-eating Cardinal is a year-round resident in the eastern and central United States; the male (far right) is bright red.

in the mud picked up on the feet of marsh and pond birds. Still other seed, such as that of the tickseeds (*Bidens* spp.), has tiny hooks that allow it to attach to feathers and enjoy a considerable ride away from the parent plant.

FICKLE VISITORS AND FLEXIBLE PALATES

Be prepared for inconsistency in the food preferences and appetites of birds. They will patronize some fruit-bearing plants immediately, yet ignore other fruits until they season naturally and become less astringent, or until other preferred food resources have been exhausted. While one year a fruiting shrub may attract a resident flock of waxwings; another year, it will fail to draw much at all in the way of feathered visitors (though always providing a welcome touch of color for the garden). In fact, birds are not only fickle but they also are surprisingly flexible, and when times are lean, they will accept food that they would otherwise ignore. For the early-spring migrants, such as phoebes and bluebirds, which sometimes get caught in a cold snap when most insects are dormant, the lingering berries in the yard will prove highly attractive as a vital, emergency food source. Even in the summer, when insects are abundant, some primarily insect-eating birds will then indulge themselves in berry-eating to take advantage of certain minerals and vitamins.

GARDEN SEEDS AND FRUITS FOR BIRDS

A meadow planted with native grasses and herbaceous plants—such as sunflowers (*Helianthus* spp.), wild iris (*Iris* spp.), asters (*Aster* spp.), goldenrods (*Solidago* spp.), *Coreopsis* spp., and buckwheats (*Eriogonum* spp.)—will provide the seeds that attract sparrows, juncos, buntings, and finches. Some seed heads last well into winter to serve as a source of protein and fat for birds.

Introducing berry-bearing shrubs and small trees is another productive strategy for luring a variety of birds, particularly in fall and winter. Possibilities include winterberry (*Ilex verticillata*), in the East, and toyon (*Heteromeles arbutifolia*), in the West (see The Backyard Habitat, starting on p. 304, for other species suitable for your region). There are also some exotic, non-invasive plants worth considering. Typical bird species drawn to these plants include thrushes (such as the American Robin), waxwings, jays, thrashers (and the related mimic thrushes such as the catbird), bluebirds, and occasionally, warblers and tanagers.

THIS CEDAR WAXWING (below) is feeding its chicks pin cherries (*Prunus pensylvanica*).

NIGHT DWELLERS

*When the sun sets, darkness envelopes the garden
and a new cast of wildlife characters stirs.*

Spiders freshen their webs; nocturnal animals scurry or take wing; tree frogs trill; fireflies dazzle at the meadow's edge—a different world emerges at nighttime.

ENTERING THE NIGHT WORLD

The after hours world is by no means closed to the curious gardener who is willing to adapt. Learn to rely on non-visual senses to appreciate the tell-tale sounds and fragrances that rise in importance at nighttime. And take advantage of what light is available. For example, the twilight provides an opportunity to glimpse night dwellers as they renew their activity following daytime slumber. Against the dimming sky, bats and owls take flight in silhouette. Some animals, such as the Pandora sphinx moth, are at their peak activity during this time of transition. A garden bathed in moonlight is similarly open to our perusal.

Even in starlight, our eyes can adjust to see shape and movement in the garden. The human eye achieves surprising nighttime sensitivity after only 15 to 30 minutes in darkness away from artificial lights.

NOCTURNAL FLOWERS AND THEIR ADMIRERS

Like us, most animals can't see in color at night, so it's no surprise that pale-colored flowers, especially white ones, stand out in the night garden. Some flowers glow to their full glory only at night, such as the moonflower (*Ipomoea alba*) with blooms that last a single night. Other flowers advertise nectar and pollen with bold, often exotic fragrances released only after the sun has set. Many of the lilies, flowering tobacco (*Nicotiana alata*), and, in mild-climate gardens, angel's-trumpets (*Brugmansia* spp.) and night jessamine (*Cestrum nocturnum*) are prime examples of nocturnal fragrance. The increased humidity of night air enhances such fragrances,

which communicate with potential pollinators.

Night flowers usually recess their nectar inside long, tubular blossoms, accessible to the long tongues, or probosces, of the night-flying sphinx moths (also known as hawk moths). Patient nighttime observers may spot these moths hovering like small, fluttering ghosts at flower borders.

Moths do not enjoy a monopoly on nocturnal nectar sources: for example, in the Desert Southwest, the famed saguaro cactus is pollinated by the long-tongued bat as it laps up springtime nectar.

THE LOVELY LUNA MOTH *(top), a nocturnal wanderer, is an endangered species. The pyralis firefly (above right) has a yellow flashing light on its tail. Its larvae feed on slugs and snails. True to its name, the Barn Owl (left) often nests in barns and silos.*

THE CALIFORNIA LEAF-NOSED BAT
(above) preys on various insects, including flightless ones. Some spiders, such as this green lynx spider (right), use a silk dragline when pouncing on prey.

SWEEPING THE SKY

Other animals, principally bats, naturally take advantage of night-flying insects as a food resource. The key to the bats' success is echolocation, which they employ to zero in on prey and to navigate through the landscape. Bats emit high-frequency sound waves in flight that bounce off objects ahead of them and then rebound to their perceptive ears for interpretation. They can track an insect as small as a mosquito.

Perhaps because they are active only at night, when most of us are asleep, or because they have been the featured villains in so many horror movies, bats have been saddled with a negative reputation, which does not reflect their real value in the ecology of many regions around the world. Throughout North America, small bats such as the little brown bat play a major role in the reduction of night-flying insects, particularly mosquitoes. In the tropics and desert regions, bats play a crucial role in the lives of many plants native to these

Sit outside at midnight and close your eyes; feel the grass, the air, the space.

LINDA HASSELSTROM (20th century), American writer and rancher

areas, either by pollinating flowers in their search for nectar, or by dispersing seed as they consume the fleshy fruit of cacti and tropical trees.

HAWKS OF THE NIGHT

Alongside bats, but in far fewer numbers, birds called nightjars sweep the insects out of the night air into their wide, gaping mouths. In one evening, a nightjar can capture 500 mosquitoes. Soft-edged flight feathers muffle their aerial arcs above woodland edge and garden. From fence post or branch, they sing the rich, melodious, and oft-repeated songs for which many of them are named, such as "Chuck-wills-widow", or "Whip-poor-will".

Sharing the nightjars' capacity for agile, silent flight and night-piercing calls, owls cruise the nocturnal landscape in search of larger prey. For example, the small, mottled Screech Owl is adept at capturing mice and voles, as well as grasshoppers and cutworms. It nests in tree cavities and prefers gardens with groves or orchards nearby. It doesn't actually screech, but utters an eerie whistle. The larger Barn Owl hunts over fields, farmland, and gardens, descending on as many as 20 rodents in a single night.

I never for a day gave up listening to the songs of our birds, or watching their peculiar habits, or delineating them in the best way that I could.

JOHN JAMES AUDUBON (1785–1851),
American artist and ornithologist

CHAPTER SIX

GOING BIRDING

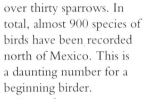

PREPARATIONS

Good preparation and some thorough groundwork
will help you make the most of your birding trips.

Most of us are birders of a kind, in that we are bound to notice the birds around us from time to time. It is unusual to find a person who cannot tell the difference between a pelican and a hawk, for instance, or who has trouble identifying a sparrow. Really, we are all just a step away from the great enjoyment birding can bring.

And what an array of birds there is to become acquainted with! In North America there are two kinds of pelicans, six types of wild geese, twenty-five "hawks", four crows, twenty-two woodpeckers, seven chickadees and over thirty sparrows. In total, almost 900 species of birds have been recorded north of Mexico. This is a daunting number for a beginning birder.

But, of course, many species have only small populations, and are found in remote places, so you are hardly likely to encounter more than a small proportion of all North American species in a single outing. On the other hand—and this is one of the joys of birding—you never know what you are going to find. In some northern states in winter you may struggle to see 10 species in an entire day, while a summer visit to the same spot may yield over 100. The key to getting the most from any outing is to be well prepared.

FIRST STEPS
It's best to begin slowly. Start by browsing through The Habitat Birdfinder (p. 134) at home to become familiar with the various groups and species you are likely to come across. Don't be discouraged by the great diversity. Think about the kind of environment you live in, select a corresponding habitat in The Habitat Birdfinder, and read the entries that relate to the birds you are most likely to see.

FIELD GUIDES *The prime purpose of a field guide (left) is to help you through the vital first step in birding: to identify your bird.*

A BIRDER'S VEST *(above) is a useful item of clothing. Its many pockets are ideal for field guides and other birding paraphernalia, such as pocket knives, notebooks, and magnifying glasses (top).*

The next step is to study an area in your neighborhood, such as a park, using the information in this chapter to help you develop your identification skills. Parks with lakes are particularly rewarding as most waterbirds are large, easily observed, and distinctively marked—three desirable attributes. You are also likely to find exotic visitors in such parks, which might be a little confusing, but don't be put off.

Once you have mastered some basic skills you will be ready to go further afield. Be thorough, but don't get frustrated when birds disappear before you have clinched their ID! Another new bird will be nearby.

O to mount again where

erst I haunted;

Where the old red hills

are bird-enchanted…

Robert Louis Stevenson
(1850–94), Scottish novelist
and poet

Field Guides

The Habitat Birdfinder introduces you to over 200 of the most commonly encountered North American species and is a great place to start your birding. Fairly soon, however, you are likely to want to acquire a complete field guide to North American birds. After binoculars, a good field guide will be your most important birding tool. A wide range of guides is available.

BIRDING GEAR *As in any other out-door activity, staying warm and comfortable is an important consideration. A wide range of clothing and accessories is readily available for birding, from rain-proof jackets, back-packs, and sturdy boots (far right) to field bags and carry-pouches (right) for your field guide.*

At first the organization of a field guide may seem odd, as the birds will not be presented in any obviously logical order, such as alphabetically or large-to-small. This is because birds (and other vertebrate animals) are classified by scientists in taxonomic order (see p. 20).

Out in the field you will become aware of the usefulness of this in at least one respect: physically similar birds are grouped together,

A STARTING POINT *A good place to start birding is at a local pond or lake, as waterbirds are often fairly easy to identify. However, particularly if you are in a park, watch out for exotic species that may mislead you.*

and these, of course, are the ones that you are most likely to confuse.

Once you identify a bird and know its name, you will find that more information is available in your guide.

GETTING EQUIPPED

In addition to a field guide, the only other essential piece of equipment for a birder is a good pair of binoculars (see p. 112). Otherwise, use the clothing and provisions that you would take on any hike or field trip.

Bear in mind, however, that birding may involve sitting or standing in one spot for long periods. Warm clothing will therefore be important in colder areas. If it's hot, be wary of the sun's rays: brimmed hats and sunscreen will protect you but if you are at sea, remember that the sun may be twice as intense as it is on land.

If you are likely to be out in the rain, remember to take something along to dry the lenses of your binoculars, spotting scope, or spectacles. A baby diaper is extremely effective— after all, they were invented to soak up moisture. Avoid rainwear that squeaks, as it will alert the birds to your presence.

CHOOSING BINOCULARS

As your most important piece of birding equipment,

binoculars should be chosen with

a good deal of care.

Many people have an old pair of binoculars at home, but if they have been lying around for some time they may well have been knocked out of alignment. Unless they are particularly valuable, you may be better off investing in a new pair rather than paying for expensive repairs.

When buying binoculars, the following features should be considered carefully.

MAGNIFICATION

All binoculars feature a set of numbers such as 7 x 40. The first number denotes the power of the binoculars: a 7x pair of binoculars will make a bird look seven times larger than it appears to the naked eye; a 10x pair will make the bird look 10 times larger, and so on.

Anything less than 7x is of little benefit. 10x binoculars will give you a great view, but you may have trouble keeping the image steady— the greater the magnification, the more any hand tremor is accentuated. So, depending on how steady a hand you have, you should select a pair between 7x and 10x.

BRIGHTNESS AND WEIGHT

The second number that appears on your binoculars— 40 in the above example— denotes the diameter of the objective (front) lenses. The larger these are, the more light will enter the binoculars and the brighter the image will be. However, the larger the objective lenses are, the heavier the binoculars will be.

SIZE AND WEIGHT *are important considerations in choosing binoculars, but the pair you buy must also deliver a bright, crisp image at both short and long ranges.*

CONSTRUCTION AND WEIGHT

There are two types of binoculars—porro prisms and roof prisms (see below)—and their designs have a bearing on their weight and price.

Until the 1980s, the best binoculars were porro prisms. Porro designs are still popular and, in general, dominate the lower end of the price range ($40 to $400). Many provide bright, clear viewing and, in some cases, good close focus.

Recently, however, new technology has allowed manufacturers to create roof prisms that provide the same power and clarity in a more compact design. Roof prisms are therefore lighter but tend to be more expensive.

DURABILITY

Porro designs tend to be frailer than roof prisms. Even with average usage, some part

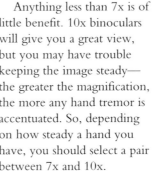

IN CLOSE-UP *A 7x pair of binoculars will magnify the image you see seven times (top inset). A 10x pair will give you a larger image (bottom inset), but at this magnification you may have trouble keeping the image steady.*

of the frame may eventually break or a prism may slip out of alignment.

Many binoculars now feature rubber armoring for protection. However, there is a tendency for some rubber eyecups to crack and break, and for bubbles to form in armored panels.

CLOSE FOCUS

A good pair of birding binoculars should focus on objects that are as close as 14 feet (4.2 m), and the closer they can focus, the better. Some roof prism models, designed for birding, will focus to 12 feet (3.7 m) but some binoculars have a minimum viewing distance of 23 feet (7 m) or more, which is totally impractical.

PRICE

There are good, robust binoculars available at the lower end of the price range, but, as with most equipment of this kind, you get what you pay for and top-quality binoculars are a joy to use. On the other hand, as binoculars are easily damaged, you should buy only what you can afford to replace.

COMFORT

Before buying binoculars, talk to someone who owns the model you have in mind, or

USING BINOCULARS

When aiming binoculars, it is important to find an object (or at least a specific area) first with the naked eye and to keep watching it while bringing the binoculars up to the appropriate line-of-sight. Practice aligning your binoculars to what you are looking at. You will take longer to find what you want if you search the landscape aimlessly.

If you turn your binoculars round, they can function as a microscope for making monsters out of ladybugs or examining flowers.

try to find a salesperson who is a binocular specialist and ask them for guidance.

In the shop, hang the binoculars around your neck to check their weight: if they feel heavy, they'll feel a good deal heavier at the end of a day in the field. Look through them and roll the focus wheel to be sure all parts are running smoothly. Check how well they focus on objects close by.

How well do the eyepieces fit your eyes? If you wear glasses, can you use them with your glasses? Comfort and ease of use are as important as power. Last but not least, check what kind of warranty the manufacturer will provide.

MAINTENANCE

Binoculars must be properly aligned and kept clean. Use a soft cloth to wipe oily dust and lunch crumbs from the lenses. Q-tips are good for small, hard-to-reach crannies.

ROOF AND PORRO PRISM *binoculars both use prisms to fold the light path passing through them. However, the roof prism design (far left) achieves a slimmer style and reduced weight by means of a more complex prism configuration than that found in the somewhat simpler (and consequently less expensive) porro prism design (near left).*

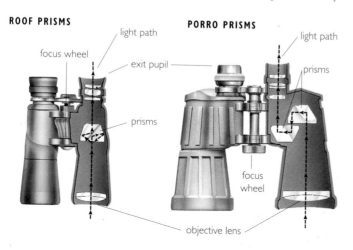

ROOF PRISMS

focus wheel

light path

exit pupil

prisms

PORRO PRISMS

light path

prisms

focus wheel

objective lens

CHOOSING *a* SPOTTING SCOPE

If you plan to do a good deal of long-range viewing in open areas, such as in grasslands or at the seashore, you may find it worthwhile to invest in a spotting scope.

Having used binoculars in the field for a while, you may decide you would like to buy a spotting scope. A spotting scope will complement your binoculars, rather than replace them, as only in certain environments and for particular activities will a spotting scope prove more effective.

In particular, spotting scopes are excellent for identifying distant, perched raptors or for scanning flocks of shorebirds. They are also useful for close scrutiny of nesting activity and birds at feeders. They are less effective for observing small, fast-moving forest birds.

A wide range of brands and models of spotting scopes is available and, as a general rule, you get what you pay for— the more expensive ones give brighter, sharper images and their optics and construction are more rugged. Given the expense, it's a good idea to

THE RIGHT FIT *You may find that scopes with offset eyepieces (below) are more comfortable to use as you don't have to stoop so low to see through them. On the other hand, straight scopes (below left) are generally easier to aim.*

talk to other birders about the spotting scopes they like to use and even try looking through them.

After settling on a make and model, you still need to consider configuration and eyepiece power.

CONFIGURATION

Spotting scopes are available in two forms: either with an eyepiece aligned with the barrel or one that is offset by 45 degrees.

You may find straight scopes easier to aim, but, on the other hand, offset scopes are often more

SMALL FRY *Setting the tripod low is not merely a convenience for younger birders (left), it also makes the spotting scope more stable, improving the view for all concerned.*

TRIPODS

Choosing a tripod is a matter of finding just the right compromise between stability and weight. The heavier your tripod is, the more stable it will be, but, on the other hand, the heavier it is, the less convenient it will be to take on birding outings. There are also a number of other features that may have a bearing on your decision.

Probably the most important single element is the head. Tripods are mostly made for cameras and have all sorts of knobs and screws for adjusting the head to various positions. Birders need rapid-action controls, and the fewer there are the better. A single handle with a grip-tightener for locking, and vertical and horizontal lock screws are all you need. The handle should be on the opposite side of the head from the eye you normally look through.

The fixtures at the junction of each telescoping section of the legs of your tripod must be sturdy. Screw locks are usually stronger and last longer than flip-locks, but flip-locks allow quick set-up and collapse. Tubular legs are normally steadier than square ones and you may appreciate the difference when birding on windy days.

comfortable to use as you may not have to stoop so low to look through them. Try the different types out and think about how you will be using your scope. Weigh carefully the pros and cons of the two types before you buy.

EYEPIECE POWER

The most common magnifications are: 15x; 22x wide angle; 30x; 40x; and 20x to 60x zoom.

A spotting scope at lowest power (15x) is hardly worth the expense if you are proficient with 10x binoculars. A 40x eyepiece may give a nice view of a hawk ¼ mile away, for instance, but will not be particularly effective for scanning shorebird flocks.

A zoom lens may seem a good compromise, and there are many worthwhile models available, but some cheaper zoom eyepieces are optically incorrect, giving fuzzy images, and most of them lose their light–gathering ability quickly as the power increases.

All things considered, the best all–round magnification is in the region of 25x to 30x.

USING YOUR SPOTTING SCOPE

Spotting scopes have a smaller field of view than binoculars and are, therefore, even more difficult to master. Once you have your scope, it's a good idea to practice using it at home before you go on a birding trip.

Aim at a stationary object like a telephone pole or your neighbor's fuchsia, trying to locate the object and focus on it as quickly as you can.

ON THE ROAD *Car window clamps for spotting scopes (below) facilitate birding on the move, allowing you to stop and take a close look at birds such as this Yellow-headed Blackbird (below right). If you don't have a clamp, a plump beanbag flopped over the open window will do much the same job.*

I find it hard to see anything about a bird that it does not want seen. It demands my full attention.

ANNIE DILLARD (b. 1945), American poet and essayist

GOING AFIELD

*An effective birder is one who has a good idea of when
and where to go looking, and who causes the birds
a minimum of disturbance.*

From the beginner's viewpoint in particular, birds can seem very difficult to even get close to. However, providing you go looking for them within their range and at the right time of year, and keep in mind the following information, you will find that a large number of birds can be located with just a little careful planning.

Birds are always more conspicuous first thing in the morning, for then they are at their most active, and are generally in full song, often singing from prominent perches. This is particularly the case in spring, when most male (and some female) landbirds sing from perches or perform showy displays.

In winter, swimming birds gather together on oceans, bays, lakes, and rivers where various species may be studied side-by-side. During spring and fall migration, shorebirds, hawks, seabirds, and many small songbirds become gregarious and may be observed in single-species and mixed flocks.

GONE BIRDING *The father of the modern outdoor movement, John Muir (right), pictured on a field trip with Theodore Roosevelt, another keen birder.*

Fields, meadows, and particularly forests may seem birdless until you find a flock. To locate flocks, scan open ground near brushy areas or weedy fields, or listen for the calls of the birds—as they forage they remain in constant vocal communication.

HABITATS

The best first step to take in a search for a particular bird is to find out what kind of habitat and niche it favors (see pp. 30 and 136). Within habitats, often the best places to look for birds are what could be termed "boundary areas" (known as ecotones), such as forest edges, the fringes of meadows, and reed beds on lakes, as many species prefer to remain constantly within reach of cover.

APPROACHING BIRDS

While some birds may be approached openly, many are timid and will flee at the first hint of danger. To many, such a hint is the sense of some-

BIRDING ETHICS

It is important that all birders are aware of their responsibilities in relation to birds and to the natural environment in general. The members of the American Birding Association pledge to adhere to the following "general guidelines of good birding behavior".

Birders must always act in ways that do not endanger the welfare of birds or other wildlife.
• Observe and photograph birds without knowingly disturbing them in any significant way.
• Avoid chasing or repeatedly flushing birds.
• Only sparingly use recordings and similar methods of attracting birds and do not use these methods in heavily birded areas.
• Keep an appropriate distance from nests and nesting colonies so as not to disturb them or expose them to danger.
• Refrain from handling birds or eggs unless engaged in recognized research activities.
A complete version of this code can be obtained from the American Birding Association.

WATCHING *treetop birds in level woodland (left) is often uncomfortable. Look for a slope or similar vantage point from which to watch with greater comfort. Always keep your distance from nests or hatchlings like these Least Bitterns (above left).*

FIELD TACTICS *An experienced birder will look first along the edges of habitats, where visibility is least obstructed and the greatest variety of birds is to be found. In grasslands (above left), this tactic may reveal birds such as the Scissor-tailed Flycatcher (above), while the edges of wetlands (left) are the haunt of birds like the Great Blue Heron (below left).*

Your first observations of birds and their behavior can be done by simply learning to drift gently through a wood: a naturalist in a hurry never learns anything of value.

GERALD DURRELL (b. 1925)
English naturalist and writer

thing unusual happening in their environment. A sudden movement, an unfamiliar sound, a flash of light, or the shape of a predator (you) outlined against the sky can all alarm the birds and result in their departure.

When arriving at a birding spot by car, shut off the motor at once. If possible, remain in the car. Birds are much less fearful of a car that does not move than they are of people running around and aiming things at them. If you get out, try not to slam the doors.

In a new habitat, look around and plan your approach before advancing. Avoid walking into the sun as this will make it hard for you to see clearly. Move slowly and avoid talking loudly or snapping twigs. Look into a clearing before you step into it. Standing still in one spot for some time is often the most effective tactic, particularly in woodlands.

Try to avoid breaking the horizon line with the outline of your body. Earth-toned clothes may camouflage you to some extent. Use cover wherever possible: hide behind vegetation, a rock, or even a car. Remember, however, that the bird's observation skills are far better than yours and it will almost always know you are there. The key is to move around in a way that will not alarm it. If you can assure the bird that you pose no threat, it will usually tolerate your presence.

Once you have obtained a good view, back off and leave quietly. Birds have a hard enough time finding places to rest and forage in peace without birders putting them under more pressure.

HUNTERS

Be very careful during the hunting season as each year people are killed or wounded by hunters mistaking them for quarry. If you do hear hunters, try to head away from them. If they are already close to you, shout to them to warn them of your presence. Do not try to hide—if you do, you are far more likely to be shot at.

IDENTIFYING BIRDS:
the BASICS

By learning to focus on particular features of the birds you see, you can become proficient in identifying all but the most difficult species.

Frequently, novice birders are dismayed by the huge number of species listed in field guides. But of the total check-list of any given locality, less than half the species of regularly occurring birds are likely to be present at any given time.

When you are trying to identify a bird, always start by considering what you see in front of you. Don't reach immediately for your guide to see what you ought to be seeing or whether the bird looks like any others in your book. Describe the bird to yourself and try to draw on information you already have in your head. Consider the following questions.

FAMILY TRAITS
What family or group does the bird belong to?
Most families of birds share certain physical characteristics and if you can be sure what group a bird belongs to you are well on your way to making a positive identifi-cation. Familiarizing yourself with the information on pp. 138–143 will assist you greatly in this respect.

What size is the bird?
The size of a lone bird may be hard to deduce, but try matching it to one you know. Is it bigger or smaller than a robin? Is it similar to the size of a crow? Size comparisons are, of course, easiest when the mystery bird is with something you know.

BEHAVIOR
What is the bird doing?
Because different groups of

BEHAVIOR *Only nuthatches (above) move down tree trunks head first, a behavior so distinctive that the family can be identified by this feature alone.*

birds demonstrate different behaviors, what a bird is doing may help to identify it. Is it pecking at the ground, leaf-gleaning in a tree, or making short flights to and from an exposed perch? Is it swimming and surface diving? Drilling in mud at the edge of a pond or flying in a V-formation?

Is the bird alone or in a group?
During fall and winter, most small sandpipers join huge flocks of their own and similar species. Insect-eaters such as chickadees, kinglets, nuthatches, creepers, and vireos come together to increase foraging efficiency and predator avoidance. Other birds are solitary, except during the breeding season.

How much it enhances the richness of the forest to see in it some beautiful bird which you never detected before!

HENRY DAVID THOREAU (1817–62), American naturalist and writer

FAMILY TRAITS *Most people are able to recognize an owl and a duck (above) when they see them. Once you have established which family a bird belongs to, you are well on your way to making a positive identification.*

PHYSICAL FEATURES

What distinguishing features does the bird have?

To really pin down a species you have to learn to recognize its field marks.

Field marks are those characteristics of a species that, taken together, distinguish that bird from others. Usually they are plumage features. Pay particular attention to the following parts of the bird:

• eyebrow (supercilium)
• rump
• outer tail feathers
• wingbars

Make sure you are familiar with the names used for the different parts of a bird's body and the tracts of feathers that make up its plumage (see p. 24). In The Habitat Birdfinder, the identifying marks are highlighted in the Field Notes boxes. Always bear in mind that patterns are more significant than colors.

EYE MARKINGS *The pattern of the eyebrow (supercilium) or eye-ring often distinguishes a species, as with the Black-capped Vireo (left), the Northern Wheatear (center), and the White-throated Sparrow (right).*

WINGBARS *are often important field marks. For example, they help to distinguish this Black-throated Green Warbler (right) from the Wilson's Warbler (left).*

OUTER TAIL FEATHERS *are field marks in many species. Frequently the distinguishing mark is a lighter tip or sides.*

TIME AND PLACE

Where are you and what time of year is it? What kind of habitat are you in?

Always make a note of where you are, what time of year and day it is, and what kind of habitat the bird is in. It is important that you have noted these details as they may help you confirm a sighting. Many birds are common only within a particular range at particular times of year and favor a specific habitat. Most field guides indicate the distributions of species and their habitat preferences.

ROGER TORY PETERSON *Author of the first compact field guides, Roger Tory Peterson (right) has probably done more to introduce people to birding than any other single person.*

ROGER TORY PETERSON

The first compact, mass-market field guides were written and illustrated by Roger Tory Peterson, and were first published in 1934. These guides introduced the innovative and influential system of "field marks".

A bird's field marks are those physical features that distinguish it from all other species. In Peterson's guides, these marks are highlighted both in the text and in the accompanying illustrations.

Peterson's system was so successful that its principles were adopted during the Second World War to assist allied troops in identifying aircraft. Almost all contemporary field guides use field marks to assist in identification.

IDENTIFYING BIRDS: CASES

The following cases—one from each of the six habitats in The Habitat

Birdfinder—show how to put the advice on the previous pages into practice.

DOWNY WOODPECKER

We hear a weak tapping noise and a black-and-white head peeks out from behind a tree trunk. Sidestepping around, we see that the bird is clinging to the trunk with its claws and using its tail to provide further support. As we watch, we see that it is drumming its narrow, sharp beak against the bark. This is unquestionably a woodpecker, but which one?

What stands out in the bird's generally black-and-white patterned plumage is an obvious, solid white line down the middle of its back. This alone indicates that it is either a Hairy or a Downy woodpecker. Looking more closely, we note that our bird has black spots on its tail. These mean that it can only be a Downy.

YELLOW-RUMPED WARBLER

During a winter walk in a wood beside a river, a sharp chip note followed quickly by another attracts our attention to a group of small birds flitting through the trees. From a distance, these birds seem plain and colorless. Sparrows and finches are common in woods but they would appear brownish, not gray like these birds. The habitat, color, and call suggest that these are warblers.

Only a few warblers remain in North America in winter, so we don't have too many birds to consider. On closer inspection our generally nondescript birds show a flash of color: a small, bright yellow mark on the rump. Few warblers have a yellow rump, so that is a help. Any other features? A small fleck of yellow on the crown. That clinches it: the only bird with both these features is the Yellow-rumped Warbler.

KILLDEER

Driving along a country road through prairie, we spot a couple of brownish, long-legged, robin-sized birds standing in the middle of a field. As we watch, the birds suddenly sprint along the ground, their legs a blur, and then, even more abruptly, stop dead. This action, repeated over and over as we watch, is characteristic of plovers.

Not many plovers feed in dry open areas such as grasslands. As we sight the birds from the front, we are able to identify them positively. Both birds display two distinctive black bands across their white chests—a feature that distinguishes them as Killdeers.

BLUE-WINGED TEAL

As we pass a marshy pond in the countryside, we note a group of birds swimming and splashing in the water. About half of the group are brown and mottled. The shape of their bills instantly identifies them as ducks of some kind. (All other birds found on open water have pointed bills.) This should be easy!

The birds we are observing are tipping up or "dabbling". As they tip forward, we can see that they are kicking at the surface to keep themselves submerged. This is significant

as ducks can generally be divided into two groups—those that dabble and those that dive. Among the dabblers, the males are usually more distinct than the females. The brown birds must therefore be the females. The rest have slaty blue faces which bear prominent bold white crescents. The combination of dabbling behavior and the white crescent on the face confirms beyond doubt that these are Blue-winged Teals.

HERRING GULL

On a walk along the seashore on a pleasant winter afternoon, we notice several crow-sized birds squabbling over scraps of fish thrown to them by fishermen on the pier. The birds have a white head and body, and a yellow bill. The seashore environment, the plumage features, the scavenging behavior of the birds, and their tolerance of humans all imply that these are gulls.

Juvenile and immature gulls are tricky to identify (see p. 268), but adults are more straight-forward. The pale gray back and white head of these birds indicate that they are adults. The next things to check when looking at gulls are the bill, the legs, and the wingtips. Looking through our binoculars, we see that these gulls have a red spot on their yellow bills, pink legs, and white-spotted black wingtips. These features identify the birds as Herring Gulls.

CURVE-BILLED THRASHER

On an early morning walk in the desert, our attention is drawn to a bird singing on top of a saguaro cactus. The song is a long, rich, scratchy, warbling song, and some phrases are repeated before the sequence starts again. The bird is slender, with a long bill, and has a strikingly long tail. These features suggest a member of the Mimidae family (Mocking-birds and Thrashers) but which one?

The bird's plumage seems to lack distinct markings. So what other features can we use to identify it? The bill quite obviously curves downwards. And although they are faint, there are some dusky spots on the bird's chest. After a while, the bird flies off. As it does so, we note pale tips to its tail feathers. These clinch it: the combination of decurved bill, mottling on the chest, and pale tail feathers is found only on the Curve-billed Thrasher.

BIRDING *by* EAR

If you are able to learn the vocalizations of the birds

in your area, you will be able to identify many more of them than

if you were relying on your eyes alone.

Birding by ear is a learned discipline. Because each bird species has its own range of vocalizations and because birds frequently vocalize in areas of thick vegetation, a person who can identify each voice will be able to record many more birds in a given area than one birding only by sight.

During spring, each territorial male sings persistently from several perches, seldom leaving his area. At such times, an experienced birder can estimate the number of territories in an area simply by counting singers.

LEARNING

People gifted with a musical memory and perfect pitch can remember a bird's song or call after hearing it only once. The rest of us have to work at it! Listening to tapes may be helpful—many commercial cassettes are available at bird stores—but listen to only a few songs at a time. If you try to learn too many in a session, they tend to sound very much the same.

The best method for learning bird sounds is to go where the birds are and to watch them vocalize. You will probably find that you are able to retain the visual and audible connection—at least for a while.

REMEMBERING

The easiest way to remember a song or call is to compare it with one you already know. For example: "This song sounds like a robin's but is more abrupt and rolls along through shorter phrases," or "This call note is like the Song Sparrow's but is louder and more metallic." Occasionally, when you hear an unfamiliar bird voice, you may find it useful to record it in the field for later identification at home, by comparing it with tapes of known species.

Some field guides (notably those published by Golden Press) contain sonograms—graphs representing bird calls—(see p. 37), which some people find very helpful.

It is truly wonderful how

love-telling the small voices

of these birds are, and how

far they reach through the

woods into one another's

hearts and into ours.

JOHN MUIR (1838–1914), Scottish-born American naturalist and writer

PARABOLIC REFLECTORS *are often used in the field to obtain high-quality recordings (above). An Eastern Meadowlark in full song (top).*

TED PARKER

Far-and-away the world's expert on the birdlife of South America, the late Ted Parker was able to identify over 3,000 species of birds by ear.

Many tropical birds live in thick vegetation (either beneath ground cover or within the dense canopy of tall forest) and are very hard to see, so visual censusing simply does not work. Identifying the little voices in the jungle is the only way to know what's there.

Ted could be dropped into a rainforest containing hundreds of birds and emerge an hour or two later with a thorough analysis of the avifauna.

A chief scientist for Conservation International, Ted was working on a program assessing the faunal and floral qualities of tropical rainforests when, in August 1993, the plane that had been leased for aerial surveys hit a fog-veiled mountain, killing Ted and a number of other team members. With his death, a large part of our knowledge of South American birds was lost.

RECORDING BIRDS

As recently as twenty years ago, to record a bird song or call one needed an umbrella-sized cone called a parabolic reflector, a microphone, and a cumbersome reel-to-reel recorder. Nowadays, of course, small, lightweight directional microphones and digital recorders do the same job far more effectively.

For best results when recording bird sounds, try to find a bird that is vocalizing where there are no other sounds. Running water, other birds, wind, airplanes, whispering humans, and rustling leaves will all cause interference. Indeed, it's only when you try to record a bird singing that you fully appreciate just what a noisy world we live in!

It is a good idea to find a quiet spot in advance and then, on recording day, have your equipment set up and ready to go before dawn.

ATTRACTING BIRDS WITH SOUNDS

Many birders play tapes of bird calls in the field in order to attract birds, and this is often very effective. However, as birds will assume that the recording is the call of a territorial rival, repeated playing can place them under extra strain. You should therefore use tapes sparingly.

Another way of attracting birds with sounds is by using techniques known as spishing—making a *spssh, spssh* sound with your lips—and squeaking—kissing the back of your hand to produce crude but effective imitations of calls. Small birds, such as warblers, sparrows, wrens and chickadees, will gather round apparently fascinated by these sounds.

For a similar effect you can also use a "squeaker", a gadget, available from birding stores, consisting of a cylinder with a resin-coated wooden plug that squeaks when the plug is rotated.

INSTANT REPLAY *Portable recorders (left and far left) allow you to record the calls of birds—such as this Marsh Wren (above)—in the field and then listen to them at home. One way to learn more about recording is to attend a course like Cornell Laboratory of Ornithology's annual sound recording workshop (below).*

KEEPING NOTES *and* RECORDS

From short notes on scraps of paper to exhaustive, computerized compendiums, a birder's records can take many forms.

Some birders become habitual listers. Almost all keep at least one list of all the species that they have seen.

A list may take the form of scribbled notes in the margin of one trusty field guide, or it may be checked off in one of the many printed lists available from birding organizations. It may record all the birds you have seen on your travels or only the birds you have seen in your region, local park, or even just your backyard—a local list can be every bit as challenging as a national or world list.

Many active birders start a new list each year, month, or even week. Breaking out a clean, unmarked checklist on January First can instill a good deal of vigor in even the most jaded birder!

Nowadays a respectable life list might cover 300 to 400 species, though many avid, well-traveled birders have been able to notch up 700 or more. At the top

end of the scale, a few listers have managed to see over 7000 species!

JOURNALS

One way to get more out of your adventures in birding is to keep a journal recording the details of places visited and wildlife observed.

Use a robust and, if possible, waterproof notebook. Write in it in pencil rather than pen. Pencil is more appropriate for sketching and won't run if the journal gets wet.

Use your journal to record not just the species seen but an estimate of the numbers present, the time and weather when you saw them, and any other relevant observations

A VISUAL REFERENCE *When you are out birding and see a bird that you are unable to identify, it's a good idea to make notes and even do a quick sketch of the bird in your notebook. Note the time and the place, what kind of habitat you are in, and any distinctive plumage or behavioral features of the bird (right). With this information at hand, you can then take time at home to consult field guides and other reference works in order to positively identify the bird—and add another species to your life list!*

(see p. 118). Such notes will help you if you wish to do further research on a bird's identity at home or if you intend to report a rare sighting to your local birding organization.

Many people choose to enliven their birding notes with sketches, pressed flowers, and other jottings. All of this will make your journal a valuable reference source and something to treasure throughout your birding career.

OTHER TYPES OF RECORDS

In addition to maintaining a running narrative on trips afield, many birders also keep a computer file, loose-leaf

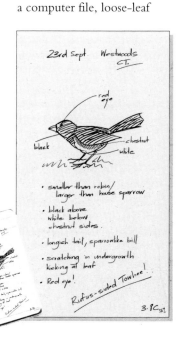

23rd Sept Westwoods CT.

red eye

black   chestnut white

- smaller than robin/ larger than house sparrow
- black above white below chestnut sides.
- longish tail, sparrowlike bill
- scratching in undergrowth kicking at leaf
- Red eye!

Rufus-sided Towhee!

3.8C

BIRDER'S LISTS *Printed "tick" lists (below) are now available for most regions, but many birders still prefer a traditional notebook (left).*

binder or card index arranged according to species. Looking, for example, under Red-necked Grebe, a well-traveled birder would find several entries detailing encounters with this species.

COMPUTERS

There are many software programs designed for recording bird sightings. Some incorporate complete world or American species lists. Some feature information on the abundance of species in different areas at different times of year.

Many field guides, birding reference books, and encyclopedias of birds are now also available on CD-ROM.

GREAT AMERICAN BIRD ARTISTS

The first serious American ornithological work and one of the great works of bird art was the *Natural History of Carolina, Florida and the Bahamas* by the English artist and naturalist Mark Catesby (1683–1749). Catesby undertook two extended journeys to the Americas between 1712 and 1726, and ultimately succeeded in illustrating around one quarter of all species found in the eastern United States. His two sumptuously illustrated folios were published in London in 1731 and 1743.

Not until the beginning of the nineteenth century was Catesby's work bettered. Alexander Wilson (1766–1813), a weaver, school master, and poet, arrived in America from Scotland in 1794. He was so overwhelmed by the beauty and variety of the birdlife that, despite little training in either art or ornithology, he began work on a large-scale guide to American birds. The first volume of Wilson's superb *American Ornithology* was published in 1808, with eight other volumes appearing subsequently.

To finance his work, Wilson sought sponsors by displaying published volumes wherever he went. On one of his trips he approached a storekeeper by the name of John James Audubon (1785–1851). Audubon had arrived in America from France in 1803 and, unknown to Wilson, was at work on a similar project. Initially dismayed, Audubon was subsequently inspired by the meeting to work even harder at his plan to paint every bird in America.

Published serially from 1827 to 1838, to great acclaim, the four volumes of *Birds of America* were a landmark in bird art and are now among the most valuable books in the world.

PORTRAIT PAINTERS TO THE BIRDS
An illustration of a Bald Eagle by the English artist Mark Catesby (top). America's first great ornithologists, Alexander Wilson (above right) and John James Audubon (right), alongside a more recent successor, Louis Aggassiz Fuertes (above).

Like Audubon, Louis Aggassiz Fuertes (1874–1927) was not only an exceptional artist but an avid and observant naturalist. One ability that set him apart from his peers was his acute memory. After studying his subjects closely in the wild, he would draw them hours later with astounding accuracy. Fuertes' publications are now among the most highly regarded of all bird books.

PHOTOGRAPHING BIRDS

Bird photography can be immensely satisfying, but for beginners it can also be frustrating. Good results require a significant investment of time, money, and patience.

The sense of satisfaction achieved by taking a good color slide or print of a bird—perfectly composed, accurately exposed, crackling sharp, and with good saturated colors—is enormous, and most birders want to try their hand at capturing their quarry on film at some time or other.

Bird photography is, however, harder than it might seem. Suitable equipment is quite expensive, and outstanding results need technical commitment. Perhaps the best single piece of advice is: choose your equipment with great care.

CAMERAS

Cameras come in two basic styles, usually referred to as rangefinders and single lens reflexes (SLR). Rangefinder cameras are unsuitable for bird photography for several reasons, but especially because you cannot normally change lenses with this type of camera, so you cannot use a telephoto lens.

The recommended style and format is therefore an SLR that uses 35 mm film, preferably one with automatic exposure control and focusing capability.

FOCAL LENGTH

The most important variable to consider when choosing a lens for bird photography is its focal length. Usually expressed in millimeters, this is what governs the size of the image of the bird on the film. With a 35 mm camera, you can roughly equate this with the magnification of your binoculars by dividing the focal length of the lens by 50: a 400 mm lens, for example, is roughly the equivalent of 8x binoculars. (This only applies to 35 mm cameras; for other formats the formula is different.)

In a simple lens, the focal length is roughly the same as the length of the barrel, which means that a 1,000 mm simple telephoto lens would be about 3 feet (1 m) long. Sophisticated design in modern lenses has resulted in substantial improvement in this respect, but lenses suitable for bird photography are nevertheless long and heavy.

The greater the focal length, the harder it is to maintain focus and to "target" your bird in the finder. Beyond about 400 mm you will need a tripod (see p. 114), as you will find that you simply cannot hold the lens steady enough by hand to get worthwhile results.

A QUESTION OF BALANCE

A Night Heron (above right) perches on some high-quality camera equipment. Experienced bird photographers use a tripod whenever possible, even with birds as tame and cooperative as this Brown Pelican (left).

THE F-STOP

The second critical parameter is the f-stop, which measures the light-gathering capability of the lens. The smaller the number, the wider the lens opens, the more light is let into the camera, and the quicker the image will be processed. An f4 lens is therefore better (that is, faster) than an f5.6. On the other hand, the smaller the number, the bigger, heavier, and more expensive the lens.

ZOOM AND MIRROR LENSES

Zoom lenses are those in which the focal length is variable (75 to 125 mm is a typical range). Mirror lenses (so-called because the wizardry inside is done with mirrors, not lenses), are much smaller, lighter, and more compact than normal tele-photo lenses, but their f-stop is fixed. Such considerations are not that important in bird photography, however, as you will usually find yourself operating the lens at maximum zoom, in order to get as close as possible to the bird, and with the aperture wide open (that is, at its lowest f-setting), in

MIRROR LENSES *(top) are more compact than other lenses, whereas zoom lenses (center) provide increased flexibility. If you can afford it, this 600mm lens (right) will provide the ultimate in power and image clarity.*

order to record the image as quickly as possible.

You can extend the focal length of your lens by using a telextender, a small lens that attaches to the back of your telephoto before you mount it on the camera. These are convenient, but you pay for the increased range with some reduction in image quality and speed. You can also buy a mounting collar that allows you to mount your camera onto a spotting scope.

FILM

The most important difference in film types is in speed. High speed films (indicated by higher numbers) allow you to use a faster shutter speed and are there-fore better for catching birds in motion, but they tend to give you grainier pictures.

Store film in the coolest place you can find (the refri-gerator is fine), and protect it from marked temperature changes when you use it.

If you want the very best results, get it processed by a custom lab (check the Yellow Pages for one near you) rather than by the corner drugstore.

VIDEO

Something to consider carefully before investing in photographic equipment is whether you wish to opt for a video camera instead. The latest video cameras are small and easy to use, and you may feel that capturing a bird's appearance, sound, and motion outweighs consider-ations of image quality.

You may well find yourself getting much more enjoyment out of your video tapes of birds than from still photographs. With a few video cameras (the more expensive models) you can even interchange lenses with your still camera, thus getting the best of both worlds.

FIELD OF VIEW *A group of budding bird photographers (above) sets its sights on a Great Egret (right).*

BEYOND BASIC BIRDING

The best way to broaden your birding experience is to get to know other birders through clubs, birding tours, and other group activities.

In most areas of North America there are local birding organizations, ranging from chapters of the National Audubon Society to university ornithological societies and small birding clubs. Most of these groups organize meetings and field trips, and they may help you to become involved in other aspects of birding such as censuses and research projects.

MOVING ON *Joining a club (above) is the first move to make if you are serious about birding. Organized tours will take you to a wide range of places, from mountain-top hawk watches (below) to tropical wetlands (bottom).*

National and state parks, too, offer a range of naturalist-led walks, some specializing in birds. Some city museums, colleges, and universities offer classes in ornithology or birding (field ornithology). There is even a college level correspondence course run by the Cornell Laboratory of Ornithology, which is highly recommended, especially for people living in isolated areas.

The principal organization for birders in North America is the American Birding Association. If you join the association you will be put in touch with thousands of other like-minded birding enthusiasts and provided with a variety of useful sources of information in the form of journals and newsletters.

TRAVEL

A whole continent filled with superb and diverse birding areas awaits you. For a selection of the top sites that you will find rewarding to visit, see p. 132. If you want to explore these and other areas on your own, there are many birdfinding guides and birding groups available for almost every region.

If you prefer to go on an organized tour, there is a huge range of companies and trips from which to choose. Most are inclusive, with similar travel arrangements. The big difference will probably be in the leader or tour guide—some are excellent, some can be a disappointment. Ask other birders for recommendations.

SPECIALTY BIRDING

Some people focus their birding activities on one kind of bird. For example, hawk-watching is a popular form of specialized birding. Diurnal raptors (hawks, eagles, ospreys, kites, and so on) follow well-established migration routes (often over mountains where these birds ride the rising air currents), and along these routes there

are localities, known as hawk watches, where hundreds, even thousands, of raptors may be seen in a single day.

Pelagic (open sea) trips to watch seabirds are also popular. Many species of seabirds which cannot normally be seen from land may be observed from ocean-

COUNTING BIRDS *Researchers often welcome the help of volunteers in the routine work of censusing (above).*

going boats on one- or two-day trips. Again, a wide range of trips is on offer, but if you are planning your first pelagic birding trip, be sure the organizer tells you exactly what is involved and how to prepare for it.

BIRDING AS SPORT
One fun activity undertaken by many birders is known as a "big day". The aim is to record as many species as possible between one midnight and the next within a clearly defined area and following strict rules.

This can be done as a competition between members of a group or as a group effort aimed at improving on previous tallies. Frequently, it is done to raise money for a birding group or for conservation efforts, with each species recorded bringing in a small sum from sponsors.

RESEARCH
A number of national censuses and feeder-watch programs are organized each year and all birders can participate. Perhaps the best known of these censuses are the Audubon Society's CBCs (Christmas Bird Counts).

Each CBC takes place on one day between mid-December and the first week of January and covers one of nearly 1,700 circles around North America, each of them 15 miles (24 km) in diameter. Participants record all the species they see that day within their circle.

The information gathered during the CBCs has given rise to a database that is one of the most important birding resources in the world. To take part in a CBC, you should contact the National Audubon Society.

Other important censuses include the Breeding Bird Surveys, run by the US and Canadian Fish and Wildlife services, and the Breeding Bird Atlas Projects that take

BIRD AID *Many regions have organizations dedicated to nursing back to health injured and abandoned birds (below). One way of monitoring the movements of birds is by banding (right). A metal leg-ring bearing an address and a number (above right) will identify a bird if it should be found again.*

Birds are Nature's most vital and potent expressions.

FRANK M. CHAPMAN
(1864–1945), American ornithologist

FRANK M. CHAPMAN *(above) organized the first Christmas Bird Count on Christmas Day 1900, as a protest against traditional Christmas bird shoots. As curator of ornithology at the American Museum of Natural History and editor of various journals, Chapman did as much as any ornithologist to encourage members of the public to take up birding.*

place from time to time in many states and provinces.

Observatories and banding stations also conduct research which requires volunteer participation. Each year, the American Birding Association lists volunteer opportunities available through government agencies such as the US Forest Service and the US Bureau of Land Management.

BIRDS *in* DANGER

Although public attitudes to conservation have changed radically in the past one hundred years, many bird species are still in grave danger of extinction.

For early ornithologists the gun was as important a tool as writing and sketching materials, as most of their studies were based on dead specimens. Early in his career, John James Audubon (see p. 125) said "I consider birds few if I can shoot less than a hundred a day".

Even in the nineteenth century the wholesale slaughter of America's birds continued in the name of sport and fashion, but the attitude of the ornithological community began to change.

OVERHUNTING *exterminated the Passenger Pigeon, a species once so numerous that flocks of millions (below right) were a common sight. At the height of this destruction, in the 1880s, Frank Chapman (see p. 129) undertook a survey of headwear in New York and found that of the 700 hats that he counted, 542 sported mounted birds. Of these, he recognized at least 20 species.*

CONSERVATION GROUPS

These changing attitudes led to the foundation of the first American conservation groups. The most significant of these was the Audubon Society, founded in 1886 in New York City by George Bird Grinnell. Similar groups throughout North America adopted its name and were amalgamated in 1905 under the banner of the National Association of Audubon Societies (it was renamed the National Audubon Society in 1935).

During the early 1900s, Audubon Society members fought vigorously for the protection of endangered species. Some campaigners were prepared to put their own lives on the line and, tragically, three wardens lost their lives in disputes with hunters.

Ultimately, however, the campaigns led to the establish-

HABITAT DESTRUCTION *today threatens many birds, such as the Burrowing Owl (left).*

ment of wildlife sanctuaries throughout the country, and saved a number of species including the Great and Snowy egrets. They also gave rise to the first bird protection laws, introduced in New York City in 1895 and adopted by 32 states during the next ten years.

Unfortunately, legislation came too late for some birds. The last Carolina Parakeet and the last Passenger Pigeon both died in September 1914 at the Cincinnati Zoo.

A NEW THREAT

In the early 1960s it became clear that we were poisoning our continental wildlife through widespread use of pesticides such as DDT. These "miracle" sprays were great for growing insect-free

EXTINCT SPECIES

Labrador Duck, Great Auk, Passenger Pigeon, Carolina Parakeet

SOME ENDANGERED SPECIES

Species	Range	Status	Causes
Wood Stork	Southern US	Faltering	Habitat destruction
Whooping Crane	Alberta to Texas	Recovering	Habitat destruction; shooting
Piping Plover	East	Faltering	Forced out of habitat by humans
Eskimo Curlew	North America	May be extinct	Overhunting
California Condor	California	Extinct in the wild	Pesticides; displaced by humans
Ivory-billed Woodpecker	Southeastern US	Probably extinct	Habitat destruction
Black-capped Vireo	Oklahoma to Mexico	In danger	Nest parasitism; habitat destruction
Bachman's Warbler	Southeastern US	Probably extinct	Habitat destruction
Kirtland's Warbler	Michigan to Bahamas	Faltering	Habitat destruction; nest parasitism

produce but were devastating to apex predators (animals and birds at the top of the food chain). For birds such as Brown Pelicans, Ospreys and Peregrine Falcons, the absorption of DDT caused them to lay eggs with shells too thin to incubate or eggs with no shells at all. As a result, populations of all three species plummeted.

By the time Rachel Carson's prophetic *Silent Spring* (see p. 36) alerted politicians and public to the danger, much damage had already been done.

CONTEMPORARY THREATS

There is no question that the most serious contemporary threat to birds is the continuing destruction of habitat. Numbers of many migratory species have dropped dramatically as their habitats in their summer homes in the US and Canada and their winter residences in Latin America have been cleared for agriculture and urban development.

Other threats to the survival of native species are also a result of human intervention. Clearance of native vegetation has allowed nest parasites like the Brown-

headed Cowbird to thrive (see pp. 41 and 233), and some populations have been wiped out by cats. Human structures too have taken their toll: huge numbers of birds die annually as a result of collisions with plate-glass windows (see p. 53).

ON THE BRIGHT SIDE

Illegal shooting and trapping is now rare in North America, and legislation prohibits misuse of pesticides. Many wildlife agencies have implemented cowbird control programs, and many private organizations are buying property to protect habitats and care for animals and birds.

Organizations such as The National Audubon Society,

UNDER SIEGE *The California Condor (above) is now extinct in the wild, while the number of free-living Whooping Cranes (above left) remains dangerously low even after decades of support. The Kirtland's Warbler (top) is in a precarious position as a result of habitat loss.*

The Nature Conservancy, BirdLife International, and Partners in Flight continue to campaign effectively for endangered species and habitats. To counterbalance continuing habitat destruction, it is imperative that these efforts are not only continued but stepped up. If you are interested in helping, the best way to start is to contact one of these groups or join a birding organization in your local area.

TOP BIRDING SITES

North America offers an extraordinary range of habitat types, a superb system of national parks, and some of the world's top birding areas.

It is not easy to make a selection of top birding sites because there are so many of them scattered around the continent. Here, however, are ten of our favorites. Not only will you be able to see numerous bird species at each site, you should also be able to sit back, relax and enjoy the beautiful scenery of each area.

❶

❶ **SAINT PAUL ISLAND,** ▶ **PRIBILOF ISLANDS, ALASKA** *Reached by biweekly flights from Anchorage. Nesting seabirds (fulmars, kittiwakes, murres, auklets, and puffins) may be viewed and photographed at close range and, during migration, Asiatic strays may show up. Lapland Longspurs, Arctic Foxes, reindeer, fascinating local history, and amazing wildflowers (above right) are all part of the package.*

◀ ❸ **MONTEREY BAY, CALIFORNIA** *A diversity of habitats makes this a great year-round birding spot. The shoreline (left) is frequented by Black Turnstones, Wandering Tattlers, and oystercatchers, and you will hear Pygmy Nuthatches and Chestnut-backed Chickadees calling from the nearby cypresses. Also the departure point for some great pelagic trips.*

❷ **MANNING PROVINCIAL PARK, BRITISH COLUMBIA** *Excellent for mountain species including Ruffed, Blue, and Spruce grouse; Black Swifts; and Calliope Hummingbirds (below). Many warblers and flycatchers also occur in summer. A beautiful park with quite stunning mountain scenery. Summer is really the only time to visit.* ▼

LOCAL LISTS

The following list will give you some idea of the number of species you can expect to find in different regions of North America.

Texas	600
California	580
Arizona	500
British Columbia	450
Alaska	445
Ontario	430
Nova Scotia	410
Saskatchewan	375
South Dakota	370
Prince Edward Island	280

◀ ❹ **PAWNEE NATIONAL GRASSLANDS, COLORADO** *One of the last remaining areas of shortgrass prairie left in North America. In summer, specialties include Chestnut-collared and McCown's Longspurs and Lark Buntings. Keep an eye out too for nesting Swainson's and Ferruginous (left) hawks, and herds of American Pronghorns.*

❺ **SANTA ANA NATIONAL** ▶ **WILDLIFE REFUGE, TEXAS** *This refuge features a remarkably high concentration of wildlife and is home to a number of East Mexican birds found nowhere else in the US, including the Hook-billed Kite, Altamira Oriole, Great Kiskadee, Parauque, Green Jay (right), Groove-billed Ani, Plain Chachalaca, and Tropical Parula.*

⑥ CHURCHILL, MANITOBA

Located where boreal forest merges with tundra, Churchill attracts astonishing numbers of migrating (late May to early June), then nesting (late June through August), waterbirds. The chance of spotting a Polar Bear keeps visitors on their toes.

⑦ POINT PELEE, ONTARIO

Arguably the best place in North America to observe northbound landbird migration in spring (mid-May is best). If the weather is right, warblers, thrushes, vireos, buntings, orioles, and tanagers amass here, sometimes in astounding numbers.

⑧ CAPE MAY, NEW JERSEY *If*

Point Pelee is the best place to witness northbound migration in the spring, Cape May is the place to be for southbound migration in the fall. Nowhere will you see more passing waterbirds, songbirds, and birds of prey. Hawkwatching here can be exhilarating.

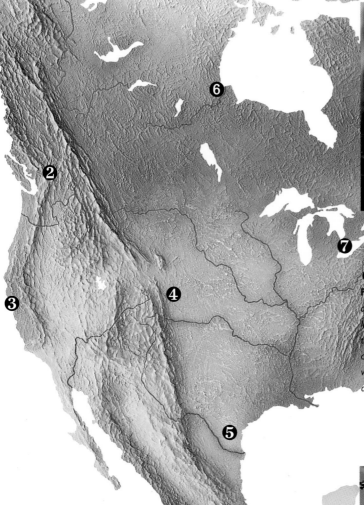

⑨ EVERGLADES NATIONAL PARK, FLORIDA

Even under the siege of habitat loss, the Everglades is a wetlands showcase. An attractive system of trails, boardwalks, and roads allows close observation of some fascinating wildlife, including numerous ibis, herons, and egrets, and alligators and turtles.

⑩ THE DRY TORTUGAS, FLORIDA

These low coralline islands support large numbers of nesting Sooty Terns and Brown Noddies. Other visitors include Masked and Brown boobies, White-tailed Tropicbirds, and Magnificent Frigatebirds. In spring, a wide variety of landbird migrants break their northward journey here, and they are usually easy to approach and photograph.

O quick quick quick, quick hear the song-sparrow,

Swamp-sparrow, fox-sparrow, vesper-sparrow

At dawn and dusk. Follow the dance

Of the goldfinch at noon. Leave to chance

The Blackburnian warbler, the shy one. Hail

With shrill whistle the note of the quail, the bob-white...

All are delectable. Sweet sweet sweet...

Landscapes, T.S. ELIOT (1888–1965),
British poet and critic

INTRODUCTION

In North America there are over 850 species of birds. How does a beginning birder start getting to know them? Our Habitat Birdfinder offers you the perfect introduction—to all the main bird groups and to over 200 of the most commonly encountered species.

Getting to grips with the large number of species that may be encountered in North America can be a daunting task. A good way to start is to learn something about the general characteristics that distinguish groups of related birds.

THE TAXONOMIC APPROACH

On the following pages you will find concise but informative descriptions of the main bird groups in North America. These include information on shared physical features; behavioral characteristics; differences in plumage between males and females, and from season to season; and the number of species in that group found in North America compared with the world as a whole.

It may be a little hard to digest all of this information at once, but it is worth persevering as it will give you a good foundation on which you can build.

You will probably be surprised at how much you already know. For example, you probably recognize a duck or an owl when you see one. You may not be able to say exactly what species it is, but you at least know it right away as a duck or an owl.

Greater familiarity with the shared characteristics of bird groups will help you narrow down the identity of an unknown bird in the field. Knowing how many species there are in a group will mean that you are aware just how many similar birds there are. And an awareness of plumage cycles and differences will mean you are better placed to make a more precise identification. For all these reasons, it makes sense to read this section carefully and return to it again and again.

THE HABITAT APPROACH

Learning about families and other groups will give you a good grounding in American birds, but groups can be large and widespread. Furthermore, you will quickly want to start naming the individual species that you see around you. So how can you predict what species you are likely to see in your area? One answer is to consider birds in relation to their habitats.

FAMILY TRAITS *Most of us recognize an owl—like this Burrowing Owl (top)—immediately, even though we may not know the exact species. It takes only a little more practice to learn to recognize the family traits of many less familiar birds, such as the Marsh Wren (right).*

Birds do not occur at random across the landscape. Instead, each species has its own set of environmental requirements and preferences, based on what it eats and where it nests (see p. 30). Most of the species that you find in grasslands, for instance, do not normally occur in woodlands, and vice versa.

This concept sometimes holds good for entire groups of birds: if you want to look for a duck, for example, you go to a lake or marsh, not to a dry grassland or a wooded park. But it is generally true at

START WITH THE HABITAT

Many birds are restricted to an easily recognizable habitat, offering a useful aid to identification. You will normally find Pied-billed Grebes, for example, only in a lake or marsh.

the species level as well: the Short-eared Owl, for example, lives in grasslands, while its close relative the Long-eared Owl lives in forests and woodlands.

We have therefore arranged our selection of the most commonly encountered North American birds into six habitat categories: urban areas, woodlands, grasslands, wetlands, seashores, and deserts. These are broad, widespread, familiar environments, and it should be easy for you to relate them to the kind of area you live in. This in turn will help you familiarize yourself with the birds you are most likely to see around you.

PITFALLS

The habitat approach is ideal for the beginner; however, it does have its limitations, and to use the approach to best effect it is important to be aware of them.

In the first place, birds don't always relate to their environment in ways that make sense to humans. Some occur in many habitats, while others are found only in very restricted environments. Some dwell in different habitats at different times of the year.

Moreover, the concept of habitat alone may give us an incomplete notion of how the bird relates to its environment, and we need the concept of niche to complete it. For example, both vireos and towhees occur in woodlands (often the very same patch of woodland), but towhees are seen on the ground and in bushes whereas vireos are usually seen only in the leafy crowns of trees.

To help you deal with this, preferences for particular niches are described where relevant within the species profiles. Furthermore, each habitat is introduced by two sections, the first of which presents a typical scene from that habitat and highlights commonly used niches. The second recommends strategies and equipment that may assist you within a particular environment.

A TWO-PRONGED APPROACH

Both approaches—the taxonomic and the habitat—have advantages and disadvantages. On the whole, it is best to view them as complementary: by exploiting them both fully you will rapidly improve your birding knowledge and your identification skills.

Family Groups
138

Urban Areas
145

Downtown Areas, Parks, Gardens, Vacant Lots

Woodlands
167

Forests, Clearings, Riparian Groves, Edges, Thickets

Grasslands
207

Prairies, Open Fields, Farmland

Wetlands
235

Lakes, Marshes, Reservoirs, Rivers, Swamps

Seashores
267

Beaches, Sand Dunes, Coastal Cliffs, Estuaries, Mangroves

Deserts
289

Scrublands, Chaparral, Mesas, Sagebrush Plains

FAMILY GROUPS

All North American bird species belong to broad family groups. A sound knowledge of these groups and their shared characteristics is a real boon to any birder.

In taxonomy, bird species are organized into groups at different levels: order, family, subfamily, genus, and so on (see p. 20). To most birders, groups of certain species will be better known at one level than another.

For example, we tend to think of thrushes as one group and wood-warblers as another, even though the thrushes constitute a family while the wood-warblers are only a subfamily; we think of owls as one group even though there are two distinct families. It is simply more straightforward and more useful for us to think of the birds in these groups, even if they are not at the same taxonomic level.

We have therefore arranged the birds of North America into the groups that we feel will be most familiar to birders and most easily grasped by beginners. These groups are listed in traditional taxonomic order.

Each group name in our list is highlighted in bold. Scientific names of families and subfamilies are given. These names can prove useful when consulting other publications.

A useful starting point when considering groups is to think of birds as either passerines (songbirds) or non-passerines, as passerines make up over half of all species.

Familiarizing yourself with the traditional taxonomic sequence will also help you to navigate through other sources of information on birds, as most field guides (including this one), handbooks, and bird lists use similar sequences.

NON-PASSERINES

Loons (Gaviidae) are strongly aquatic birds that dive beneath the surface for their food and come ashore only to nest. To some extent, they resemble ducks and cormorants, but they ride low in the water and their bill is pointed and often quite stout.
♀♂⫙ **4/5** ➤ 270

Grebes (Podicipedidae) resemble small loons and, like them, are strongly aquatic, inhabiting wetlands generally. One distinctive feature is their apparent lack of a tail— their bodies end in a powder-puff effect of loose feathers.
♀♂⫙ **7/20** ➤ 238–9

The three families of seabirds—**albatrosses** (Diomedeidae), **shearwaters and petrels** (Procellariidae), and **storm petrels** (Hydrobatidae)—are often known as tubenoses because their nostrils are set in tubes on top of the bill. Strictly pelagic, they seldom come within sight of land except when breeding.
♀♂⫙ **30/105** ➤ 271

KEY TO SYMBOLS

♀♂	No difference in plumage between males and females	⫙	No seasonal variation in plumage
♂♀	Males and females have different plumage	⫕	Seasonal variation in plumage
♂♀	Plumage difference between sexes in some species but not in others	⫙	Seasonal variation in plumage in some species but not in others
7/20	Number of species in the group in North America/ the world	➤23	Page references for species in the group that feature in The Habitat Birdfinder

Cormorants (Phalacrocoracidae) are mainly black in plumage and their longish bills are distinctly hooked at the tip. They swim low in the water, dive for their food, and inhabit fresh and salt water alike. There are several related groups with few species and widely differing appearance: **anhingas** (Anhingidae) resemble cormorants but have longer tails and pointed, spear-like bills; **pelicans** (Pelecanidae) have huge, pouch-like bills; **gannets and boobies** (Sulidae) inhabit coastal waters and dive for fish in spectacular plunges from high above the sea.
♀♂ **18/62** ➤ 240, 272–3

Herons, egrets, and bitterns (Ardeidae); **storks** (Ciconiidae); and **ibises and spoonbills** (Threskiornithidae) are all long-legged, long-necked, long-billed, and short-tailed birds that wade in shallow water in search of much of their food. Many egrets are entirely white but dull reds and grays are common among herons. Bitterns may be brown and streaked. Ibises have downward-curving bills; spoonbills have the bill shape their name suggests; and the only American stork has a naked, featherless head and upper neck.
♀♂ **35/117** ➤ 210, 241–5, 274

Ducks, geese, and swans (Anatidae) all have some recognizable variation of the familiar duck bill, which is difficult to describe concisely but is instantly recognizable. Most lose their flight feathers all at once, so are flightless for a few weeks every year while the new feathers grow.

Male ducks often have a striking courtship plumage.
♀♂ **55/150** ➤ 246–56, 275

The diurnal **birds of prey** are often known collectively as raptors. It is convenient to include the New World vultures and condors (Cathartidae) in this group although they are not related. Key subgroups are the hawks, kites, and eagles (Accipitridae) and falcons (Falconidae). Raptors are extremely variable in plumage, and in identification subtle details of flight silhouette (length of tail, breadth of wing, and so on) are often far more important than color pattern.
♂♀ **35/292** ➤ 172–4, 211–15, 257–8

Of the **gamebirds** (Phasianidae) only the Wild Turkey, grouse, and quail are native to the North American continent; partridges and pheasants have been introduced. All are chicken-like birds that feed almost exclusively on the ground.
♂♀ **24/257** ➤ 175, 216, 292

In body form, **crakes, rails, and coots** (Rallidae) look faintly chicken-like but for the most part inhabit swamps and marshes. Shy and elusive, most are seldom seen by the casual observer. Their tails are frequently cocked high, and persistently flicked. Allied to the crakes and rails are the single species of Limpkin (Aramidae) and the two American cranes (Gruidae), the Sandhill Crane and Whooping Crane.
♀♂ **12/158** ➤ 259

Top to bottom: Green Heron (Ardeidae); Purple Gallinule (Rallidae); Sage Grouse (Phasianidae); Cinnamon Teal (Anatidae)

139

Anyone familiar with the Killdeer should have little difficulty recognizing any of the other **plovers** (Charadriidae). These are birds of coasts and open country, with long, pointed wings, rather large dark eyes and a pigeon-like bill. Plovers have a characteristic habit of dashing over the sand or mud on twinkling feet, with head held low, then periodically coming to an abrupt halt, as though called smartly to attention.

♂♀ **10/64** ➤ 217, 276

The **sandpipers** and their relatives (Scolopacidae) mostly inhabit seashores, especially tidal mudflats. Many are strongly migratory, nesting in the High Arctic and traveling south in fall. Most are gregarious and habitually congregate in large mixed roosting flocks at high tide, scattering to feed over exposed mudflats as the tide recedes. Plumage is mainly dull brown or gray, and many species are extremely difficult to identify. The slender bill ranges from very long to quite short, and may be straight, strongly down-curved, or even slightly upcurved. An important first step in identifying shorebirds is to carefully note length and shape

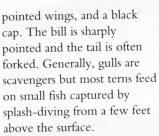

Right: Black-necked Stilt (Recurvirostridae); below: Sanderlings (Scolopacidae); bottom left: Common Murre (Alcidae).

of bill; whether there is a white rump or not; and whether there is a white stripe down the length of the upper wing (wingbar) or not.

♂♀ **52/87** ➤ 260, 276–80

Closely related are two other small but distinctive groups: **stilts and avocets** (Recurvirostridae) and **oystercatchers** (Haematopodidae). The former are common on prairie sloughs and similar wetlands, especially in the west and south; they are mainly black-and-white in plumage, and have very long legs. The latter live along coastlines and have long, stout, chisel-like beaks.

♂♀ **4/23**

Almost everyone knows what **seagulls** (Laridae) look like but there are many different species (and quite a few live nowhere near the sea). Furthermore, most take several years to reach maturity, going through a series of different immature plumages, which make species identification a matter of considerable intricacy. A typical adult gull is white below and gray above, and some have black heads.

Terns are similar to gulls but usually smaller and slimmer, with long, slender,

pointed wings, and a black cap. The bill is sharply pointed and the tail is often forked. Generally, gulls are scavengers but most terns feed on small fish captured by splash-diving from a few feet above the surface.

There are two smaller groups closely related to gulls but very distinctive in appearance: one **skimmer** (Rynchopinae) occurs in the southern US and looks a bit like a large tern, but the lower mandible is much longer than the upper. **Skuas and jaegers** (Stercorariinae) look rather like dark brown gulls but specialize in piracy, bullying and harassing other seabirds until they abandon their catch.

♂♀ **46/99** ➤ 281–7

The family Alcidae includes **murres, guillemots, and puffins**. Alcids are exclusively marine birds that catch their food underwater. Their small wings lend their flight a distinctively buzzy appearance, low to the water. Many species congregate in large colonies on seacliffs to nest. They are well represented in the Arctic, but several species extend southward, especially along the Pacific coast to Mexico.

♂♀ **20/23** ➤ 288

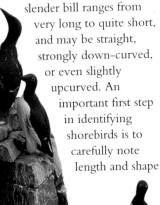

Left: White-winged Dove (Columbidae); above: Anna's Hummingbird (Trochilidae); below left: Great Horned Owl (Strigidae); below right: Gila Woodpecker (Picidae)

Pigeons and doves (Columbidae) come in a range of colors and sizes, but all resemble the ordinary street pigeon closely enough to make confusion unlikely at the group level.
♂♀ **15/302** ➤ 198, 218, 293

The **cuckoos** (Cuculidae) are a worldwide group with relatively few species in North America; the group includes the anis and the Greater Roadrunner. These are all generally slender, long-tailed birds with somewhat curved bills.
♂♀ **6/130** ➤ 294

There are, in fact, two distinct groups of **owls**— barn owls (Tytonidae) and

"typical" owls (Strigidae)— but they are so similar in most respects that the distinction is more or less academic. A typical owl is a nocturnal bird of prey with remarkably well-developed night-vision and acute hearing; and strong,

curved talons. Their eyes are forward-facing, like those of humans and unlike most other birds.
♂♀ **19/149** ➤ 176–7, 219

Nightjars (Caprimulgidae) are for most people disembodied voices in the night. They catch flying insects at night but spend the rest of the day on the forest or woodland floor, trusting entirely to their extra-ordinarily cryptic coloration to avoid detection.
♂♀ **8/79** ➤ 220

Swifts (Apodidae) quite closely resemble swallows in general appearance and behavior, though they are not related. They spend almost all of their time in the air, feeding on small flying insects. They have compact, cigar-shaped bodies and long, narrow, scythe-like wings. They typically fly much higher than swallows and martins.
♂♀ **4/94** ➤ 149

Hummingbirds (Trochilidae) are unmistakable. No other bird beats its wings so rapidly (up to 200 beats per second) that they are visible only as a blur. The hummingbird hovers and flies in all directions with equal facility,

in much the same way as a helicopter.
♂♀ **18/353** ➤ 150, 295

The only common and widespread **kingfisher** (Alcedinidae) in North America is the Belted Kingfisher. Kingfishers perch in trees overhanging rivers and streams and catch fish by splash-diving.
♂♀ **3/92** ➤ 261

A typical **woodpecker** (Picidae) clasps a tree trunk with strong-clawed feet, leans back to throw much of its weight onto its stiffened, spine-tipped tail feathers, and uses this tripod stance as a fulcrum from which to batter away at the bark with its rather heavy, chisel-like bill. Males often have some small patch of red on the head.
♂♀ **21/221** ➤ 151, 178–9

141

PASSERINES

The **tyrant flycatchers** (Tyrannidae) are an exclusively American family with a distinctive habit of perching bolt upright on some vantage point and sallying forth to catch flying insects with an audible snap of the bill. Most are drab and inconspicuous in plumage, and lack complex songs—though it is often easier to identify a tyrant flycatcher by its call than by its plumage.
♂♀ **35/390** ➤ 180, 221–2, 262

Larks (Alaudidae) are small, inconspicuous, brownish birds of open country. Most occur in Eurasia and Africa, and only the Horned Lark is common in North America.
♂♀ **2/79** ➤ 223

Swallows and martins (Hirundinidae) are small, slender birds that catch insects in midair, more or less sucking them up as they fly in graceful swoops, flurries, and glides usually at no great height over open ground. When not feeding they may perch in twittering flocks along telephone lines.
♂♀ **9/81** ➤ 152–3, 263

Jays, magpies, crows, nutcrackers, and **ravens** all belong to the group

Corvidae. Jays are often brightly colored, but crows and ravens are black. Most are big, bold, conspicuous, and versatile songbirds, and they appear in most habitats.
♂♀ **17/126** ➤ 154, 224–5, 296

The **chickadees and titmice** (Paridae) are sometimes the most obvious small songbirds in the winter woods across North America. Small, intensely active, acrobatic birds, many share a similar color pattern consisting of a dark cap, white cheeks, and a small black bib across the lower throat. Similar to these but plainer are the **bushtits** (Aetithalidae).
♂♀ **10/47** ➤ 155–6, 297

Both **nuthatches** (Sittidae) and **creepers** (Certhiidae) are usually instantly recognizable by their behavior alone: nuthatches are the only birds to creep headfirst down tree trunks, and treecreepers are the only small birds that creep up the trunks of trees.
♂♀ **5/30** ➤ 181

Wrens (Troglodytidae) are small, drab, brown birds that usually inhabit undergrowth or very low vegetation. They are active, have high-pitched, vigorous songs. Many species habitually

carry the tail cocked above the back.
♂♀ **9/61** ➤ 157, 298–9

The few North American members of the enormous, essentially Old World assemblage of **warblers** (Sylviidae) are very small, energetic birds of forests and woodlands. This group includes kinglets and gnatcatchers. Kinglets are birds of coniferous forest, given to dangling and fluttering acrobatically at the very tips of branches, nervously flicking their wings. The gnatcatchers are equally small but bluish above, with long slender tails that are often held cocked.
♂♀ **6/384** ➤ 182–3

Thrushes (Turdidae) are medium-sized songbirds that spend much of their time in the middle levels of wood-lands. They are soberly colored, and often have strikingly beautiful, evocative songs. They include the bluebirds and the Townsend's Solitaire, as well as the familiar American Robin.
♂♀ **17/316** ➤ 158, 184

The **mockingbirds and thrashers** (Mimidae) somewhat resemble thrushes except they have curved billsand long tails. Many

Left to right: Steller's Jay (Corvidae); Cedar Waxwing (Bombycillidae); Eastern Kingbird (Tyrannidae)

Left: Red-winged Blackbird (Icterinae);
below: Evening Grosbeak (Cardinalinae)

frequent undergrowth, and their songs often include mimicry of other birds.
♂♀ **10/32** ➤ 159, 300

Across North America there are only two resident species of **pipits** (Motacillidae), a group otherwise widespread in Eurasia and Africa. These are small, drab, streaked birds resembling larks, except that they have slender bills and frequently wag their tails.
♂♀ **5/54**

Waxwings (Bombycillidae) are slender, elegant, crested birds with soft silky plumage and yellow tail-tips. They are gregarious, and feed largely on fruit. Allied to them is the Phainopepla (Ptilogonatidae) of the southwest.
♂♀ **3/8** ➤ 160, 301

The most characteristic feature of the **shrikes** (Laniidae) is that they seem like a songbird version of a hawk: they select the highest perches available in open country as a vantage point from which to look for large insects, mice, or small birds.
♂♀ **2/74**

Vireos (Vireonidae) often sing persistently, even through the heat of a summer's day when other birds are silent. Though common and widespread, they are seldom noticed, as they spend most of their time high in the canopy of trees.
♂♀ **11/44** ➤ 185–6

Strongly migratory, **wood-warblers** (Parulinae) of one species or another (and often several together) are common in summer in all kinds of woodlands and forests across North America. Spring males often have bright colors and distinctive patterns, and spring females—though duller— look similar enough not to present identification difficulties. In fall, however, many molt into a drab plumage that makes most look much alike. The fall warblers are a challenge to the identification skills of any birder.
♂♀ **53/126** ➤ 187–96, 264

One of the largest groups, **New World sparrows** (Emberizinae) are present in virtually all habitats from suburban gardens to arctic tundra and southern salt marshes. A group of similar birds is Cardinalinae, including the **grosbeaks and buntings**. Most are small, brown and streaked, and have short, conical bills.
♂♀ **60/319** ➤ 162–5, 198–204, 226–9, 302–3

Male **tanagers** (Thraupinae) are among the most brilliant and intensely colored of all American songbirds. Females are plain and duller in color. All spend much of their time in the canopy of trees. In contrast to the orioles, the bill is moderately long, fairly stout, and usually yellowish rather than black.
♂♀ **4/242** ➤ 197

The **cowbirds, blackbirds, grackles, and orioles** all belong to an exclusively American group, the Icterinae. Many are birds of open country (though orioles are strongly arboreal), and a number are familiar in suburban and rural areas.
♂♀ **20/95** ➤ 166, 205–6, 230–3, 265–6

The **finches** (Fringillidae) are very like the weavers and sparrows in size and appear-ance but are, on the whole, more brightly colored, and have stout, seed-cracking bills.
♂♀ **16/124** ➤ 167, 234

The **weavers** (Ploceidae), **starlings** (Sturnidae), **Old World sparrows** (Passeridae) are Old World groups with no native members in North America. Several, however, have been introduced, notably the House Sparrow and the European Starling.
♂♀ **4/261** ➤ 161, 168

USING *the* HABITAT BIRDFINDER

The following pages present 141 of the most commonly encountered species, arranged according to the habitat that they favor. In many cases, similar or related species are also discussed, bringing the total number of birds featured to over 200. Each page incorporates the features shown here.

A clear photograph of the species in typical plumage and attitude. Captions indicate, where relevant, the sex, age, seasonal plumage, and subspecies.

The habitat code indicates which type of environment the bird most often frequents. See the key on page 137.

The name of the group of birds—family or subfamily—that the species belongs to.

The common and scientific names of the species. Within each habitat, the species are arranged in taxonomic order.

The map shows the bird's breeding distribution in yellow and its winter range in blue. Green indicates that the species is resident.

The calendar bar highlights the period during which the eggs are normally in the nest.

The text provides important information on where and how you are likely to encounter the bird; its behavioral characteristics, life cycle, and migration patterns; and how to identify the species in the field, including how to distinguish it from any similar species.

Accurate, full-color illustrations show field marks; plumage variations; similar species and subspecies; and behavioral characteristics.

Quick-reference Field Notes include:
- The size of the bird from the bill tip to the end of the tail
- Distinctive plumage and behavioral features
- ▲ Information on similar species that may confuse you
- Form and location of nest
- Number and color of eggs in a clutch

Gaviidae: Loons

Common Loon
Gavia immer

In the north, Common Loons are often seen nesting on large freshwater lakes, where their loud, yodeling calls are a sign of summer. Some of these birds also spend the winter on inland waters, especially the Great Lakes. For most people, however, loons are birds of the coasts.

All loons in winter are dark above and white below, and it is important to note the shape of the head and bill. The Common Loon has a large, angular head and a stout, straightish bill. These features, along with a distinct whitish area around its eyes in winter, distinguish it from the smaller Pacific Loon (*Gavia pacifica*; 22–26" [56–66 cm]), which nests in the far northwest and is common along the Pacific coast in winter.

The Pacific Loon has a puffier, more rounded head, and a slighter bill than the Common.

In summer the adult Pacific has a pale gray head and hindneck, and a blackish foreneck bordered by white stripes, while the Common Loon has a black head and neck with two striped white cross-bands.

Pacific Loons tend to fly low over the ocean and, unlike Commons, often occur in fair-sized flocks. Common Loons can also be distinguished in flight by their large feet that stick out behind them like paddles.

Common (winter)

Common (breeding)

Pacific (breeding)

FIELD NOTES
- 26–33" (66–84 cm)
- Pointed bill
- Large, angular head
- Rides low in water
- Darker than most other loons
- ▲ Difficult to distinguish from several other loon species in winter
- Bowl of grass and twigs, on land or anchored to vegetation
- 1–3; olive-brown with fine dark flecks

270

Adult (breeding plumage)

144

Urban Areas

BIRDING *in* URBAN AREAS

From the relatively sterile concrete and glass environment of downtown business districts to the suburbs with their gardens and shade trees, opportunities for urban birding abound.

It is a mistake to think that if you live in a city there will be few opportunities to observe birds. Urban birding can be extremely rewarding. Even if you live in an apartment block you will normally not be too far from a park, a formal garden, a reservoir, or even some wasteground, all of which attract their share of birdlife.

If you have your own garden then chances are that you are already aware of various bird residents and visitors, and the information and suggestions in Chapter Two will add to the pleasure of your backyard birding.

YOUR LOCAL PATCH

Learning to recognize and appreciate the variations in common local birds is the first step to becoming a good birder, and building up a degree of familiarity with one area is the best way to form a reference base to build upon when you visit other habitats and regions. Even in urban areas, if you look carefully around your neighborhood you will find a surprising range of habitats. Corners of your town or city that you may pay little attention to from day to day—a piece of open wasteground, a small ornamental garden—may prove very interesting from a birding point of view.

Once an area becomes your "local patch", you will soon learn when certain species of migrants arrive in the spring and fall, which birds are most common in winter, which species start to sing when, and so on. With time and patience, you can learn a great deal about bird behavior and nesting biology right on your own doorstep.

URBAN SPECIALISTS *Herring Gulls (above left), Common Grackles (above), and Canada Geese (left) are all among the birds that have thrived in urban areas across much of North America.*

IN THE CITY *New York's Central Park (left) attracts a host of migrant birds. High on a city skyscraper (below), a researcher checks a Peregrine Falcon chick. Hummingbirds (right) are easily attracted to almost any suburban garden.*

RARE VISITORS

While relatively few species of birds live permanently in cities, or are regular visitors, a quite remarkable number of different species have been recorded in towns and cities at one time or another.

This is in part due to the fact that all urban areas are fragmented environments that can contain a broad range of habitat types, and these habitats attract a correspondingly varied range of species. In particular, many migrating and vagrant birds (birds that are lost or off course) will make temporary use of any small pocket of suitable habitat that they can find, even in the center of a city.

These migrants and vagrants are far more likely to be detected in urban areas than in more remote regions. In cities and suburbs there are often hundreds or thousands of birdwatchers, and there is a good chance of any visiting rarity being noted. Indeed, a number of birding groups in North America have

well-organized "hotlines" that you can telephone to receive a recorded and regularly updated summary of the rarities "in town tonight".

Many a birder has accumulated a very respectable life list based solely on the species seen over the years in his or her own home town.

LOCAL RESOURCES

For birders, one great advantage of living in an urban area is that you will almost certainly have access to local resources such as birding clubs and educational institutions that may hold classes relating to birding.

Most of these clubs have the equivalent of an activities officer, who organizes birding trips and excursions, typically ranging from half-day walks in a local park to two-week expeditions to somewhere as remote as the Pribilof Islands. Many trips are

designed as outings for beginners, and some are bound to fit your own particular circumstances.

With a guidebook such as this one you can identify many species on your own, but nothing equals having an experienced birder explain to you—on the spot, while the bird is in view—just what you should be looking for.

■ Adults

Rock Dove

Columba livia

Rock Doves, also known as Feral Pigeons, are among the birds most familiar to city dwellers throughout North America. They are native to Eurasia, where they inhabit rocky seacoasts and desert canyons. An outstanding example of a bird that was domesticated for showing and racing purposes, this species has "gone wild" in the New World, with the result that there are healthy populations in most towns and cities in North America.

Many city dwellers enjoy feeding these birds, so they have become extremely tame and are sometimes quite a nuisance, large numbers of them nesting on window sills and in enclosed areas. However, the Rock Dove's tameness provides many opportunities for observing interesting aspects of bird behavior (often difficult and time-consuming when watching wild birds). These include social hierarchy in feeding groups (individual recognition is made easy by the pigeons' varied plumages), courtship, and even drinking. Pigeons are among the very few birds that drink by sucking up water.

J F M A M J J A S O N D

FIELD NOTES
- ■ 12–14" (30.5–35.5 cm)
  - ■ White rump
  - ■ Double black wingbar
  - ■ Plumage very varied
- ▲ Band-tailed Pigeon (western forests) is bigger, has gray rump, plain upperwings, yellow bill and white collar
- Shallow saucer of sticks on a ledge
- 1–2; white

plumage variations

■ Adult

Chimney Swift

Chaetura pelagica

Each summer, after wintering in South America, the Chimney Swift returns to eastern North America. Look for it over towns, open country, woodlands, and lakes, and listen for its high-pitched twittering calls. These often draw attention to it high overhead, where it might otherwise be missed.

Swifts are supreme aerialists, well adapted for a life on the wing. In this way they resemble swallows, but although the two families look alike and are often seen together, they are not closely related. The Chimney Swift can be distinguished from swallows by its more rapid, stiff wingbeats; faster and more direct flight; and overall blackish plumage.

The Chimney Swift originally nested in hollow trees but, as its name implies, it has readily adapted to nesting on walls of chimneys and other buildings.

The slightly smaller Vaux's (rhymes with "corks" or "corks's") Swift (*Chaetura vauxi*; 4½" [11.5 cm]), the Chimney Swift's counterpart in the west, favors open conifer woods and canyons.

J F M A M J J A S O N D

Vaux's

going to roost

Chimney

FIELD NOTES

■ 4¾–5" (12–12.5 cm)
■ Aerial; dark and featureless overall
■ Squared-off tail
▲ Vaux's Swift (west) almost identical
❀ Half saucer of twigs glued together with saliva, on a building
● 3–6; white

149

Female

Ruby-throated Hummingbird

Archilochus colubris

The Ruby-throated is the only hummingbird in eastern North America, and it occurs in woodlands, parks, and gardens. Seeing hummingbirds in the field can be difficult since they are small and fly at great speed. Your best chance of seeing one is at a hummingbird feeder. You will then be able to see how tiny they are and admire their iridescent plumage and remarkable flight.

Like most hummers in North America, the Ruby-throated migrates south in winter to Mexico and Central America for the warm climate and ready supply of nectar-rich flowers.

The female Ruby-throated is green above and whitish below, with white corners to her tail, and lacks the male's ruby red throat patch (or gorget). During the breeding season, males display in front of females with a rocking, pendulum-like flight.

The very similar Black-chinned Hummingbird (*Archilochus alexandri*; 3¼–3½" [8–9 cm]) is the western counterpart of the Ruby-throated. It occurs in drier areas but also visits hummingbird feeders in gardens. The females of the two species are almost impossible to tell apart. (See also p.98.)

J F M A M J J A S O N D

Ruby-throated ♂

Ruby ♀ on nest

Black-chinned ♂

FIELD NOTES

- 3¼–3½" (8–9 cm)
- Male: Green flanks and ruby-red throat patch
- Female: No throat patch; white corners to tail
- ▲ Male Black-chinned (west) has black and violet gorget
- Cup of lichens, spider's silk, plant down
- 2; white

■ Male

Downy Woodpecker

Picoides pubescens

This small woodpecker is common and widespread in deciduous and mixed woodlands, parks, and gardens. In winter, it regularly visits bird feeders, where it is partial to suet, and joins feeding flocks (known as guilds) of small woodland birds such as chickadees and titmice.

Equally widespread, but less often seen in gardens, is the Hairy Woodpecker (*Picoides villosus*; 7½–9½" [19–24 cm]), a larger version of the Downy.

J F M A M J J A S O N D

Telling these two species apart can be quite difficult. Basically, if you can see the bill it's a Hairy, and if you can't it's a Downy. Note also that the Downy has black bars on its white outer tail feathers (which the Hairy lacks), and that the Hairy shouts rather than speaks its sharp call.

Occasionally, you may be rewarded by views of a Hairy and a Downy side by side—the difference in bill size is then obvious. Note that western birds of both species generally have less white on their wings than eastern birds.

Hairy ♂

Hairy & Downy (from above)

FIELD NOTES

■ 6–6½" (15–16.5 cm)

■ White back stripe Hairy Woodpecker has larger bill and lacks black bars on outer tail feathers

🌿 Hole in tree lined with wood chips

🥚 3–6; white

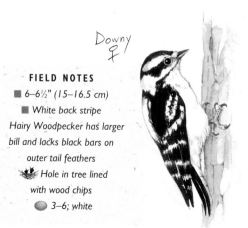

Downy ♀

151

Adult male

Purple Martin

Progne subis

The male Purple Martin, in his glossy blue-black plumage, is one of the most handsome birds in North America. In the east this large swallow is a familiar sight during summer in urban areas, especially around "martin houses"—condominium-style nestboxes erected on poles. In the west, the species occurs more locally and favors natural nest sites such as holes in dead tree limbs.

The best way to find Purple Martins in the west is to check dead trees along ridges or to visit ponds and lakes where swallows gather to drink, swooping down to dip their bills into the water. Purple Martins stand out as they are significantly larger than other swallows.

Purple Martins spend the winter in South America, return to Florida in February, and reach Canada in May. By October, this fine bird has once again departed from North America.

J F M A M J J A S O N D

FIELD NOTES

- 7½–8" (19–20.5 cm)—noticeably larger than other swallows
- Male: Overall glossy blue-black plumage
- Female: Brownish, pale-bellied
- Cavity in dead tree or nestbox lined with grass, mud, and feathers
- 3–8; white

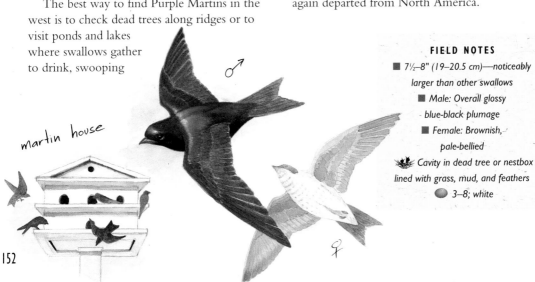

martin house

Adult

Barn Swallow

Hirundo rustica

A familiar summer visitor to urban and rural areas across North America, the Barn Swallow is often welcomed as a herald of spring. This graceful bird, identified by its long tail streamers (short or lacking in the juvenile), nests singly or in small colonies on buildings, where it builds a cup-like nest of mud.

Also widespread and common in summer is the closely related Cliff Swallow (*Hirundo pyrrhonota*; 5–5½" [12.5–14 cm]), identified by its chunkier build, squared-off tail and pale rump. The Cliff Swallow's nest is a gourd-shaped mud structure built under eaves or bridges, and colonies sometimes number up to a thousand pairs.

Like all swallows, these two species are masters of the air, where they swoop and glide, apparently effortlessly, for hours on end. As they fly, they dip down to the surface of lakes and rivers to drink and bathe. They also feed as they fly, their wide gapes enabling them to catch insects on the wing.

J F M A M J J A S O N D

Barn

Cliff

Cliff Swallows at nest

FIELD NOTES

- ■ 5–5½" (12.5–14 cm)
- ■ Glossy blue above, reddish below
- ■ Deeply forked tail with streamers
- ▲ Cliff Swallow has pale rump, square tail
- 🪺 Mud cup lined with grass and feathers, on a building
- 🥚 4–7; white spotted with browns

153

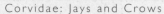

Adult

Blue Jay

Cyanocitta cristata

The handsome, unmistakable Blue Jay is a common and familiar bird in parks and gardens from the Atlantic coast to the Great Plains, and often visits bird feeders in winter.

Its counterpart in the west is the Steller's Jay (*Cyanocitta stelleri*; 11–12" [28–30.5 cm]), which takes over from the Rockies to the Pacific coast. The Steller's tends to be more of a forest bird although, like most jays, it can be tame at campgrounds and picnic areas. Northwestern Steller's Jays tend to be darker, while southern birds have a white crescent above each eye.

Best known for their loud and raucous calls, both jays are also accomplished vocalists whose repertoires range from convincing imitations of hawk screams to occasional soft, sweet warbling songs. Tracking down a scolding group of jays can frequently lead to a hawk or a roosting owl, as jays often mob these birds.

Both jays (but particularly the Blue Jay) vary their diet in summer by stealing other birds' eggs, while in fall they conceal acorns in the ground for times of hardship during winter.

J F M A M J J A S O N D

FIELD NOTES
- 10–11" (25.5–28 cm)
- Blue and white plumage and crest
- Steller's Jay (west) has blackish head
- Cup of twigs and grass at mid to upper levels in tree
- 3–7; greenish to bluish, marked with browns

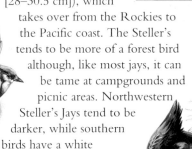

Blue Jay

northern form

southern form

Steller's Jay

154

Adult

Black-capped Chickadee

Parus atricapillus

Chickadees are frequent winter visitors to bird feeders, where they are noted for their acrobatic behavior. The Black-capped Chickadee is a familiar bird in gardens and woodlands across northern North America, where its *chick-a-dee-dee-dee* call can be heard throughout the year. In the southeastern US, the Black-capped is replaced by the slightly smaller but virtually identical (even experts argue about how to tell the two apart!)

Carolina Chickadee (*Parus carolinensis*; 4¼–4¾" [11–12 cm]).

Tracking down the call of a chickadee can transform a late fall or winter walk through a wooded area into an exciting experience, as it may lead you to woodpeckers, titmice, nuthatches, creepers, kinglets, and warblers, all moving and feeding together, with the chickadees acting as a nucleus species. Following the chickadees' scolding calls may also lead you to an owl on its daytime roost, as chickadees are known to mob these birds.

FIELD NOTES

■ 4¾–5¾" (12–14.5 cm)

■ Black cap and bib

■ Grayish back

▲ Carolina Chickadee (southeast) almost identical

✹ Tree cavity lined with grass, feathers

⬤ 5–10; white dotted with reddish browns

chickadees at feeder (with Evening Grosbeaks)

155

Tufted Titmouse

Parus bicolor

In the New World, titmice are simply crested chickadees. The Tufted Titmouse is a readily identifiable, familiar visitor to bird feeders in the east and its *peter peter peter* song is a common sound in parks and woodlands. Should titmice be regular winter visitors to your garden, you may be able to persuade them to stay all year by erecting a suitable nestbox.

If you live in south Texas or are a visitor there, note that the local Tufted Titmice have a whitish forehead and black crest. At one time they were considered a separate species—the Black-crested Titmouse.

In deciduous and mixed woodlands of the west, especially among oaks, you can find the

Tufted's western counterpart, the well-named Plain Titmouse (*Parus inornatus*; 5½" [14 cm]), which often visits gardens during winter.

Like chickadees, titmice are regular members of mixed-species feeding flocks in woodlands in winter.

J F **M A M** J J **A S O** N D

eastern form

south-western form

Plain Titmouse

FIELD NOTES
- 5–6" (12.5–15 cm)
- Gray and white with crest
- ▲ Number of similar species in southwest
- Tree cavity lined with grass, feathers
- 4–8; white flecked with browns

Adult

House Wren

Troglodytes aedon

A lively, chortling song or an insistent, scolding chatter often attracts attention to this small, fairly drab-looking brown bird with its slender bill, long tail, and the dark barring on the wings that is characteristic of wrens. The House Wren is common and widespread in North America, and different populations live all the way to Tierra del Fuego at the southern tip of South America. Like most small wrens, it can be difficult to see as it slips in and out of thickets and brush piles.

House Wrens nest in cavities, and the male builds several dummy nests of sticks from which the female chooses one, lines it with fine grass, and makes it home. Sometimes a pair will destroy the eggs of other wrens nesting nearby. This species can be attracted to nestboxes in gardens, but the entrance hole must be small enough to keep out starlings and House Sparrows. In winter, most House Wrens migrate to the southern US and Mexico.

J F M A M J J A S O N D

at nest box

FIELD NOTES

- 4½–5" (11.5–12.5 cm)
- Small, brown; skulking
- Barred wings and tail
- Foundation of sticks lined with fine material, in cavity
- 5–12; white dotted with browns

Adult male

American Robin

Turdus migratorius

Perhaps the most familiar and widespread North American bird, the American Robin—found in urban and forested areas from coast to coast—needs little introduction. Its melodic, caroling song usually starts before dawn and is considered a harbinger of spring in much of the north.

The American Robin's brick red chest reminded early European settlers of the small, red-breasted Robin of the Old World. It would be more correct to call the New World species the American Thrush, but few ornithologists would have the nerve to suggest that its name be changed!

This is the only widespread large thrush in North America and although the sexes are similar in

appearance, by looking carefully you may note that the male has a blacker head and brighter plumage. The juvenile is paler than the adult and has dark brown spotting on its chest; its bill is dark, changing to yellow in winter.

J F M A M J J A S O N D

FIELD NOTES
■ 9–10" (23–25.5 cm)
■ Brick red breast
■ Juvenile: Paler with spotting on chest
▲ Varied Thrush (western forests) has dark breast band
❋ Cup of grass, mud, low to high in bush or tree
● 3–7; unmarked pale blue

adult feeding fledglings

■ Adult

Northern Mockingbird

Mimus polyglottos

The English translation of the Northern Mockingbird's scientific name—"many-tongued mimic"—sums up well the best-known quality of this slender, long-tailed, gray and white bird. Its remarkable song, characterized by frequent three- to six-times repetition of phrases, is heard all over rural regions in the southern US, and in recent years the species' range has expanded into much of New England. As well as imitating other birds, mockingbirds incorporate a variety of sounds, such as barking dogs, into their repertoire, which they give day or night, from a perch or in flight.

J F M A M J J A S O N D

If you watch a Northern Mockingbird running around on a lawn, you may see it flash its white wing patches. This is apparently a way to flush out insect prey and is also useful in distracting predators from the nest.

As with all members of the family Mimidae, the sexes are alike in appearance. The juvenile Northern Mockingbird can be identified by the dusky spotting on its chest and by its dusky eyes.

FIELD NOTES
- ■ 9–10" (23–25.5 cm)
- ■ Active and noisy
- ■ Slender, long-tailed
- ■ Bold, white wing patches
- Cup of twigs, grass, wool at low to mid levels in bush or tree
- 2–6; pale bluish, heavily marked with browns

white wing patches

Mockingbird attacking cat!

159

Adult

Cedar Waxwing

Bombycilla cedrorum

The first sign of Cedar Waxwings is often high-pitched, sibilant calls overhead. On looking up, you may then see a tightly packed group of pointed-winged, short-tailed birds wheeling around in the sky. (In flight they resemble the European Starling.) With luck, the flock will then land to reveal one of the most beautiful of all birds, with its sleek plumage in soft pastel shades and a tufted crest above its narrow, black mask. The name "waxwing" comes from the waxy red tips on its inner wing feathers. Juvenile Cedar Waxwings have streaked underparts.

While they nest in northern North America, Cedar Waxwings move south in winter (some reaching as far as Panama) and

Cedar

J F M A M J J A S O N D

frequently visit parks and gardens to feed at berry-bearing trees and shrubs.

A good way to attract these birds to your garden is to plant cedars (*Cedrus*), and rowans (*Sorbus aucuparia*), as the berries of these plants are their favored food. In summer, Cedar Waxwings often eat insects, caught as the birds fly.

juvenile

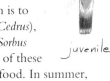

FIELD NOTES
- ■ 6–7" (15–18 cm)
- ■ Smooth, elegant, crested
- ■ Yellow-tipped tail
- ■ White undertail coverts
- ▲ Bohemian Waxwing (northern forests) is larger and has brick red undertail coverts
- Cup of twigs, grass, moss at mid to upper levels in tree
- 2–6; pale blue with dark markings

Bohemian

160

Adults (breeding plumage)

European Starling

Sturnus vulgaris

Whether feeding and squabbling in city parks, or flying in vast swarms to roost in the urban warmth of down-town areas, starlings are a familiar sight in cities across North America. Sixty European Starlings, natives of the Old World, were introduced into New York's Central Park in 1890, and their offspring has multiplied to the 200-million-plus starlings we see today.

These birds are easy to watch and provide a good opportunity to observe how summer and winter plumages

J F M A M J J A S O N D

can vary. Most songbirds molt twice a year, but the starling has a single molt in late summer (after breeding), when the glossy adult and the dull gray juvenile acquire new blackish feathers marked profusely with pale spots. The spots then wear off through the winter, to be replaced by the purple and green sheens of breeding starlings. The bird's bill is darker in winter and changes to bright yellow in breeding birds.

FIELD NOTES
- 8–9" (20.5–23 cm)
- Stocky, stub-tailed bird
- Glossy black plumage
- Winter: Speckled plumage, dark bill
- Summer: Yellow bill
- Cup of grass and twigs in cavity
- 4–8; pale blue

winter plumage

juvenile

161

■ Adult male

Northern Cardinal

Cardinalis cardinalis

The Northern Cardinal is characteristic of eastern North America, and the male, with his stout red bill, black face, and tufted crest, is unmistakable. In spring and summer, he sings his loud song of bright whistles from a prominent perch, and in winter he adds a splash of color to many a snow-covered bird feeder.

J F M A M J J A S O N D

The female and juvenile are pale grayish brown overall with some red in their wings and tail; the female has a reddish pink bill, and the juvenile's bill is dark gray. In late summer, the young male molts into his all-red plumage and his bill turns red.

There is a separate population of Northern Cardinals in the brushy washes of the southwestern deserts, where the closely related Pyrrhuloxia (p. 302) also occurs. The Northern Cardinal can be seen, too, in Hawaii, where it was introduced by homesick Americans from the eastern US.

winter ♂
(on holly)

juvenile
♂

FIELD NOTES
- ■ 8–9" (20.5–23 cm)
- ■ Male: Stout red bill, black face and tufted crest—unmistakable
- ■ Female: Paler brownish color; reddish pink bill
- 🍂 Bowl of twigs, grass at low to mid levels in thicket or bush
- 🥚 2–5; whitish marked with browns and grays

♀

Adult

California Towhee

Pipilo crissalis

This large, plain brown sparrow is common in urban and rural California where you may see it hopping on the ground, often with its long, dark tail held cocked; the cinnamon undertail coverts are a distinctive field mark. California Towhees often feed in areas of open ground but quickly run for cover— under a bush or a parked car—when disturbed.

Until a few years ago, this bird was considered to be the same species as the Canyon Towhee (*Pipilo fuscus*; 7½–9" [19–23 cm]) of the interior southwest, and the species was at that time known as the Brown Towhee. It has been shown, however, that the two types look and sound different,

and ornithologists now recognize two distinct species whose ranges do not overlap.

The California Towhee gives a loud metallic *chink* call, while the Canyon Towhee's call is a two-syllable, complaining *ch-eh*. The Canyon Towhee, less often found in urban gardens than the Californian species, is further distinguished by its rustier cap and a dark spot on the center of its chest.

| J | F | M | A | M | J | J | A | S | O | N | D |

California

Canyon

FIELD NOTES

- ■ 7½–9" (19–23 cm)
- ■ Plain, brownish
- ▲ Canyon Towhee (southwest interior) has rustier cap and dark spot on chest
- 🪹 Bulky bowl of twigs, grass at low to mid levels in bush or tree
- 🥚 2–6; pale bluish marked with browns, grays, and black

163

■ Adult

Song Sparrow
Melospiza melodia

In spring and summer, the Song Sparrow sings a varied arrangement of chips and trills from a low perch on a bush or post. During other seasons, although common and widespread, the Song Sparrow does not draw attention to itself. Look for it in and near brushy thickets, especially in damp areas.

This is one of the most variable birds in North America, and some 31 subspecies have been identified, from the huge (7" [18 cm]) birds of the Aleutian Islands in Alaska to the pale birds of the southwestern deserts, which have sparse, rusty spots on their chest.

The "typical" Song Sparrow is gray and brown above (its broad gray supercilium, or eyebrow, is a good field mark) and its underparts are white marked with blackish streaks which often form a dark spot in the center of its chest. The juvenile has a pale yellowish, or buffy, wash to its face and underparts, which are less distinctly streaked than those of the adult.

| J | F | M | A | M | J | J | A | S | O | N | D |

in full song!

FIELD NOTES
■ 5½–7" (14–18 cm)
■ Broad gray supercilium (eyebrow)
■ Blackish streaks on chest—often form spot in center of chest
▲ Similar to many other sparrows
❀ Cup of grass, weeds on or near ground in grass or thicket
● 2–6; pale bluish to greenish white, marked with reddish browns

Song Sparrow

Aleutian

164

■ Adult

White-throated Sparrow

Zonotrichia albicollis

The sweet, whistled *Old Sam Peabody, Peabody, Peabody* song of the White-throated Sparrow is a characteristic sound in the bird's summer home in Canada's coniferous forests. In winter, this common species migrates southward, mainly to the eastern US, although small numbers also spend the winter in the south and west.

| J | F | M | A | M | J | J | A | S | O | N | D |

If you live in the east, following up a rustling sound in the bushes of your local park or woodland in winter may well reveal a flock of White-throated Sparrows. You may also be able to find them if you can recognize and follow their high-pitched, lisping *tseet* call.

The adult has a brightly marked head with a clean-cut, white throat patch and a yellow spot forward of the eyes; the supercilium (eyebrow) varies from white to buff. The immature has dark streaking on its chest; its throat may be pale gray; and its head pattern, while similar to the adult, is more subdued.

buff-striped adult

white-striped adult

FIELD NOTES

- ■ 6–7" (15–18 cm)
- ■ Clean-cut, white throat patch
- ■ Yellow spot in front of eye
- ▲ White-crowned Sparrow—
  see p. 203
- ✿ Cup of grass, pine needles on or near ground in thicket
- ● 3–6; pale bluish marked with browns and black

immature

■ Adult

Common Grackle

Quiscalus quiscula

The Common Grackle is a familiar and common blackbird in the east, where it lives in urban areas, farmland, and open woodlands. As with other blackbirds, males are slightly larger and brighter than females, although at a distance the sexes appear similar. Seen close up, the males have particularly glossy plumage. This varies from an overall bronze color in birds of New England and west of the Appalachian Mountains, to purplish in birds east and south of the Appalachians. Adults have pale yellow eyes but these are dusky in the sooty brown plumaged juveniles. The birds have long slender tails that are broader toward the tip.

The Common Grackle could be confused with the Rusty Blackbird (*Euphagus carolinus*; 8" [21 cm]), common in the east, and Brewer's Blackbird (*E. cyanocephalus*; 8½–9½" [21.5–24 cm]), common in the west, but both are shorter-tailed than the Common Grackle.

J F M A M J J A S O N D

shear tooth

purple form

bronzed form

FIELD NOTES
- ■ 10–12" (25.5–30.5 cm)
- ■ Black, glossy blue-green and bronze
- ■ Long slender tail, broader toward tip, carried folded lengthwise
- ▲ Rusty Blackbird (east) and Brewer's Blackbird (west) similar but shorter-tailed
- Cup of sticks and grass in tree or building
- 4–5; pale green or brown with dark markings

Adult male

House Finch

Carpodacus mexicanus

Native to the semi-arid lands of western North America and Mexico, House Finches were released on Long Island, New York, in the 1940s. They have since spread into much of the eastern US and southeastern Canada, and their range apparently continues to expand in the east, where they compete with another introduced species, the House Sparrow (p. 168), for nest sites and food.

The House Finch is a common visitor to birdfeeders, where the drab female may be overlooked among House Sparrows. Note her plain face and wings and the extensive dusky streaking on her underparts. The male is more conspicuous by virtue of his red brow, bib, and rump. On some males this red tends to orange or yellow. The juvenile resembles the female, and the young male attains adult-like plumage by fall. The House Finch's song is a prolonged warble, ranging from a scratchy to a fairly melodic sound.

| J | F | M | A | M | J | J | A | S | O | N | D |

House Finch ♂

House Sparrows

♀

FIELD NOTES

■ 5½–6" (14–15 cm)

■ Male: Red brow, bib, and rump

■ Female and juvenile: Paler; dusky streaking on underparts

▲ Purple Finch (north and west) similar, but male lacks streaked flanks and female has white streak above eye

❀ Cup of grass, twigs in cavity or dense foliage

● 2–6; bluish white flecked with browns

167

Adult female

House Sparrow

Passer domesticus

Introduced to New York in the middle of the nineteenth century, the House Sparrow, also known as the English Sparrow, has spread through most of the Americas. It likes to live near humans and, with the Rock Dove (Feral Pigeon), is perhaps the bird most familiar to city dwellers. Its chirps and chatters may be heard all over town, from wooded parks and gardens to ledges high on skyscrapers.

The male is quite handsome, with his chestnut-colored head stripes and black bib. In winter his bill is dusky pale brownish but in summer it becomes black. If you would like to practice taking notes and sketching birds in the field, the female House Sparrow is a good subject to start with, providing an excellent introduction to bird anatomy and the subtleties of bird behavior. This superficially nondescript bird can puzzle even experienced birders when they encounter it out of context.

J F M A M J J A S O N D

♂

FIELD NOTES
- 5½–6" (14–15 cm)
- Male: Gray crown, gray rump
- Female and juvenile: Dingy gray
- ▲ In St Louis and Illinois beware of confusion with the Eurasian Tree Sparrow
- Bulky dome of grass and straw in a cavity or dense foliage
- 2–6; whitish with brown spots

dustbathing
♀

168

Woodlands

BIRDING in WOODLANDS

North American woodlands contain a wealth of birdlife. However, dense foliage can make it difficult to locate many species, so you may be able to identify some only by their calls. Moreover, what you hear and see will depend very much on the time of year.

In winter, the northern woods are home only to those birds that eat foods which last through cold weather, such as seeds, and insects that shelter under tree bark. These birds often congregate in wandering, mixed feeding parties of several species—woodpeckers, nuthatches, creepers, chickadees, and others—all moving through the woods together in search of food. You might walk for an hour or more through a forest that seems to be entirely empty of birdlife, then suddenly encounter such a flock. For a few moments the trees will be crowded with birds, but the encounter will usually be brief because the birds keep moving along. Soon their soft calls will die away in the distance and the woods will become silent again.

In the warmer climates of the south and west, you'll find a greater diversity of species in winter, including a few warblers and flycatchers.

In spring and summer there is food for many more birds, and flycatchers, thrushes, vireos, warblers, and a host of other birds return from their winter homes in the New World tropics (the Neotropics) to nest. The spring and fall migration periods (mainly April to May and August to October) are therefore the best times to see the most species, particularly if you live in the south.

WOODLAND WATCHERS *A group of birders takes a close look at a woodland bird. Stiff necks are an occupational hazard of forest birding, as so many of the birds are situated directly above you!*

HABITAT PREFERENCES *Some species frequent only one type of forest—either deciduous or coniferous. White-breasted Nuthatches (above right) prefer deciduous woods; Gray Jays (right) favor conifers.*

KNOWING THE HABITAT

In woodlands, perhaps more than in other habitats, it pays to learn something about the details of the environment, in particular the names of the trees and other plants that you will see around you.

Many bird species are closely associated with specific trees and bushes. If you take time to learn the names of these plants and note which birds you see on or near them, you will soon be able to predict, just by studying the surrounding flora, which birds are likely to inhabit a particular area of forest.

In the text of The Habitat Birdfinder we indicate, where relevant, which trees and plants each species is most closely associated with.

TRACKING BY EAR

Unlike marshlands and open country, where birds can be readily seen, woodlands may at first seem less rich in birdlife, since birds can easily remain out of sight in the foliage. In these conditions, your hearing becomes an important aspect of birding.

It takes practice to learn the songs and calls of different species (see p. 122). A useful way to start is to listen to recordings of songs and calls at home.

When in your local woods, try tracking down the sources of songs and calls for yourself. At first, identifying the bird by sight will be easier than by its call, but as you match the most common songs and calls

WOODLAND BIRDS *may live mostly on the ground, as the American Woodcock (above) does, in the middle layers of foliage, as the Black-capped Chickadee (left) does, or high in the canopy, as the Red-eyed Vireo (below left) does.*

with the species that make them you will soon be able to identify those birds as soon as you hear them. In turn, you will be able to distinguish the songs of species that are new to you.

Learning something of the meaning or context of bird calls in woods can also be useful. For example, small woodland birds have a characteristic alarm note they use if a hawk is in the area, and the scolding notes they make on discovering an owl at its daytime roost can often lead you to the owl itself.

STEALTH AND STRATEGY

You need to move quietly in woodlands, not so much for fear of scaring birds away as for your own ability to concentrate on what you can hear. Look for a trail or some little-used country track to wander along, because then you don't need to keep watching where you put your feet, and you make less noise than when you go crashing through the woods.

Remember to keep scanning all levels of the forest. Some species are birds of the treetops

and seldom come low. Others prefer the middle levels, and quite a few species are almost always found in the understory or on the ground.

Woodland birds vary widely in their response to a human observer. Some are extremely wary, while a few are inquisitive, and may even follow you as you go. If you are patient and move carefully, or, better yet, sit still for a while, many woodland birds will accept your presence. The trick is not to crowd the

bird, or trigger its "startle" response. Once startled into flight, the bird is unlikely to allow you within range again.

■ Adult

Sharp-shinned Hawk

Accipiter striatus

The Sharp-shin, or "Sharpie" as it is often known, is the most common small woodland hawk across much of North America. Like other accipiters (from the genus name), it preys mainly on small birds, and may visit gardens to take birds from feeders—a spectacular sight to witness.

To tell the Sharp-shin from small falcons such as the American Kestrel (p. 215), note its broad, rounded wings and its flight style—bursts of quick flapping followed by a glide. Adults are blue-gray above, barred with orange-red below, while juveniles are brown above and streaked reddish below.

J F M A M J J A S O N D

The larger Cooper's Hawk (*Accipiter cooperii*; 15–20" [38–51 cm]), of the US and southern Canada, is generally less common than the Sharpie, and favors more open woodlands and, in winter, semi-open country. Many papers have been written on how to tell these two species apart, but experts still disagree at times. The Sharpie has a proportionately smaller head and a shorter, squarer tail than the Cooper's, but you may find it easier to simply write "accipiter species" in your notebook.

immature

Sharp-shinned ♂

Coopers ♂

FIELD NOTES

11–14" (28–35.5 cm)

- ■ Squared or slightly notched tail tip
- ■ Females: Clearly larger than males
- ▲ Cooper's Hawk has more rounded tail and larger head
- Stick platform at mid to upper levels in tree
- 3–6; whitish marked with browns

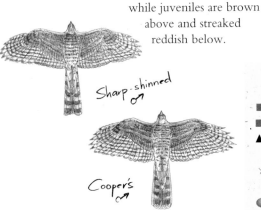

Adult

Red-shouldered Hawk

Buteo lineatus

A medium-sized buteo, the Red-shouldered Hawk is common in eastern woodlands and hunts mainly from perches such as roadside wires, from where it drops on small mammals and reptiles. Its persistent screaming *kyaah kyaah kyaah* call often draws attention to it. A brighter-marked race occurs in the west.

The other medium-sized buteo widespread in the east is the Broad-winged Hawk (*Buteo platypterus*; 15–17" [38–43 cm]) which is present only in summer, as it migrates south to the tropics for the winter. It has broader, more pointed wings and a shorter tail than the Red-shoulder and spends more time soaring; its wingbeats are looser and more measured. The Red-shoulder is larger and often flies with bursts of quick flapping followed by glides, suggesting an accipiter.

J F M A M J J A S O N D

Watching Red-shoulders in winter, when you can be sure there are no Broad-wings around, is a good way to start learning the field marks of these two similar species.

Broad-winged

Red-shouldered

FIELD NOTES

■ 18–22" (45.5–56 cm)
■ Reddish shoulders
■ Dark wings, barred white
■ Reddish wing-linings, dark bars on underside of tail
▲ Broad-winged Hawk has broader, more pointed wings, shorter tail
🪹 Stick platform at mid to upper levels in tree
🥚 1–4; whitish marked with browns

immature

173

■ Adult

Red-tailed Hawk

Buteo jamaicensis

This buteo, the most widespread and familiar hawk in North America, is found in woodlands, farmlands, deserts, and wooded urban areas. As well as hunting from perches such as roadside phone poles, Red-tails often hunt while flying. At times, the Red-tail hangs, or hovers, in the wind, like a giant kestrel, and then drops down on its prey, usually a rodent.

J F M A M J J A S O N D

The Red-tail is highly variable in plumage. Most birds are dark above and pale below, but some are dark all over. Adults have a rufous, or orange-red, tail, and a V-shaped area of pale mottling on the back is a good field mark on perched birds. The juvenile Red-tail, like many young hawks, is proportionately longer-winged and longer-tailed than the adult, and its tail is brownish above with numerous dark bars.

The Red-tail's silhouette is useful as a yardstick for comparison with less common species.

dark form (Harlan's)

pale form (Krider's)

from below

FIELD NOTES
- ■ 19–23" (48–58.5 cm)
- ■ Most common and widespread buteo
- ■ Reddish tail
- ■ V-shaped pale mottling on back
- ■ Pale underparts, streaked belly
- ▲ Plumage extremely variable
- Stick platform at mid to upper levels in tree
- 1–5; whitish flecked with browns

174

Adult male

Ruffed Grouse

Bonasa umbellus

The Ruffed Grouse is typical of deciduous and mixed forests across northern North America, and is often encountered at the side of a quiet road, especially early and late in the day.

Finding one in the woods is really a matter of luck, since this bird's cryptic plumage helps it blend in with leaves on the forest floor. A good way to detect Ruffed Grouse is to listen for the "drumming" of the male's display, which he does from a low perch, in spring. The sound is made by air rushing through his wingtips as he beats them rapidly.

Ruffed Grouse are found in two forms: redder birds are more common in warmer climates, and grayer birds prevail where the climate is cool.

| J | F | M | A | M | J | J | A | S | O | N | D |

In the coniferous forests of the north, the Ruffed Grouse tends to be replaced by the Spruce Grouse (*Dendragapus canadensis*; 14–16" [35.5–40.5 cm]). In the Rocky Mountains, males of this species—known locally as the Franklin's Grouse—have white tips to their upper tail coverts and lack the orange tail tip of male Spruce Grouse elsewhere.

'ruff'

FIELD NOTES

- ■ 16–18" (40.5–45.5 cm)
- ■ Black ruff on side of neck
- ■ Reddish or pale grayish tail with conspicuous dark band near tip
- ▲ Spruce Grouse is darker, looks more compact, and has blackish tail with brownish-red tip
- ❧ Hollow in ground, lined with leaves, pine needles
- ● 8–14; buff, sometimes flecked with browns

Spruce ♂

Ruffed ♂

175

Adult

Great Horned Owl

Bubo virginianus

The low *hoo h-hoo, hoohoo* of this spectacular large owl is a familiar sound in much of North America, where the bird appears equally at home in woods and deserts. The Great Horned Owl is often seen perched at dusk on roadside phone poles, wires, or even television aerials. In open country, these birds often use the perches that Red-tailed Hawks use in the daytime. This owl's cryptic plumage varies in color from the pale,

J F M A M J J A S O N D

frosty gray birds of the Canadian tundra to the dark, heavily marked birds of the wet Pacific coast forests. All Great Horned Owls can be distinguished from other large owls by their widely spaced ear tufts, their fluffy white throat bib, and the dark cross-barring on their underparts.

If Great Horned Owls are nesting near your house, you will hear the persistent begging shrieks of the juveniles for a month or more in summer, often beginning in late afternoon and continuing till dawn.

bringing food to young

FIELD NOTES

- 19–24" (48–61 cm)
- Very big and bulky
- Yellow eyes
- Conspicuous, widely spaced ear tufts
- White throat bib
- Old nest of hawk or crow; cavity in tree or rocks
- 1–6; white

Adult

Barred Owl

Strix varia

The large, brown-eyed Barred Owl is common in the deep woods of the east, especially in river valleys, and also occurs across Canada as far as the west coast, from where its range is expanding south into California. Its western counterpart is the Spotted Owl (*Strix occidentalis*; 17–19" [43–48 cm]), famous for its key role in the battle to save the old growth forests of the Pacific northwest.

The Barred Owl has dark barring across its chest, with dark vertical streaks on the rest of its underparts, while the Spotted Owl has spots and bars all down its underparts.

Both species give a varied series of barking hoots: the Barred Owl says *Who cooks for-you? Who cooks for-you-all?*, while the Spotted has a shorter *Who, cooks for, you-OU!* call.

You may hear these birds in the late afternoon and therefore be able to track them down in daylight. If you are fortunate enough to find them roosting during the day, they can be remarkably tame, and usually allow you to come quite close.

J F M A M J J A S O N D

Spotted Owl

Barred Owl nestlings

FIELD NOTES
- 18–22" (45.5–56 cm)
- Chunky build
- Dark eyes
- Barring on chest; streaked belly
- ▲ Spotted Owl (west) is darker with marbled and spotted underparts
- Tree cavity or stump; old nest of hawk or squirrel
- 1–4; white

Adult male

Acorn Woodpecker

Melanerpes formicivorus

One of the most handsome woodpeckers in North America, the unmistakable, "clown-faced" Acorn Woodpecker is common in oak woods of the west and southwest. It is a notably social woodpecker, and often the first clues to its presence are its burry chattering and rhythmic laughing calls. It lives in groups of up to 15 birds centered around their famous "granaries", where acorns are wedged into holes in trunks. Up to 50,000 acorns have been counted in a single hiding place! Studies have shown that these communities of Acorn Woodpeckers are composed largely of siblings, their cousins, and parents.

JFMAMJJASOND

Up to four males may mate with one female, and all eggs are laid in a single nest. All members of the community are involved in incubating and feeding the young. As well as feeding on insects on trunks, Acorn Woodpeckers may be seen flycatching in lazy, soaring flights.

♂ (flying)

FIELD NOTES
- 8¼–9¼" (21–23.5 cm)
- Unmistakable
- White eye contrasts with black cheek
- White rump and white flash near each wingtip
- Female: Black patch at front of red crown
- Hole excavated in tree
- 4–6; white

Adult male (Red-shafted)

Northern Flicker

Colaptes auratus

The Flicker is the most common and conspicuous large woodpecker over much of the continent, and has three distinct subspecies that were once considered to be separate species: the Yellow-shafted Flicker of the east ("shafted" refers to the wing- and tail-feather shafts), the Red-shafted Flicker of the west, and the Gilded Flicker (with golden yellow shafts) of the southwestern deserts. Hybridization of these forms is now common.

Flickers live in open woodlands and can often be seen feeding on lawns, where they search with their long tongues for ants. Males can be identified by their "mustache" marks: black in the Yellow-shafted, and red in the Red-shafted and the Gilded.

In all of these forms, the white rump is conspicuous in flight.

The Flicker's strident call, a loud *wick wick wick*, is a common sound in woodlands during spring.

| J | F | M | A | M | J | J | A | S | O | N | D |

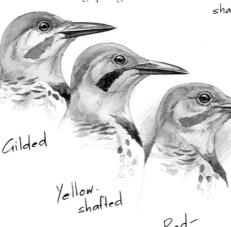

Yellow-shafted in flight

FIELD NOTES

- 10–12" (25.5–30.5 cm)
- Barred, brownish back
- Red or yellow "shafts"
- Bold black crescent across chest
- ▲ Three different populations with variations in color of crown, nape, and "mustache" marks
- Hole excavated in tree
- 3–10; white

Gilded

Yellow-shafted

Red-shafted

Adult

Great Crested Flycatcher

Myiarchus crinitus

Like almost all flycatchers in North America, this fairly large species is present here only in summer. It is common in woods and residential areas in the east but often stays out of sight in the canopy where it can be detected by its call—loud bickering chatters and an ascending, emphatic whistled *wheeep!*

In the west you'll find the closely related and similar-looking Ash-throated Flycatcher (*Myiarchus cinarascens*; 7½–8" [19-20.5 cm]) which inhabits drier, more open habitats, especially riparian groves, and is seen more easily. Its calls include a bright *ka-brick* and a quiet *pic*.

Where both species occur, note the darker upperparts of the Great Crested, and its darker gray throat and chest which contrast strongly with the yellow belly. By comparison, the Ash-throated appears washed-out overall. Both species have bright orange-red in their wings and tail.

J F M A M J J A S O N D

Great Crested

FIELD NOTES

■ 8–8¾" (20.5–22 cm)

■ Dark gray throat and chest

■ Yellow belly

■ Orange-red in wings and tail

▲ Ash-throated Flycatcher more washed-out overall with smaller, all-black bill

✿ Cavity in tree or post

⬭ 3–8; cream scrawled with browns

■ Adult

White-breasted Nuthatch

Sitta carolinensis

A nasal note, repeated steadily—*neh-neh-neh*—is often the first clue that a White-breasted Nuthatch is close by. These small birds creep along trunks and branches, both head-up and head-down, as they forage under loose bark and in tree crevices. Often they accompany mixed-species flocks of chickadees and titmice in the winter woods, and they will visit bird feeders.

The White-breasted Nuthatch occurs in most woodland and forest habitats, and in the west it is found in dry oak and pine-oak woods.

J F M A M J J A S O N D

The smaller Red-breasted Nuthatch (*Sitta canadensis*; 4¼–4½" [11–11.5 cm]), also widespread across North America, prefers conifers, and therefore nests mainly in the north and west. It moves into the south in winter where it is noted as an irruptive migrant; that is, one whose winter abundance varies greatly from year to year. The Red-breasted is identified by its mostly orangey underparts. In both species, the male's cap is glossy black while the female's is dark gray to blackish.

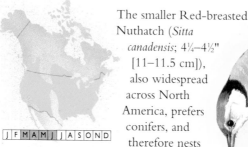

White-breasted ♀

FIELD NOTES

■ 5¼–5½" (13–14 cm)

■ White face surrounds black eye

■ Forages up and down tree trunks

▲ Red-breasted Nuthatch has orangey chest, and black line through eye

 Bed of grass and bark in cavity at mid to upper levels in tree

● 4–8; whitish, speckled with reddish browns

Red-breasted ♂

181

Ruby-crowned Kinglet

Regulus calendula

Kinglets, among the smallest of North American birds, are olive above and pale below, with two white wingbars. The Ruby-crowned Kinglet has a plain face with a broken white eye-ring. The male has a red crown-patch which can only be seen when the crown feathers are raised.

This kinglet frequents northern and western forests in summer, while in winter it often joins mixed-species feeding flocks of chickadees and warblers. Listen for the Ruby-crowned's dry chattering *ch-cht* call and look for a tiny, active bird that often hovers briefly while picking at twigs and leaves for food. In the same habitats you may also

find the Golden-crowned Kinglet (*Regulus satrapa*; 3¾–4" [9.5–10 cm]). It has a yellow crown stripe, dark face stripes, and a whitish eyebrow; the male also has a red crown patch.

The Golden-crowned's very high-pitched *see-see-see* call will help you locate it, particularly in summer, high amid the dense foliage of the firs and spruces it favors for nesting. Some of these birds remain as far north as southern Canada through the winter—much farther north than the Ruby-crowned.

crest exposed

Golden-crowned

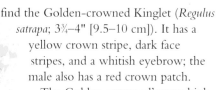

Golden-crowned ♂

Ruby-crowned ♂

J F M A M J J A S O N D

FIELD NOTES

■ 4–4¼" (10–11 cm)

■ Tiny, active

■ Plain with two white wingbars

■ Broken white eye-ring

▲ Golden-crowned Kinglet has striped face

❀ Pouch of moss, lichen, spider's silk at mid to upper levels in tree

● 5–10; whitish finely marked with browns

Adult

Blue-gray Gnatcatcher

Polioptila caerulea

The tiny Blue-gray Gnatcatcher nests in open woodland, chaparral, and pinyon-juniper woods. In winter it favors mixed woodland and brushy thickets. It is an active bird that cocks and flicks its long, white-sided tail as it moves through the trees, and it often hovers like a kinglet to pick at the undersides of leaves or twigs. It joins mixed-species feeding flocks in the south in winter when, as in summer, it can be detected by following up its nasal, mewing *meehr* call.

J F M A M J J A S O N D

Its song is a high-pitched, squeaky and scratchy warble.

In summer the male can be distinguished by his narrow black brow, but in winter he has a plain blue-gray face with a white eye-ring, like the female.

Along with many small songbirds in the east, the Blue-gray Gnatcatcher is often host to the Brown-headed Cowbird, which lays its eggs in the nests of other species. The nest of the Blue-gray Gnatcatcher is remarkable: a tiny cup of lichens and other fine materials slung between twigs.

underside of tail

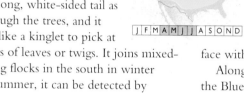

FIELD NOTES

- 4–5½" (10–14 cm)
- Long black tail with white edge
- Blue-gray above, white below
- Summer male: Narrow black brow
- Cup of lichen and fine grasses slung in a fork
- 3–6; pale bluish speckled with reddish brown

183

■ Female

Eastern Bluebird

Sialia sialis

Bluebirds are among the most colorful birds in North America. In summer, look for them in open woods, especially where there are pines. In fall and winter, they occur in family groups or small flocks in open farmland and grassland where they often perch on roadside wires and fences. Bluebirds hunt from a perch or while hovering, then drop to the ground to pick up insects.

Eastern ♂

West of the Great Plains, the Eastern Bluebird is replaced by the closely related and very similar Western Bluebird (*Sialia mexicana*; 6½–7" [16.5–18 cm]).

J F M A M J J A S O N D

The male Eastern has an orange-red throat and chest (paler in the southern Arizona race), and an all-blue back. The male Western is identified by his blue throat, and he often shows some orange-red on his back. The females of both species are similar to one another, but if you look carefully you will see hints of the male plumage features: a pale orangey throat in the Eastern, and a grayish throat in the Western.

Bluebird populations have declined in recent decades, apparently largely because of competition with starlings for nest holes, but specially designed bluebird nestboxes have helped populations recover in some areas.

Eastern ♀

FIELD NOTES

- ■ 6½–7" (16.5–18 cm)
- ■ Familiar and unmistakable
- ■ Bright blue above, reddish below
- ▲ Western Bluebird (west of Great Plains) is similar but has blue throat and some red on back
- 🪺 Cavity in tree; nestbox
- 🥚 2–6; pale blue to white

Western ♂

Adults

Red-eyed Vireo

Vireo olivaceus

The mellow, repetitive song of the Red-eyed Vireo is often heard on long summer days in eastern woodlands and among suburban shade trees. If you track down the persistent singer (the song may suggest an American Robin but tends to be weaker and more continuous), you will find a small, fairly drab bird, a little chunkier than a warbler.

The Red-eyed Vireo's upperparts are olive and its underparts silky whitish, but the red eyes and the dark lines above and below the whitish eyebrow are its distinctive features (though in fall young birds have brownish eyes). It is a

neotropical migrant; that is, it migrates north to breed and raise its young among the rich insect life of the North American summer, then moves south to the Neotropics (the New World tropics) for the winter. Red-eyed Vireos in fact fly all the way to the Amazon Basin.

Like all vireos, the Red-eyed Vireo weaves its deep, cup-shaped nest from fine grass, spider's silk and strips of bark, and suspends it from a fork in a tree.

J F M A M J J A S O N D

Red-eyed Vireo

FIELD NOTES
- 5½–6" (14–15 cm)
- Red eye
- Black line through eye and along edge of gray crown
- No wingbars
- Cup of grass and bark suspended in fork in mid to upper levels of tree
- 3–5; white with brown flecks

185

■ Adult

Warbling Vireo

Vireo gilvus

A scratchy, fairly rapid warbling song is often the first indication that Warbling Vireos have arrived back from their wintering grounds in Mexico and northern Central America. The first migrants reach California in March, and arrive in Canada by May. Most have departed again from North America by the beginning of October.

These rather nondescript vireos nest in open deciduous woods and riparian groves where, like many vireos, their persistent songs give them away. The Warbling Vireo's head and upperparts are plain grayish, and its underparts are dirty whitish. A broad whitish brow is its best field mark. Fresh-plumaged birds in fall can be washed with olive above and yellow below, looking surprisingly bright if you are used to breeding birds in their dull summer colors. Juveniles have two pale cinnamon wingbars.

The Warbling Vireo, like many small songbirds, often plays unsuspecting host to the Brown-headed Cowbird, which lays its eggs in the nests of other species.

J F M A M J J A S O N D

FIELD NOTES

■ 4¾–5¼" (12–13 cm)
■ Broad whitish brow
■ Plain grayish head
■ Smaller, paler and grayer than Red-eyed Vireo
▲ Philadelphia Vireo (east) has yellowish throat and breast, and dull buffy wingbar
❀ Cup of fine grass, spider's silk, bark strips suspended in fork in mid to upper levels of tree
● 3–5; white with brown flecks

Warbling Vireo

Philadelphia Vireo

Adult (western form)

Orange-crowned Warbler

Vermivora celata

This fairly plain warbler is a common breeding species in the west and north, but is common only as a winter migrant in the east and south. It favors brushy woodland, forest edges, and chaparral.

As is typical of most species in the genus *Vermivora*, the Orange-crowned has a sharply pointed bill and lacks bold wing and tail markings. Its orange crown patch is usually concealed. The Orange-crowned's song is a rapid trill that fades abruptly.

J F M A M J J A S O N D

Like many species with a widespread range in North America, the Orange-crowned shows marked regional variation in its plumage: western birds are brightest, and can be quite a strong yellow overall, while eastern birds tend to be a duller, grayish olive overall and have a gray hood. Two useful field marks for all subspecies are the face pattern (narrow pale eyebrows and pale eye-crescents), and the bright yellow undertail coverts.

The Orange-crowned is often confused with the Yellow Warbler and the Wilson's Warbler (pp. 190 and 196).

FIELD NOTES

■ 4½–5" (11.5–12.5 cm)

■ Dullest of all the wood-warblers

■ Narrow pale eyebrows and pale eye-crescents

■ Bright yellow undertail coverts

▲ Yellow and Wilson's warblers—see pp. 190 and 196

Cup of grass and bark on or near ground

3–6; white marked with reddish browns

eastern form

western form

187

■ Adult

Nashville Warbler

Vermivora ruficapilla

The Nashville Warbler is one of a pair of birds that replace each other geographically as breeding species and which some ornithologists consider to be races of a single species. The other bird is the Virginia's Warbler (*Vermivora virginae*; 4–4½" [10–11.5 cm]), and both are plain warblers in the genus *Vermivora*.

The Nashville nests in open mixed woodlands, often in boggy areas, while the Virginia's favors pinyon-juniper woods with a brushy understory. Experienced

J F M A M J J A S O N D

birders can find both of these birds by their songs, but, unless you have a well-trained ear, learning any more than the most distinctive songs of the many warbler species that nest in North America is a real challenge. Both of these species give a metallic *pink* note that may help you locate them as they feed low in bushes, wagging their tails as they hop about.

The Nashville has a gray hood and white eye-ring, and is otherwise olive above and yellow below. Males tend to be brighter than females. The Virginia's Warbler is distinguished by its overall gray plumage, and lacks olive on the back. Some males have a yellow chest. Like the Nashville, the Virginia's has a white eye-ring and yellow tail coverts.

FIELD NOTES

■ 4¼–4¾" (11–12 cm)

■ Bright yellow below, olive above

■ Gray head with white eye-ring

■ Virginia's Warbler gray overall, lacks olive on back

❀ Cup of grass and bark strips well hidden on or near ground

● 3–5; white speckled with reddish browns

Virginia's Warbler ♂

Nashville at nest

Adult female

Northern Parula

Parula americana

One of the smallest North American warblers, and one of the most attractive, the Northern Parula is common in summer in deciduous and coniferous woodlands of the east, especially near water. An important feature of its nesting habitat is the hanging moss or lichens (especially old-man's beard in the north and Spanish moss in the south) in which the nest is hollowed out.

The Parula's song—a high-pitched, wiry buzz that rises and ends abruptly—

J F M A M J J A S O N D

is fairly easy to learn, as warbler songs go. Tracking down the song will lead you to the handsome male, with his slate- and rust-colored chest bands. The female appears duller overall and lacks the chest bands, but she shares with the male the distinctive olive back patch, white eye-crescents, and bright yellowish underside to the bill.

The Parula is an early migrant, moving into the southeast in March and starting to head south in early August.

FIELD NOTES
- 4–4¼" (10–11 cm)
- Bluish above with two white wingbars
- Olive patch on back
- White eye-crescents
- Male: Rusty chest bands
- Deep pocket hollowed out of moss, in tree
- 3–7; white flecked with browns

189

Adult male

Yellow Warbler

Dendroica petechia

One of the most widespread warblers in North America in summer, the Yellow Warbler nests in second-growth woodlands, groves of willows and alders, and orchards, often near water. It is a well-named bird, the male's face and underparts being bright yellow. The reddish streaks on the male's chest are a good field mark. The female is duller than the male but is still yellowish overall, her head and upperparts washed with olive.

In fall, some immatures are notably dull and can easily be confused with the Orange-crowned and Wilson's warblers (pp. 187 and 196).

J F M A M J J A S O N D

The Yellow Warbler has a blank-looking face with a yellowish eye-ring and lacks the Orange-crowned's distinctive pale eyebrow and sharply pointed bill. It also lacks the Wilson's capped effect and longer, cocked tail.

The Yellow Warbler's bright song has been phrased as *sweet sweet sweet, I'm so sweet* but is variable and sounds similar to the songs of several other warblers.

FIELD NOTES
- ■ 4½–5" (11.5–12.5 cm)
- ■ Almost entirely yellow
- ■ Prominent black eye
- ■ Male: Reddish streaks on chest
- ▲ Orange-crowned and Wilson's warblers (see p. 187 and 196)
- Cup of grass and lichens at mid to upper levels in tree
- ● 3–6; whitish marked with browns and grays

Wilson's ♂

Yellow ♂

Orange-crowned ♂

 Adult male (breeding plumage)

Chestnut-sided Warbler

Dendroica pensylvanica

In summer, the handsome Chestnut-sided Warbler inhabits second-growth woodlands and overgrown brushy fields in eastern North America, where the male sings his loud clear song, sometimes written as *so pleased, so pleased, so pleased to* MEETCHA. Although fairly common today, the Chestnut-sided was apparently quite rare 200 years ago, when the heavily forested eastern US offered little suitable habitat.

In spring and summer, the Chestnut-sided is readily identified by its yellow crown, black eyestripe and mustache, and chestnut sides. After molting in late summer, however, this bird looks quite different and can surprise even experienced birders with its pale gray face and underparts, a white eye-ring, a bright greenish cap and back, and two pale yellow wingbars. Adults in fall may show some chestnut on their sides.

| J | F | M | A | M | J | J | A | S | O | N | D |

fall ♂

FIELD NOTES

- 4½–5" (11.5–12.5 cm)
- *Breeding plumage: Yellow crown; black eyestripe and mustache; chestnut sides*
- *Fall plumage: Greenish above with two yellow wingbars; grayish face and underparts; white eye-ring*
- Cup of weed stems, grass, and bark strips low in shrub or sapling
- 3–5; whitish marked with browns

breeding plumage ♀

191

Immature Myrtle (winter plumage)

Yellow-rumped Warbler

Dendroica coronata

Sometimes known as the "butterbutt", the Yellow-rumped Warbler is one of only a few warblers that remain in North America during winter. It is abundant on both coasts of the US and in winter frequents woodlands, gardens, and overgrown fields. A flock of Yellow-rumps flying up from a field is a common winter sight. In summer, Yellow-rumps are found mainly in coniferous forests.

The two distinct subspecies of Yellow-rumped Warbler—the Myrtle Warbler, nesting in the north and east, and the Audubon's Warbler, nesting in the west—were formerly considered separate species, but they interbreed freely where their ranges meet in southwestern Canada. In summer, the males

J F M A M J J A S O N D

of the white-throated Myrtle and the yellow-throated Audubon's look quite different from one another. Females and winter birds show more subdued features than the summer males: note the pale brow of the Myrtle versus the broken whitish eye-ring of the Audubon's.

The often heard *chip* note of the Yellow-rump is useful to learn as a base for comparison with other warbler calls.

Myrtle breeding ♂

Audubon's ♀

Audubon's breeding ♂

FIELD NOTES

- 5–5½" (12.5–14 cm)
- Bright yellow rump
- Breeding plumage: Bright yellow patch on crown and sides of chest; yellow (western birds) or white (eastern birds) throat
- Cup of fine twigs, grass, rootlets low to high in tree
- 3–5; whitish marked with browns

Immature

Townsend's Warbler

Dendroica townsendi

The attractive Townsend's Warbler nests in coniferous forests of the west. Its closely related counterpart, the Black-throated Green Warbler (*Dendroica virens*; 4½–5" [11.5–12.5 cm]), nests in mixed and coniferous forests of the north and east. Some Townsend's winter in coastal California, but others, and the Black-throated Green, spend the winter in Mexico and Central America.

Both species spend much time high in trees and may be easily missed if you don't know their songs—varied series of about five hoarse or buzzy notes. Look for these birds feeding down low at forest edges, drinking at pools or creeks, or in mixed-species flocks in late summer and fall. The males have an extensive black bib. This is smaller in females and may be almost lacking in some fall immatures. The dark mask on the yellow face of Townsend's is a field mark among western warblers; the yellow face and green back of the Black-throated Green are distinctive features among eastern warblers.

J F M A M J J A S O N D

Townsend's
♂

Townsend's
♀

Black-throated
Green ♂

Black-throated
Green ♀

FIELD NOTES
■ 4½–5" (11.5–12.5 cm)
■ Yellow face with dark mask
▲ Black-throated Green Warbler (north and east) has yellow face, green back
❀ Cup of grass, moss, bark strips at mid to upper levels in tree
● 3–5; white marked with browns

Adult male (breeding plumage)

Black-and-white Warbler

Mniotilta varia

The Black-and-white Warbler is readily identifiable, not only because of its striking, black-and-white striped plumage, but also because of its distinctive, nuthatch-like behavior—creeping up and down trunks and along branches, gleaning insects and larvae from the bark.

Black-and-whites nest in deciduous and mixed forests in much of the north and east, where they may be found by tracking down a high-pitched but not particularly fast song of six to eight *wee-see* phrases.

The male has a black mask and throat in summer but after breeding he molts and his throat becomes white. Females and immatures have a white face and throat, with a dusky stripe behind the eye.

Black-and-whites are early migrants, moving north in spring, since their feeding style doesn't require the foliage to be leafed out. They arrive back in the southern US in March, with some returning to Mexico as early as the middle of July.

J F M A M J J A S O N D

nuthatch-like behavior

♂ *winter*

♀

FIELD NOTES

■ 4½–5" (11.5–12.5 cm)

■ Creeps along branches and trunks like a nuthatch

■ Streaked black and white all over

■ White throat

■ Breeding male: Black throat and mask

❀ Cup of grass and bark strips on or near ground at base of stump or shrub

● 4–5; whitish speckled with browns

194

American Redstart

Setophaga ruticilla

Named for the male's red start, an old English word for tail, the Redstart is one of the most common warblers in North America in summer. Redstarts favor deciduous and mixed second-growth woodlands where they set up territories after returning from wintering in Mexico, Central America, or the Caribbean.

These are notably active and restless warblers: they often fan their long tails and droop their wings as they flit about, showing off the male's flame-colored and the female's yellow wing and tail patches. Unlike most warblers, Redstarts have stiff, hair-like feathers (rictal bristles) around their gape, which help them catch flying insects.

Male songbirds usually molt from their immature plumage to an adult-like plumage by the spring, but Redstarts are an exception. In their first summer, male Redstarts resemble females, although they tend to show a few black flecks on the head and chest and have brighter, more orangey, flashes at the sides of their chest. Adult male Redstarts are also unusual in that they look the same in winter as in summer.

rictal bristles

| J | F | M | A | M | J | J | A | S | O | N | D |

FIELD NOTES

- 4¾–5¼" (12–13 cm)
- Constantly fans tail and droops wings
- Male: Glossy black and bright orange
- Females and immatures: Same pattern as male in dull olive and primrose yellow
- Cup of grass, lichens, bark strips, low to high in bush or tree
- 2–5; whitish marked with browns

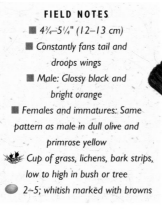

♂

Adult male

Wilson's Warbler

Wilsonia pusilla

The Wilson's Warbler is a small, active bird that nests in riverside thickets of willows and alders in northern and western North America. In much of the east it is an infrequent migrant, but in the west it is quite common.

The first impression of a Wilson's is usually a small, bright yellow bird flitting around the lower parts of a bush or a tree. A closer look reveals its longish tail, often held cocked, and a big, beady, dark eye. The male has a neat, glossy, black cap, while the female has either a smaller blackish cap or an olive head, the same color as her back. Western birds are bright yellow below and have an almost golden yellow face, while

J F M A M J J A S O N D

eastern birds are duller overall. The Wilson's Warbler is similar to the Orange-crowned and the Yellow Warbler, and telling these species apart is often difficult (see pp. 187 and 90). If you live in the west, where there are relatively few species of warblers, the Wilson's song—an intensifying series of chips that fades abruptly—is one you may soon learn.

By the end of September, most Wilson's have left the US for their winter homes in Mexico and Central America.

_western ♀

eastern ♀

FIELD NOTES
- 4¼–4¾" (11–12 cm)
- Bright yellow below, olive above
- Prominent dark eye
- Male: Glossy black cap
- Cup of grass and weed stalks, well hidden on or near ground
- 4–6; whitish speckled with browns

Adult male

Scarlet Tanager

Piranga olivacea

Scarlet Tanagers are long-distance migrants that spend winter in South America and move north in summer to nest in the deciduous and mixed woodlands of eastern North America. The Western Tanager (*Piranga ludoviciana*; 6½–7¼" [16.5–18.5 cm]) replaces the Scarlet in the deciduous and coniferous woodlands of western North America.

The unmistakable breeding males of these two species are among the most colorful of all North American birds. The females and immatures are duller—olive and yellowish overall, the Western having two distinct pale wingbars. After nesting, the male Scarlet molts into a more somber,

female-like plumage but he can still be distinguished by his black wings.

Despite their bright colors, tanagers are sometimes hard to spot, as they perch high in the canopy and move around little. Familiarity with the songs of these two species will help you locate them. The Scarlet has a caroling song that suggests an American Robin, while the Western repeats a leisurely series of three or four burry phrases.

J F M A M J J A S O N D

Western Tanager ♂

FIELD NOTES

- 6½–7" (16.5–18 cm)
- Breeding male: Brilliant red with black wings (all plumages) and tail
- Female: Olive and yellow overall
- ▲ Females difficult to distinguish
- Cup of twigs, grass, rootlets at mid to upper levels in tree
- 3–5; pale bluish speckled with browns

♀ Scarlet

Scarlet winter ♂

Scarlet ♂ in molt

197

▶ Adult male

Rose-breasted Grosbeak

Pheucticus ludovicianus

The Rose-breasted Grosbeak and the closely related Black-headed Grosbeak (*Pheucticus melanocephalus*; 6½–7½" [16.5–19 cm]) are east–west counterparts that exhibit a striking example of delayed plumage maturation. In their first summer, young males do not attain their fully adult plumage, as most songbirds do. Instead, the immatures look variably intermediate between the adult

male and the more somber female, and thus tend to be at a disadvantage when competing for mates against the brilliantly colored adult males.

Both species nest in summer in deciduous woodlands, often along watercourses. The Rose-breasted is found east of the Great Plains, and the Black-headed to the west. In the Plains themselves the planting of trees in an otherwise open region has enabled the two grosbeaks to come into contact and hybridize, bringing into question whether they are really separate species.

Their songs consist of rich warbling phrases that suggest the American Robin, and the males have the unusual habit of singing from the nest while incubating the eggs.

J F M A M J J A S O N D

FIELD NOTES

■ 7–8" (18–20.5 cm)

■ Boldly patterned— adult male unmistakable

■ Pale, massive, triangular bill

▲ Replaced in west by Black-headed Grosbeak, females and immatures of which more strongly washed with orange and less heavily streaked below

❀ Cup of twigs, grass, rootlets, low to high in bush or tree

● 2–5; pale bluish speckled with browns

Rose-breasted ♀

Black-headed ♂

198

Adult male

Indigo Bunting

Passerina cyanea

On a summer's day, a flash of bright blue across a trail or road may indicate the presence of a male Indigo Bunting. Stopping at such a sight, you may hear his pleasant song of sweet to buzzy couplets, which is given throughout the summer. The handsome Indigo Bunting returns in April from its winter home in Mexico and Central America, to nest in the woodlands and overgrown fields of the east and south. The female is brown overall, paler below, with diffuse dusky streaking on her chest. After nesting, the male's bright blue is molted for an overall brown plumage punctuated with blue patches.

While the Indigo Bunting is widely seen in summer, as with many neotropical migrants (species that spend the winter in the tropics), little is known about its life in winter, and it was discovered only recently that this species has a complex molting strategy. First year birds have two molts in fall—one before and one after migrating—and another in late winter when they attain adult-like plumage.

♂ molting

J F M A M J J A S O N D

♂

♀

FIELD NOTES

■ 4¾–5¼" (12–13 cm)

■ Breeding male: Deep blue, tending to look black in poor or deceptive light

■ Female: Brown overall with dusky streaks on chest

▲ Lazuli Bunting (western counterpart) has two pale wingbars

Cup of grass, bark strips, at low to mid levels in a tangle or shrub

3–6; bluish white

Adult (western form)

Rufous-sided Towhee

Pipilo erythropthalmus

White-eyed
Florida form

Until as recently as the 1950s, there were believed to be two species of "rufous-sided" towhees in North America: the Red-eyed Towhee of the east, and the Spotted Towhee of the west. While these two forms look and even sound quite different, where they meet in the middle of the country they interbreed freely and are now considered to be a single species.

As the old name suggests, western birds have white spots on their backs and wings. Eastern males, on the other hand, are solidly black above and the females brown above. Another geographical trait in this large and colorful sparrow is that birds in Florida often have whitish, not red, eyes.

Rufous-sided Towhees are common, though often fairly secretive, in open brushy woodlands, thickets, chaparral, and gardens across North America. Listen for them scratching in dry leaf litter, which they do with a distinctive jump-and-kick motion, thrusting both feet back to move leaves and reveal food. Eastern birds call a rising *tow-hee*, while western birds give a mewing *rreeah*.

J F M A M J J A S O N D

western form

eastern form

FIELD NOTES
- 7½–9" (19–23 cm)
- White underparts
- Chestnut flanks
- Dark back and head
- ▲ Eye color and white spotting on back varies geographically
- Cup of grass, and rootlets, on or near ground in clump of grass or bush
- 2–6; whitish speckled with reddish browns

Adult (breeding plumage)

Chipping Sparrow

Spizella passerina

This slender, long-tailed sparrow is a common summer resident in open woods, forest edges, parks, and mountain meadows throughout much of North America, particularly in and around pines. In winter, after migrating south, it is often found in brushy fields and in scrub.

The Chipping Sparrow forages on the ground in open, grassy areas but takes cover in bushes or trees if disturbed. It sings from a prominent perch in a pine or other tree. Its song—a dry trill on one pitch—may suggest the song of another eastern pine woods bird, the Pine Warbler.

Occasionally, a male Chipping Sparrow may mate with two females. After nesting, both male and female lose their distinctive orange-red cap and gray face for a browner, streaky head pattern that is similar to that of several other winter sparrows, and

their bill turns from black (summer) to pinkish (winter). Note, however, the fairly prominent white or pale brow, and the gray rump—good field marks in both summer and winter. Juveniles, like most young sparrows, are streaky and brownish overall but tend to have a trace of the adult face pattern.

| J | F | M | A | M | J | J | A | S | O | N | D |

winter ♂

juvenile

FIELD NOTES

■ 5–5½" (12.5–14 cm)
■ White brow
■ Gray rump
■ Breeding male: Chestnut cap, black bill, bold white eyebrow
▲ Winter females and immatures similar to many other sparrows
Cup of grass, weeds, from ground to fairly high in tree
3–5; pale bluish with dark markings

201

■ Adult

Fox Sparrow

Passerella iliaca

The Fox Sparrow is a good example of how much a widespread songbird can vary in appearance in different parts of North America. Some 18 races of this large sparrow, which nests in dense underbrush of coniferous and mixed woodlands, have been described. In the north (and in the east in winter) you'll see a bird with bright orange-red wings and tail; a broad blue-gray brow; and blue-gray patches on the sides of its neck. In the Rockies, Fox Sparrows tend to have a gray head and back and a reddish tail, and some have very stout bills. Birds nesting in the wet forests of the Pacific northwest have a darker head and upperparts, with the tail only slightly brighter and redder. All forms have a deep-based bill that is paler (gray to orange) below, and coarse, triangular–shaped dark spots on their underparts.

Fox Sparrows are most familiar as winter visitors to the brushy understory of woods and gardens. Although they tend to keep out of sight, they may be detected by their strong, smacking *tssk!* call and the scratching sound they make while kicking in the leaf litter like a towhee.

J F M A M J J A S O N D

western form

Rocky Mountains

eastern form

FIELD NOTES

- ■ 6½–7½" (16.5–19 cm)
- ■ Dark spots on underparts
- ■ Reddish rump and tail
- ■ Scratches around in leaf litter
- ▲ Wide geographical variation in plumage
- ✿ Cup of twigs, moss, grass on or near ground in thicket
- ● 2–5; pale greenish marked with browns

Adult

White-crowned Sparrow

Zonotrichia leucophrys

A familiar winter visitor to parks, open woodlands, and gardens across much of the US, the White-crowned Sparrow nests mostly in the temperate climate of the far north and the mountains of the west. One race, however, shows a remarkable adaptation to a local microclimate on the coast of central California. There, the cool, foggy summers, caused by cold air over the ocean waters meeting hot air from the interior, moderate what would otherwise be too hot a climate. Move a mile or so from the coast, away from the fog's influence, and you won't find a single nesting White-crown!

The closely related Golden-crowned Sparrow (*Zonotrichia atricapilla*; 6½–7¼" [16.5–18.5 cm]) nests in thickets at the timberline in the northwest and is a common winter visitor to the west alongside White-crowns. Adults of the two species are distinctive (compare also the White-crowned with the White-throated Sparrow, p. 165).

As with other sparrows, note that the immatures show distinctive traces of the adult head patterns.

J F M A M J J A S O N D

immature Golden-crowned

immature White-crowned

FIELD NOTES

■ 6¼–7" (16–18 cm)

■ Black-and-white striped head

▲ Immatures difficult—compare carefully with Golden-crowned Sparrow

▲ White-throated Sparrow (p. 165) has yellow patch in front of eye, and white chin marked off with gray

🪺 Cup of twigs, grass, and moss, on or near ground in bush or small tree

🥚 3–5; pale bluish to whitish, speckled with browns

Golden-crowned ♂

Adult (eastern form)

Dark-eyed Junco

Junco hyemalis

This sparrow shows some of the greatest geographic plumage variations of any bird in North America. At least five types are identifiable: the Slate-colored Junco of the north and east, with its gray hood, upperparts and sides; the Oregon Junco of the west, with blackish hood, orange-red back, and pinkish sides; the Pink-sided Junco of the central Rockies, with gray hood, orange-red back, and pink sides; the White-winged Junco of the Black Hills, with blue-gray hood, upperparts, and sides, and two white wingbars; and the Gray-headed Junco of the southern Rockies, which is gray overall with an orange-red back patch. Juvenile juncos are streaky overall and look quite different from adults.

Dark-eyed Juncos nest in coniferous and mixed woodlands, and in winter also visit parks and gardens where they often occur in flocks and feed on the ground. The junco's song is a ringing trill, and flocks make high-pitched twitters, especially when disturbed. As they fly up, juncos flash their characteristic, bright white outer tail feathers.

J F M A M J J A S O N D

white tail feathers

Slate-colored

Oregon form

juvenile

FIELD NOTES

■ 5½–6" (14–15 cm)
■ Blackish tail with white outer feathers, conspicuous in flight
■ Pinkish bill
▲ Strong regional variations in color
🪺 Cup of grass, twigs, and rootlets, on ground, in bank, under stump, or in brushpile
⬮ 3–6; bluish white speckled with browns

204

Adult male (breeding plumage)

Orchard Oriole

Icterus spurius

In spring, in open woodlands, orchards, and among suburban shade trees of the southeast, a loud scratchy warble, sung from a perch or during a display flight over the treetops, may attract your attention to a singing male Orchard Oriole. This is the smallest North American oriole, and the male's deep chestnut plumage is its main distinguishing feature. The female and immature look quite similar to other species of orioles, particularly the Hooded Oriole of the southwest. Note, however, the Orchard's small size and relatively shorter, more slender,

J F M A M J J A S O N D

and slightly downward-curved bill. The young male's black bib separates him from the plain-faced female.

This is one of only two species of New World orioles that have been known to nest in colonies. On one 7-acre tract in Louisiana, a total of 114 nests were found!

Orchard Orioles are early fall migrants, and families may begin heading south, to their winter home in Mexico, in July.

immature ♂

FIELD NOTES

- 6–6¾" (15–17 cm)
- *Male: Black and chestnut— unmistakable*
- ▲ *Female and immature similar to other orioles (especially Hooded) but note shorter bill and tail*
- *Cup of grass suspended in fork in tree*
- *3–7; pale bluish marked with browns and grays*

205

Adult male (Baltimore race)

Northern Oriole

Icterus galbula

Found in summer in deciduous and mixed woodlands, this is the most common and familiar North American oriole. The two very different-looking races of the Northern Oriole—the Baltimore Oriole in the east, and the Bullock's Oriole in the west (their ranges separated by the Great Plains)—were considered separate species for many years. With the planting of trees as shelter belts around homesteads on the plains these two orioles came into contact and ornithologists found that they interbred readily. Thus the two were united as a single species, although most birders still refer to them by their old names.

Males in their first summer look like adult females, with some black in their face and throat. Immatures of the two forms are alike and are not easily told apart.

The Northern Oriole's song is a somewhat disjointed series of rich whistles which may be interspersed with rough chatters, especially in Bullock's Orioles. In fall, these orioles migrate south to spend the winter in Mexico and Central America.

J F M A M J J A S O N D

Bullock's

Baltimore
♀

FIELD NOTES

■ 7–8" (18–20.5 cm)

■ Male: Flame orange and black, almost unmistakable

▲ Females and immatures nondescript, but with definite hint of orange

❀ Pouch of grass and bark strips, slung in fork of tree

● 3–6; bluish white marked with dark scrawls

Grasslands

BIRDING *in* GRASSLANDS

The open vistas of grasslands allow easy observation of numerous birds, from hawks perched on overhead wires to larks foraging in farmland. Other species, however, require a more cautious approach.

An excellent way to go birding in open country is by car. Many species are conspicuous along roadsides, and the car acts as a blind, from which you can watch birds more closely than if you were on foot. Driving is also often the best way to spot species that occur in low densities or that have large hunting territories, as is the case with hawks in winter.

However you get around, it is always good birding policy to keep an eye on utility wires, poles, and fences as these all provide perches for many species of birds. For example, in summer, the best place to spot kingbirds is usually on roadside wires, while in winter, poles and pylons are favored roosting and even hunting perches for many hawks. In some areas, particularly the southwest,

ravens nest readily on pylons—tree substitutes in a wide open environment.

It pays to stop and scan any freshly ploughed field you may pass. Ploughing, of course, brings to the surface many insects, grubs, worms, and similar subsurface fauna. These quickly attract birds, ranging from gulls to larks and longspurs. Depending on the season, there are several species of birds

OUT IN THE OPEN *Mist gradually clears over a meadow, home to many grassland species such as the American Goldfinch (above right). This bird is especially attracted to rough pasture and wasteground, where weeds such as thistles abound. Tall grass shelters many birds, like the female Red-winged Blackbird (top). A group of birders (above) explores one of the richest of all grassland habitats—the arctic tundra.*

(some plovers and longspurs, for example) that prefer ploughed fields, when available, to grasslands.

Do not assume that all the birds in a group are of one species. Many open country birds are gregarious outside the breeding season, and any rare vagrant that happens to be in the area is quite likely to attach itself to a group of some common local species.

Note that the presence of hedges and scattered trees will greatly increase the diversity of birds you can find.

SEASONAL CHANGES

In fall and winter, fields provide food for many species that migrate to grasslands after nesting in other habitats. If you pass through an area of open grassland or farmland regularly, from late summer through the winter you'll see a greater variety of species than at other times of the year, in particular more hawks, kestrels, sparrows, blackbirds, and finches. These numbers reflect both the population increase following the nesting season, and the migration of other species into a habitat that is good for feeding but would not be a suitable nesting habitat.

TALLGRASS TACTICS

Grasslands, with their unrestricted views, provide certain obvious advantages over woods and forests. However, these advantages do not apply to all birds all year round. In spring and summer, the males of most grassland species sing and are therefore fairly easy to find and identify, but during other seasons some birds, such as sparrows, can be hard to see, let alone identify.

If you are walking with a friend and flush a sparrow from the grass, watch where it comes back down. One of you can then keep an eye on the spot while the other walks part of the distance toward it. If the walker then stops and relocates the spot, the watcher can catch up. In this way you can walk up on the bird without ever losing sight of it, or at least where it landed.

ALPINE MEADOWS *support rosy-finches, ptarmigans, and several other high-country specialist birds.*

USING COVER

When you are out in open country with hedges, or with a bordering wood, walking along the hedge or beside the trees will make you less conspicuous. Furthermore, such areas are rich in birdlife.

GRASSLAND GEAR

Little is required in the way of specialized equipment for birding in grassland areas—just an efficient pair of binoculars. Spotting scopes do however come in handy in open areas where you may be some distance from a bird. Special mounts are available that allow you to clamp your scope to the glass of a half-open car window, enabling you to use the scope from your mobile blind.

GRASSLAND BIRDING *(left) requires a steady hand, as many species are easy to spot but hard to get close to. The Eastern Kingbird (above) is one of many birds that habitually perch on fence wires.*

Adult (breeding plumage)

Cattle Egret

Bubulcus ibis

While today the Cattle Egret is common across much of the south, 50 years ago it was almost unknown in North America. Its colonization of the New World has been remarkable. The first Cattle Egrets seen in the Americas were in Surinam in 1877, and to get there they had presumably crossed the Atlantic from Africa. In the New World they found cleared grasslands and cattle typical of their native environment. They crossed the Caribbean to Florida in the 1940s and a second front moved north through Central America in the 1950s. By the early 1970s, Cattle Egrets were well-established in the southern US, and their range seems to be still expanding.

J F M A M J J A S O N D

This small heron is identified by its stocky shape and its habit of following cattle to feed on insects they flush up. Flocks have learned to accompany tractors for the same reason. For most of the year, Cattle Egrets are white overall with dark legs and a yellow bill. At the start of the breeding season they attain buffy plumes on their head, chest, and back; the bill becomes reddish; and the legs change color to orange.

winter plumage

breeding plumage

FIELD NOTES

- 18–21" (45.5–53.5 cm)
- Small and stocky
- Distinctive "heavy-jowled" look
- Breeding plumage: Golden buff wash on crown, lower breast, and back
- Platform of sticks in tree or reed bed, often with other herons
- 2–6; unmarked pale blue

Adult

Black Vulture

Coragyps atratus

A characteristic bird of the open skies of the southeast, the Black Vulture is identified by its naked gray head, its broad wings with a large white patch on each wingtip, and its relatively short, squared tail. It flies with a distinctive flap-flap-flap-glide movement, the wingbeats hurried and the glides usually short, holding its wings flat or only slightly raised above the body while gliding. Its shape, combined with its way of flying, will enable you, with practice, to identify the Black Vulture at long range and to distinguish it from the Turkey Vulture (p. 212).

Black Vultures are social. Often you'll see groups of them soaring in tight circles or hopping and running with a gamboling gait at garbage dumps, fishing wharves, or on beaches where dead creatures wash up. If you look carefully, particularly in fall, you may notice that some Black Vultures have an all-gray bill while others have a distinct pale tip to their bill. The former are young of that year, the latter adults.

J F M A M J J A S O N D

immature

adult

FIELD NOTES
- 22–26" (56–66 cm)
- Naked gray head
- Broad wings, short tail
- Wings held almost flat in flight
- Hollow at base of tree, or on cliff
- 1–3; pale greenish, usually marked with browns

211

Adult

Turkey Vulture

Cathartes aura

Although it withdraws from the northern part of its range in winter, migrating as far south as South America, the Turkey Vulture is a familiar sight in North American skies. It is best distinguished from the Black Vulture (p. 211) by its shape and flight manner. The Turkey Vulture has longer wings and tail. It glides and soars for long periods with its wings held in a shallow V-shape, tilting, or rocking, from side to side. It seldom flaps its wings, but when it does, the wingbeats are deep and smooth, not quick and hurried like those of the Black Vulture. From below, note also its two-tone wings.

Adults have naked reddish heads while juveniles have naked gray heads, similar to the Black Vulture. Generally, this species is seen singly or in small groups, and tends to fly lower than the Black, an indication of its ability to locate food by smell. In contrast, the Black Vulture hunts only by sight.

J F M A M J J A S O N D

two-tone wings

adult

juvenile

FIELD NOTES
- ■ 26–30" (66–76 cm)
- ■ Naked red head
- ■ Broad wings, long tail
- ■ Wings held in V-shape in flight
- Hollow at base of tree, in old log, or on cliff
- 1–3; whitish heavily marked with browns and grays

212

Adult female

Northern Harrier

Circus cyaneus

The Northern Harrier, formerly called the Marsh Hawk, is widespread in grasslands and over open fields, especially in marshy areas. It hunts low to the ground, quartering back and forth with its wings held in a shallow V-shape, braking and turning with aerobatic agility. It perches readily on the ground or on fence posts, but, unlike many hawks, rarely if ever perches higher.

juvenile
(showing facial disks)

The Harrier's bold, white rump band and owl-like facial disks are good field marks. The male is gray overall with black wingtips; the larger female is mostly brown. Juveniles show a rich orangey color on their underparts.

In winter, several harriers may hunt over a small area, and communal winter roosts of up to 80 or 90 birds have been recorded. In display, the male flies high and tumbles and swoops while giving a rapid yelping chatter. For most of the year, however, harriers are silent.

white rump

J	F	M	A	M	J	J	A	S	O	N	D

FIELD NOTES
- 18–22" (45.5–56 cm)
- Long wings and tail
- White rump
- Slow sailing flight, often low over grassland or marsh
- Platform of sticks and grass on ground
- 3–9; bluish white, occasionally with brownish flecks

213

■ Adult

Swainson's Hawk

Buteo swainsoni

The Swainson's Hawk is noted for its remarkable long-distance migration, with most of the population spending the winter on the grasslands of Argentina. On their journey there, these birds move through Mexico and Central America in flocks that may number thousands, and often travel with Turkey Vultures and Broad-winged Hawks. The Swainson's Hawk returns to North America in March to nest in the grasslands and prairies of the west, and is a fairly common summer resident.

dark morph

Like several North American hawks, the Swainson's comes in many different plumages, known as color morphs, and juveniles look different from adults. The most common plumage is the distinctive light morph of the adult. The Swainson's has long, relatively narrow and tapered wings, testimony to its long-distance migration. Often the wing linings are paler than the underside of the flight feathers.

immature

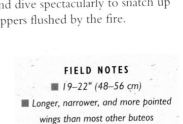

The Swainson's hunts while soaring, its wings held in a distinct shallow V, and it often hangs in the wind. Flocks may gather at burning fields and dive spectacularly to snatch up grasshoppers flushed by the fire.

| J | F | M | A | M | J | J | A | S | O | N | D |

gathering over grassfire

FIELD NOTES

- ■ 19–22" (48–56 cm)
- ■ Longer, narrower, and more pointed wings than most other buteos
- ■ Plumage very variable, but usually has dark "bib" contrasting with paler chin and underparts
- ❀ Platform of sticks, usually low in lone tree or bush
- ⬭ 2–4; whitish, often marked with browns

Adult female

American Kestrel

Falco sparverius

Formerly known as the Sparrow Hawk, this familiar small falcon occurs throughout the Americas. It is a common sight perched on roadside wires or hunting, with its characteristic hovering flight, over fields and roadside verges. The pointed wings of the American Kestrel and other falcons distinguish them from hawks, which have broader, rounded wings.

The male American Kestrel, with his blue wings and orange-red tail, is one of the most attractive of all North American birds. The female's upperparts and tail are more uniform: orange-red, barred with black. As with many raptors, males are smaller than females.

One explanation for this difference in size is that it enables the male and female to hunt for different-sized prey, since any food of a fixed size may be insufficient to support both sexes. But why is the male not the larger bird? As female falcons and hawks do most, if

not all, of the incubating of the eggs, their larger size helps them stay at the nest for longer periods. Furthermore, the male feeds the female while she is at the nest, and the smaller prey that he catches tends to be more abundant than the larger prey caught by the female.

J F M A M J J A S O N D

hovering over field

♀

♂

FIELD NOTES

- 10–11½" (25.5–29 cm)
- Small, common, widespread; hovers
- Orange-red back and tail
- Male: Blue-gray wings
- Cavity in tree, cliff, or building
- 3–7; cream blotched with browns

Adults

Northern Bobwhite

Colinus virginianus

The loud, sharp *bob-white!* or *h-hoo wheet!* call of the Northern Bobwhite is often heard in farmland and rural areas of the east where this bird lives in fields, brushy areas, and open woods. Populations at the northern edge of its range fluctuate, depending on how severe the winters are. In the west, this gamebird has been introduced into Washington state.

For much of the year, Bobwhites occur in groups, or coveys, of up to 25 birds, but in the spring the birds form territorial pairs. Bobwhites usually run for cover if disturbed, but, when startled, they flush into the air with a whirr of their wings and fly a short distance out of sight across a hedge or into brush.

The female is less boldly patterned than the male and has a buffy brow and throat patch. A distinct race of Bobwhite, the so-called Masked Bobwhite, with a blackish face and throat, used to occur in the deserts of southern Arizona. It was wiped out in the early 1900s as a result of overgrazing of cattle, but attempts are being made to reintroduce it from Mexico.

J F M A M J J A S O N D

downy young

'Masked' form

eastern form ♀

FIELD NOTES

- 8–10" (20.5–25.5 cm)
- Small, mottled, strongly reddish in overall hue
- White throat
- Distinctive call
- Well-hidden depression in ground, lined and concealed with grass
- 7–16; whitish

216

Adult

Killdeer

Charadrius vociferus

This striking and often noisy bird is actually a shorebird, but it is common across North America in farmland and other open areas such as playing fields, airfields, and riverbanks. Its name comes from its plaintive screaming and wailing cries, in particular the *kill-dee-eu* given in alarm or in display flight as the male circles with slow, deep wingbeats.

If you approach newly hatched Killdeer chicks too closely, the parents may give a broken-wing display, which is designed to distract predators. The adult Killdeer shuffles and runs along the ground, allowing you to come quite close, while holding out one wing as if it is broken and the bird cannot fly. Although interesting to observe, if this happens you should obviously move away to prevent further disturbance.

Killdeers are readily told from other plovers (which all tend to be found near water) by their two black chest bands and their long orangey tail with its black-and-white tip. Unlike many shorebirds, the Killdeer looks much the same in all plumages, although the downy chick has only a single black chest band.

Like other plovers, Killdeers feed with a distinctive stop-start action: standing still, then running and picking at the ground, then standing still again.

J F M A M J J A S O N D

FIELD NOTES
- 9½–10" (24–25.5 cm)
- Common and noisy
- Bright reddish rump
- Double black breast band
- Scrape in ground lined with small pebbles and grass
- 3–5; buff, marked with browns and black

broken-wing (distraction) display

217

■ Adult

Mourning Dove

Zenaida macroura

This elegant, medium-sized dove is common across North America in farmland, parks, gardens, open woodland, and irrigated desert areas. Flocks in fall and winter may number hundreds, especially in the south.

The Mourning Dove's name derives from its low, mournful, cooing call which may be written as *wh'hooo hoo hoo hooo*. It is overall a fairly plain dove, its long tapered tail being a field mark. The male is slightly brighter than the female and has a powdery blue-gray area on his nape and a rosy sheen on the sides of his neck. Juveniles have distinctly scaly-looking plumage and a shorter tail than the adults.

Like most doves of open country, the Mourning Dove is a strong, fast flier that flushes up with a whirring whistle of its wings. In display, single birds and pairs climb fairly high with slow wingbeats and then glide smoothly toward the ground with their wings held bowed down. Especially in dry regions, Mourning Doves may fly several miles to good feeding areas or the nearest water source, often at or before first light and again at dusk. Thus, if you are often out early or drive home at dusk through open country, you will soon come to recognize the birds' silhouettes.

♀

FIELD NOTES

■ 10–12" (25.5–30.5 cm)

■ Pinkish brown overall

■ Long, tapered, white-tipped tail

✸ Shallow bowl of sticks in tree or bush, or on ledge

● 1–4; white

♂

218

Adult

Barn Owl

Tyto alba

One of the most widespread birds in the world, the Barn Owl occurs in open country of rural and urban areas throughout much of the Americas, although it is absent from higher latitudes, including most of Canada. It is most frequently seen hunting at dusk or at night along highways, where the grassy verges and median strips are home to its main prey, rodents. Lit up by headlights, the Barn Owl's white underparts, combined with its silent, hovering flight, give it an almost ghost-like appearance.

Sadly, a combination of traffic casualties, the loss of trees and old buildings where the owls nest and roost, and, until recently, the effects of pesticides, have caused a decline in Barn Owl numbers in many regions. However, the use of nestboxes in some areas, for example around New York City, has helped maintain other populations of this beautiful species.

JFMAMJJASOND

The Barn Owl belongs to the family Tytonidae, which is distinct from all other owl families in North America. One feature of this family is that the downy young molt directly into adult-like plumage. Another feature is their pectinate, or comb-like, central toenail, which is used for preening.

The Barn Owl has one of the most blood-curdling calls of any North American bird: a loud, hissing shriek, often given in flight.

pectinate toenail

FIELD NOTES
- 14–16" (35.5–40.5 cm)
- Plain white below, mottled tan above
- Dark eyes set in white, heart-shaped face
- Cavity in tree, cliff, or old building
- 3–11; white

Barn Owl chicks

219

Adult

Common Nighthawk

Chordeiles minor

A sharp nasal *beehnk* heard at dusk may attract your attention skyward to a high-flying bird that suggests a swift in shape but is larger, with slower, more erratic flight. If you watch for a while it may dive steeply and at the bottom of the stoop make a low *boom* sound. This is the Common Nighthawk, a summer visitor to much of North America—from the open plains of the west to the cities of the east.

During summer, in the deserts and open dry lands of the southwest you'll find the very similar and closely related Lesser Nighthawk (*Chordeiles acutipennis*; 8–9" [20.5–23 cm]). This bird's song is a prolonged, churring, toad-like trill and, unlike the Common Nighthawk's song, it is given while the bird is perched on the ground.

Identifying these two species by sight alone is difficult since, as with most night birds, their plumage camouflages them

during the daytime, rather than acting as a visual signal, as is the case with other birds. Although hard to judge, the white bar on the nighthawk's wing is nearer the wingtip in the Lesser than in the Common. The Common looks longer-winged, its wings tend to be more pointed, and its flight is rangier and less fluttery.

J F M A M J J A S O N D

Lesser ♂

Common ♂

broad gape

FIELD NOTES

- 9–10" (23–25.5 cm)
- Common in many towns and suburbs
- White wingbar
- ▲ Lesser Nighthawk (southwest) has shorter, blunter wings and subtly different placement of white wingbar
- Scrape on open ground; flat roof
- 2; cream to pale cinnamon, flecked with browns

■ Adult

Eastern Kingbird

Tyrannus tyrannus

Kingbirds are large, conspicuous flycatchers of open country, and you'll often see them in summer on roadside wires and fences. Eight species of kingbirds nest in North America, and all of them are migratory, wintering from Mexico to South America. The Eastern Kingbird is common across much of North America and is a distinctive-looking bird with blackish upperparts, white underparts, and a bold white tip to its tail.

Although kingbirds are strongly territorial when nesting, in migration and in winter they form flocks that feed and roost together. Unlike many songbirds, kingbirds often migrate by day so that in spring and fall you may see a flock drop into a nearby tree, feed, and then move on.

The most spectacular kingbird in North America is the Scissor-tailed Flycatcher (*Tyrannus forficatus*; 7½–14" [19–35.5 cm]), a fairly small-bodied bird with a long, forked tail. The Scissor-tail nests in Texas and adjacent states where it is a common roadside bird in open ranchland. It usually shows only a soft pink wash on its belly when perched but in flight it reveals a bright pink flash on its flanks. Its spectacular tail is longest in the adult male, shortest in the immature.

Eastern ♂ on wire

J F M A M J J A S O N D

FIELD NOTES

- 7¾–8¼" (19.5–21 cm)
- Common and conspicuous
- Slate-gray above, white below
- Broad white band at tail tip
- Bulky cup of grass, weeds, in bush or tree
- 3–5; whitish, marked with browns

Scissor-tailed Flycatcher

221

Adult

Western Kingbird

Tyrannus verticalis

The Western Kingbird is common in summer across farmland of the midwest and west, and in many areas it may be found alongside the Eastern Kingbird (p. 221). The Western's distinctive features are its pale gray head and chest and its square-tipped black tail with white sides.

While these white sides can be hard to see, or even missing if the tail is molting, the nasal *pik* call will always enable you to identify it. All kingbirds in fact have distinctive calls, and their full songs, or "dawn songs" as they are often known, are given mainly at or before first light.

Another yellow-bellied kingbird, similar to the Western, is Cassin's Kingbird (*Tyrannus vociferans*; 8–9" [20.5–23 cm]). The Cassin's is

J F M A M J J A S O N D

typical of dry habitats of the interior west, and occurs north to southern Montana and central California. It is distinguished from the Western Kingbird by its dusky gray head and chest which offset a cottony white chin patch, or bib. Its tail is blackish and squared, with a paler tip, and lacks the bright white sides of the Western. The Cassin's call—a burry, slightly explosive *ch-beehr*—is also a good way to identify this bird.

Western

Cassin's Kingbird

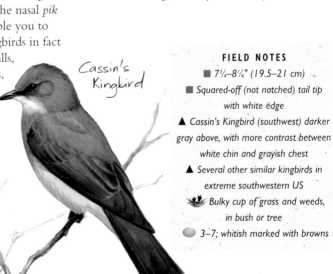

FIELD NOTES

■ 7¾–8¼" (19.5–21 cm)

■ Squared-off (not notched) tail tip with white edge

▲ Cassin's Kingbird (southwest) darker gray above, with more contrast between white chin and grayish chest

▲ Several other similar kingbirds in extreme southwestern US

🪺 Bulky cup of grass and weeds, in bush or tree

🥚 3–7; whitish marked with browns

Adult

Horned Lark

Eremophila alpestris

Male Horned Larks draw attention to themselves when singing their high-pitched tinkling song, either from a low rise on the ground or in a prolonged song flight high overhead. At other times, both males and females tend to be inconspicuous, blending well with their background and running away or crouching quietly when disturbed. If alarmed, they take off in a low, undulating flight, usually giving a few high-pitched tinkling call notes as they go.

chick

JFMAMJJASOND

The Horned Lark occurs in many open habitats, from the arctic tundra to the southwestern deserts, and from ploughed fields to beaches. In winter these birds may gather in flocks of over a hundred birds.

Like many widespread songbirds, the Horned Lark's plumage varies considerably from place to place. In all areas, however, the black mask, black chest band, and black forehead band that runs into short "horns" in the male, are distinctive field marks.

The juvenile Horned Lark, with its pale-spotted upperparts and little trace of the distinctive face pattern, looks strikingly different from the adult and is often a source of confusion when first encountered.

northern race

prairie race

FIELD NOTES
- 6½–7½" (16.5–19 cm)
- Whitish or yellowish face and throat
- Black face pattern
- ▲ Numerous subspecies, varying slightly in color
- Hollow in ground, lined with grass
- 2–5; grayish white speckled with browns

223

Black-billed Magpie

Pica pica

A striking, long-tailed bird, the Black-billed Magpie is found in farmland, rangeland, and open woodland of the interior west and northwest, where its raucous, chattering calls are a common sound.

A good example of biogeographic differentiation (the evolution of an isolated population into a separate species) is the closely related Yellow-billed Magpie (*Pica nuttallii*; 17–21" [43–53.5 cm]), which is common in the valleys of central California and is separated from the range of the Black-billed by high mountains that have little or no suitable habitat for magpies. The Yellow-billed Magpie is the only species of bird restricted to the state of California and, as its name suggests, it is readily identified by its

yellow bill (which may be dusky in immatures). If you look closely you may also see a yellow crescent of naked skin below its eyes.

Magpies often form loose flocks of up to 20 birds outside the breeding season, and both species may also nest in loose colonies. In areas where magpies are common, their bulky nests, used year after year, are conspicuous features of the landscape.

J F M A M J J A S O N D

Yellow-billed

nest

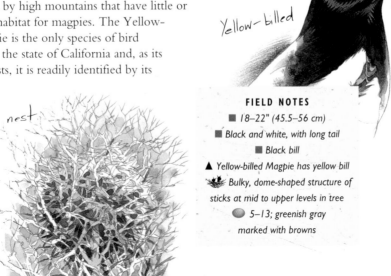

FIELD NOTES

■ 18–22" (45.5–56 cm)

■ Black and white, with long tail

■ Black bill

▲ Yellow-billed Magpie has yellow bill

✹ Bulky, dome-shaped structure of sticks at mid to upper levels in tree

⬭ 5–13; greenish gray marked with browns

Adults

American Crow

Corvus brachyrhynchos

The American Crow is a familiar sight across most of North America in farmland and rural and urban areas. In the coastal northwest (north of Washington state) it is replaced by the very similar but slightly smaller Northwestern Crow (*Corvus caurinus*; 16" [40.5 cm]), which some ornithologists consider to be simply a subspecies of the American.

Crows are social birds, especially in winter when feeding and roosting flocks may number

| J | F | M | A | M | J | J | A | S | O | N | D |

thousands. If you watch a flock of crows feeding, you may notice one or two birds positioned on posts or other prominent perches while the rest of the flock feeds. These sentinels keep watch for signs of danger and thus allow the flock to forage more efficiently.

Of the five crows in North America, the only other widespread species is the Common Raven (*Corvus corax*; 22–26½" [56–67 cm]) of the north and west. It is larger and more heavily built than the American Crow (ravens are simply large crows) and has a graduated, or wedge-shaped tail tip, unlike the squared-off tail tip of other crows. It also has a larger bill and shaggier throat than the American Crow.

American Crow

Common Raven

FIELD NOTES
■ 16–20" (40.5–51 cm)
■ Black
■ Only common corvid across most of North America
▲ Common Raven (Canada and western US) is larger, with wedge-shaped tail, heavy bill
▲ Several other species of crows locally common in restricted ranges
❀ Bulky cup of sticks in tree, or on utility pole
● 3–7; greenish marked with browns and grays

Common Raven

225

Dickcissel

Spiza americana

Although a common summer resident in the prairie states and provinces of the midwest, the Dickcissel is notoriously unpredictable in its abundance in a given area from year to year, being common some years and rare or even absent in others.

Dickcissels nest in grainfields and open weedy meadows where the males sing their buzzy *dick-cizz-l* song from fences or other low perches. In flight the Dickcissel gives a distinctive call: a wet, buzzy *dzzzrt*. Often these gregarious birds travel in vast flocks, especially during migration and when in their winter grounds in the tropics. At a distance, these flocks look like undulating clouds of insects.

While the male is relatively distinctive, the female and immature resemble a female House Sparrow. Note, however, the Dickcissel's longer and more conical bill, dark whisker mark, and orange-red shoulders. Young birds also often have dark streaks on their chest and flanks.

J F M A M J J A S O N D

immature

FIELD NOTES

- 5¾–6¼" (14.5–16 cm)
- Yellowish eyebrow
- Stout grayish bill
- Reddish wingpatch
- Bulky cup of grass in clump of grass, hedge, or low bush
- 3–5; pale blue

flock of Dickcissels

Adult

Lark Sparrow

Chondestes grammacus

The attractive Lark Sparrow, a summer resident in farmlands, prairies, and rural areas, is one of the most readily identifiable sparrows, with its harlequin-like face pattern and bold white tail edging. Its name derives from its pleasant, lark-like song which is a varied series of rich chips, buzzes, and trills that may be given in a song flight.

Most sparrows fly fairly low when, for example, flushed up from the grass. Lark Sparrows, however, commonly fly overhead with a strong, gently undulating flight, and can often be spotted in the sky if you learn their distinctive, high-pitched, slightly metallic *tik* call.

Like most young sparrows, the juvenile Lark Sparrow has fine dusky streaking across its chest and shows a trace of the adult's distinctive head pattern, although brown replaces the adult's chestnut areas.

J F M A M J J A S O N D

Another sparrow with white in its tail is the Vesper Sparrow (*Pooecetes gramineus*; 5½–6" [14–15 cm]), widespread in summer in open grassy habitats across North America. It is streaky brown overall with orange-red shoulders and white tail sides, and it often shows a distinct, narrow, whitish eye-ring.

Lark Sparrow

Vesper Sparrow

FIELD NOTES
- 6–6½" (15–16.5 cm)
- Whitish underparts with black central spot
- Harlequin-like head pattern
- ▲ Juveniles difficult to distinguish from other nondescript sparrow species
- Cup of grass on ground in grass or weeds
- 3–6; whitish with blackish marks

227

Adult male (breeding plumage)

Lark Bunting
Calamospiza melanocorys

Driving across the prairie states and provinces in summer, you'll often see the handsome male Lark Bunting singing from fences or in his distinctive, hovering, song flight. As this species is not highly territorial, frequently several males sing in one small area.

The female is similar to several sparrows, but note her stout bill, which is black above and blue-gray below, and her whitish wing panel. After nesting, the male molts into a female-like plumage though with more black in the throat and more white in the wings. The only similar bird in this habitat in summer is the male Bobolink (p. 230), which has a blond hood and whitish rump.

In fall and winter, Lark Buntings form large flocks that may be seen feeding along roadsides in brushy and grassy ranchland. These flocks fly in a distinctive and fairly compact formation, with a general undulating movement. As they fly, the birds give their, soft, slightly nasal *whew* or *hoo-ee* call.

J F M A M J J A S O N D

winter ♂

winter ♂

♀

FIELD NOTES
- 6¼–6¾" (16–17 cm)
- Stocky
- White wing patch
- Stout bill
- Summer male: Black
- Cup of grass in depression in ground
- 3–7; pale bluish, sometimes with rusty spotting

Adult

Savannah Sparrow

Passerculus sandwichensis

One of the most widespread North American birds, the Savannah Sparrow is a typical streaky brown sparrow. It is found in fields, grasslands, marshes, and grassy dunes, and tends to be somewhat skulking. In spring, the male draws attention to himself with his song of a few high-pitched chips running into a trilled buzz, given from a low perch. At other times, you will most often see the Savannah Sparrow as a small, streaky brown bird that flushes up from close range, flies a short distance, and then drops back down to cover. However, unlike many grassland and marshland sparrows which are silent when flushed, the Savannah often calls as it flies off, giving a high-pitched *tsip*. It may also perch briefly on a grass stalk, low bush, or fence before dropping back to cover.

In most of its range, it has a small pinkish bill, streaked chest, and pale buffy or whitish eyebrow with a yellowish wash forward of the eyes.

Some birds of the northeast Atlantic coast (sometimes called the Ipswich Sparrow) are larger and paler overall with little or no yellow in their face, while those in the salt marshes of southern California are darker and more heavily streaked.

J F M A M J J A S O N D

dark form

Ipswich form

pale form (deserts)

FIELD NOTES
- ■ 5–6" (12.5–15 cm)
- ■ Common and widespread
- ■ Brown and streaky
- ■ Pink bill and legs
- ■ Yellowish brow
- ▲ Very variable
- Cup of grass in hollow in ground
- 3–6; whitish to pale greenish blue, marked with browns

229

Adult male

Bobolink

Dolichonyx oryzivorus

Named for the male's bubbling *bob-o-link bob-o-link…* song, this blackbird nests in hayfields and open weedy grasslands. The males often sing in a fluttering display flight and may mate with more than one female. This is thought to reflect the female's preference for a male with high quality territory over males with poor territories. Males with good territories are therefore able to attract more than one mate.

J F M A M J J A S O N D

As with many northern-breeding songbirds, after nesting the male molts into a plumage resembling that of the female and the immature: buffy overall, streaked with dark brown on the face, back, and sides. This plumage suggests a sparrow, but note the Bobolink's relatively large size and its plain underparts with their dark streaks only down the sides and not extending across the chest. In all plumages the Bobolink has a distinctly spiky-looking tail.

A good way to find Bobolinks during their migration is to listen for their nasal *eenk* call note which is often given in flight.

FIELD NOTES

- 6–7" (15–18 cm)
- Male: Entirely black below; white rump and shoulders; buff nape
- Female: Yellowish; heavily streaked above and on flanks
- Cup of grass in hollow in tall grass or crops
- 4–7; pale gray to brownish, marked with browns

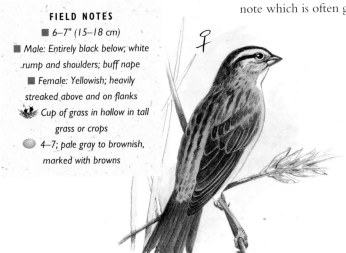

spiky tail

Adult

Eastern Meadowlark

Sturna magna

Eastern Meadowlarks are familiar and conspicuous songbirds of open country. In the midwest and southwest, their range overlaps that of their western counterpart, the Western Meadowlark (*Sturna neglecta*; 7½–9½" [19–24 cm]).

Both species are commonly found in open fields. They are most often seen perched on fenceposts, and seldom on overhead wires.

white tail sides

J F M A M J J A S O N D

Identifying a silent meadowlark is a challenge, even for experts. The male Western can sometimes be distinguished from the Eastern by the more extensive yellow in his cheeks, but both meadowlarks are more easily identified by their songs and calls.

The Eastern sings a pleasant song usually of three or four plaintive whistled notes such as *see seer seee-u* or *see seeu see-u-seu*, while the Western Meadowlark's song is fluty and more complex, typically running into a warbled ending—*whee hir weedle-e whi-chee*. The two species also have distinct call notes, the Eastern giving a raspy *zzzrt* and the Western a low *chuk*.

As the birds fly, note the bright white tail sides of both species, often best seen as they take off or land.

Eastern ♂

Western ♂

Western ♀

FIELD NOTES
- 7½–9½" (19–24 cm)
- Bright yellow underparts
- White tail sides
- Bold, black V-shaped breast band
- ▲ Eastern and Western similar
- Cup of grass, often with dome, in depression in ground
- 3–7; whitish, marked with browns

231

Adult

Great-tailed Grackle

Quiscalus mexicanus

Until the early 1960s, the Great-tailed Grackle was considered the same species as the Boat-tailed Grackle (*Quiscalus major*, 13–16" [33–40.5 cm]) of the coastal US from New England to eastern Texas. However, studies conducted in Louisiana showed that the two nest alongside one another without interbreeding and they are now considered separate species.

The Great-tailed can be told by its larger size and pale yellow eyes. The Boat-taileds of the Gulf coast have pale brownish eyes (though Atlantic coast Boat-taileds often have pale yellowish eyes). The vocalizations and displays of the two also differ, although both have a varied repertoire of loud clucks, whistles, shrieks, and chatters. The Great-tailed is expanding its range in the southwest, following the spread of agriculture and irrigated urban areas. Except in Florida, the Boat-tailed occurs only along or near the coast, and is often associated with salt marshes.

J F M A M J J A S O N D

Boat-tailed ♂

Great-tailed

Great-tailed ♀

FIELD NOTES

■ 10½–18½" (26.5–47 cm)

■ Long, full tail

■ Golden yellow eyes

■ Flat crown

🪺 Bulky cup of grass low to high in bush or tree

🥚 3–4; pale grayish with dark markings

Brown-headed Cowbird

Molothrus ater

The Brown-headed Cowbird's most famous or infamous attribute is that it is a brood parasite—the female lays eggs in the nests of other birds and takes no part in the rearing of her young. Brown-headed Cowbird eggs have been recorded in the nests of some 220 species, ranging from ducks to hummingbirds! The female cowbird has been estimated to lay an average of 80 eggs—40 per year for two years. Although only about 3 percent of eggs end up as adults, this still means that an average of 2.4 adults are produced by each female, so the species continues to increase in number.

Originally a bird of the Great Plains, where it lived around buffalo, this cowbird has spread dramatically across North America, following the clearance of forest for farms and pastures. This has allowed it to parasitize many more species, some of them poorly adapted to such behavior.

The male Cowbird makes a high-pitched whistle, while the female's spluttering chatter often gives her presence away. The female and juvenile Brown-headed Cowbirds are a plain gray-brown overall, though paler on the head and underparts. They both have a fairly stubby bill and a pale eye-ring.

J F M A M J J A S O N D

Bell's Vireo feeding cowbird chicks

FIELD NOTES

- 6½–7½" (16.5–19 cm)
- Stocky, with stubby bill and rather short tail
- Male: Black with brown head
- Female: Gray-brown, paler below
- Juvenile: Similar to adult female but streaked below
- Eggs laid in other species' nests
- Bluish white, densely speckled with browns

233

American Goldfinch

Carduelis tristis

The American Goldfinch is a common bird of weedy fields, farmland, open woodlands, and urban areas. In all these areas it is often found feeding on thistle seeds. While the summer male is one of the most colorful American birds, after breeding, both male and female molt into a more somber winter plumage like that of the immatures. In winter, American Goldfinches frequently visit garden birdfeeders to eat seeds.

In much of the southwest, the American Goldfinch is only a winter visitor and is replaced as a nesting bird by the Lesser Goldfinch (*Carduelis psaltria*; 4–4½" [10–11.5 cm]). Male Lessers in the west have green backs and a black cap, while those in the east have a black head and back. In all plumages, Lessers differ from American Goldfinches in having a

white flash at the base of the primaries on the closed wing, and in their pale yellowish (versus whitish) undertail coverts. Both species are accomplished singers and their pleasant twittering songs often include mimicry of other species' calls.

J F M A M J J A S O N D

Lesser

♀

♂ (western form)

FIELD NOTES
- 4½–5" (11.5–12.5 cm)
- Adult breeding male unmistakable
- White undertail coverts and lack of streaking constant in all plumages
- ▲ Lesser Goldfinches have yellowish undertail coverts, greenish backs, and males are entirely black-capped
- Cup of fine plant material, such as thistledown, in bush or tree
- 4–6; unmarked bluish white

at feeder

234

Wetlands

BIRDING *in* WETLANDS

Clearly delineated habitats and a diversity of highly visible species make wetland environments ideal places to study the social behavior of birds, their feeding tactics, and annual migration cycles.

Wetlands provide some of the most exciting habitats for birding because they contain all sorts of spectacular and easily observed species, such as pelicans, herons, egrets, geese, ducks, Ospreys, and shorebirds. Another appealing aspect of birding on an area of water is that it is a finite region, distinct from the surrounding land, enabling you to keep track of day-to-day changes in the diversity and numbers of birds present.

On a walk in the woods or fields you may see more warblers or sparrows one day than another but you will be unable to tell whether there are really more birds because at any one time many birds may be hidden from view. In contrast, if you see 20 ducks and 10 coots on a lake one day, and 50 ducks and no coots the next, you can be fairly certain that the variation is real rather than apparent.

PASSING THROUGH

Many wetlands are wintering areas or transit points for vast numbers of ducks and shorebirds that nest in Alaska and the Canadian arctic.

Southbound migrants appear as early as late June, heralding a stream of avian traffic that extends well into November. Some remain for the winter, others continue southward into Central or South America. In spring, some birds begin moving north again as soon as ice-free conditions permit, while many others are still moving north as late as early June.

It can be fascinating to note these day-to-day changes in your notebook, and over the years to compare arrival and departure dates for various species. You also may come to see how day-to-day changes relate to weather factors and thus learn how to predict which days are best for birding.

COEXISTENCE

The self-contained nature of many wetland habitats will also allow you to observe the intricacy with which the total resources of a habitat are parcelled out to different kinds of birds.

There is almost sure to be at least one small, short-legged species that forages over the muddy margins but does not actually wade (a sandpiper, perhaps).

WILDLIFE REFUGES *A huge range of highly visible birds can be observed in wetlands, from these ducks "dabbling" for food (below) to the White Ibis (right), seen here in a mangrove swamp.*

BIRD SPECTACULARS *Wetlands are the stage for many of the most spectacular sights in nature. Events such as the migrations of Snow Geese (right) attract birders from all around the country (above).*

Then there will be a slightly longer-legged species that can cover a wider area because it can wade in shallow water (yellowlegs, for example). And there will also be longer-legged birds that can reach deeper water to take full advantage of an even larger percentage of the wetland's total area (stilts or herons). Other birds—terns, for example—can cover the total surface area, but only at the cost of staying airborne for long periods. Some ducks habitually feed in the shallows, others "upend" in somewhat deeper water, while still others dive for food, exploiting resources that cannot be reached by other birds. Birds such as rails have narrow bodies that enable them to slip easily between stems in reedbeds on the margins of the wetland.

More than other habitats, wetlands illustrate that, far from being distributed haphazardly, birds live in clearly structured communities. It can be absorbing to work out the way wetland birds are distributed and how they operate.

GETTING AROUND

Some wetland areas can be difficult to reach. Power-boats, of course, involve far too much noise to be of any use to the birder but— depending on the kind of wetland—puttering about quietly in a canoe or kayak can be a wonderful way of observing waterbirds at close range without disturbing them unduly.

Alternatively, you may be able to find a causeway or dike to use as a vantage point to scan the wetland with your binoculars or spotting scope. Otherwise, wading may be the only way of exploring the marsh, but this often results in wet feet.

You can, of course, wear rubber boots or waders, but a little-known corollary of Murphy's Law states that the depth of the water you want to wade across is always one inch higher than the top of your boots. That's why experienced birders often keep a pair of sneakers and an old towel in the trunk of the car.

One final recommendation for wetland birding: don't forget the insect repellent!

WETLAND RESERVES *are so popular with visitors that boardwalks (left) and blinds have become necessary controls in their management. Canoes (above) can also provide effective and unobtrusive transport through these areas.*

Adult (breeding plumage)

Pied-billed Grebe

Podilymbus podiceps

Common across much of North America, this small, chunky grebe can be found on lakes and ponds with marshy vegetation. Generally, it avoids open water, such as stone-banked reservoirs or estuaries, but in winter it may be found occasionally in these habitats, especially if smaller lakes freeze over. Like all grebes, it dives well and can be elusive, especially in the nesting season when its presence may be given away only by varied whinnying and clucking calls coming from the reeds.

J F M A M J J A S O N D

The Pied-billed Grebe is identified by its large head and thick pale bill which, in breeding birds, has a black vertical band, hence the name "pied-billed". The immature and non-breeding adult lack the black band on the bill and have a whitish throat. The downy young have black-and-white striped heads and often ride on their parents' backs.

An interesting aspect of grebe biology is that these fish-eating birds also consume many feathers—in fact, as much as half of the stomach contents of a grebe may be feathers. It is thought that the feathers form soft balls that protect the stomach against damage from the sharp fish bones that the grebe's gizzard is unable to break down.

juvenile

FIELD NOTES
- 11–13" (28–33 cm)
- Stocky, large-headed
- Stout bill: white with black ring in summer, otherwise dull yellowish
- Platform of aquatic vegetation, floating or anchored to reeds
- 2–10; bluish white

with chicks

Adult (breeding plumage)

Western Grebe

Aechmophorus occidentalis

This elegant grebe nests in colonies on lakes in much of the west. After breeding, most of the population migrates to spend the winter along the west coast, where you can also see non-breeding birds throughout the summer.

If you watch birds at a nesting lake long enough, you may be fortunate to see this species' spectacular and elaborate courtship display. This involves "rushing", when two or more birds run upright across the water, and the "weed dance", when two birds face one another with weed in their bills and make a number of ritualistic displays.

Until recently, it was widely believed that there were two forms of the Western Grebe: a dark form, with dark feathering extending below the eyes, and a light form, with white feathering extending above and in front of the eyes. However, studies have shown that the two rarely interbreed

JFMAMJJASOND

and they are now considered separate species, the Western Grebe having the dark feathering, and the Clark's Grebe (*Aechmophorus clarkii*) the light.

The face patterns are best seen on breeding birds and most of the time you'll find it easier to identify the two species by the color of the bill. The Western has a greenish yellow bill while the Clark's has a brighter, orange-yellow bill.

Western

Clark's

grebes 'rushing'

FIELD NOTES

- 20–24" (51–61cm)
- Large, with graceful neck and slender bill
- Blackish above, white below
- ▲ Clark's Grebe has brighter, orange-yellow bill
- Platform of aquatic vegetation, floating or anchored to reeds
- 2–7; unmarked bluish white

239

■ Adults

American White Pelican

Pelecanus erythrorhynchos

With a wingspan of up to 9½ feet (3 meters), this unmistakable bird is one of North America's largest, and there are few more spectacular sights than a flock of White Pelicans, wheeling and turning in unison. These birds nest mostly in colonies at large lakes in the interior west and then migrate to lagoons and estuaries along the coasts of the southern US and Mexico for the winter.

Unlike the coastal, saltwater Brown Pelican, which dives from the air, White Pelicans feed while swimming, putting their heads and bills under water to scoop up fish. Often several birds will swim together in a line, rounding up fish in shallow water and so maximizing their catch.

J F M A M J J A S O N D

During the nesting season, White Pelicans develop a horn-like growth on their bill. This growth is shed after the eggs have been laid. Immatures differ from adults in having a paler, grayish to flesh-colored bill, paler orange legs, and a brownish wash to their upperwing coverts. They resemble adults by the end of their second year.

bill showing 'horn'

FIELD NOTES
■ 57–65" (145–165 cm)

■ Large, mainly white, with large pouched bill—unmistakable

🪺 Depression in ground, sometimes built up with dirt

🥚 1–6; dull white

Adults

Great Blue Heron

Ardea herodias

Found in almost all wetland habitats, this is the most familiar large wading bird in North America. Like many conspicuous and widespread wading birds, the Great Blue Heron nests in relatively few colonies throughout its range, and non-breeding immatures occur in summer at many localities far from nesting populations.

JFMAMJJASOND

The Great Blue is unmistakable throughout most of its range, but in the Florida Keys you may find an all-white form, formerly considered a separate species. To distinguish this white form from the smaller Great Egret (p. 242), note the dull yellowish bill and pale legs of the heron.

The immature Great Blue has an all-dark crown and is duller overall than the adult. It attains full adult plumage when it is three years old.

Great Blue Herons are most often seen slowly stalking at the side of a lake or marsh, or standing still in fairly deep water where their long legs enable them to feed. In some areas you may see them feeding in fields or on lawns, where they hunt gophers and mice. If disturbed, the Great Blue takes off heavily and flies away with slow deep wingbeats, often giving a deep, throaty call as it goes.

white form

immature

FIELD NOTES

■ 40–50" (101.5–127 cm)

■ Large, gray

▲ White form, locally common in southern Florida, may be confused with Great Egret but has pale legs

🪶 Platform of sticks in trees, on ground, or on cliffs

🥚 3–7; pale greenish

Adult

Great Egret

Casmerodius albus

Formerly known as both the American Egret and the Common Egret, this is the large white heron seen across much of North America. These birds occur at lakes, lagoons, and along rivers and coasts, and like most herons, they nest in colonies which may include several other species of waterbirds.

J F M A M J J A S O N D

Besides its size, the Great Egret's field marks are its bright yellow beak and its all-black legs and feet—note, however, that the space between the eye and the bill (the lore) on an adult becomes bright green for a brief period at the start of the breeding season.

Great Egrets feed by standing still and waiting, or by stalking slowly, and their statuesque posture while feeding distinguishes them from the Snowy Egret (p. 243).

In the second half of the nineteenth century, huge demand from the fashion industry for the plumes of breeding egrets caused egret populations to be devastated through hunting. Protective legislation introduced at the start of the twentieth century, following campaigns by the Audubon Society (whose symbol is the Great Egret) and others, has helped egret populations recover.

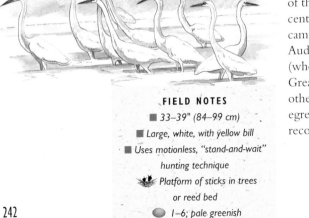

FIELD NOTES

- 33–39" (84–99 cm)
- Large, white, with yellow bill
- Uses motionless, "stand-and-wait" hunting technique
- Platform of sticks in trees or reed bed
- 1–6; pale greenish

breeding plumage

242

Adult

Snowy Egret

Egretta thula

The Snowy Egret sometimes dashes around with its wings partly spread, and when it does, it presents a notable contrast to the much more sedate Great Egret. The rapid movement of the Snowy is thought to startle fish into revealing themselves, while the spread wings may shadow the water's surface, enabling the bird to see its prey more clearly.

Common to lakes, marshes, and coasts in North America, this small, white egret is identified by its all-black bill, yellow lores, and black legs with yellow feet or "golden slippers".

J F M A M J J A S O N D

In the southeast, especially along the coast, you'll also find the Little Blue Heron (*Egretta caerulea*; 20–24" [51–61 cm]). The adult is distinctive, with its overall dark bluish plumage. Immature Little Blue Herons are much harder to identify because they are all white and can easily be confused with Snowy Egrets. Unlike the Snowy, the Little Blue usually has a bicolored bill.

immature
Little
Blue

Little Blue
Heron

FIELD NOTES

- 19–23" (48–58.5 cm)
- Small, white
- Black bill and legs, yellow feet
- Hunts briskly in shallow water
- Platform of sticks on ground, or in trees
- 1–6; pale greenish

243

Immature

Green Heron

Butorides virescens

Although widespread and common, this crow-sized heron tends not to be as conspicuous as the larger herons and egrets, since it prefers wooded marshes and pools and avoids wide open habitats. Nonetheless, if you walk quietly and are observant, you may well see Green Herons (formerly known as Green-backed Herons) hunched quietly at the edges of ponds and marshes. Often they are detected by their calls: a sharp barking *kyow!* which they give when flushed, and varied barking and clucking chatters.

adult

In flight, the Green Heron is distinguished by its small size, compact shape, and dark plumage; and the yellow feet projecting beyond the tail are often quite conspicuous. Its main field marks are its chestnut-colored face and neck, its dark cap, and its yellow legs. In good light, the chalky greenish cast that gives the bird its name is visible on its back. This is most evident in breeding birds, which also have bright reddish orange legs. The immature is duller overall than the adult and has dark and pale streaking on its neck and chest.

J F M A M J J A S O N D

FIELD NOTES
- 15–17" (38–43 cm)
- Small
- Yellowish legs
- Looks all dark at a distance
- Platform of sticks in reeds or trees
- 3–6; pale greenish

fishing

244

Adult

Black-crowned Night-Heron

Nycticorax nycticorax

As the name implies, this heron is mostly nocturnal, although it can often be seen during the day, feeding along the edges of lakes or coastal lagoons, or roosting in trees near water. The Black-crowned's barking *wok!* frequently draws attention to it at dusk when these birds leave their roosts and set out to hunt for food. (This is when most herons are heading in the opposite direction—back to their roosts.)

Yellow-crowned

Black-crowned

J F M A M J J A S O N D

The Black-crowned stands with a characteristic hunched posture that helps distinguish it from the closely related, taller-standing Yellow-crowned Night-Heron (*Nycticorax violaceus*; 20–23" [51–58.5 cm]) of the southeast. In flight, note that the longer legs of the Yellow-crowned project noticeably beyond its tail whereas the feet of the Black-crowned can only just be seen. Immatures of these two species look very similar, being brown overall with pale spotting on their upperparts. They are often best told apart by their shape, but note also that the Yellow-crowned's thicker bill is all-black while the immature Black-crowned has a yellowish base to its bill.

Yellow-crowned

FIELD NOTES
- ■ 22–25" (56–63.5 cm)
- ■ Adult: black cap and back, gray wings, white underparts
- ▲ Immature easily confused with Yellow-crowned Night-Heron and American Bittern
- ✿ Platform of sticks in trees, in marshes
- ● 1–6; pale greenish

immature Black-crowned

245

Adult (foreground) and immature

Snow Goose

Chen caerulescens

Few sights in the bird world are as breathtaking as a cacophonous blizzard of thousands of Snow Geese taking to the air or alighting in a field. After breeding in the arctic tundra, this goose migrates south to spend the winter at traditional wintering grounds in parts of the US, and in southwest British Columbia.

J F M A M J J A S O N D

Because of the commercial value of geese to hunters, a large part of the work of many wildlife refuges across North America involves protecting populations of Snow and other geese during the migrations in fall and early spring, as well as in winter. Visiting these refuges, especially in the hunting season before the great majority of geese disperse away from the safety of protected sites, is the best way to see Snow Geese and many other waterfowl.

blue
form

The Snow Goose comes in two forms (morphs): the more common white form and the blue form, at one time considered a separate species known as the Blue Goose. Blue morph Snow Geese occur mainly in the midwest and on the Great Plains.

The immature Snow Goose is dirty whitish overall in the white form and dusky brownish overall in the blue form. Many immatures do not attain adult-like plumage by spring.

immature
(white form)

FIELD NOTES
- 25–30" (63.5–76 cm)
- White form: Plain white with black wingtips
- Blue form: Dark bluish gray with (adults only) white head
- Depression in ground lined with grass and down
- 4–7; creamy white

246

Adults

Canada Goose

Branta canadensis

Perhaps the most familiar goose to most North Americans, the Canada Goose is famous for its geographic variation—some of the largest subspecies are nearly twice as big as the smallest.

From eight to eleven subspecies are generally recognized. For practical purposes these can be broken down into small, medium, and large birds. In general, the smaller races, which are a quarter the size of the largest birds, give higher-pitched, yelping or cackling calls, and the larger birds give more drawn-out honking calls. The small races are therefore often known as "cackling geese", whereas the larger races are known as "honkers".

All Canada Geese have the diagnostic white "chinstrap" and are varying shades of brownish below. The young look much like the adults.

J F M A M J J A S O N D

The large and medium-sized races are fairly widespread whereas the small cacklers breed only in the far north and winter locally in the west and midwest.

As with other geese, Canada Geese often fly in a distinctive V-formation that aids streamlining, and family parties stay together throughout the winter.

'cackling' Canada Goose

'honker'

FIELD NOTES
- 22–45" (56–114.5 cm)
- Black head and neck
- White patch under chin
- Depression in ground built up with grass and lined with feathers
- 2–12; dull white

247

Adult male (breeding plumage)

Wood Duck

Aix sponsa

That the Wood Duck is now common in much of eastern North America is a tribute to a highly successful conservation policy. Early in the twentieth century, Wood Ducks were threatened with extinction through over-hunting, drainage of wetlands, and felling of forests. Their rarity led to a moratorium on hunting for 23 years, from 1918 to 1941, and a program of close habitat management. Since Wood Ducks nest in tree cavities, nestboxes have also played a particularly important role in re-establishing the species in many areas.

Many people's first encounter with a Wood Duck is hearing a rising squeal and seeing a pair of ducks with long, squared-off tails rise up from a wooded

J F M A M J J A S O N D

pond and circle overhead. If this happens and you remain still, they may land nearby, giving you the opportunity of viewing one of the most handsome birds you are likely to encounter in wetlands.

The ornate male is unmistakable for much of the year. After nesting he molts into a drab female-like plumage but keeps his distinctive red bill. Good field marks of the female are her bushy pointed crest and her bold white eye-ring.

chicks leaving nest

♀

FIELD NOTES
- 17–19" (43–48 cm)
- Male: Unmistakable, with bold, intricate pattern and bright colors
- Female: Dull; grayish head with white patch around eye
- Hollow in tree
- 9–12; off-white

Adult male (breeding plumage)

Mallard

Anas platyrhynchos

The Mallard is the most widespread and familiar duck in the Northern Hemisphere. Since it is often tame and found in city parks, it can provide an excellent opportunity to learn the important basics of duck breeding biology, plumage, and molt—lessons that will serve you well when identifying less familiar species.

Mallards are the ancestors of all breeds of domestic or farmyard ducks except the Muscovy. Wild and feral birds may interbreed in parks, giving rise to an array of plumages ranging from typical male Mallards, with their green head, white neck band, and mahogany breast, to birds that are mostly white. Females are dull and mottled like most female dabbling ducks.

In the east you'll also find the closely related Black Duck (*Anas rubripes*; 21–24" [53.5–61 cm]). As this bird sometimes interbreeds with the Mallard, some ornithologists consider it a subspecies of the Mallard. The male does not have brightly colored plumage—both sexes resemble dark female Mallards. Black Ducks, however, have white on only the trailing edge of their deep blue speculum. The Mallard's speculum has a white border on both sides.

J F M A M J J A S O N D

dabbling Mallard

♂

speculum

FIELD NOTES

■ 20–23" (51–58.5 cm)

■ Male: Glossy green head, mahogany breast, narrow white collar

▲ Female difficult to distinguish from Black Duck, but Mallard has white on both sides of speculum

❀ Cup of leaves and grass on ground, lined with down

● 5–14; greenish white

American Black Duck

249

Adult male (breeding plumage)

Green-winged Teal

Anas crecca

Teals are small dabbling ducks, and the Green-winged Teal is common across North America. It nests in tall grass and reeds around lakes and marshes, and in winter it favors muddy channels in marshes and estuaries for feeding. Non-breeding Green-winged Teals often occur in fairly large flocks that fly rapidly in tightly grouped formation. They associate with other dabbling ducks while feeding, but, although a single teal may fly with Mallards or other ducks, the species tend to separate in flight.

The handsome, full-plumaged male is unmistakable, while the female is told from most ducks by her small size. In flight, she is readily separated from the Blue-winged and Cinnamon teals by her brownish (not pale bluish) forewings and the bright green inner square on the speculum (wingpatch).

J F M A M J J A S O N D

While swimming, the three teals can look very similar, but note the female Green-winged's relatively small bill and whitish undertail coverts.

breeding ♂

♀

♀ Green-winged Teal & ducklings

FIELD NOTES
- 14–15" (35.5–38 cm)
- Very small
- Male: Chestnut and bottle-green head
- ▲ Female difficult to distinguish from other teals, but has plain head, whitish undertail coverts, and green speculum
- Depression in ground lined with grass
- 7–15; cream

■ Adult male (breeding plumage)

Northern Pintail

Anas acuta

After the Mallard and perhaps the Lesser Scaup, the elegant Pintail is one of the most abundant ducks in North America. Like most dabbling ducks, Pintails nest mainly on freshwater lakes and marshes in the north and west. They migrate south in winter to the west and south coasts, where large groups may be found in favored estuaries and coastal lagoons.

The Pintail's long neck enables it to feed, by up-ending, in deeper water than other dabbling ducks. In nuptial plumage, the male, with his attenuated, pin-like central tail feathers making up almost a quarter of his total length, is unmistakable.

J F M A M J J A S O N D

The female is generally paler and grayer than other dabbling ducks, and has something of the male's elegant, long-necked and long-tailed appearance. In flight, the female Pintail's best field mark is the white edge on the brown speculum (wingpatch) of her upperwing.

FIELD NOTES

■ 20–26" (51–66 cm)
■ Slim and elegant
■ Long slender neck
■ Male: Brown head, white foreneck
■ Female: Plain head, pointed tail, gray legs
🪺 Depression in ground lined with grass, leaves
🥚 6–12; cream

♀

up-ending

breeding ♂

♀

251

Adult male (breeding plumage)

Blue-winged Teal

Anas discors

Common across much of North America, although less so along the west coast, the Blue-winged Teal is one of the long-distance migrants of the duck world, with some birds flying as far as Argentina in the winter. In parts of the west, you are likely to find the closely related Cinnamon Teal (*Anas cyanoptera*; 15–16" [38–40.5 cm]).

J F M A M J J A S O N D

The males of these two species are readily separable in nuptial plumage: the male Blue-winged has a bold white crescent on his slaty blue face, and the poorly named male Cinnamon

Teal is chestnut (not cinnamon) overall. Females, juveniles, and non-breeding males of these two species are difficult to tell apart and can puzzle even expert birders. Note that the Cinnamon Teal is often a warmer brown overall and has a broader, more spatulate bill that suggests the Northern Shoveler. In flight, both are readily told from the Green-winged Teal by their pale bluish forewings, which are brightest in the adult males.

Blue-winged ♂

Cinnamon Teal ♀

Blue-winged Teal ♀

Cinnamon Teal ♂

FIELD NOTES

- 15–16" (38–40.5 cm)
- Male: Slaty gray face with white crescent
- Female: Pale spot at base of bill
- Basket-like structure of dead grass on ground
- 6–15; creamy white

Northern Shoveler

Anas clypeata

By virtue of its shovel-like bill, the Northern Shoveler is one of the most distinctive North American ducks. In profile the heavy bill is longer than the head—a distinguishing mark among the dabbling ducks. The size of the bill causes the bird to hold its head slightly drooped in flight. When feeding (usually in shallow water), the Northern Shoveler extends its neck forward and dabbles its bill just under the water's surface. The small comb-like teeth along the sides of the bill are used as a strainer, retaining food items.

The male Northern Shoveler in nuptial plumage is one of the most handsome North American ducks. The female, like other female dabblers, is mottled brown overall.

Unlike most dabbling ducks, the immature Northern Shoveler does not attain adult male plumage until late winter. You may therefore see the distinctive immature male plumage—similar to a dull adult but with a mottled whitish crescent forward of the eyes—right through the New Year.

♀

♂

♂ immature

FIELD NOTES
- 17–20" (43–51 cm)
- Large, spatulate bill
- Male: Green head, white chest, chestnut flanks
- Female: Plain, sober-hued, best identified by distinctive bill
- Depression in ground, lined with grass
- 6–14; pale buff color

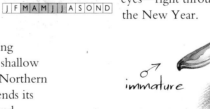

spatulate bill

253

Lesser Scaup

Aythya affinis

Lesser Scaups are a common sight on lakes and reservoirs across much of North America in winter, when they may form large flocks and associate with other diving ducks. Large numbers also spend the winter in protected estuaries and lagoons along both coasts. In summer, they nest mainly on small prairie lakes. Like other diving ducks, scaups spend much of the day sleeping because they feed at night, their bill tucked into their back.

The closely related Ring-necked Duck (*Aythya collaris*; 16–18" [40.5–45.5 cm]) may be found with Lesser Scaups, although it tends not to occur in large flocks and prefers less open habitats, such as small ponds and lakes in woodlands.

J F M A M J J A S O N D

Unlike dabbling ducks, diving ducks run along the water to take off. In flight, the scaup shows a white wingstripe compared with the pale gray stripe on the Ring-necked Duck's wings. The female Ring-necked lacks the bold white patch at the base of the scaup's plain bill. She has a gray face, narrow white eye-ring, and banded bill. In all plumages, note the distinctive head and bill shapes of these two species.

Lesser Scaup ♀

Ring-neck

FIELD NOTES

■ 15–17" (38–43 cm)

■ White, not gray, wingbar

▲ Ring-necked Duck has high-peaked crown as opposed to Lesser Scaup's more rounded head

❀ Hollow in ground lined with grass and down

● 6–15; dark olive-buff

Adult female

Bufflehead

Bucephala albeola

The sprightly, fast-flying Bufflehead is the smallest North American diving duck. Unlike most diving ducks, however, it can take off from the water without running along the surface. Buffleheads are common in winter on lakes, reservoirs, coastal lagoons, and in estuaries and sheltered harbors. They usually occur in small flocks and readily associate with other diving ducks.

The females and first-winter males are identified by their small size and the white patch on the sides of the head. In flight, the male shows the white inner half of his upperwings, whereas the female and immature have a white patch on the secondary wing feathers.

In the same genus is the Common Goldeneye (*Bucephala clangula*; 17–20" [43–51 cm]), which occurs in much the same range and habitats as the Bufflehead. Frequently, the two species are

seen side by side. The adult male Goldeneye is identified by the large, round white spot in front of his eyes. The female and immature have a brown knobby head. By midwinter the immature male often shows a whitish spot in front of his eyes.

J F M A M J J A S O N D

FIELD NOTES
- 14–16" (35.5–40.5 cm)
- Male: Tubby with big, dark green and white head
- Female: Dark gray head with horizontal white cheek patch
- Cavity in tree, often old Flicker hole
- 6–11; cream

Common Goldeneye

255

Ruddy Duck

Oxyura jamaicensis

The distinctive Ruddy Duck is a compact duck with a "stiff" tail that is often held cocked, especially when the bird is sleeping. In winter both sexes have pale cheeks, but the female's cheeks have a dark bar across them. The male attains his full chestnut breeding plumage by March, and this is lost again by the end of the summer.

Many ducks dive but the Ruddy sinks slowly below the surface, scarcely leaving a ripple. In display, the male "bubbles", striking his bill against his inflated chest to disperse bubbles into the surrounding water.

Ruddies are common in many areas: they nest on marshy ponds and lakes with reedy edges, and spend the winter on lakes, lagoons, and reservoirs. Throughout the year, non-breeding birds may occur in flocks which tend to keep somewhat apart from other ducks.

Although strong fliers, Ruddy Ducks take to the air infrequently. In flight their upperparts are uniformly dark, lacking the white markings found on many other ducks.

J F M A M J J A S O N D

diving

winter ♀

winter ♂

FIELD NOTES

- 14–16" (35.5–40.5 cm)
- Dumpy shape
- Prominent "stiff" tail, carried flat or cocked
- Male: Mainly chestnut, with blue bill, black cap, white cheeks
- Female: Brownish gray body, horizontal dark bar across cheek
- Basket-like structure of marsh grass anchored to reeds
- 5–10; creamy white

256

Adult

Osprey

Pandion haliaetus

From a distance, an Osprey circling high over the water, with its crooked wings and whitish underparts, may suggest a large gull. Note, however, the dark wrist marks on the Osprey's blunter-tipped wings, and its dark eyestripe. Also, unlike gulls, the Osprey hovers. If you watch for a while, you may witness the spectacular sight of an Osprey diving feet-first into the water, coming up with a fish and carrying it off aligned head first, in its talons.

While today the Osprey is common in summer across much of North America, from the 1950s through the 1970s many populations declined drastically. This was largely as a result of the misuse of pesticides—such as DDT, which caused thinning of birds' eggshells and thus reproductive failure. The banning of DDT in the early 1970s, and the provision of nesting platforms, helped the Osprey recover.

J F M A M J J A S O N D

The male and female Osprey look alike, although the female often has a necklace of brown streaks across her chest. The juvenile is distinguished in fall by the extensive pale tips on the feathers of its upperparts.

dark wrist mark

artificial nest-platform

FIELD NOTES

- 22–26" (56–66 cm)
- Dark brown above, white below
- Dark wrist marks on underwing
- Carries wings in distinctive arched posture
- Bulky platform of sticks in tree, on cliff, or on ground
- 2–4; pinkish, heavily marked with browns

257

Adult

Bald Eagle

Haliaeetus leucocephalus

Although the Bald Eagle is considered a threatened species in many areas, if you live in the northwest you have a good chance of seeing this impressive raptor along the coast or at large lakes. In fall, Bald Eagles gather at favored feeding grounds, in particular certain salmon-spawning grounds in Alaska and British Columbia, where up to 3,000 eagles may gather. Elsewhere, in the east and south, Bald Eagles are local and uncommon, although for the most part their populations are increasing following a decline linked, like the decline of the Osprey, to pesticides such as DDT.

In 1782 the Bald Eagle won the contest between it and the Wild Turkey to become the national bird of the US, and was picked for its fierce demeanor. In fact, Bald Eagles tend to be quite timid and often feed on carrion. They hunt mostly from perches overlooking water, and plunge like Ospreys to catch fish with their talons before returning to a perch to eat them.

J F M A M J J A S O N D

adult

In flight, at a distance, the Bald Eagle can be told from the Turkey Vulture (p. 212) by its more massive, barn-door-like shape, and its broader wings that are held flat rather than distinctly raised, as is the case with the Turkey Vulture. The immature Bald Eagle is mostly dark brown, with some whitish mottling under its wings. After four years it attains the white-headed, white-tailed adult plumage.

immature

adult

immature

FIELD NOTES
- 30–40" (76–101.5 cm)
- White head and tail
- ▲ Immatures easily confused with Golden Eagle
- Bulky mass of sticks in tree, on cliff
- 1–3; dull white

258

American Coot

Fulica americana

The widespread American Coot is one of the most common and conspicuous birds on North American lakes and ponds. Unlike ducks, which tend to be wary and fly off when you approach them, coots seem tolerant of people and will nest even at small ponds in city parks. They swim with a slight head-jerking motion that will enable you to pick them out at long range from swimming ducks, and they have to patter and splash frantically along the water's surface to gain momentum for flight.

In winter, coots may gather in large groups, or "rafts", on open water, but in the nesting season they can be quite shy, keeping to dense reeds and only giving away their presence by their gruff clucks and chatters.

J F M A M J J A S O N D

The juvenile coot looks very different from the adult. It lacks a bare forehead shield and is paler and grayer overall, with a whitish face and neck. By winter, the young resemble adults.

In marshes and ponds, especially in the east and south, you'll also find the Common Moorhen (*Gallinula chloropus*; 13–14" [33–35.5 cm]), which skulks more than the coot and is rarely seen on open water or in groups. The moorhen is readily told from a coot by its red and yellow bill and the white stripe along its sides. Like coots, moorhens feed while walking along the shores of ponds and while swimming.

juvenile Coot

Common Moorhen

FIELD NOTES
- ■ 14–16" (35.5–40.5 cm)
- ■ Mainly black
- ■ White bill
- Platform of marsh plants, anchored to reeds
- 6–12; pale buff with dark speckling

259

■ Adult (breeding plumage)

Spotted Sandpiper

Actitis macularia

At first glance, this small bird, with its brown and white plumage and white wingstripe, may appear like any typical sandpiper, but certain characteristics make the Spotted one of the most distinctive North American shorebirds. If you watch a Spotted Sandpiper for more than a few seconds, you'll notice that it walks with a persistent bobbing action, wagging its rear end up and down and often continuing to bob when standing still. And in flight, the Spotted's wingbeats are stiff and shallow, so that the wings are flicked quickly and held bowed below the body.

The Spotted is also set apart from other small sandpipers by the fact that it does not occur in large flocks and tends to be found alone rather than with other shorebirds. During migration and in winter, you may find Spotteds at lakes, estuaries, reservoirs, and rocky coasts, as well as along rivers, which is where they nest in summer.

The spots for which this species is named are only present in the summer plumage. The base of the bill and the legs are yellowish to dull pinkish in winter, as opposed to bright orangey pink in nesting birds.

breeding

J F M A M J J A S O N D

FIELD NOTES

- ■ 6½–7" (16.5–18 cm)
- ■ Underparts spotted in summer, plain whitish in winter
- ■ Teeters and bobs almost constantly
- ■ Flies with rapid shallow beats of stiff, slightly bowed wings
- ❀ Hollow in ground, hidden by grass
- ● 1–4; buff marked with browns

winter

Belted Kingfisher

Ceryle alcyon

The machine-gun-like rattling call of the Belted Kingfisher is a distinctive sound in wetlands across North America, and will attract your attention to a medium-sized bird with a large, bushy head and stout, pointed bill. The male has a single blue-gray band across his white underparts, while the female has a rusty band below the gray band.

Kingfishers are often seen perched on trees or wires overlooking water, from where they plunge head-first to catch fish in their bills. They also hunt by hovering, often fairly high over the water, swooping down when they spot a fish.

J F M A M J J A S O N D

Juvenile kingfishers are taught to fish by their parents, who drop dead fish into the water for the young to retrieve. After about ten days training, the young have learned to catch live food and are then chased away from the territory by the parents.

Kingfishers are solitary through the winter, when they may often be seen along seacoasts, and some birds overwinter as far north as ice-free water allows.

diving for fish

FIELD NOTES
- 12–13" (30.5–33 cm)
- Large shaggy head
- Heavy, pointed bill
- White underparts with blue-gray band across chest
- Female: Additional chestnut band across lower chest
- Burrow excavated in bank
- 5–8; unmarked white

261

Adult

Eastern Phoebe

Sayornis phoebe

Phoebes are relatively hardy flycatchers that overwinter in North America, at least in the south, when other flycatchers migrate to the tropics. In part this is because they eat insects associated with year-round habitats, such as ponds and streams, rather than with short-lived spring and summer foliage. In much of the north and east, a familiar sight in summer is an Eastern Phoebe perched on a post or tree over water, attracting attention to itself with its high-pitched, sharp *peek!* call.

Like many small flycatchers, the Eastern Phoebe is fairly nondescript, which is a help when identifying it, since it lacks even the pale eye-ring and distinct pale wingbars of most small flycatchers. Other useful field marks are its dark head and the way that it wags, or dips, its tail down (not up) while perched.

J F M A M J J A S O N D

In the southwest its counterpart is the closely related Black Phoebe (*Sayornis nigricans*; 6–7" [15–18 cm]) which has the same habits and a very similar call note to the Eastern Phoebe. The Black Phoebe is almost all black, with a white belly. The juvenile has distinct cinnamon wingbars.

juvenile Black Phoebe

Black Phoebe

FIELD NOTES
- 6¼–6¾" (16–17 cm)
- Dingy white underparts
- Dark head
- Alert, upright stance
- Persistently jerks tail slowly downward
- Cup of mud and grass on rock ledge, or building
- 3–8; whitish

Adult

Tree Swallow

Tachycineta bicolor

In summer, Tree Swallows are common in most wooded habitats near water, especially where dead branches provide nest sites. (Tree Swallows also use nestboxes readily.) During migration, in fall, Tree Swallows may be seen in vast flocks that cloud the sky like insect swarms. As they eat berries in addition to insects, these swallows are able to overwinter in areas north of where purely insectivorous swallows can survive.

Most adult Tree Swallows are readily told from other North American swallows by their steely blue upperparts and white underparts. However, juveniles and immatures are brownish above and may have a dusky wash across the chest, and females too, at least in their first summer, are brownish above rather than glossy blue. Thus they may be confused with the two North American species of brown-backed swallows, the Bank

Swallow (*Riparia riparia*; 4¾–5¼" [12–13 cm]) and the Northern Rough-winged Swallow (*Stelgidopteryx serripennis*; 5–5½" [12.5– 14 cm]), both of which nest in holes in banks or cliffs. The smaller Bank Swallow has a clean-cut brown chest band, while the Rough-winged has a dusky throat and a squarer-tipped tail.

J F M A M J J A S O N D

juvenile Tree Swallow

Rough-winged Swallow

Bank Swallow

Tree Swallow

FIELD NOTES

- 5¼–5¾" (13–14.5 cm)
- Glossy green-blue upperparts, white underparts
- ▲ Females and immatures may be confused with Bank and Northern Rough-winged swallows (see above)
- Cup of grass in cavity
- 4–6; white

263

Adult male

Common Yellowthroat

Geothlypis trichas

The bright warbled *witchety-witchety-witchety* song of the Common Yellowthroat often gives away the presence of this attractive warbler, which is common in summer in marshes and damp meadows and, during migration, in brushy fields and gardens often far from water. Another way to locate Yellowthroats is to learn their call note, a fairly gruff *chek*. If you then "spish" (make a lisping sound like *psssh-psssh...*), Yellowthroats will often respond by hopping up and flying toward you to investigate the noise. No one knows why birds respond to spishing this way, but it seems to work particularly well with Yellowthroats.

The male is readily identified by his bold black mask, bordered above by a narrow band that may be white, gray, or pale yellow. The female is fairly nondescript: her upperparts are olive and her underparts yellow, the yellow being brightest on the bib and on the undertail coverts. Young males in fall look like females but often show traces of the black mask.

J F M A M J J A S O N D

♀

immature

FIELD NOTES

■ 4½–5¼" (11.5–13 cm)

■ *Male: Olive above, bright yellow below, with bold black mask*

▲ *Female similar to other female and immature warblers, but note ground-haunting habits, plain tail, and yellowish throat and upper chest*

❧ *Bulky cup of grass, on or near ground in marshy vegetation*

⬮ *3–5; whitish speckled with browns*

Adult male

Red-winged Blackbird

Agelaius phoeniceus

Red-winged Blackbirds are a familiar sight across North America, where they nest in marshes, roadside ditches, grainfields, and damp meadows. In winter, they may form flocks of thousands, even millions, which swarm over fields to feed, often in company with cowbirds, grackles, and other blackbirds.

In spring, the male Red-winged can often be seen singing his song, a strangled gurgle, from a roadside perch or in a low fluttering flight. As he sings, he displays his brilliant red shoulders, or "epaulets", which are bordered with a yellowish band.

The female is dark brown and heavily streaked, especially on the underparts. Young males resemble females until their second year.

The closely related and very similar Tricolored Blackbird (*Agelaius tricolor*; 7–9" [18–23 cm]) is found only in California and adjacent Oregon and northern Baja.

The male Tricolored is distinctive in that his dark red shoulders are bordered by a white band rather than a yellowish band, but telling the female Tricolored and Red-winged blackbirds apart is a challenge even for experts.

J F M A M J J A S O N D

Red-winged ♀

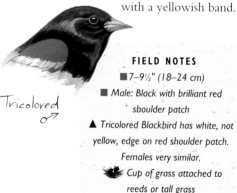

Tricolored ♂

FIELD NOTES
- 7–9½" (18–24 cm)
- Male: Black with brilliant red shoulder patch
- ▲ Tricolored Blackbird has white, not yellow, edge on red shoulder patch. Females very similar.
- Cup of grass attached to reeds or tall grass
- 3–5; pale blue with dark markings

Red-winged ♂

265

Adult male

Yellow-headed Blackbird

Xanthocephalus xanthocephalus

The unmistakable male Yellow-headed Blackbird is one of the most striking songbirds you are likely to see in a wetland habitat. As with many blackbirds, the female is smaller and more somberly colored than the male: she is dark brown overall with a yellow face and chest, and lacks the male's bold white forewing patch. Juveniles of both sexes have a golden-buff head and chest but soon molt into an adult-female-like immature plumage. The juvenile male tends to be brighter than the female and by spring looks similar to the adult male.

Yellow-headed Blackbirds are rare in the east but common in western and central North America. They nest in large, dense colonies, and often the reed beds are filled with the sound of thousands of them making their strangled, honking gurgles that pass for songs. In migration and winter, Yellow-heads remain highly gregarious and may

join with other blackbirds feeding in fields. Also, as is frequently the case with winter blackbirds, males and females may form separate flocks, so you may come across a flock of thousands of male Yellow-headed Blackbirds—truly an incredible sight!

J F M A M J J A S O N D

FIELD NOTES

- 7½–10" (19–25.5 cm)
- Male: Black with bright yellow head and upper chest
- Female: Dark brown overall with yellow face and chest
- Deep basket of grass woven into reeds
- 3–5; pale grayish, marked with browns

Seashores

BIRDING *at* SEASHORES

Seashores are demanding birding environments. You may study your garden or local patch for the sheer pleasure of watching birds going about their daily affairs, but seacoasts are where you go for the thrill of having your identification skills challenged and extended.

Birding would not be the fun it is if all birds were easy to identify, and seashores are where you will come up against three of the five most challenging groups of birds: gulls, migratory shorebirds, and seabirds (the fourth and fifth groups are the flycatchers and the fall warblers).

GULLS
Everyone knows a seagull when they see one, but the sheer number of species makes positive identification difficult. In addition, each gull takes between two and four years to reach maturity, each year giving rise to a different plumage. And to compound the problem further, most species have distinct winter and summer plumages (and this sometimes applies to the immatures as well!). Thus the birder is faced with a quite bewildering array of alternatives. Working through all these possibilities is the real problem; once you've done that, making a positive identification just takes time. At least gulls are (usually) fearless enough to let you look at them closely.

Critical points you should note when trying to identify a strange gull are:
- color and shape of bill
- leg color
- wingtip pattern
- whether it has a dark tail band

SHOREBIRDS
Migratory shorebirds are less cooperative than gulls. They are generally extremely wary, and habitually congregate in large flocks, often of mixed

COASTAL HABITATS *are often dominated by gulls, like this mixed group loafing on a rock platform in Monterey Bay (above) and the soaring Laughing Gull (right). In more remote parts of North America, such as Alaska's Pribilof Islands, you will find more exotic species including the Parakeet Auklet (above right).*

AT THE SEASHORE *the spotting scope (left) really comes into its own. Its greater power is particularly useful when it comes to identifying small shorebirds such as Sanderlings (below) as they scuttle before the surf.*

species, making them difficult to single out for study. Identification often has to be made at long distance. Like gulls, there are many species. In breeding plumage they are generally very distinctive, but juveniles and birds in winter plumage are often similar. In a few cases the similarities are such that positive identification depends almost literally on a feather-by-feather analysis or a detailed examination of the extremely subtle variations in relative size and form. For the most part, however, you are half way there if you carefully note:

- leg color
- length and shape of bill
- pattern of upperwing (if any)
- whether it has a white rump

SEABIRDS

The third problematic group is the seabirds, especially the tubenoses. There are two difficulties with tubenoses. Firstly, these are pelagic birds that generally remain far offshore. Viewing opportunities from land are therefore limited, and few of us get out to sea often enough to become familiar with them. Secondly, many species have similar plumage, differing, rather, in nuances of flight style and body proportions, which are difficult to describe in words.

You really need on-the-spot, one-to-one help from an expert to master identification of these birds. Birding groups in many cities and towns along the coast regularly organize pelagic trips, chartering a boat to ferry birders far out to sea to look at tubenoses. In such a group, you are sure to find experts familiar with seabirds.

TIDES

Birds living on either land or sea can, like us, run their lives according to the cycle of day and night, but birds living at the interface between the two must pay attention to the tides. Many feed at low tide and sleep while the tide is high; others do the opposite. If you live on the coast or often go birding at the seashore, you'll be aware of the importance of tides.

Low tide is generally the best time for birding, being when birds come together to feed on exposed beaches and mud flats. But in places with an extensive inter-tidal zone you may choose to go birding when the tide is rising, as it will push birds in close enough for you to see them clearly. In some areas, shorebirds gather at high-tide roosts where you can watch them before the tide recedes

and they set off again to feed. Local knowledge will help you make the most of your trip.

SEASHORE GEAR

Tidal flats, estuaries, and similar localities are places where the spotting scope really comes into its own, giving you greater "reach" than most binoculars can deliver. Many coastal birds are wary and highly mobile, and it is often more difficult to follow a particular bird at the seashore than it is in, say, grasslands. You will be called upon to exercise your identification skills at greater distances than in almost any other habitat.

Magnifications somewhere between 20x and 40x are probably best for seashore conditions. If you go much above this you start to magnify atmospheric conditions rather than birds. A spotting scope is almost useless without a tripod, especially on seashores where it may be windy and wet. For more information on spotting scopes and tripods, see p. 114.

Common Loon

Gavia immer

I n the north, Common Loons are often seen nesting on large freshwater lakes, where their loud, yodeling calls are a sign of summer. Some of these birds also spend the winter on inland waters, especially the Great Lakes. For most people, however, loons are birds of the coasts.

All loons in winter are dark above and white below, and it is important to note the shape of the head and bill. The Common Loon has a large, angular head and a stout, straightish bill. These features, along with a distinct whitish area around its eyes in winter, distinguish it from the smaller Pacific Loon (*Gavia pacifica*; 22–26" [56–66 cm]), which nests in the far northwest and is common along the Pacific coast in winter.

The Pacific Loon has a puffier, more rounded head, and a slighter bill than the Common.

J F M A M J J A S O N D

In summer the adult Pacific has a pale gray head and hindneck, and a blackish foreneck bordered by white stripes, while the Common Loon has a black head and neck with two striped white cross-bands.

Pacific Loons tend to fly low over the ocean and, unlike Commons, often occur in fair-sized flocks. Common Loons can also be distinguished in flight by their large feet that stick out behind them like paddles.

Common (winter)

FIELD NOTES
- 26–33" (66–84 cm)
- Pointed bill
- Large, angular head
- Rides low in water
- Darker than most other loons
- ▲ Difficult to distinguish from several other loon species in winter
- Bowl of grass and twigs, on land or anchored to vegetation
- 1–3; olive-brown with fine dark flecks

Common (breeding)

Pacific (breeding)

Adult

Sooty Shearwater

Puffinus griseus

In August and September, you may look offshore from a beach in California, Oregon, or Washington and see large flocks of long-winged, all-dark birds gliding and skimming the surface of the sea—"shearing" the waves. You may also see them milling around, or sitting in "rafts" on the water, looking from a distance like a dark slick. These are Sooty Shearwaters, among the most abundant birds in the world.

Sooties nest on islands in the southern oceans and after breeding (in US winter) migrate north to the North Pacific and North Atlantic oceans. They are common off both coasts, more so off the west, and are most numerous in summer,

J F M A M J J A S O N D

although small numbers of non-breeding immatures remain in North American waters year-round.

If you take a boat trip offshore in the Pacific, the Sooty Shearwater will be among the seabirds you are most likely to encounter, and it serves as a useful comparison with other species. If you get a good view of a Sooty, you'll note that when it banks up and shows its underside there is a silvery flash under the wings. Like other shearwaters and petrels, the Sooty has a "tubenose"—the nostrils are encased in tubes on top of the bill—through which salt from the sea water that the bird drinks is exuded.

tubenose bill

raft of sooties

FIELD NOTES

- 17–18" (43–45.5 cm)
- Conspicuous white underwings
- ▲ Several similar all-dark shearwater species off west coast
- Burrow in ground
- 1; white

271

Adult with chick

Brown Pelican

Pelecanus occidentalis

In the 1960s and 1970s, the Brown Pelican had become a rare sight along the US coasts. This drastic decline resulted from the use of pesticides such as DDT which caused eggshell thinning and reproductive failure. With the banning of DDT in North America, Brown Pelican populations have recovered and today this impressive bird is again common along southern coasts. If you look off the beaches you can often see pelicans flying low in lines, gliding just above the waves, and if you live near a fishing harbor you will almost certainly be familiar with tame pelicans sitting around on the wharves.

Brown Pelicans feed by plunge-diving from flight, either at a shallow angle, as they skim the water, or more steeply from high overhead.

In fact, the adult Brown Pelican is overall silvery gray with a whitish head and neck. Prior to nesting, the hindneck of adults becomes dark reddish on Atlantic coast birds, or a darker reddish brown on Pacific coast birds. Immatures are brownish overall and take three years to attain adult plumage.

J F M A M J J A S O N D

winter

FIELD NOTES

- 44–54" (112–137 cm)
- Very large
- Huge pouched bill
- Plumage silvery gray
- Platform of sticks and grass in tree or on cliff
- 2–3; chalky white

summer

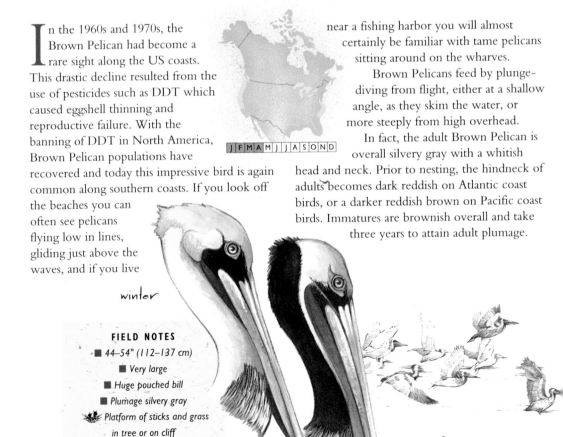

Adult (breeding plumage)

Double-crested Cormorant

Phalacrocorax auritus

The Double-crested Cormorant is the most widespread cormorant in North America, being found at inland lakes across the continent as well as along both coasts. It is most common at estuaries and lakes adjacent to the coast and rarely ventures far offshore.

At a distance, you can tell cormorants from loons by the way cormorants hold their hooked bills tilted up a little, and by the way they jump as they dive. Also, cormorants don't hold their necks drooped like loons when flying.

For most of the year, adults, like other cormorants, are blackish overall. Before nesting, the adults attain tufted white crests on either side of the head (hence the name). Immatures are dark brown with a pale foreneck and chest. The extensive bright yellow-orange throat pouch is a field mark in all plumages.

Along the Pacific coast, you'll also find the similar Brandt's Cormorant (*Phalacrocorax penicillatus*; 29–33" [73–84 cm]), strictly a bird

Double-crested

Brandt's

J F M A M J J A S O N D

of salt water. The adult Brandt's has a blue-gray throat pouch bordered by a band of buffy feathers. To distinguish between these birds in flight, note that the Double-crested holds its head raised, giving it a kink-necked look, while the Brandt's holds its head and neck out in a straight line.

Brandt's

Double-crested

FIELD NOTES
- 28–32" (71–81 cm)
- Orange throat pouch (all year)
- Carries neck kinked in flight
- Breeding adult: Two wispy crests on crown (whitish in west, black in east)
- Platform of sticks and seaweed on cliff or in tree
- 2–7; chalky pale blue

273

Adult

White Ibis

Eudocimus albus

White Ibises are gregarious wading birds that inhabit coastal saltmarshes, mangrove swamps, and adjacent freshwater lagoons in the southeastern US. Unlike herons, they fly with rapid, shallow wingbeats interspersed with glides, and they hold their neck outstretched. They may be seen flying in lines or V-shaped formations, especially early and late in the day when commuting to and from roosting sites. The downward-curving bill and probing feeding action

J F M A M J J A S O N D

distinguish the White Ibis from egrets.

In the breeding season, adult White Ibises develop a bright red wattle under their bill. The immature looks mostly brown, but in flight its white rump and uppertail coverts are conspicuous. Note the black wingtips of the adult as it flies.

Another spectacular wading bird found in similar habitats along the Gulf coast of the southern US is the unmistakable Roseate Spoonbill (*Ajaia ajaja*; 28–31" [71–79 cm]). The immature spoonbill is overall whitish with only a faint pinkish tinge, and attains the bright plumage and naked head of the adult over three years.

White Ibis

adult

immature

Roseate Spoonbill

FIELD NOTES
- ■ 21–25" (53–63.5 cm)
- ■ Almost entirely white
- ■ Dull pink to scarlet (depending on season) legs and curved bill
- ■ Immatures: Brown above, white below; curved, dull pink bill
- 🪹 Platform of sticks in tree
- 🥚 3–4; greenish white, spotted with browns

Surf Scoter

Melanitta nigra

Surf Scoters are a common sight off beaches along both Atlantic and Pacific coasts of North America, mainly in winter. As the name suggests, they can often be seen feeding in the surf of breaking waves, or sleeping in rafts just beyond the surf zone. Small numbers also occur in estuaries, harbors, and lagoons along the coast. In summer, Surf Scoters nest on the tundra of the far north, although some non-breeding immatures remain on the coasts throughout the year.

The distinctive male is one of the most handsome ducks. The all-brown female and immature may be confused with the closely related but generally less abundant White-winged Scoter (*Melanitta fusca*; 20–23" [51–58.5 cm]).

Note, however, that the whitish mark forward of the eye on the Surf Scoter is shaped like a vertical rectangle, while on the female White-winged it is a rounder spot. Also, the female Surf Scoter has a steeper forehead and flatter crown than the White-winged. In flight, or when scoters sit up and flap their wings, the bold white wingpatch on the White-winged is a good field mark.

White-winged ♂

JFMAMJJASOND

Surf ♀

White-Winged ♀

FIELD NOTES
- 18–20" (45.5–51 cm)
- Breeding male: Black; colorful bill; white forehead and nape
- Breeding females, immatures, winter males: Brown; two white spots on head
- ▲ White-winged Scoter has white patch on wing (revealed in flight)
- Depression in ground, built up with weeds
- 5–8; buff

raft of Surf Scoters

Juvenile

Black-bellied Plover

Pluvialis squatarola

This, the largest North American plover, is common on beaches and mud flats along coasts from August to May, with fewer birds present in June and July. During migration, some birds occur inland at lakes and on ploughed fields.

The Black-bellied Plover is often located by its plaintive *clee-oo-ee* call. As well as the black belly, breeding adults attain a black face and throat bordered by a bold white stripe. Winter birds and juveniles are overall grayish above and whitish below.

winter

Golden

breeding

J F M A M J J A S O N D

In flight, note the white rump, bold white wingbar, and black axillars or "armpits" that distinguish the Black-bellied from the American Golden-Plover (*Pluvialis dominica*; 9½–10" [24–25.5 cm]). Goldens nest in the far north and spend the winter in South America. They occur as migrants in fields and at lakes through the center of North America in spring, and along the Atlantic coast in fall. Their upperparts in flight appear uniform, and their underwings are plain gray.

winter

Black-bellied

breeding

American Golden

Black-bellied

FIELD NOTES

- 10½–11½" (26.5–29 cm)
- White rump
- Bold white wingbar
- Black "armpits"
- Breeding plumage: Bold black underparts
- Scrape in ground, lined with grass
- 3–4; buffy brown with dark markings

Adult (winter plumage)

Willet

Catoptrophorus semipalmatus

For much of the year, this large sandpiper is dull grayish overall and when standing it resembles many other shorebirds. However, when it takes to the air the Willet is immediately distinguished by its flashy black-and-white wing pattern. Its loud shrieking *will-will-et* call will identify it in the breeding season.

| J | F | M | A | M | J | J | A | S | O | N | D |

FIELD NOTES
- 12½–14" (31.5–35.5 cm)
- Noisy, conspicuous
- Unmistakable in flight—bold black and white patches clearly visible
- Summer: Mottled above and below
- Winter: Smooth grayish above, whitish below
- Scrape in ground, lined with grass
- 4–5; olive marked with browns

Willets are common on beaches and at estuaries and lagoons along both coasts from July to May. They also nest along much of the Atlantic and Gulf coasts, as well as at lakes and marshes in the interior west. After nesting, females leave their chicks in the care of the male bird and set off on their migration, so the first southbound migrants you see are likely to be females. Breeding birds are more variegated than birds in plain winter plumage, having dark and white streaking and barring on the face, neck, and chest, and dark markings on the back. As with other shorebirds, juveniles can be distinguished from adults in fall by their neat, fresh plumage (as opposed to the worn, faded, breeding plumage of the adults), which is brownish above with fine pale flecks.

winter

breeding

277

Ruddy Turnstone

Arenaria interpres

As the name indicates, turnstones use their short, slightly wedge-shaped bills to turn over stones, seaweed, and other beach debris to look for prey. The chunky, medium-sized Ruddy is a distinctive shorebird, seen frequently on sandy beaches, rocky coasts, and jetties throughout the year, most commonly from August to May. It tends to avoid muddy shores and estuaries. In summer, it nests on the arctic tundra.

The breeding adult is strikingly marked, while juveniles and winter birds are duller: note their plump shape, short bill, reddish legs, and dark circular patches at the sides of the chest.

On the west coast you'll also find the Black Turnstone (*Arenaria melanocephala*; 8½–9" [21.5–23 cm]), which favors rocky coasts and headlands. The Black is darker overall than the Ruddy, and has a solidly dark chest and duller, grayish to pale pinkish legs. In flight, both turnstones display a bold, angular pattern of white patches on their upperparts, and both have distinctive dry, chattering or rattling calls.

J F M A M J J A S O N D

Ruddy (breeding)

Black (breeding)

Black Turnstone

Ruddy Turnstone (winter)

FIELD NOTES

- 8½–9" (21.5–23 cm)
- Distinctive tortoise-shell pattern of black, white, and orange-red
- Blackish bib
- Reddish legs
- ▲ Black Turnstone has largely dark head and chest
- Scrape in tundra
- 3–4; olive marked with dark browns

Adult (winter plumage)

Sanderling

Calidris alba

A group of Sanderlings feeding at the tideline is a common sight on sandy beaches. Watch for them running after the receding waves to pick at food washed up, then racing back up the beach ahead of the advancing waves. Like many arctic-nesting shorebirds, Sanderlings are most common on the coast from August to May, with smaller numbers, mainly non-breeding immatures, present during June and July. Among small sandpipers, winter Sanderlings are characteristically pallid. Breeding birds and juvenile Sanderlings look quite different from winter birds. In breeding plumage (seen on migrants in May) the face, chest, and upperparts are overall bright reddish, while juveniles have a white face and underparts; a dark cap; and dark, spangled upperparts.

The Sanderling is an exception among sandpipers in that it is the only one that lacks a hind toe.

The Dunlin (*Calidris alpina*; 7¾–8½" [19.5–21.5 cm]) is a common, equally widespread sandpiper, similar in size to the Sanderling but with a longer, slightly downward-curving bill. Its winter plumage is brownish gray above (and on the chest), darker than the Sanderling, and spring adults have a black belly patch. Dunlins favor mud flats and estuaries and often occur in large flocks.

sanderling chicks

juvenile sanderling

breeding

Dunlin (winter)

FIELD NOTES

■ 7–7½" (18–19 cm)

■ Pale gray with bold white wingbar

■ Black bill and legs

■ Trots up and down beach, staying just out of reach of waves

▲ Other small sandpipers usually darker with less distinct wingbars

✿ Scrape in ground, lined with moss

⬭ 3–4; olive marked with browns

279

Western Sandpiper

Calidris mauri

Least (winter)

Small sandpipers, of which there are five common species in North America, are known as "peeps". Two of these winter in North America—the Western Sandpiper and the Least Sandpiper.

The Western is common in winter on both coasts at estuaries, lagoons, and on mudflats. In some areas, huge flocks occur, wheeling in flight over the water like rippling silvery sheets, or covering the mudflats with a carpet of intense, twittering activity.

The Western is identified by its long, slightly downward-curving bill and its black legs. Winter Westerns are grayish above, and white below. Juveniles, common in August and September, have reddish and pale gray upperparts.

J F M A M J J A S O N D

Breeding adults have a reddish cap and cheeks, and dark spots down their sides.

The other peep common in winter is the Least Sandpiper (*Calidris minutilla*; 5¼–5¾" [13–14.5 cm]). Although Leasts prefer drier and marshier areas than Westerns and are more commonly seen inland, the two species often occur together. Note the Least's browner plumage and yellowish legs.

FIELD NOTES
- 6–6½" (15–16.5 cm)
- Tapered bill with faint droop at tip
- Often has orange-red tinge along shoulders
- ▲ Difficult to distinguish from other small sandpipers
- Scrape in ground, lined with grass
- 4; buff marked with browns

Adult (breeding plumage)

Laughing Gull

Larus atricilla

The Laughing Gull is common along the Atlantic and Gulf coasts, where it occurs on beaches, at estuaries, and in fields. For a gull, it is at the small end of medium-sized, and is termed a "three-year gull"—it molts into its adult plumage in three years (see p. 268).

Characteristic features of the adult are its size, dark gray back, and the dark bill that droops slightly at the tip. Breeding birds attain a blackish hood, while winter birds have a whitish head with a dusky smudge behind the eye. Juveniles are brownish above and have a brownish chest band. They attain a gray back in their first winter, and by their second winter they are similar to adults.

The closely related Franklin's Gull (*Larus pipixcan*; 14–15" [35.5– 38 cm]) migrates up the center of North America, from its winter grounds in the southern hemisphere, to nest on the northern prairies. The adult has bold white markings on its wingtips in contrast to the solid black wingtips of the Laughing Gull.

J F M A M J J A S O N D

Franklin's (breeding)

Laughing (winter)

Franklin's (winter)

1st winter Laughing

FIELD NOTES

- ■ 15–17" (38–43 cm)
- ■ Slate gray with black-tipped wings
- ■ Comparatively long slender bill, red in breeding adult
- ■ Winter adult: White head with light gray wash across nape
- ▲ Two successive immature plumages
- 🪹 Scrape in ground, built up with seaweed
- ⬭ 3–4; olive marked with browns

281

Herring Gull

Larus argentatus

The Herring Gull is a large, four-year gull (see p. 268) common on the coast, especially the Atlantic coast, as well as at lakes and reservoirs across much of North America. You'll see it feeding at fishing harbors and on beaches, as well as at garbage dumps and in ploughed fields away from the coast. In the afternoons, watch for birds flying inland to bathe in fresh water. Later in the day a steady procession of birds flying toward their communal roosts is a common sight.

spot

J F M A M J J A S O N D

The adult Herring Gull is distinguished by its large size, pale gray back, black wingtips, and pink legs; note also that its bill has a red spot near the tip. Like other large white-headed gulls, winter adults have extensive dusky mottling on their head and chest. First-year birds are mottled brownish and have a blackish bill. They attain a pale gray back in their second year. In their third year they look similar to adults but usually have some black near the bill tip, less white on the wingtips, and some black still in the tail.

FIELD NOTES
- 22–27" (56–69 cm)
- Pinkish legs
- Yellow bill with red spot on lower mandible
- Black wingtips with white spots
- ▲ Intricate series of three immature plumages
- Scrape in ground built up with weeds
- 2–3; pale bluish to brownish, with dark markings

2nd winter

1st winter

Adult (winter plumage)

Ring-billed Gull

Larus delawarensis

Found throughout much of North America—on beaches, estuaries, inland lakes, reservoirs, and even supermarket parking lots—the Ring-billed Gull is a medium-sized, three-year gull (see p. 268). This bird is often quite tame and will beg and scavenge at picnic tables and on beaches.

J F M A M J J A S O N D

The adult is distinctive, with its pale, silvery gray back, yellow bill with a black ring, and greenish yellow legs. Like virtually all juvenile gulls, the young Ring-billed is overall mottled brownish. In its first winter it attains a gray back, and the legs and black-tipped bill are pale pinkish. By its second winter the immature looks similar to the adult but lacks the bold white spots in the wingtips and usually shows some black in the tail. Non-breeding immatures remain on coasts away from the nesting range.

adult

Close up, the immatures look like immature Herring Gulls (p. 248), but note the Ring-billed's smaller and lighter-looking bill, and smaller overall size.

FIELD NOTES

- 17–20" (43–51 cm)
- Yellow bill with narrow black band
- Greenish yellow legs
- ▲ Two successive immature plumages
- Scrape in ground, built up with grass
- 2–4; buff marked with browns

immature (1st winter)

283

Adult (breeding plumage)

Western Gull

Larus occidentalis

Found along much of the Pacific coast throughout the year, the Western Gull is a large, four-year gull (see p. 268). The adult has pink legs and a dark gray back (always obviously darker than that of the Herring Gull). The plumage stages from juvenile to adult parallel those of the Herring Gull (p. 282).

In the Pacific northwest, the Western is replaced by the closely related Glaucous-winged Gull (*Larus glaucescens*; 22–28" [56–71 cm]), which in winter occurs south along the Pacific coast to California. The adult Glaucous-winged has pink legs, a pale gray back, and gray, not black, wingtips; the immature always has paler wingtips than the Western.

In some areas, especially along the coast of northern Washington state, Western and Glaucous-winged gulls hybridize extensively at mixed colonies. Not surprisingly, some ornithologists consider these two large gulls to be a single species.

J F M A M J J A S O N D

Glaucous-winged adult

Glaucous-winged (1st winter)

Western (1st winter)

FIELD NOTES

- ■ 21–26" (53.5–66 cm)
- ■ Slate gray mantle and upperwings
- ■ Pink legs
- ▲ Three successive immature plumages
- ▲ Hybridizes with Glaucous-winged Gull
- Shallow scrape built up with weeds and grass
- 1–5; buff to pale gray, with dark markings

Adult (breeding plumage)

Great Black-backed Gull

Larus marinus

The largest gull in the world, the Great Black-backed Gull is a voracious feeder and readily eats fairly large young ducks and other birds, which it can swallow whole in a few gulps. The Great Black-back inhabits the harbors, beaches, and rocky coasts of the northeast. It is expanding its breeding range south, and in winter it is occasionally seen on the Gulf coast. Some birds can be found year-round on the Great Lakes.

This is a four-year gull (see p. 268), readily identified by its large size and massive bill. Among the common, large eastern gulls, the adult's black back is distinctive. The first-year bird looks like other immature large gulls, but note that compared with a young Herring Gull (p. 282) its upperparts are more neatly

checkered, its tail has a black band of wavy lines rather than a solid dark band, and its head often looks whiter. The second-year bird has dark gray feathers on its back.

J F M A M J J A S O N D

with prey

FIELD NOTES

■ 25–31" (63.5–79 cm)

■ Very large (bigger than most raptors)

■ Large, stout yellow bill with red spot on lower mandible

▲ Three successive immature plumages

🪺 Scrape in ground, built up with seaweed

🥚 1–4; olive marked with browns

1st year

2nd year

3rd year

285

Adult (breeding plumage)

Caspian Tern

Sterna caspia

A deep, throaty, slightly scratchy *rrah* call often draws attention to an adult Caspian Tern flying overhead. This is the largest tern, about the size of a medium-sized gull, and is readily identified by its stout, carrot-red bill, black cap, and the large dark patch under each wingtip, visible when the bird is in flight.

J F M A M J J A S O N D

Caspian Terns are locally common in summer at beaches and coastal lagoons, as well as at lakes and along inland rivers. In late summer, you may see juveniles accompanying their parents on migration, following after them and begging with high-pitched whistles that are quite different from the adult's deep call.

The slightly smaller Royal Tern (*Sterna maxima*; 17–19" [43–48 cm]) is common on the southeast coast and also occurs on the coast of southern California. It has a stout, bright-orange bill and lacks the Caspian's big dark patch under the wingtips. For much of the year, Royal Terns have a large white forehead patch; on the Caspian this area is streaked dark gray and white.

Royal Tern
(winter)

Caspian Tern
(winter)

FIELD NOTES
- 20–22" (51–56 cm)
- Large, gull-like
- Long, stout red bill
- Scrape in sand, often lined with grass
- 1–4; buff, marked with browns

Caspian
(summer)

Royal
(summer)

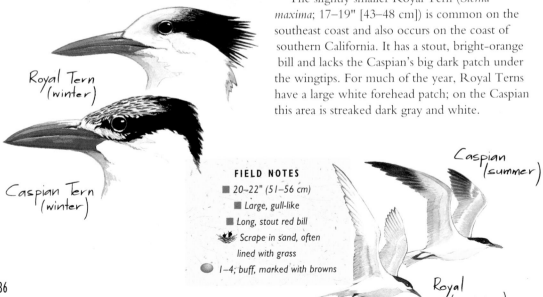

Forster's Tern

Sterna forsteri

The Forster's Tern nests at interior lakes and marshes, as well as along the Atlantic and Gulf coasts. It is the only tern commonly seen in winter at lagoons and estuaries along both coasts—most species migrate south to Mexico or beyond. In winter and immature plumages, when the bill is black, the bold, black mask is a field mark. Breeding birds have an orangey red bill with an extensive black tip. In most plumages, the pale silvery upper surface of the wings is a good field mark.

The similar Common Tern (*Sterna hirundo*; 11½–13½" [29–34 cm]) nests along the northeast coast as well as at lakes in the northern interior and is a common migrant along both coasts. Breeding Commons

have a red bill with a small black tip, and lack the silvery upperwings of the Forster's. Immatures and winter adults have dark bills. Unlike the Forster's, their dark mask extends around the back of the head in a partial cap, and, when at rest, they show a dark bar along the shoulder.

J F M A M J J A S O N D

FIELD NOTES

- 12½–17" (31.5–43 cm)
- Summer: Black cap; orange-red bill and legs; pale upperwings, lacking noticeable markings
- ▲ In winter difficult to distinguish from Arctic and Common Terns, but normally only Forster's present in winter in US
- On floating raft of reeds, or scrape in ground
- 2–5; buff marked with browns

Common (summer)

Forster's (summer)

Forster's Tern (winter)

287

Adult (breeding plumage)

Common Murre

Uria aalge

Alcids are heavy-bodied, small-winged pelagic birds, 20 species of which occur in North America, most of them in the Pacific Ocean. The Common Murre is the most widespread member of this family. Murres nest in large colonies on rocky headlands and offshore islands and spend the winter at sea. Away from colonies, they are most often seen flying fast and low over the sea, or swimming singly or in loose groups in inshore waters, where they dive for fish.

Overall, Common Murres are similar to small loons but are stockier and shorter-necked. The summer adult has a dark head and neck while the immature and winter adult have a white face and neck with a dark stripe below the eye. The males accompany the young after they fledge, and adult-juvenile "pairs" are a common sight in late summer.

| J | F | M | A | M | J | J | A | S | O | N | D |

The other auk most commonly seen off the west coast is the Pigeon Guillemot (*Cepphus columba*; 13–14" [33–35.5 cm]) which stays close to land throughout the year. Summer birds are all-black with a white wing patch; winter birds and juveniles are peppered black and white, with a less conspicuous white wingpatch.

juvenile

adult

FIELD NOTES
- ■ 16–17" (40.5–43 cm)
- ■ Brownish black above, white below
- ▲ Thick-billed Murre (far north) larger and blacker with stouter bill; white underparts rise to sharp point on throat (straight across in Common Murre)
- ▲ Winter birds difficult to distinguish
- ✹ Bare cliff ledge
- ● I; white to brown, marked with dark browns

288

Pigeon Guillemot (summer)

Deserts

BIRDING *in* DESERTS

The extremely harsh climate and localized vegetation of deserts support a specialized and distinctive community of bird species, many of which seldom occur in any other type of habitat.

Woodland and wetland birds move around the continent enough for you to have some hope of seeing many of them, at least as vagrants or casual visitors, in your local marsh or woodlot. To see certain bird species you have to go to the desert. Most birders who don't live in the southwest will therefore, sooner or later, want to travel to desert country to see this particular avifauna for themselves.

Deserts have been aptly described as very cold places where the sun is very hot. Chilly nights may be followed by noon-time temperatures approaching 100° Fahrenheit (38° Celsius). Being out and about early is important, particularly in spring and summer, as most desert birds suspend their activities through the heat of the day. By mid-morning, birds that have been active earlier seem to melt into their surroundings, and can be difficult to locate.

As in woodlands and grasslands, finding birds by song is therefore important. Because vegetation is sparse, territories can be large and many birds, such as thrashers, have songs that carry long distances. Limited vegetation usually means you can walk in a fairly direct line towards a singing bird, but always be aware of where the trail is and where you parked your car.

WHERE TO LOOK

Keep scanning the skies. A vulture or hawk soaring high in the air may be looking for lunch—but the bird will also be a good deal cooler up there than it is on the ground.

Keep an eye open for water, a scarce commodity in deserts. An intermittent stream or a small pool with shade trees can be a really active spot for birds throughout the heat of the day, and from the birder's point of view it sure beats walking around under the blazing sun and not seeing anything.

DESERT GEAR

A wide-brimmed hat or baseball cap not only protects you from the sun, but by shading your face it makes spotting birds in the harsh glare just that little bit easier. An effective sunscreen is very important, and remember to protect the back of your neck. A water-bottle hooked to your belt or a couple of soft drinks slung into a knapsack is by no means a bad idea either.

SOUTHWESTERN DESERTS
combine spectacular scenery (above) and exotic birds such as the Roadrunner (right) in a memorable experience for visiting birders.

290

Desert birds have a way of leading you on, and you may well find yourself much farther away from your car than you intended to be!

If you happen to live in, or do most of your birding in, a desert area, this may influence your choice of binoculars (p. 112). In the deep shade of woodland or forest, wide angles and big, bright images are important, both for locating the bird in the field of view and enjoying the image when you have it. But wide angles and large images come at the cost of sizeable chunks of glass inside the binoculars, and glass is very heavy. As light is seldom a problem in desert regions during the day, you may find that binoculars with a narrower field of view and less magnification will deliver the kind of image you are comfortable with, and they will be easier to carry around.

DESERT BIRDS *include the Cactus Wren (right), and the Gambel's Quail (below left). Many desert species use saguaros (below) as sources of food and nesting sites.*

HOT SPOTS *When birding in deserts (above), make sure you protect yourself from the frequently fierce sun by wearing a hat and applying an effective sunscreen.*

California Quail

Callipepla californica

The crowing *ka KA-kwah* or *chi CA-go* of the California Quail is a familiar sound throughout much of that state. These attractive, plump birds are common in chaparral; scrub and open woodland; desert edges; and in suburban areas, where they will come to seed put out in gardens. In the absence of introduced predators, such as feral cats, they can become quite tame. In wilder areas you may see them as they flush up in a twittering whir of wings from close-by in the brush.

J F M A M J J A S O N D

Through much of the year, California Quail occur in groups, or coveys, of 10 to 20 or more birds. In spring, these break up into pairs and the males give their crowing song from fence posts and atop bushes.

The closely related Gambel's Quail (*Callipepla gambelii*; 9½–10½" [24–26.5 cm]) is found only in deserts of the interior southwest, from southeastern California to western Texas. It looks and sounds like the California Quail but is a little paler and grayer and has chestnut sides and a creamy belly. The two species seldom occur together.

FIELD NOTES
- 9–10" (23–25.5 cm)
- Black forward-tilted head plume
- Brown flanks, streaked white
- Prominent black scales on belly
- ▲ Gambel's Quail (southwest) has chestnut flanks
- Scrape in ground, lined with leaves and grass
- 6–17; cream, spotted with browns

Adult

White-winged Dove

Zenaida asiatica

Common in summer in the southern deserts, especially alongside streams, White-winged Doves are often found nesting in large colonies. Around these colonies the White-winged's display flight can be a common sight: the bird climbs up with clapping wingbeats, then glides back down again.

nest

On hot summer days this dove's slightly burry cooing *who koo-koo-koo* or *Who cooks-for you?* call can be heard almost continually, even when many birds are silent. A longer, more complex series of moaning coos that slows toward the end of the song may also be heard. In winter, most White-winged Doves migrate south to warmer latitudes in Mexico.

J F M A M J J A S O N D

Like Mourning Doves in open habitats, White-winged Doves may fly long distances each day to drink from the nearest creek or pool. In flight, the bold white band on their wings is a striking field mark. Their tail is shorter and broader than the Mourning Dove's tail and has bold white corners, easily seen as the bird lands or takes off.

White-winged Dove

Mourning Dove

FIELD NOTES
- 10½–12" (26.5–30.5 cm)
- Large white wing patches
- Platform of twigs in bush or tree
- 1–4; creamy white

293

Greater Roadrunner

Geococcyx californianus

This large, ground-dwelling cuckoo is so unmistakable that it has even found its way into the world of cartoons. Many people who know the cartoon character are surprised to learn that such a bird really exists! Although typical of the southwestern deserts, Roadrunners also occur in open woodland, chaparral, and farmland where they run after snakes, lizards, and rodents, which they dispatch with their stout, pointed bills.

J F M A M J J A S O N D

Most people encounter a Roadrunner by chance as it runs along or across a road. If you set out to track down a Roadrunner, you may find it quite a challenge. Listen for their low, moaning, slightly dove-like "song" of five to eight coos that descends from high to low pitch, or scan the tops of bushes, fence posts, or rocks early in the day when Roadrunners perch up high to sunbathe.

The male and female look alike, and the young can be told by the gray, rather than blue and red, naked facial skin. If you see a Roadrunner fly, note the bold band of white across the wing and the long tail with bold white spots at the feather tips.

sunbathing

FIELD NOTES

- 20–24" (51–61 cm)
- *Unmistakable*
- *Platform of sticks in low tree or cactus*
- *2–6; chalky white*

Roadrunner and rattler

294

Adult male

Anna's Hummingbird

Calypte anna

The wiry, high-pitched, often prolonged warble of the Anna's Hummingbird is a common sound in chaparral and other scrub, and in suburban parks and gardens. This song makes the Anna's an exception among North American hummingbirds, as no other North American hummer sings. In the tropics, however, most hummers sing, so it is really the North

J F M A M J J A S O N D

American species, which use display flights instead of song to attract mates, that are in the minority. The Anna's also uses a display flight, during which the male makes steep dives from high in the air. The male is identified by his iridescent reddish gorget (throat patch) and forecrown.

Anna's ♀

With the planting of flowering trees beside roads and houses in the desert, the breeding range of the Anna's has recently expanded into southern Arizona. (See also p.98.)

In the deserts of southern California and Arizona you'll also find the closely related Costa's Hummingbird (*Calypte costae*; 3–3½" [7.5–9 cm]). The male has an elongated purple gorget (throat patch) and forecrown and can often be found by tracking down the very high-pitched, thin, whining whistle that he gives while making high oval loops in his display flight. Females of both Anna's and Costa's look like females of other small hummingbirds and even experts have difficulty telling them all apart.

Costa's ♂

FIELD NOTES

■ 3½–4" (9–10 cm)

■ Male: Rose-red head and throat

▲ Female very difficult to distinguish from Black-chinned and Costa's, but is larger, usually has darker, grayer breast, and streaks of rose-red on throat

❀ Cup of lichens, spiders' silk, plant down

● 2; white

295

Adult

Scrub Jay

Aphelocoma coeulescens

Scrub Jays are common in chaparral and suburban areas of California, and in arid scrublands of the interior west. Usually you'll find them singly or in pairs, often perching conspicuously on roadside wires or atop bushes. From their perches they keep an eye out for lizards and insects which they then fly down to seize. They're also notorious nest raiders, pouncing on the eggs or nestlings of many songbirds.

An isolated population of Scrub Jays, sometimes considered a separate species, exists in central

J F M A M J J A S O N D

Florida. These Florida Scrub Jays are renowned for being cooperative breeders, a group of birds, usually related, helping to raise the brood of the one nesting pair in the group.

Male and female Scrub Jays look alike. The juvenile has duskier, less blue, upperparts which bear only a trace of the adult's dark mask.

stealing eggs

on roadside wires

FIELD NOTES

- 11–13" (28–33 cm)
- Blue head, lacking crest
- Grayish or brownish back
- Streaked blue-gray chest band
- Bulky cup of sticks in bush or tree
- 2–7; bluish green, marked with browns and greens

Bushtit

Psaltriparus minimus

A tiny, active, fluffy ball of feathers with a long tail, the Bushtit is common in chaparral, open woodland, and suburban parks and gardens. It is usually detected by following up an excited-sounding, high-pitched twittering. As often as not, you'll then find not one Bushtit but a flock of 10 to 25 or more birds that feed in an acrobatic, chickadee-like manner, swinging from foliage to pick under leaves and in spider's webs. Flocks tend to feed in a tree or bush for a while and then move on, flying across a trail or other open area, allowing the observer to count just how many birds are creating all that twittering fuss.

Males have dark eyes and females have pale eyes. Coastal Bushtits have a brownish cap while interior birds have a grayish cap. Some male birds in West Texas and southern Arizona have black cheeks.

The Verdin (*Auriparus flaviceps*; 4–4¼" [10–11 cm]) is a superficially similar bird of the southern deserts. Usually it occurs singly or in pairs, and it is identified by its yellow head. The young Verdin, however, is overall pale grayish and is told from the longer-tailed Bushtit by its sharply pointed (not small and stubby) bill.

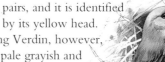

Verdin

nest

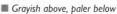

FIELD NOTES

- 4¼–4½" (11–11.5 cm)
- Tiny, plain, strongly gregarious
- Grayish above, paler below
- Brown cap (coastal birds) or gray cap (interior birds)
- Gourd-shaped hanging pouch with entrance hole near top
- 5–13; white

Bushtit ♀

Black-cheeked form ♂

Cactus Wren

Campylorhynchus brunneicapillus

I n the southern deserts, throughout the year and at any time of day, a loud, gruff, prolonged chattering *grru grru grru…* or *cha-cha-cha…* can be heard. This is the sound of the Cactus Wren, the largest North American wren and an exception in a family of small, somewhat skulking birds typified by the House Wren (page 157).

| J | F | M | A | M | J | J | A | S | O | N | D |

Cactus Wrens tend to be conspicuous and are found in pairs or small groups, foraging in cacti and small bushes. Sometimes they feed on the ground, where they dig like thrashers in the sand with their bills. They sing from a prominent perch atop a bush or post and build conspicuous, bulky, domed nests of sticks, typically in a cactus. Each Cactus Wren builds several such nests— one for the eggs and the others for sleeping in. These birds also occur in brush alongside rivers and streams, and in residential areas where they may nest in man-made structures.

The juvenile Cactus Wren lacks the adult's bold patch of black blotches on the chest, and its underparts are buffy white with evenly spaced fine dusky spots.

Cactus Wren nest

FIELD NOTES

- 7–7½" (18–19 cm)
- Strongly barred wings and tail
- Conspicuous white eyebrow
- Bulky dome of sticks in cactus or bush
- 3–7; cream speckled with browns

juvenile

Adult

Rock Wren

Salpinctes obsoletus

Rock Wrens, as the name suggests, are found in rocky areas, from steep-walled canyons to broken, rocky and stony slopes, and even at times on sea cliffs. Your first encounter with one may be hearing its bright, springy *ch-reer* call or its song: a varied series of buzzes, trills, chips, and whistles, each usually repeated a few times, suggesting a quiet mockingbird song. This will lead to what is, at first sight a small, rather plain bird which typically bobs or hops over the rocks. A closer view will reveal subtly attractive plumage, with fine silvery flecks on the upperparts and fine dusky streaks on the underparts. The most distinctive feature is the Rock Wren's fairly long tail, with a blackish subterminal band and pale cinnamon tail corners.

J F M A M J J A S O N D

Often in the same habitat, particularly on cliffs and in canyons, you'll come across the Canyon Wren (*Catherpes mexicanus*; 5–5½" [12.5–14 cm]) whose presence is also most often given away by its call— a springy, nasal *bzeeihr*—or by its song—a beautiful, descending series of whistles that cascades from canyon walls but can be hard to trace. The bright white bib and orange-red tail of this handsome bird are good field marks.

cocked tail

FIELD NOTES

- 5¼–5¾" (13–14.5 cm)
- Grayish above
- Cinnamon rump and tail
- Very pale underparts
- Faintly streaked chest
- Cup of grass in burrow or rock crevice
- 4–10; white flecked with browns

Canyon Wren

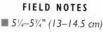

299

Adult

Curve-billed Thrasher

Toxostoma curvirostre

The Curve-billed Thrasher is a common and relatively conspicuous thrasher found in deserts, brushy riverside washes, and residential areas of the southwest. It is often seen perched on cacti or posts by the roadside, or flying low between bushes or across the road. As it lands and fans its tail, note the pale tips to the tail corners.

Like many birds, Curve-billed Thrashers are often heard before they are seen: listen for a bright, emphatic *whit whuit!* or *whit whuit whuit* call, and a varied, rich to slightly scratchy warbling song that may be prolonged and often includes repetition of phrases. The song carries a long way and often you'll be able to spot the bird atop a cactus or other prominent perch from quite far off.

Good field marks of the Curve-billed Thrasher are the all-black bill which usually appears downward-curving; the bright orange eyes; and the diffuse dusky mottling, or spotting, on the chest. Young birds look similar to adults but their eyes are duller and their bill can be notably shorter and barely curved.

J F M A M J J A S O N D

FIELD NOTES

- 10–11" (25.5–28 cm)
- Mottled chest
- Moderately long, all-dark, strongly curved bill
- Bulky cup of twigs and grass in cactus or bush
- 2–4; pale bluish green, spotted with browns

adult

juvenile

Phainopepla

Phainopepla nitens

This attractive crested bird, whose name means "shining robe", is a member of a small family of birds found from the US southwest (one species) to Central America (three species). Members of this family all have "silky" plumage (hence the common name of the family), and are closely related to the waxwings (p. 160).

Phainopeplas are most often seen perched prominently atop bushes and trees, or flying over open areas with a weak, jerky flight, which reveals the male's striking white wingpatches. Overall, males are black and females are gray.

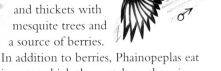

J F M A M J J A S O N D

The best places to look for Phainopeplas are desert washes and thickets with mesquite trees and a source of berries. In addition to berries, Phainopeplas eat insects, which they catch on the wing.

Phainopeplas are not particularly vocal, but their mellow *whiut?* call is distinctive and may help locate them. Their song is a short, quiet warble that does not attract attention. Juveniles resemble females; in their first summer males can be blotched black and gray.

FIELD NOTES
- 6¾–7¾" (17–19.5 cm)
- Small spiky crest and long tail
- Red eyes
- Male: Black, with white wingpatch noticeable only in flight
- Female: Plain gray
- Cup of fine plant material saddled in tree
- 2–4; whitish marked with browns

Pyrrhuloxia

Cardinalis sinuatus

The name Pyrrhuloxia derives from two Greek words—*pyrrhos*, meaning "flame-colored", and *loxos*, meaning "slanted"—which allude to the bird's pinkish red plumage and curved, parrot-like bill. The Pyrrhuloxia inhabits thorny desert washes, agricultural land with brushy hedges, suburban areas, and thickets. It resembles the Northern Cardinal (p. 162) and its song of loud, rich whistles, given from a prominent perch atop a tree or from a phone wire, sounds like the song of the Cardinal. In fact, where these two closely related species occur together it can be very difficult to identify them by their songs. If not singing, the Pyrrhuloxia can be hard to find: listen for a slightly metallic, Cardinal-like *tik*

J F M A M J J A S O N D

and a scratching sound in the leaf litter that may give away its presence.

Pyrrhuloxias sometimes form small flocks in winter when, like Northern Cardinals, they visit garden birdfeeders. The Pyrrhuloxia is a distinctive bird, grayer than the female Cardinal and with a yellowish bill and spikier crest. As with the Cardinal, the juvenile resembles the female but has a grayish bill.

♀

♂

♂ Cardinal

FIELD NOTES

- 7½–8½" (19–21.5 cm)
- Short, deep, arched bill
- Cup of twigs and grass in bush
- 2–5; greenish white, marked with browns

Black-throated Sparrow

Amphispiza bilineata

The Black-throated Sparrow is an attractive sparrow found in rocky deserts with cacti and low bushes—habitats often shared with the Cactus Wren (p. 298) and the Verdin (p. 297). It is best found by tuning into its high-pitched, thin, tinkling calls. On tracking these calls down, you'll find the birds running on the ground with their tails cocked, or flying low from bush to bush. Alternatively, if you make a "spishing" sound (see p. 123) this will often bring the birds into sight as they pop up and look about to see where the sound came from.

The Black-throated's song is a high-pitched warble with intermittent trills, normally given from a low bush.

In sandier deserts with sagebrush, and also in chaparral, you'll find the closely related Sage Sparrow (*Amphispiza belli*; 5½–6¼" [14–16 cm]) which is similar to the Black-throated in its calls and behavior. Its song is a jangling or tinkling warble. Sage Sparrows of California's chaparral are notably darker than the paler, sandier-colored birds of the Great Basin sagebrush flats.

Juveniles of these two species lack the adult's bold markings, and both have fine dusky streaks on their pale chests. Note that the Black-throated has a long, bold, whitish eyebrow while the Sage has a short whitish brow mostly forward of the eye.

J F M A M J J A S O N D

Sage Sparrow juvenile

Black-throated juvenile

Sage ♂

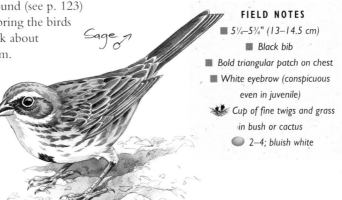

FIELD NOTES
- 5¼–5¾" (13–14.5 cm)
- Black bib
- Bold triangular patch on chest
- White eyebrow (conspicuous even in juvenile)
- Cup of fine twigs and grass in bush or cactus
- 2–4; bluish white

303

Everybody needs beauty as well as bread,

places to play in and pray in, where Nature may heal

and cheer and give strength to body and soul alike.

JOHN MUIR (1838–1914),
Scottish-born American naturalist and writer

CHAPTER EIGHT

The BACKYARD
HABITAT

THE SIX REGIONS

Gardening climates and distribution patterns of natural vegetation have determined our regional divisions.

The native plants in The Backyard Habitat have been grouped into six regions within the United States and Canada. These regions have been established based upon distribution patterns of the natural vegetation, combined with the gardening climates that distinguish various parts of the continent. Thus, for instance, the long, relatively rainless summers of the West Coast are distinct from the higher elevation arid regions of the Mountains and Basins.

Each region opens with a double-page artist's impression of a habitat garden showing typical plants and the visitors they are likely to attract.

Concluding each regional group of plants is a list of an additional 20 plants that are good choices for a regional habitat garden; included in this list will be a few plants that are not native to the region, but are well-adapted, well-behaved (non-invasive), and are attractive to wildlife.

A small version of the regional map is reproduced for each species featured in The Backyard Habitat. The map shows in green those regions in which the plant can be found growing natively. Any other regions in which it might be expected to be easily cultivated are in orange. Be aware that each species is likely to have a natural range much smaller than the entire region or regions shown, particularly in those regions where there is a wide range in elevation, as in the Mountains and Basins. Plants will be found growing naturally where conditions are most suitable for their growth. For example, water lovers will be found in the arid west, but only where there is a dependable supply of water, as along a stream. The paper birch and the claretcup cactus are both adapted to the West Coast region, though neither is native there. However, they will not grow together; the birch needing the cool summers of the north, while the cactus prefers the warm winters of the south. It is always best to check the regional map, the hardiness zones, and the water needs to determine if a particular plant will work in your garden.

PLANT CHOICES

The plants discussed in The Backyard Habitat have been chosen to give an appropriate representation of plants native to each region. In the Northeast and Southeast, where forests are the dominant natural climax vegetation type, trees are presented in greater numbers than in the Prairies or Desert Southwest, where native trees are relatively few and climax vegetation is dominated by grasses or shrubs.

PURPLE CONEFLOWER (Echinacea purpurea) *(top); the distinctive giant swallowtail butterfly (above); natural desert garden features mesquite, penstemons, and verbena (right).*

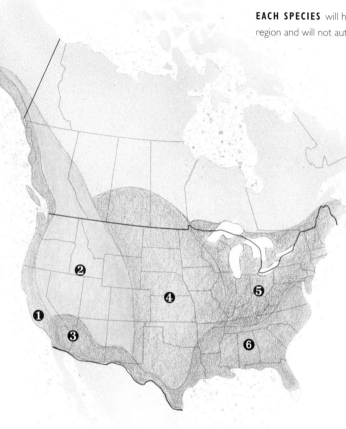

EACH SPECIES will have a natural range within its specific region and will not automatically cover that entire region.

In all regions, a broad selection of plant types has been included to serve the needs of those starting a new garden or adding to existing gardens.

Gardeners with any type of garden, be it big or small, damp or dry, sunny or shady, should be able to find plants that suit their circumstances and will attract wildlife to the garden.

KNOW YOUR REGION

The West Coast is a narrow band noted for dryer summers and wetter winters.

The Mountains and Basins include the "cold desert" of the Great Basin states and the adjoining, relatively arid, mountains from the Rockies to the eastern Sierra Nevadas and Cascades.

The Desert Southwest is limited to the warmer Mojave, Sonora, and Chihuahua Deserts to the south.

The Prairies follow the original distribution of the grasslands of the Great Plains.

The Northeast includes the forests and meadows of colder portions of the eastern states.

The Southeast represents the hot, humid, and relatively low-lying lands of the eastern states and the Gulf Coast.

	REGIONAL KEY	
❶	*The West Coast*	*309*
❷	*Mountains and Basins*	*335*
❸	*The Desert Southwest*	*363*
❹	*The Prairies*	*385*
❺	*The Northeast*	*411*
❻	*The Southeast*	*437*

USING *the* BACKYARD HABITAT

P resented on the following pages are native plants that will attract wildlife to the natural garden. They are grouped into six regions: West Coast, Mountains and Basins, Desert Southwest, Prairies, Northeast, and Southeast. A chart at the end of each section lists 20 additional species.

The **common and scientific name** of the plant. Plants are grouped first by type and then in alphabetical order by scientific name within each group.

The **color banding** identifies each of the six regions of The Backyard Habitat.

The **family** in which the plant is placed; and its type (cacti, grass, herbaceous flower, shrub, tree, or vine).

A **photo** of the species discussed; captions are included if the text discusses more than one species.

The **map** shows the plant's native region(s) in green. Any other region(s) to which it has become adapted are shown in orange.

The **text** provides important information on the plant's flowers, foliage, and fruits, including color and season; the preferred soil and propagation method; and which visitors are attracted to the plant, for what reason, and when.

The **calendar bar** highlights the best periods for dividing, taking cuttings, transplanting, or starting seeds.

Accurate, full-color **illustrations** highlight aspects of the flower and fruit, or show visitors to the plant; the sex is noted for birds.

Asteraceae: Sunflowers ❧ Herbaceous flower

Maximilian's Sunflower

Helianthus maximiliani

M aximilian's sunflower makes a real show in the fall landscape. It blooms late, often into October, and the numerous stems lined with many bright yellow flowers create quite a display. It is named after Maximilian Alexander Philipp of Wied-Neuwied, who collected many plants on an expedition up the Missouri River in 1833 and 1834. This is a long-lived perennial that is considered native throughout the Great Plains, but it is most associated with the tallgrass prairies, where there is relatively ample moisture. In dry locations, this sunflower is much smaller than on moist sites. It has become a significant part of northern New Mexico landscaping, where it adds to the dramatic

yellow fall flowers of rabbitbrush (*Chrysothamnus* spp.), various senecios, and the wonderful blue of Bigelow's asters (*Machaeranthera bigelovii*). Maximilian's sunflower is adapted to a wide range of soils. Propagation is usually by seed.

The flowers attract numerous butterflies. Colorful lazuli buntings and white-crowned sparrows feed on the seeds, which have been grown as a source of excellent birdseed.

FIELD NOTES
- Zones 2–8
- Perennial
- 5–10' (1.5–3 m)
- Full sun
- Moderate

white-crowned sparrow

394

Quick-reference Field Notes include:
- The USDA hardiness zone range in which the plant performs best (from coldest to mildest zone).
- Annual or perennial (if the plant is herbaceous).
- Deciduous, semi-evergreen, or evergreen (if the plant is woody).
- The height of the plant.
- ☀ Sun or shade preferences of the plant.

The plant's normal water needs, once established—within its native range.
Low–little or no water beyond natural rainfall.
Medium–occasional water, especially when rainfall is lighter than normal for your area.
High–frequent water, except when rainfall is higher than normal for your area.

The West Coast

THE WEST COAST
The California Dry-summer Garden

The West Coast is comprised of a long region from the crest of the Sierra Nevada and Cascade ranges, in the east, to the Pacific Ocean, in the west, and from the border with Baja California, in the south, to the coastline of Alaska, to the north. Thus defined, the region embraces extremes in climate from short growing seasons with extreme winter cold, to mild, subtropical conditions with a nearly continuous growing season and little frost.

The population is concentrated in the milder coastal zones that experience relatively minor temperature fluctuations throughout the year. The greatest concentration of people is, in fact, in the Mediterranean climate of California, where mild winters and springs represent the rainy season; and dry, warm to hot summers, the drought season.

Xeriscape is the key word, meaning a garden that needs little or no supplemental water. California xeriscape gardens feature a multitude of small trees and flowering shrubs that enliven the scene in spring and attract a wide array of colorful pollinators—honey-, bumble-, and solitary native bees; wasps; hover and bee-flies; butterflies; and hummingbirds. They also offer shelter and housing to tree-dwellers.

The California garden showcases spring-flowering perennials, annuals, bulbs, and native bunchgrasses, which are important to pollinators through a long and varied spring, starting in late February and continuing to early June. This is followed by a quiet time, when many flowers die back to underground roots, and perennial grasses provide texture and color with their leaves. Seeds and seedpods attract various wildlife, such as the many kinds of seed-eating birds and forest mammals, including squirrels and chipmunks. Grasses also provide nesting sites for ground-dwelling birds.

Most shrubs are evergreen but grow little in summer. Some offer colorful, fleshy fruits in summer and fall, which are irresistible to fruit-feeding birds and small mammals. Shrub foliage is also attractive to deer, and it may be necessary to take protective measures, or the growth of the plant will be jeopardized.

A small pond can serve as a precious water supply. Ponds are places of quiet beauty; a periphery for wildflowers that prefer to have wet "feet"; and a welcome source of sustenance to birds, butterflies, and small mammals. They are effective in attracting wildlife to the garden during the day as well as night.

Twining brodiaea (*Dichelostemma volubile*)

Brodiaeas

Brodiaea, Dichelostemma, and Triteleia *spp.*

Easily adapted to summer-dry gardens, these western natives grow from bulb-like corms, and multiply readily by means of cormlets. Their colorful flowers appear through the spring months; by selecting several kinds you can keep the floral pageant going from March to mid-June. Flowers come in a wide variety of colors: blue, purple, white, yellow, pink, and red with green (firecracker brodiaea, *Dichelostemma ida-maia*), with most being a shade of blue or purple. Seeds spill from seedpods in May to July. Each plant has two to four long, lance-shaped leaves, which often shrivel by flowering time.

Brodiaeas can be planted throughout an open meadow or border. They are best planted in drifts for floral impact. Propagation is from seed (which takes three to four years to bloom) or cormlets. Soil should be a well-drained loam, although sand is best.

The flowers lure a wide variety of beautiful butterflies, especially the spectacular swallowtails, and also bees and bee-flies. Pocket gophers are attracted to the edible corms. It is wise to take protective measures, such as placing corms in wire baskets.

J F M A M J J A S O N D

anise swallowtail butterfly

FIELD NOTES
■ Zones 7–10
(a few to zones 5–6)
■ Perennial
■ 2"–2' (5–60 cm)
☀ Most like full sun; some accept light shade
🜄 Low

Douglas Iris

Iris douglasiana

The widely spreading clumps of glossy, deep green, sword-shaped leaves look good all year. Douglas iris's rhizomatous colonies should be divided every three years or so. The delicate, orchid-like blossoms light up meadows in early to mid-spring. Flower color varies from lavender to deep blue, white to pale yellow, and flowering occurs at different times, according to locale. By selecting several forms you may extend garden bloom. Many hybrids are available, but many of these are not so drought tolerant nor as delicate as the true species. Elongated fruits ripen about three weeks after the flowers bloom.

J F M A M J J A S O N D

Propagation is by root division and seed (stratification may improve the percentage of germination). Douglas iris prefers a well-drained soil, and it is tolerant of rocky soil. Plant it throughout a meadow or toward the front of a mixed border. It will tolerate light shade. Bees, bumblebees, bee-flies, checkerspot, copper, and swallowtail butterflies, and Costa's and Anna's hummingbirds feed on the flower nectar. The rhizomes and leaves are poisonous to livestock and not attractive to deer.

seedpods

bumblebee

FIELD NOTES
■ Zones 8–10
■ Perennial (evergreen)
■ 8–18" (20–45 cm)
☀ Full sun, especially near coast; light shade elsewhere
◊ Low

313

Leopard Lily

Lilium pardalinum

The graceful stems of leopard lily emerge in spring, and slowly grow to several feet tall, carrying narrow, smooth-edged, spirally arranged leaves. The flower buds swell and open toward spring's end, revealing large, nodding (or hanging), orange or red-orange with yellow-centered blossoms, with beautifully recurved petals sprinkled with dark brown or black-purple spots, such as those on a leopard's coat. The fruits ripen about a month after flowering. Papery seedpods appear in mid- to late summer.

Propagation is by bulb scales, divisions, or seed, but the plants will take three or more years to reach blooming size.

Leopard lily prefers a well-drained soil, with the ability to retain moisture. A perfect position for leopard lily is along the periphery of a stream or pond, in light shade. Plant the bulbs between rocks.

papery seedpods

Leopard lily flowers attract beautiful pollinators, such as large butterflies (including monarchs, admirals, and mourning cloaks), sphinx moths, Allen's and Rufous hummingbirds, and bumblebees. Bulbs are eagerly sought by pocket gophers. Deer love to browse the stems and especially the flower buds, so it may be necessary to protect your plants with wire cages.

| J | F | M | A | M | J | J | A | S | O | N | D |

FIELD NOTES

- Zones 5–10
- Perennial
- 3–6' (1–1.8 m)
- ☀ Full sun near coast–filtered sun inland
- 💧 Moderate

mourning cloak butterfly

314

Lupinus arboreus

Lupines

Lupinus spp.

Lupines range from annual to perennial to small shrub, according to kind. All are characterized by their palmately compound leaves, the leaflets splayed out like the fingers on a hand. The leaves are sometimes covered with silky to felted white hairs. The showy, pea-like flowers are arranged in whorls or spirals up long spikes and come in many beautiful colors, including cream and white, with blues and purples predominating. The harlequin lupine (*L. stiversii*) is striking for its pink and bright yellow color combination. Lupine roots bear nodules that add nitrogen to the soil after the plants have died, helping to enrich impoverished soils. Lupines all lend beautiful color and form to the landscape from early spring well into summer. Choose several species to prolong your floral pageant.

Propagation is from seed, which should be soaked and/or stratified, particularly if the seed is not fresh. Lupines prefer a sandy or well-drained soil. Meadow lupine (*L. polyphyllus*) requires a moist soil. Nonwoody lupines are best massed in a meadow or border; shrubby lupines can be planted in front of taller shrubs.

| J | F | M | A | M | J | J | A | S | O | N | D |

Bumblebees and a wide variety of butterflies, such as the common hairstreak and acmon blue, are attracted to the often-fragrant lupine flowers. Over 40 different species of lupine provide larval food for the common blue butterfly.

common blue butterfly

FIELD NOTES

- ■ Zones 3–10 for perennials; 5–10 for shrubby species; all zones for annuals
- ■ Annual or perennial
- ■ Evergreen
- ■ 4"–5' (10–150 cm)
- ☀ Most need full sun
- ◗ Low–moderate

315

Scarlet Monkeyflower

Mimulus cardinalis

Scarlet monkeyflower grows along stream banks. Easy to grow, its rather floppy, flowering branches bear a long succession of scarlet-red blossoms in summer and fall. The flowers look as though they are yawning, for the two lips of the petals are spread in such a way that the lower lip is curved backward and the upper lip stands straight up. This arrangement, together with the vivid flame-colored blossoms, make it an excellent hummingbird-pollinated flower. Opposite, pale green leaves grow up the stems.

Propagation is by root division or from seed. Scarlet monkeyflower prefers sandy or well-drained soil and tolerates rocky areas.

Plant beautiful clumps by a water feature, in light shade. Old flower stalks should be cut back to promote new flowering. Seedpods follow three weeks after flowering.

Scarlet monkeyflower blooms are very attractive to Anna's, Costa's, Allen's, and Rufous hummingbirds, especially late in the summer season. Common checkerspot and buckeye butterflies lay their eggs on the leaves.

J F M A M J J A S O N D

rufous hummingbird ♂

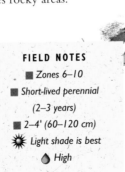

FIELD NOTES

- Zones 6–10
- Short-lived perennial (2–3 years)
- 2–4' (60–120 cm)
- Light shade is best
- High

Foothill Penstemon

Penstemon heterophyllus

O f the numerous ornamental penstemons available, foot-hill penstemon is one of the best. It grows rapidly, blooms prolifically from late spring through summer, and adapts readily to gardens. The several leafy stems carry long wands of yellow buds and showy blue to purple flowers. Nearly linear, smooth-edged, pale green to whitish-green leaves grow up the stems. Flower color may change with age and from plant to plant; sometimes, there are tints of rose-purple, at other times, clear blue. Foothill penstemon blooms longer when it receives summer water, but with a shortened lifespan. This does not matter, for the plants are easily propagated from tip cuttings (with some older, woodier growth at the base desirable), or from seed. Seedpods ripen three weeks or so after the flowers finish blooming. Foothill penstemon is excellent in rock gardens, at the front of mixed borders, or between bunchgrasses in meadows. It likes a well-drained soil, and sandy or rocky soil is fine.

A wide range of pollinators visits the flowers, including native bees, bee-flies, wasps, and hummingbirds.

| J | F | M | A | M | J | J | A | S | O | N | D |

native bee

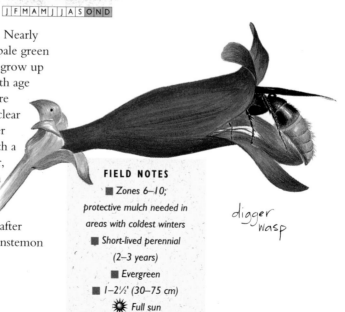

digger wasp

FIELD NOTES
- Zones 6–10; protective mulch needed in areas with coldest winters
- Short-lived perennial (2–3 years)
- Evergreen
- 1–2½' (30–75 cm)
- ☀ Full sun
- ◊ Low

317

California Fuchsia

Zauschneria spp.

California or hummingbird fuchsia is a subshrubby perennial with widely traveling roots. Its stems bear myriad, narrow, pale green to grayish-white leaves; plants may be upright and bushy or prostrate and groundcovering. The trumpet-shaped, scarlet flowers appear from midsummer through fall, depending when the first hard frosts occur. Pink and white cultivars are also available. The flowers are followed two weeks later by fruits, which are long, slender capsules that split into four segments to release numerous seeds covered with tufts of white hair. California fuchsia needs to be cut back to the ground when it goes dormant in late fall, which makes it a great companion to early spring flowers that will be finished by the time *Zauschneria* gets going.

Propagation is from seed (which may self-sow), or by root divisions. Sandy or rocky soils are ideal for California fuchsia. Plant it where there is plenty of room for it to spread, such as through a wildflower meadow.

California fuchsia's chief charm is the long succession of scarlet flowers that are irresistible to all kinds of hummingbird, providing them with a regular source of food in late summer and fall.

J F M A M J J A S O N D

Anna's Hummingbird ♂

FIELD NOTES

■ Zones 6–10

■ Perennial

■ Winter dormant

■ 6–18" (15–45 cm) tall

☀ Full sun

💧 Low

Sonoma manzanita (Arctostaphylos densiflora "Sentinel")

Manzanita

Arctostaphylos spp.

Manzanitas fill several niches in the garden because of their variety of forms. Kinnikinnick (*A. uva-ursi*) provides a drought-tolerant evergreen groundcover, while the bigberry manzanita (*A. glauca*) may grow to a small tree. Plant manzanitas in the background of the garden, with other drought-tolerant shrubs, but not in the shade of trees. Groundcover species are fine in light shade from shrubs or small trees. All manzanitas feature smooth to flaky, polished, red-purple bark and tough, evergreen leaves (which may vary from silvery white to vivid green or gray-green) Masses of nodding, urn-shaped, white or pink flowers bloom from winter through early spring, according to kind. The late spring through summer fruits resemble little apples, hence the common name (manzanita is Spanish for "little apples").

Propagation is from scarified or stratified seed. Cuttings may be taken in fall using bottom heat. Manzanita favors sandy to loamy soil, but with excellent drainage. Some species prefer acid soil.

J F M A M J J A S O N D

A wide range of animals, from bears and coyotes to fruit-eating birds (such as California Thrashers, Rufous-sided Towhees, and Fox Sparrows) are fond of the fruits; butterflies, bee-flies, flies, and small bees frequent the flowers from late winter to early spring.

winter–spring flowers

Fox Sparrow

FIELD NOTES

■ Zones 5–10, *according to species*

■ Evergreen

■ 4"–20' (10 cm–6 m)

☀ *Most want full sun (strictly coastal species prefer light shade)*

◊ *Low*

319

Salal

Gaultheria shallon

The semiprostrate to upright, zigzaggy stems of salal weave intricate shrubberies and hedges along the edge of coastal forests. They will do likewise in the garden, enlarging their territory by means of their wandering roots. The handsome, large, evergreen leaves are stiff and decorative. Modest clusters of hanging, bell-shaped, white to pale pink blossoms, with pink sepals, appear in May to July, followed in July to September by large, near-black, edible "berries".

J F M A M J J A S O N D

Propagation is by root division and seed, which should be stratified for one to two months. Well-drained acidic loams and sands, conditions as for rhododendrons, camellias, or azaleas, best suit salal. Plant salal as an informal hedge or wandering shrub along a forest border; it is best planted under conifers, such as Douglas fir (*Pseudotsuga menziesii*).

summer fruits

A wide variety of fruit-eating birds, bears, and small rodents, such as Sonoma and Townsend chipmunks, eat the fruits. Various small bees, flies, and hover flies are attracted to the flower nectar. Browsing mule deer can be a pest and you may need to take steps to protect the plant.

mule deer

320

FIELD NOTES

■ Zones 7–10

■ Evergreen

■ 1–10' (30–300 cm)

☀ Moderate–full shade

💧 Moderate–high

Toyon

Heteromeles arbutifolia

Toyon, or California holly, grows into a large shrub or small tree in well-drained soils and with hot summer temperatures. The tough, serrated, dark green leaves are attractive and a good replacement for true holly (*Ilex aquifolium*), as are the brightly hued, red-orange berries that ripen in late fall. Berries sometimes remain on the plant through winter and early spring, when they feed northward-bound migrating birds. The rounded to pyramidal clusters of tiny, whitish flowers appear at the end of spring.

Toyon is best planted at the back of a meadow or border, with other drought-tolerant shrubs, or in front of oaks. It prefers a well-drained soil. Propagation is from semihardwood cuttings (using bottom heat). Seed should be stratified for one to two months.

| J | F | M | A | M | J | J | A | S | O | N | D |

Fall to winter resident birds, such as Yellow-rumped Warblers, California Thrashers, starlings, Rufous-sided Towhees, and House Sparrows are attracted to toyon in fall. Beetles, wasps, hover flies, butterflies, and bees are attracted in early summer to the abundance of nectar in the masses of tiny blossoms.

California Thrasher ♂

FIELD NOTES
- Zones 6–10
- Evergreen
- 10–30' (3–9 m)
- Full sun–light shade
- Low

321

California Coffeeberry

Rhamnus californica

California coffeeberry is an easy to grow, densely branched shrub ranging from coastal forms with sprawling branches, which may be wind-pruned to less than a foot tall; to inland shrubs with many upright branches, which may grow to over 10' (3 m). The attractive leaves vary from deep green to a dusky, pale green according to location. Tiny, greenish-yellow, star-like blossoms are hardly noticed in late spring, but the fleshy berries add interest as they turn from green to red to deep purple in early fall.

Propagation is by layering, from hardwood cuttings and seed (which should be stratified for one to two months). California coffeeberry prefers a sandy or well-drained soil, and requires minimal water. It can be placed in front of taller shrubs in the garden, in company with smaller manzanitas and ceanothuses.

J F M A M J J A S O N D

Fruit-eating birds, such as Cedar Waxwings, robins, and Black-headed Grosbeaks, seek out the berries, and wasps, beetles, and hover flies visit the flowers to feed on their nectar. The dense branches provide cover for cottontail and other rabbits, and deer are fond of the young leaves. The pale swallowtail butterfly lays its eggs on the leaves.

fall fruits

FIELD NOTES
- Zones 5–10
- Evergreen
- 1–12' (30 cm–4 m)
- Full sun–light shade
- Low

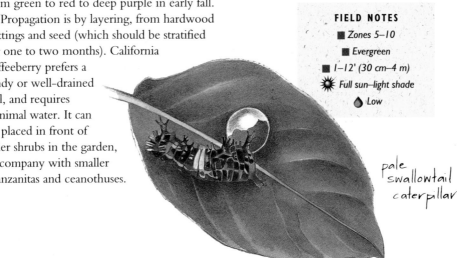

pale swallowtail caterpillar

Pink-flowering Currant

Ribes sanguineum var. glutinosum

Pink-flowering currant is a medium-sized shrub that grows rapidly to maturity in partial shade on the border of woods. Its small, pale green, maple-like leaves are sage-scented on warm days, but its best feature is the numerous trusses of hanging deep rose, pale pink, or white blossoms at winter's end. Purplish berries follow in summer.

Propagation is from cuttings in winter and early spring. It prefers a well-drained soil, but will tolerate slightly acid or neutral soil. Pink-flowering currant is ideal planted as a backdrop in a garden with light shade.

Fruit-eating birds, including Yellow-rumped Warblers, California Thrashers, House Sparrows, and starlings, and small mammals, eat the fruit in late summer and early fall, although the berries are unlikely to be their first choice when other berries are available. Colorful pollinators such as hummingbirds and bees visit the flowers for their nectar in early spring. The silenus anglewing butterfly lays its eggs on the leaves. Mule deer browse the branches, especially the new growth in early spring.

J F M A M J J A S O N D

hanging blossoms

FIELD NOTES

- ■ Zones 7–10
- ■ Deciduous
- ■ 6–12' (2–4 m)
- ☀ Best in light shade
- ◗ Low–moderate

summer fruits

323

Thimbleberry

Rubus parviflorus

Thimbleberry is a widely ranging, small to medium-sized shrub with wandering roots. Like its close sisters the black-berries and raspberries (*Rubus* spp.), it may become invasive, but forms natural, good-looking groupings and loose hedges in a suitable, spacious woodland setting. Large, pale green, downy-soft, maple-like leaves complement the single, rose-like white blossoms in May to July. Thimble-shaped, dark red berries follow in late June to September, with an exquisite taste reminiscent of raspberries.

Propagation is by root division or from seed (which must be stratified). Thimbleberry

prefers a well-drained, acid soil. Plant it along the edge of woods. It prefers a shady, garden position.

Bees, beetles, and flies visit flowers in late spring and early summer. Squirrels and fruit-eating birds, such as Swainson's and Hermit Thrushes and Black-capped Vireos, avidly seek the fruit in summer or early fall. Mule deer eat the tender new growth in early spring, so make sure you take measures to protect the plants.

J F M A M J J A S O N D

spring flower

Swainson's thrush ♂

FIELD NOTES

■ Zones 5–10

■ Deciduous

■ 4–10' (1.2–3 m)

☀ Light–fairly deep shade

◊ Low–moderate

324

Sages

Salvia spp.

The sages fill a key role in dry gardens, through their drought tolerance, late spring blooming, scented leaves, and colorful flowers. Sages range from annual thistle sage (*S. carduacea*), with elegant, ruffled, pale blue flowers, to the shrubby sages, such as white sage (*S. apiana*), with broadly elliptical, whitish leaves and tall spires of white to palest purple blossoms. All have strongly scented leaves; tiers of whorled, two-lipped blossoms; and decorative seedheads that dry on the plant. Leaf color varies from whitish to pale green or gray-green. A number of Central American species of *Salvia* have become popular garden plants across North America.

Propagation is from half-woody cuttings or seed (which should be soaked first). Sages prefer a well-drained soil; sandy to rocky is best. Plant them in the garden in full sun, as a component of a dry meadow (annual kinds), or in the middle ground next to taller shrubs (woody kinds).

Hummingbirds, bees, bumblebees, and bee-flies seek the flower nectar in spring and summer. Goldfinches, House Sparrows, and quail eat the fruits (seeds). Many sage species are considered partially deer-proof, as deer don't like the highly scented leaves.

| J | F | M | A | M | J | J | A | S | O | N | D |

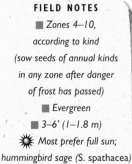

FIELD NOTES

■ Zones 4–10, according to kind (sow seeds of annual kinds in any zone after danger of frost has passed)

■ Evergreen

■ 3–6' (1–1.8 m)

☀ Most prefer full sun; hummingbird sage (S. spathacea) takes light shade

◌ Low

honeybee

325

Blue Elderberry

Sambucus mexicana

Blue elderberry is a fast-growing, graceful, large shrub or small tree. If suckers are pruned out, either one or a few main trunks may develop. The grooved bark; large leaves, which give off a strong odor when crushed; and flat-topped clusters of numerous tiny, yellowish-white blossoms distinguish blue elderberry from any other plant. The spring blossoms are fragrant up close, emitting a stronger perfume in the evening to lure night-flying insects for pollination. Strongly flavored, bluish berries follow in early summer.

J F M A M J J A S O N D

Propagation is by means of rooted suckers, semihardwood cuttings, or seed (which should be stratified for a couple of months). Elderberry prefers a well-drained soil, but a high water table is best so roots can go deep to find water under summer conditions. Plant blue elderberry in the back of the garden in a low spot if the soil drains well. Also plant it next to a water feature but not directly in soggy soils.

Long-horn beetles, sawflies, butterflies, and bees all visit the flowers in late spring to feed on their copious nectar. Many fruit-eating birds relish the ripe summer fruits, particularly Band-tailed Pigeons and House Finches.

viceroy butterfly

FIELD NOTES

■ Zones 2–10

(coldest climate may require some protection)

■ Deciduous

■ 10–45' (3–14 m)

☀ Full sun–light shade

💧 Moderate

Evergreen Huckleberry

Vaccinium ovatum

Evergreen huckleberry is a relatively slow-growing, medium-sized, compact, and handsome evergreen shrub that favors the understory of coniferous forests along the coast. The small, glossy leaves are useful for Christmas greens; the branches are laden with pale pink to white bells in mid- to late spring; and the branches carry luscious, dark purple to pale bluish berries in summer.

Plant evergreen huckleberry so that you can look up into the branches from below, as the flowers hide underneath the branches. Evergreen huckleberry is best planted along the edge of a forest or woodland as it needs shade. In the garden, plant it in the partial shade of a well-established, preferably evergreen, tree.

Propagation is from hardwood cuttings (using bottom heat), or seed (which should be stratified for a couple of months). It prefers a well-drained and acid soil.

Butterflies and several kinds of bee visit and pollinate the flowers. The delicious fruits are eaten by many birds, including Western Tanagers, White-crowned Sparrows, and Orange-crowned Warblers, as well as squirrels, chipmunks, and bears.

J F M A M J J A S O N D

Western Tanager ♂

FIELD NOTES
■ Zones 7–10
■ Evergreen
■ 4–10' (1.2–3 m)
☀ Light–medium shade
◐ Moderate

327

California Buckeye

Aesculus californica

seedpods

alifornia buckeye provides a handsome backdrop to the garden, by itself or with other small trees. It is a beautifully rounded tree with seasonal interest all year. Leafless from late summer through winter, its smooth, silvery white bark is highlighted then. The new flush of apple-green leaves is a welcome event in early spring, and candles of white to pale pinkish flowers illuminate branch tips in late May or early June. Leathery seedpods split open in fall to reveal one large, shiny brown, chestnut-like seed.

To propagate, plant fresh seed in well-drained soil in late fall to early winter. Buckeye's name derives from the resemblance of the open seedpod to a large eye. Despite their resemblance to chestnuts, buckeye seeds are deadly poisonous to humans.

Buckeye flowers attract all manner of beautiful butterflies (such as the Chalcedon checkerspot), sphinx moths, and hummingbirds. The nectar is poisonous to bees. Branches provide perches and nesting sites for birds, including Yellow-billed Cuckoos and downy Woodpeckers, although the nests are readily apparent in winter. The large seeds attract small mammals which are not affected by the toxicity.

J F M A M J J A S O N D

Chalcedon checkerspot butterfly

FIELD NOTES

- Zones 7–10
- Deciduous
- 10–30' (3–9 m)
- Full sun–very light shade
- Low–moderate

328

Madrone

Arbutus menziesii

Madrone is a sturdy evergreen tree whose crown seeks light by searching for breaks in the forest cover. A large tree, it is best planted in the background of the garden, on the level, or on a raised mound. The new bark is a striking, glossy red-orange, while the older bark crumbles into shingle-like scales. The tough, leathery leaves are silvery on their backs. White, fragrant blossoms, similar in appearance to those of lily-of-the-valley (*Convallaria majus*), appear in mid-spring. Round, red-orange, wart-covered berries appear in late fall.

This is a difficult tree to transplant, and seed should be stratified for a couple of months before planting. Plant madrone in a well-drained loam; a mildly acid soil is preferable. It may require extra water in hot, exposed situations.

The branches of madrone provide an excellent habitat for tree-nesting birds, while the crown is a good lookout post for hunting birds. Fruit-eating birds, such as Cedar Waxwings and varied thrushes, and also coyotes and squirrels, flock to the berries. Bees and bee-flies are fond of the flower nectar.

| J | F | M | A | M | J | J | A | S | O | N | D |

Varied Thrush ♂

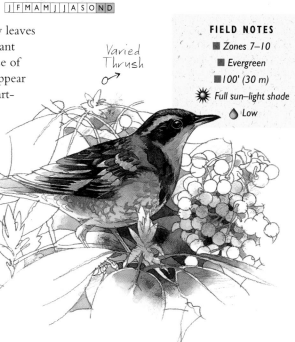

FIELD NOTES
- ◼ Zones 7–10
- ◼ Evergreen
- ◼ 100' (30 m)
- ☀ Full sun–light shade
- 💧 Low

Holly-leaf Cherry

Prunus ilicifolia

Holly-leaf cherry, or islay, grows as a dense shrub, which is prunable into a hedge, or into a small, multitrunked tree. The glossy, bright green foliage is holly-like, down to the sharply toothed leaf margins. Modest racemes of whitish flowers decorate branch tips in late spring, followed by large, plump, red-purple cherries in late summer. This shrub is ideal as a backdrop to a flower border or meadow. Plant it at the back of the garden, perhaps with other large shrubs, such as toyon (*Heteromeles arbutifolia*) and manzanitas.

Propagation is from seed (stratify briefly) or hardwood cuttings using bottom heat. Holly-leaf cherry prefers a well-drained soil; a rocky or sandy soil is suitable.

Many bees, beetles, and hover flies feed on the blossoms' nectar. Two-tailed swallowtail and Lorquin's admiral butterflies sometimes lay their eggs on the leaves. Various fruit-eating birds, such as House Finches, and small mammals, such as gray squirrels and chipmunks, relish the fruits.

J F M A M J J A S O N D

FIELD NOTES
- Zones 7–10
- Evergreen
- 50' (15 m)
- ☀ Full sun
- 💧 Low

House Finch

Douglas Fir

Pseudotsuga menziesii

Douglas fir is one of the West's truly magnificent trees. Crowns may exceed 200' (60 m) and trees may live for several hundred years. The mature bark is craggy and irregularly split; branches carry deep green, spirally arranged needles with a wonderful pine fragrance; new needles are soft and bright green. Decorative seed cones drip from branch tips, ripening from green to brown in late fall.

Propagation is from seed. Douglas fir prefers a well-drained, acid soil.

Perfect for the backdrop of a large garden, Douglas fir can be planted with compatible trees, such as madrone (*Arbutus menziesii*), tanbark oak (*Lithocarpus densiflorus*), bay-laurel (*Umbellularia californica*), and coast redwood (*Sequoia sempervirens*).

Because of Douglas fir's size, many animals shelter under its lower branches, while tree-nesting birds favor higher branches, and Osprey, eagles, and hawks perch on the tree's top to watch for prey. Bald Eagles, Band-tailed Pigeons, hummingbirds, Western-wood Peewees, and Steller's Jays nest in Douglas fir, and Ospreys nest on dead snags. Raccoons are known to nest in trunk cavities; Douglas' and gray squirrels eat the seeds. The pine white butterfly's larvae eat the needles.

J F M A M J J A S O N D

seed cone

FIELD NOTES

■ Zones 2–10; select locally grown plants for greatest adaptability

■ Evergreen

■ 50–200'+ (15–60 m)

☀ Full sun–light shade

⬧ Low–moderate

Douglas' squirrel

331

Coast Live Oak

Quercus agrifolia

The rounded canopy, large muscular trunk and primary limbs, and dense shade, typify mature coast live oaks. The leaves are glossy and evergreen and distinctive because their margins curl under, especially where leaves are subjected to bright sun.

J F M A M J J A S O N D

Sharp prickles line leaf edges. The long, dangling male catkins, reddish then becoming yellow on opening, decorate branches in early spring, while the female blossoms are tiny and seldom noticed. The fall acorns are easy to see and vary in abundance from year to year. Each acorn sits in a scaly cup and is long and pointed, often decorated with darker brown stripes.

Propagation is from seed (acorns), which should be sown when fresh. Coast live oak likes a well-drained soil. Plant this tree at the back of a garden, and allow ample room for the full development of the crown.

Great Horned Owls, Red-tailed Hawks, Scrub Jays, Bushtits, and American Robins, nest in the tree canopies. California sister, tailed copper, and California hairstreak butterflies lay their eggs on the leaves. Gall insects (midges and stingless wasps) cause the formation of diversely shaped, decorative galls on leaves, stems, and branches. Acorn and other woodpeckers, Scrub Jays, magpies, and several kinds of squirrel and chipmunk eagerly seek the acorns for food.

acorn woodpecker ♂

FIELD NOTES

- Zones 7–10
- Evergreen
- 25–50' (7.5–15 m)
- Full sun–light shade
- Low

332

California Pipevine

Aristolochia californica

California pipevine, also known as Dutchman's pipe, climbs by winding its stems around adjacent shrubs or small trees. If you train it up a tall shrub or young tree, or over a trellis, in partial shade, it will grow rapidly, quickly establishing a covering over branches and festooning them with felted, elongated, heart-shaped leaves. Vines stand out in late winter to early spring (February to early April), when the leafless stems carry the bizarre pipe-shaped, brownish, maroon, and greenish flowers with a maroon mouth. The fruits are 3" (7.5 cm) long, six-angled oval pods that ripen in early summer. The fluted seedpods are decorative in their turn by late spring.

winter–spring flower

| J | F | M | A | M | J | J | A | S | O | N | D |

Propagation is from stem cuttings in fall and winter. California pipevine likes well-drained soil, but it will accept a rocky soil. This vine is admired for its unusual flowers.

California pipevine is the exclusive food plant for the iridescent black-purple pipevine swallowtail butterfly. The adults are drawn to the vine at the time of egg laying. The flowers are pollinated by minute mycetophilid gnats, which are temporarily trapped inside the pipes.

FIELD NOTES
- Zones 7–10
- Winter deciduous
- 20' (6 m)
- Light–medium shade
- Low–moderate

pipevine swallowtail butterfly

333

Rhododendron (left); Cape honeysuckle (right)

Additional species

Plant name/flower color	Zone	Height	Visitors/attraction/season
GRASS Purple needlegrass (green, gold) *Stipa pulchra*	5–10	3–4' (90–120 cm)	birds/seeds/summer–fall
HERBACEOUS FLOWERS Wild onions (white, purple, pink) *Allium* spp.	wide range	2–12" (5–30 cm)	butterflies/flowers/spring pocket gophers/bulbs/spring
Red columbine (red–orange, yellow) *Aquilegia formosa*	7–10	2–4' (60–120 cm)	hummingbirds/flowers/ late spring and summer
Wallflowers (yellow, orange, cream) *Erysimum* spp.	5–10	1–4' (30–120 cm)	bees, butterflies/flowers/ mid-spring to early summer
California poppy (golden orange) *Eschscholzia californica*	8–10	12–18" (30–45 cm)	bees/flowers/spring
Gilia (blue, lavender, blue–violet) *Gilia* spp.	most	4–24" (10–60 cm)	bees, bumblebees, small butterflies/ flowers/mid- to late spring
Lavender (lavender, purple) *Lavandula* spp. (exotic)	7–10	2–4' (60–120 cm)	bees/flowers/late spring–summer
Hooker's evening primrose *Oenothera hookeri* (clear yellow)	most	2–8' (60–240 cm)	hummingbirds, butterflies, sphinx moths/flowers/summer
California coneflower (golden and black) *Rudbeckia californica*	7–10	3–8' (90–240 cm)	butterflies/flowers/mid- to late summer
SHRUBS Hardy fuchsia (red, purple) *Fuchsia magellanica* (exotic)	6–10	4–6' (1.2–1.8 m)	hummingbirds/flowers/all year
Island snapdragon (clear red) *Galvezia speciosa*	9–10	up to 3' (90 cm)	hummingbirds/flowers/winter–spring
Azaleas and rhododendrons (various) *Rhododendron* spp. and hybrids (exotic)	6–10	5–10' (1.5–3 m)	butterflies, hummingbirds/ flowers/late spring–summer
Fuchsia-flowered gooseberry (bright red) *Ribes speciosum*	9–10	3–6' (90–180 cm)	hummingbirds/flowers/mid-spring fruit-eating birds/berries/summer
Nootka rose (pink) *Rosa nutkana*	6–9	6' (1.8 m)	bees/flowers/spring–summer birds/fruits/fall
Snowberry (pink, white) *Symphoricarpos rivularis*	2–9	6–8' (1.8–2.4 m)	birds/fruits/winter
TREES Vine maple (red, white) *Acer circinatum*	6–9	15–25' (4.5–7.5 m)	birds/nesting/spring birds/seeds/summer–fall
Western hemlock (green) *Tsuga heterophylla*	6–9	100'+ (30 m)+	birds/seeds/fall birds/nesting/spring
California bay laurel (yellow) *Umbellularia californica*	8–10	20–50' (6–15 m)	bees/flowers/winter squirrels/fruits/fall
VINES Cape honeysuckle (orange, yellow) *Tecomaria capensis* (exotic)	9–10	8–12' (2.4–3.7 m)	hummingbirds/flowers/fall–winter
California wild grape (green) *Vitis californica*	8–10	20–30' (6–9 m)	bees/flowers/late spring birds/fruits/mid- to late fall

Mountains and Basins

MOUNTAINS AND BASINS
The Mountain Garden

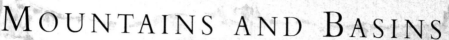

The region of the Mountains and Basins encompasses a large area of western North America between the West Coast and the Prairies, and extends from northern Arizona and New Mexico north to parts of Alaska. The major geological features are the mountain ranges—most notably, the Rockies. In between are relatively dry valleys and broad basins, such as the Great Basin of Nevada and adjoining states, which is often called a cold desert because of its low annual rainfall and cold winter temperatures. Snow is common in most areas in winter, and showers in summer, but the region is decidedly arid. Lower elevations experience intense heat in the summer, while the high elevations remain cool.

The vegetation varies from grasslands to shrub-dominated basins, to mountain slopes clothed in an open forest of needle-leaf conifers and deciduous aspens. Spring sees a grand display of wildflowers in the lowlands, while summer is the peak season for wildflowers at higher elevations. The growing season shortens as elevation increases.

Where the summers are relatively cool at the middle elevations, the mountain garden might be blessed with an existing open canopy of ponderosa pine (*Pinus ponderosa*), favored by three different species of nuthatch. On a cool north slope is a lively grove of quaking aspen (*Populus tremuloides*). In the slightly more moist soil near its base are drifts of blue Rocky Mountain columbine (*Aquilegia caerulea*), that are popular with hummingbirds. Creeping mahonia (*Mahonia repens*) carpets the ground in shadier areas beneath the trees. On the edge of a seepage, the white-flowered Saskatoon serviceberry (*Amelanchier alnifolia*) ripens its red fruits in June, providing ample food for chipmunks and birds alike. This moist area is alive in midsummer with the tall, loose spikes of fireweed (*Epilobium angustifolium*), abuzz with bees seeking the nectar.

On a dry, sunny slope, the beardlip penstemon (*Penstemon barbatus*) and the cardinal penstemon (*P. cardinalis*) attract Broad-tailed Hummingbirds, as do great drifts of scarlet gilia (*Ipomopsis aggregata*). Near the house is a small border: blanket flower (*Gaillardia aristata*) and wild white yarrow (*Achillea millefolium* var. *lanulosa*) appeal to the butterflies; wild four o'clock (*Mirabilis multiflora*) draws in the sphinx moths in the early evening; and Indian pink (*Silene laciniata*) attracts the hummingbirds.

Sideoats Grama

Bouteloua curtipendula

Sideoats grama is an attractive, long-lived bunchgrass. The seeds develop on the side of a zigzag stem and give this grass a distinctive appearance. The fall color is an attractive light brown, which is especially eye-catching when backlit by the sun. Sideoats grama is one of several grasses that make up the midgrass prairies. Color in the midgrass prairies is provided by a variety of wild flowers, such as purple prairieclover (*Petalostemon purpureum*), blanket flower (*Gaillardia aristata*), Lewis's flax (*Linum perenne* var. *lewisii*), and Mexican hat coneflower (*Ratibida columnifera*).

Sideoats grama grows in a wide range of soils. Propagate it from seed. Dry conditions favor bunchgrasses like sideoats grama, and excessive moisture may limit good growth. Wet conditions tend to favor sod-forming grasses.

Coyote, foxes, and meadowlarks are a few of the species that make their homes in midgrass meadows. Sideoats grama is also a host plant for the Dakota skipper butterfly.

| J | F | M | A | M | J | J | A | S | O | N | D |

Western Meadowlark ♂

FIELD NOTES
- Zones 3–10
- Perennial
- 1–3' (30–90 cm)
- Full sun
- Low–moderate

338

Wild White Yarrow

Achillea millefolium var. lanulosa

Wild white yarrow is a meadow wildflower with tiny flowers in flat clusters and finely divided, fragrant leaves. The flowers bloom from May to September, depending on the altitude and climate. This clump-forming plant is quite common in moderately moist areas in the ponderosa pine (*Pinus ponderosa*) forests. Nosebleed, sneezewort, knight's milfoil, bloodwort, and soldier's woundwort are a few of the names that refer to the healing nature of this plant. Some 58 different Native American groups may have used this yarrow for various medicinal treatments, and treatment of coughs, throat irritation, and bleeding were among the most common.

Wild white yarrow grows well in most soils; in fact, when there is ample moisture, this plant can sometimes spread somewhat too vigorously. Propagate it from seed or by dividing established plants.

spring-summer flowers

J F M A M J J A S O N D

Wild white yarrow is a great nectar plant, attracting a variety of butterflies, including the American copper. Deer rarely browse this plant—a very useful quality for an increasing number of gardeners—which may be because of the fragrant foliage or the taste.

American copper butterfly

FIELD NOTES

- Zones 3–9
- Perennial
- 1–2' (30–60 cm)
- ☀ Full sun or part shade
- ◊ Moderate

339

Mosquito Plant

Agastache cana

Mosquito plant is a tall wildflower with highly fragrant, very bright, pink flowers arranged in spikes. It is long-lived, and starts to bloom as early as late July and often continues into October. Both flowers and foliage bear a fragrance much like bubble gum. It is considered rare and endangered in New Mexico, where it is reported on only five sites in four counties. These sites are mountainous locations at about 5,000–6,000' (1,500–1,800 m). It also occurs in west Texas on a few sites.

J F M A M J J A S O N D

Mosquito plant is so easy to propagate from seed that it is surprising it is so rare in the wild. You can also start it easily from cuttings. It is easy to grow in most soils, though over-watering or high rainfall and high humidity are likely to cause problems. Even in semi-arid areas, it is not unusual to find a few seedlings in gardens.

White-lined sphinx moths and hummingbirds (both Rufous and Broad-tailed) are very frequent visitors. Mosquito plant is valuable for attracting hummingbirds to the garden over an extended period of time. Deer have little interest in browsing this plant. The common name refers to an alleged ability to repel mosquitoes; rubbing the leaves on skin or clothing is said to be quite effective.

Rufous ♀ Hummingbird

FIELD NOTES
- ■ Zones 5–8
- ■ Perennial
- ■ 3' (1 m)
- ☀ Full sun–part shade
- ◊ Moderate

Fireweed

Epilobium angustifolium

Fireweed, or willow-herb, is a tall wildflower with narrow leaves and showy, pink flowers in spikes. It is commonly found in disturbed areas along roads or in forest areas after either fire or logging. The flowers stand on a long, thin structure that develops into seedpods. In addition to seeds, fireweed spreads vigorously by root runners and can be invasive.

Fireweed will grow in most soils, but favors well-drained, moist situations. Propagate it from seed and from root shoots taken in spring.

Bees are attracted first to the female pollen-receptive flowers, at the bottom of the spike, which have the most nectar. They work their way up the flower spike until they encounter flowers in the male phase, where they pick up pollen before flying off to another plant in search of new pollen-receptive, nectar-rich flowers. These nectar-rich flowers make fireweed a valuable honey plant, and beekeepers have been known to search for them following forest fires or logging.

J F M A M J J A S O N D

bumblebee

fireweed seeds

FIELD NOTES

- Zones 2–9
- Perennial
- 4–5' (1.2–1.5 m)
- Full sun–full shade
- High

341

Gaillardia aristata hybrid

Blanket Flower

Gaillardia aristata

Blanket flower is a showy wildflower, often with bright red and yellow flowers, common in grasslands of the western Great Plains. The name blanket flower is a reference to the similar colors and patterns in Southwestern weaving.

J F M A M J J A S O N D

Blanket flower makes an attractive garden plant, and will bloom for a long time if the spent flowers are removed regularly. It will grow successfully in a wide range of soils, and will live longer if grown in moderately dry conditions. Propagate it from seed.

mason bee

The color contrasts in these flowers serve to attract and direct pollinators such as bees and butterflies to the nectar and pollen as quickly as possible. Not all blanket flowers have both red and yellow petals, however. Some are all yellow, with only the center being red; these blanket flowers with all-yellow petals are the sole host of a moth that exactly matches the mottled reddish centers. It was named *Schinia masoni* for John T. Mason, a Denver butterfly collector, who discovered it in 1896. The color coordination is remarkable, and the moth lives only near Boulder, Colorado.

FIELD NOTES

- Zones 3–9
- Perennial
- 2–3' (60–90 cm)
- ☀ Full sun
- ◊ Low–moderate

honeybee

342

Scarlet Gilia

Ipomopsis aggregata

Scarlet gilia is a showy wild-flower with slender trumpets of red, pink, or white flowers along a tall flower stalk. The first year following germination, a clump of lacy leaves forms close to the ground. The second year, the plant produces the familiar, tall flower stalk and brilliant flowers. By the end of the second year, seeds have been dispersed and the entire plant dies.

Scarlet gilia favors well-drained soils. Propagation is usually from seed, sown in fall or early spring so it's likely to get sufficient winter weather to allow germination. Too much rainfall and too high summer temperatures are more limiting to good growth than minimum winter temperatures. Pinching back the flower stalks will stimulate rapid regrowth, resulting in more flowers and better-quality seed.

Scarlet gilia is a classic hummingbird- and sphinx-moth-pollinated flower. Both the birds and moths are well equipped to reach into the floral tubes. The petals bend back, making entry difficult for crawling insects. In this way, the flower reserves nectar for the moths or hummingbirds. Despite these defenses, bees sometimes rob the flowers by slitting the floral tubes near the nectar. Deer will browse scarlet gilia.

J F M A M J J A S O N D

white-lined sphinx moth

FIELD NOTES

■ Zones: 3–8

■ Biennial

■ 3' (1 m)

☀ Full sun

💧 Low–moderate

343

Western Blue Flag

Iris missouriensis

Western blue flag is strikingly beautiful when it blooms during May or June. It often forms dense populations of blue flowers in meadows that are wet in spring but dry later in the season.

Western blue flag will grow in a wide range of soils. You can propagate it from seed, which is very slow; propagation is quicker by dividing the roots after blooming in July. Though it prefers plenty of water in spring, this iris will tolerate much drier conditions in summer and fall.

J F M A M J J A S O N D

bee leaving pollen

bee taking pollen

FIELD NOTES

■ Zones 2–6

■ Perennial

■ To 2' (60 cm)

☀ Full sun

◊ High–low

Bees pollinate these flowers by pushing their way between the long, upright style and sepal, or "fall", to reach the nectar near the center of the flower. In this process, they are brushed with pollen, while depositing pollen from previously visited flowers. Hummingbirds, usually considered pollination "good guys", are actually robbers of iris nectar. By probing between petals, sepals, and styles, they steal the nectar without accomplishing any pollination. Deer and most other browsers avoid all irises.

344

Wild Four o'Clock

Mirabilis multiflora

Wild, or Colorado, four o'clock is a wildflower of shrub-like proportions covered with numerous magenta flowers. There are often flowers throughout much of summer and fall. The flowers open during the late afternoon or early evening and close the following morning, unless the weather is cool and cloudy, in which case, they may remain open most of the day. This plant dies to the ground each winter.

The afternoon opening of wild four o'clock flowers offers gardeners a chance to create an interesting daily change of scenery. It has been called the immortal plant, a reference to its ability to return from the "dead" after rototilling or bulldozer activity. It will likely outlive the grandchildren of the gardener who plants it in a well-drained, sandy location.

Propagate it from seed or by digging small pieces of root in fall. Sow seed in spring or fall and transplant root pieces in fall. High rainfall and snowfall are more likely to limit good growth than minimum winter temperatures.

Plants can develop and bloom fully with no summer rainfall, drawing on moisture stored in the roots.

Wild four o'clock is pollinated by dawn-to-dusk insects, mainly sphinx moths. Some plants are reported to produce a musky fragrance several hours after dusk, probably to attract more pollinating moths.

J F M A M J J A S O N D

FIELD NOTES
- Zones 5–10
- Perennial
- To 3' (1 m)
- Full sun or light shade
- Low

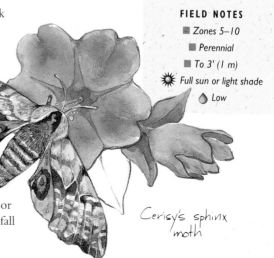

Cerisy's sphinx moth

Beardlip Penstemon

Penstemon barbatus

Beardlip penstemon, or scarlet bugler, is spectacular when its tall flower stalks are covered with bright red flowers. Its bloom time varies with altitude and from season to season: it usually blooms in mid-spring but sometimes in midsummer and in fall, too. All penstemons have five stamens (thus, the name penstemon), but the fifth stamen is often covered with hairs, resembling a bearded lip or tongue and giving rise to the names beardlip and beardtongue. The hairs actually help pick up pollen from bees as they push into the flowers looking for nectar.

J F M A M J J A S O N D

Penstemons generally grow best in relatively dry, well-drained soil. Many are short-lived, but the life can be extended by clipping all but one or two flower stalks after blooming. A few seeds from the remaining stalks are enough to produce new plants in spring. In fact, seedlings often come up with no help from the gardener. Too much rain, snow, and humidity are more limiting to good growth than minimum winter temperatures.

Beardlip penstemon is mostly pollinated by hummingbirds. Bitter substances in some penstemons discourage browsing by deer.

Broad-tailed Hummingbird

♂

FIELD NOTES
- Zones 2–9
- Perennial
- 3–4' (1–1.2 m)
- ☼ Full sun
- ◊ Low–moderate

346

Indian Pink

Silene laciniata

Indian pink, or Mexican campion, is a low-growing wildflower with delightful flowers of flaring, ragged, red petals. It is associated with partially shaded mountain slopes, frequently with pines and oaks, from west Texas to California.

This appealing little flower is easily grown in most soils that don't remain wet too long. It will grow in full sun in the North, but usually grows in part shade farther south. Indian pink is usually propagated from seed, which must be stratified to simulate winter conditions. Sow seed in fall or early spring. Too much rainfall and humidity in the eastern regions are probably more limiting to good growth than minimum winter temperatures.

Indian pink is a classic hummingbird-pollinated plant. Judging from the long period that hummingbirds remain at each flower, there must be a lot of nectar or it must be very good, or both. The flowers have backturned petals and a sticky section just below the petals that serve to repel crawling insects, who might otherwise steal the nectar without pollinating the flower.

red ants at base of flower

J F M A M J J A S O N D

FIELD NOTES

- Zones 4–8
- Perennial
- 1–2' (30–60 cm)
- Full sun–light shade
- Moderate

Scarlet Hedge Nettle

Stachys coccinea

At times, scarlet hedge nettle is covered with brilliant red flowers. It dies down during freezing weather but will continue growing in warm climates. Unlike its unpleasant namesake, it has no obnoxious stinging hairs.

Scarlet hedge nettle grows best in wet, nitrogen–rich soil, though it will survive remarkable drought by dying back and regrowing when conditions are wet again. Propagate it from cuttings or seed. Take cuttings when the plants are growing vigorously in late spring; sow seed indoors in pots and transplant seedlings in spring in cold climates, and at any time of the year in warm climates.

J F M A M J J A S O N D

Scarlet hedge nettle is likely to be the ultimate hummingbird plant: it seems to be absolutely irresistible, and it's not unusual to see humming-birds appear within minutes of setting a plant out on a patio. Because it will bloom well into the fall season, it is likely to be good for attracting hummingbirds in Flagstaff, Albuquerque, and Santa Fe, when the birds return from nesting in the central and northern Rockies.

painted lady butterfly

Black-chinned Hummingbird

FIELD NOTES
- Zones 5–11
- Perennial
- Height: 1–3' (30–90 cm)
- Full sun–light shade
- High

Showy Goldeneye

Viguiera multiflora

Showy goldeneye is a pretty wildflower that is often found on disturbed areas in ponderosa pine (*Pinus ponderosa*) forests. Numerous flowers cover this plant for many weeks during summer, and the name goldeneye refers to the yellow flower center.

Showy goldeneye is easily grown in most soils. Extremely dry and extremely wet soils limit its growth, but it produces so many seedlings in moderate moisture conditions that it should be easy to establish with the grasses of midgrass prairies. Clipping off the seed heads will prolong the already-long blooming period. Propagation is easy from seed, which can be sown directly in the garden in spring.

Although the center of these flowers appears yellow to human eyes, bees and butterflies see reflected ultraviolet light. This probably creates a vivid contrast between the flower centers and the petals that is not visible to humans. To bees and butterflies, the primary pollinators of showy goldeneye, this flower may look somewhat like blanket flower appears to humans. The pretty Gorgone crescentspot butterfly uses showy goldeneye as a host plant for its eggs, caterpillars, and chrysalises. Many other adult butterflies also visit this wildflower.

J F M A M J J A S O N D

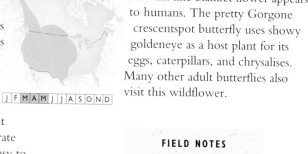

FIELD NOTES

■ Zones 3–6

■ Perennial

■ 1–3' (30–90 cm)

☀ Full sun or part shade

◐ Moderate

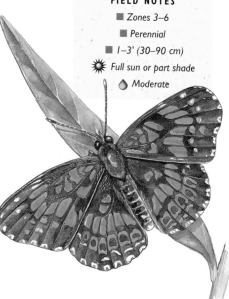

Gorgone crescentspot butterfly

349

Saskatoon Serviceberry

Amelanchier alnifolia

Saskatoon serviceberry varies from a small, thicket-forming shrub to a small tree. The attractive, white flowers appear in early spring, followed by delicious berries. The fruit ripens earlier in the season than most wild fruit, giving rise to one of the common names, Juneberry. Other names include sarviceberry, shadbush, and shadblow. Shad refers to a fish that travels upstream at the time this shrub produces masses of flowers, or "blows".

spring flowers

Saskatoon serviceberry usually grows on moist sites; at higher elevations, it is more shrubby. It is adapted to a wide range of soils, and can be propagated from seed, which must be very well cleaned to eliminate germination inhibitors in the fruit. It may also be rooted from the many suckers that develop at the base of the plant.

Deer eat the twigs and leaves. Squirrels, chipmunks, and numerous birds eat the fruits with great enthusiasm. Grow serviceberry plants in cages if you would like to keep some berries for yourself! Coral hairstreak butterfly eggs overwinter, and the caterpillars feed on the developing fruits of serviceberries.

J F M A M J J A S O N D

FIELD NOTES

- Zones 2–7
- Deciduous
- 3–40' (1–12 m)
- ☀ Full sun–part shade
- ⬤ Moderate

least chipmunk

350

Big Sagebrush

Artemisia tridentata

Extremely variable in size and shape, big, or basin, sagebrush is a pleasantly fragrant, silvery-colored shrub with three-lobed leaves. Clusters of tiny flowers are conspicuous but not showy. Blooming in August to October, bear in mind that they contribute significantly to hayfever.

Big sagebrush prefers well-drained soil, and seems to do poorly in landscaping if planted in clay soil. Do not overwater it, especially if the soil is not fast-draining. Propagate it from seed. Soil type and dry conditions are more important to good growth than minimum winter temperatures.

One of the interesting wildlife associations of this plant is the annual early spring appearance of tiny black aphids. These are followed in warmer weather by ladybugs, which eat the aphids, and finally, by ladybug larvae, which quickly finish off the remaining aphids. The whole cycle appears to be an example of leaving things alone to take care of themselves—no pesticide intervention is needed. Big sagebrush also provides protection and cover for rabbits and other small mammals.

J F M A M J J A S O N D

ladybug beetle eating aphids

FIELD NOTES

■ Zones 4–10

■ Semi-evergreen

■ 1–8' (30–240 cm)

☀ Full sun–part shade

💧 Low

351

Chrysothamnus nauseosus

Rabbitbrush

Chrysothamnus spp.

Rabbitbrush is a small- to medium-sized shrub, with brilliant yellow fall flowers. The stems and leaves can be green, gray–green, or almost white. Sometimes, the seed heads are very showy well into winter. The genus name *Chrysothamnus* comes from the Greek words *chryso* for yellow and *thamnus* for shrub.

Rabbitbrush, with its showy flowers, attractive seed heads, and variously colorful winter twigs, is an important landscape plant for dry locations. Pruning back during winter results in a more compact plant with more flowers. Rabbitbrush will adapt to a wide range of soils, but overwatering is a problem in clay. Propagation is usually by seed. Too much rain, snow, and humidity are more limiting to good plant growth than minimum winter temperatures.

J F M A M J J A S O N D

Blooming so late in the season makes rabbitbrush quite attractive to bees and butterflies, including the snout and monarch. The showy northern and sagebrush checkerspot butterflies use rabbitbrush as a host for their egg, caterpillar, chrysalis, and adult phases. Deer generally avoid browsing on this shrub. House Finches and Pine Siskins eat the seeds.

FIELD NOTES
- Zones 2–10
- Deciduous
- 2–6' (60–180 cm)
- Full sun
- Low

snout butterfly

352

Creeping Mahonia

Mahonia repens (Berberis repens)

Creeping mahonia is a low, spreading shrub, with holly-like, evergreen leaves and pretty, fragrant, yellow flowers from early to late spring. The summer and fall berries resemble grapes but have a unique flavor. Creeping mahonia is also known as creeping holly grape and Oregon grape, and there are many other similar references to holly and grapes. The leaves will change to a reddish color in fall if the plant is exposed to sun at that time of year. Native Americans used creeping mahonia to treat stomachaches, rheumatism, and, together with other plants, scorpion and spider bites.

J F M A M J J A S O N D

Creeping mahonia's chief value in the garden is as a useful groundcover that will grow in a variety of conditions. It is at its best in part sun and moderately moist situations. When fully established, it tolerates considerable traffic and makes a good plant for edges of driveways and paths. It is adaptable to nearly all soil types. Propagate it from seed or by transplanting pieces of established plants before spring growth begins (this can be as early as February in Colorado). Plants grown in shade need to be moved into full sun gradually.

Fruit-eating birds will eat the berries, and the shrubs provide shelter for both birds and mammals. Deer seldom browse on this plant.

spring flowers

summer-fall berries

FIELD NOTES
- Zones 4–9
- Evergreen
- 1–3' (30–90 cm)
- ☀ Full sun–full shade.
- ◗ Low–high

353

Pinyon Pine

Pinus edulis

Pinyon pines are large, picturesque shrubs or small trees. The needles are very resistant to loss of moisture from the dry, prevailing winds. These pines also have both shallow and deep roots to make the maximum use of soil moisture. They produce a repellent odor and taste to discourage browsing of their valuable foliage.

The pinyon pine needs full sun and grows best on well-drained soil. You can grow the trees from seed but it is a slow process. Too much rainfall and humidity, and too cool summers, are more limiting to good growth than minimum winter temperatures.

Although pinyon pines can grow quite tall and wide, you can prune them to fit the garden landscape.

Birds and mammals take a large number of seeds and store them for eating later; but enough are not eaten after being stored in good growing places that the whole system continues. Clark's Nutcrackers and Steller's and Scrub Jays all play a part in the seed distribution, but the Pinyon Jay is the primary partner in this seed distribution. Quail and Wild Turkeys also eat these seeds, as do various squirrels, voles, mice, bears, chipmunks, porcupines, and many human groups, both past and present.

J F M A M J J A S O N D

FIELD NOTES
- Zones 4–8
- Evergreen
- 10–40' (3–12 m)
- Full sun
- Moderate–low

Pinyon ♂
Jay

354

Gambel Oak

Quercus gambelii

Usually a large shrub, Gambel oak occasionally develops into a tree form and is most often found in sizeable thickets. The thickets are stimulated by fire and other disturbances such as logging. This results in vigorous, new trunks sprouting from the roots.

Gambel oak grows on a variety of soils but it favors well-drained soil. Propagate it from seed.

In the wild, the mammal and birdlife in Gambel oak shrublands is remarkable, and in gardens, creatures will be attracted to even a single Gambel oak. Scrub Jays and Rufous-sided Towhees are especially conspicuous feeders on the acorns. In winter, Scrub Jays forage in the dead leaves and branches for nymph-filled galls, while mountain and Black-capped Chickadees search the branches for insects and eggs attached to the bark. About 50 species of mammal are associated with these oak woodlands. These include

J F M A M J J A S O N D

mule deer, chipmunks, bears, and rock squirrels. The Colorado hairstreak butterfly is especially associated with Gambel oak. It lays its eggs on the bark and the caterpillars feed on the leaves. Rocky Mountain duskywing and Horace's duskywing butterflies are also associated with this oak.

Colorado hairstreak butterfly

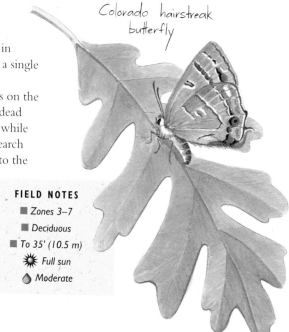

FIELD NOTES

- Zones 3–7
- Deciduous
- To 35' (10.5 m)
- ☀ Full sun
- ◔ Moderate

355

Golden Currant

Ri·bes aureum

Golden, or buffalo, currant is a medium-sized shrub with pretty, golden-yellow spring flowers. The flowers have a delightful clove-like fragrance. The currants are black, purplish, or orange and ripen during summer. Shoshone Indians used golden currant roots to treat fevers, sore throats, angina, and dysentery. The fruits were an important food for the Plains Indians, either dried, eaten fresh, or made into jelly. Even the flowers are reported to be quite tasty.

summer fruits

Golden currant is adapted to a wide range of soils. Although it prefers moderate water, it is tolerant of dry to moist conditions. Propagate it from seed; grafted selections (cultivars) ensure fragrant flowers and tasty fruit.

J F M A M J J A S O N D

A wide array of wildlife is attracted to the fruit, including skunks, squirrels, chipmunks, bears, and raccoons. Numerous birds often flock into the shrubs, finishing off the fruits in a feeding frenzy before the gardener considers them ripe enough to use. Tailed copper, gray comma, faunus anglewing, and zephyr anglewing butterflies all use currants as host plants for their egg, caterpillar, and chrysalis stages.

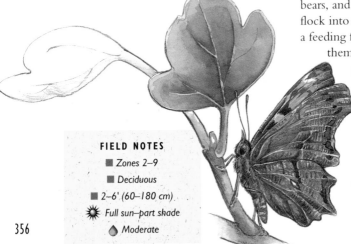

zephyr anglewing butterfly

FIELD NOTES
- Zones 2–9
- Deciduous
- 2–6' (60–180 cm)
- ☀ Full sun–part shade
- ◐ Moderate

356

Datil

Yucca baccata

Datil, or banana yucca, is an agave-like shrub with machete-like leaves, which are much broader than those of most of the other yucca species. The fruit is almost banana-like. The shallow and deep roots, together with the thick leaves, serve to utilize any available soil moisture without losing much to the hot, dry conditions that prevail where this yucca grows. Native Americans in the Southwest used datil fiber cord to make sandals, mats, nets, baskets, and blankets; and roots to make a lather for washing. They ate the fruits raw or roasted and sun-dried, or used them to make a sweet drink. They also roasted and ate the seeds and flower buds.

Datil will grow in a wide range of soils, but good drainage is important since it won't tolerate wet soil. You can propagate it from seed, a slow method, or by offsets taken from established plants. Late fall or winter is the best time for this. Too much rainfall and humidity,

and too cool summers, are more limiting to good growth than minimum winter temperatures.

Datil and other yuccas are pollinated by yucca moths, an interesting example of co-dependence, since neither can succeed without the other. Yuccas furnish protective nest sites for some birds and provide cover for numerous birds and small mammals.

J F M A M J J A S O N D

brush
mouse

FIELD NOTES
- Zones 5–10
- Evergreen
- To 3' (1 m)
- ☀ Full sun
- ◊ Low

357

Ponderosa Pine

Pinus ponderosa

Ponderosa pines are tall, majestic trees with long needles and fragrant bark, which smells like vanilla in warm weather. Their remarkable drought tolerance comes, in part, from their massive root system—at times, 35' (10.5 m) deep and 100' (30.5 m) across. Found over a broad section of the Western US, ponderosa pine is usually found above 5,600' (1,702 m) in the middle latitude of its range.

Ponderosa pines generally prefer well-drained soils. Transplant specimens in spring before the buds start growing—usually before early April. Although ponderosa pines will grow in a wide range of climates, too much rainfall is more limiting to good growth than minimum winter temperatures.

Abert's squirrels depend on fairly large areas of ponderosa pine forest. The little Brown Creeper hunts for insects in the thick, furrowed bark of these pines, and builds its nest behind pieces of loose bark. An estimated total of 57 mammals, including chipmunks, and 128 bird species, including the Pygmy Nuthatch, occur in this type of forest.

J F M A M J J A S O N D

male
cone

FIELD NOTES

- Zones 3–8
- Evergreen
- 100–200' (30–60 m)
- Full sun
- Moderate

Pygmy
Nuthatch

358

Narrowleaf Cottonwood

Populus angustifolia

N arrowleaf cottonwoods are tall, relatively narrow trees, and, as their name implies, they also have noticeably narrow leaves. They tend to grow in groves along mountain streams, usually between 3,200 and 9,900' (1,000 and 3,000 m).

All cottonwoods are considered phreatophytes (literally, "well plants"), meaning that they can survive only where the roots are able to draw on substantial amounts of subsoil moisture. The seeds of cottonwoods remain viable for only a few days, and must land on sunny, moist soil in this short time in order to germinate and grow successfully. Narrowleaf cottonwoods grow best in full sun and gravelly, well-drained soil, though they can adapt to other soils. You can propagate these trees by digging young sprouts from the roots of established trees. Transplant young trees before the leaves develop in early spring—usually, in March, April, or May, depending on altitude and climate. Beware—these trees sprout too vigorously from the roots for most urban situations.

Grouse and various songbirds, such as the Black-headed Grosbeak, eat the buds and young flowers. Beavers and other small mammals eat the buds, bark, and foliage. Mourning cloak and Compton tortoiseshell are among the many butterflies that use cottonwoods for their eggs, caterpillars, and chrysalises.

| J | F | M | A | M | J | J | A | S | O | N | D |

Black-headed Grosbeak

FIELD NOTES

- Zones 2–7
- Deciduous
- 60' (18 m)
- ☀ Full sun
- ◐ High

359

Quaking Aspen
Populus tremuloides

Considered the most widely distributed North American tree species, quaking aspens are medium size and nearly always form beautiful groves. The bark is distinctively white, and the leaves, mounted on flattened leaf stalks, flutter in the slightest breeze (hence, the tree's scientific and common names). The fall color in the Rocky Mountains is a brilliant yellow.

J F M A M J J A S O N D

Aspens are adapted to a range of soils, as long as water is always available. Transplant specimens in early spring, before the leaves develop. Aspens prefer cool summers. In areas beyond their natural range, they suffer from many pests and diseases.

It has been estimated that 500 species of animal and plant, ranging from elk to fungi, depend on aspens. Grouse and quail browse on the buds, catkins, and seeds, and numerous cavity-nesting birds occupy old-growth aspen groves, including Flammulated Owls, Northern Saw-whet Owls, Northern Pygmy Owls, Tree and Violet-green Swallows, House Wrens, Brown Creepers, Mountain Bluebirds, Pygmy Nuthatches, and Mountain Chickadees. The Red-naped Sapsucker feeds on insects extracted from the bark and enjoys the sap. Tent caterpillars, aspen leaf-miners, and many other insects depend on aspens, and in turn, become the attraction for other species.

FIELD NOTES
- Zones 1–7
- Deciduous
- 40–60' (12–18 m)
- ☀ Full sun
- ◐ High

♂

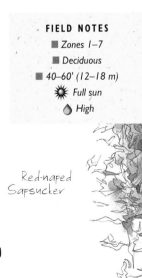

Red-naped Sapsucker

Riverbank Grape

Vitis riparia

Riverbank grape is widespread in the Mountains and Basins and Desert Southwest regions. It tends to be found near water, usually streams, and can ramble over large shrubs and small trees. It is relatively late to leaf out in spring and suffers seriously from late-spring freezes, which can eliminate the grape crops—a significant loss for wildlife. Pueblo Indians cultivated this vine for the fruits, which they ate raw or dried in the sun for eating later. The grapes make a tasty jelly, juice, and wine. The tendrils can be eaten raw as a different and distinctive tidbit, and the leaves are reported to quench thirst.

Riverbank grape is adapted to a range of soils. Propagation is usually by seed, which must be totally cleaned of germination-inhibiting chemicals in the fruit. Riverbank grape will grow well over a trellis, arbor, or fence in the garden.

J F M A M J J A S O N D

The wildlife value of this plant is immense: the grapes provide food for numerous mammals, including squirrels and raccoons, and possibly as many as 100 species of bird. In addition to food, the vines provide good cover for nests.

raccoon

FIELD NOTES
- Zones 3–8
- Deciduous
- To 20'+ (6 m+)
- ☀ Full sun
- ◍ High

361

Pale evening primrose (left); Rocky Mountain bee plant (right)

Additional species

Plant name/flower color	Zone	Height	Visitors/attraction/season
CACTI			
Porcupine prickly pear (yellow/red) *Opuntia erinacea*	5–8	6" (15 cm)	bees/flowers/spring, summer
HERBACEOUS FLOWERS			
Rocky Mountain columbine (blue) *Aquilegia caerulea*	3–8	1–2' (30–60 cm)	hummingbirds/flowers/summer
Rocky Mountain bee plant (pink/white) *Cleome serrulata*	5–9	2–4' (60–120 cm)	bees/flowers/summer, fall
Small-leaf geranium (pink) *Geranium caespitosum*	4–8	2'± (60 cm±)	bees/flowers/spring–fall
Sweet-flowered four o'clock (white) *Mirabilis longiflora*	7–10	1–3' (30–90 cm)	moths/flowers/summer, fall
Bee balm (white) *Monarda citriodora*	5–9	1–3' (30–90 cm)	bees/flowers/spring–summer
Pale evening primrose (white) *Oenothera pallida*	4–7	6–12" (15–30 cm)	moths/flowers/spring–fall
Desert penstemon (pink) *Penstemon pseudospectabilis*	5–8	4–6' (120–180 cm)	bees/flowers/spring, summer
Rocky Mountain penstemon (blue) *Penstemon strictus*	4–9	2–4' (60–120 cm)	bees/flowers/spring, summer
Wandbloom penstemon (pink) *Penstemon virgatus*	4–7	2–4' (60–120 cm)	caterpillars/leaves/spring–fall
Thread-leaf groundsel (yellow) *Senecio douglasii* var. *longilobus*	5–9	1–3' (30–90 cm)	bees, butterflies/flowers/summer, fall
Fendler's globemallow (pink) *Sphaeralcea fendleri*	4–9	2–5' (60–150 cm)	bees/flowers/summer, fall
SHRUBS			
Fernbush (white) *Chamaebatiaria millefolium*	5–8	2½–5' (75–150 cm)	bees/flowers/summer
Cliff rose (cream) *Cowania mexicana*	5–9	4–20' (1.2–6 m)	bees/flowers/spring–fall
Feather dalea (purple) *Dalea formosa*	5–9	2' (60 cm)	bees, butterflies/flowers/spring–fall
New Mexico privet (n/a) *Forestiera neomexicana*	5–9	6–10' (1.8–3 m)	birds/seeds/fall
TREES			
Utah serviceberry (white) *Amelanchier utahensis*	4–8	25' (7.5 m)	birds, mammals/fruits/fall
Engelmann spruce (n/a) *Picea engelmannii*	3–9	80–115' (24–35 m)	chickadees/cones/variable
New Mexico locust (pink) *Robinia neomexicana*	6–8	25'± (7.5 m)±	porcupines, chipmunks, Gambel's Quail/seeds/fall
VINE			
Arizona honeysuckle (red) *Lonicera arizonica*	6–9	variable	mammals/seeds/fall hummingbirds/flowers/summer

The Desert Southwest

THE DESERT SOUTHWEST
The Southwestern Garden

The warm deserts of the Southwestern United States are found from 5,000' (1,500 m), where desert meets juniper–oak woodlands, to below sea level, in the Imperial Valley.

Unlike the colder deserts farther north, moisture is measured not in snow but in rainfall, which averages 4–8" (100–200 mm) a year. The two main deserts, the Chihuahuan and the Sonoran, are mostly in Mexico but cross the border into the United States. The Chihuahuan Desert is in southwestern Texas, southern New Mexico, and southeastern Arizona, and the Sonoran Desert is in Arizona, southern Nevada, and southeastern California. The Sonoran Desert is divided into a colder portion, parts of which are called the Mojave Desert, and an almost frost-free portion, called the Lower Colorado Desert.

Each desert has signature plants and a special character of its own: the Sonoran Desert has saguaro (*Carnegiea gigantea*) and the Mojave Desert has Joshua tree (*Yucca brevifolia*). All warm deserts have desert willow (*Chilopsis linearis*), ocotillo (*Fouquieria splendens*), mesquites (*Prosopis* spp.), creosote bush (*Larrea* spp.), and some form of globemallow (*Sphaeralcea* spp.). The prettiest portions of the deserts are in the foothills, where higher elevations mean relatively cooler temperatures.

A natural desert garden is composed of small, native trees such as the desert willow and the blue palo verde (*Cercidium floridum*); flowering and evergreen shrubs, such as daleas and fairydusters (*Calliandra* spp.); succulent accents such as cacti (*Opuntia, Carnegiea* and *Ferocactus* spp.), yucca, or agave; and a myriad of small, rainy season flowers and grasses.

A drip-irrigation system will prolong bloom times and keep non-indigenous trees and cacti alive. Birds favor cacti for nesting sites, because the spines discourage predators and the pads provide food and moisture. While the plants are very small, wire cages will protect them from hungry rabbits.

It is very easy to make a Southwestern garden attractive to wildlife, because chuckwallas and other lizards, bejeweled beetles, ground squirrels, hummingbirds, quail, butterflies, and hawk moths abound in the desert. A water faucet, within sight of the house and on a timer to drip for an hour at dawn and again at sunset, will bring all the local desert creatures to your Southwestern garden.

Saguaro

Carnegiea gigantea (Cereus giganteus)

For many people, the saguaro symbolizes the Southwest, yet this tree-like cactus is native only to the Sonoran Desert. Several arms branch from a central trunk, all fleshy and succulent with stored water. The spring flowers, which appear at the tips, are white and are said to smell of ripe melon. The fruits, juicy and sweet/tart, ripen in June.

Saguaros are not easy to propagate, but a few nurseries are now attempting to produce 1–3' (30–90 cm) high plants at a reasonable price. Transplanted saguaros have a 50 percent mortality rate. Good drainage is essential, so never plant saguaro in a swale. Drip irrigation is important for the first year, while the plant gets established.

J F M A M J J A S O N D

The flowers are pollinated at night by nectar-sipping lesser long-nosed bats and long-tongued bats. Day visitors include White-winged Doves, butterflies, and hummingbirds. The fruits are eaten by bats, White-winged Doves, songbirds, humans, foxes, ringtails, and other mammals. Woodpeckers and Carpenter birds use their beaks to carve homes in the trunks. Birds of prey build nests in the branches. Fallen logs house lizards and beetles.

lesser long-nosed bat

FIELD NOTES
■ Zone 9
■ *Native to Sonoran (frost sensitive and limited)*
■ *Evergreen*
■ 20–50' (6–15 m)
☀ *Full sun*
◐ Low

Claretcup Cactus

Echinocereus triglochidiatus

Claretcup cactus, or Mojave mound, flowers may be brilliant orange, red, or magenta. Minerals in the soil rather than genes may determine the exact shade of red. The blooms are unexpectedly large for such a small plant and very profuse. They appear in early spring to early summer and are followed by 1" (2.5 cm) juicy, red fruits. The cylindrical cactus stems increase in number with age, so the plant gets wider, not taller. A tiny, nursery-propagated claretcup cactus may be 18" (45 cm) wide in a few years and ultimately 4' (1.2 m) wide.

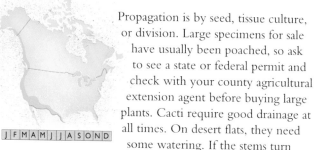

J F M A M J J A S O N D

Propagation is by seed, tissue culture, or division. Large specimens for sale have usually been poached, so ask to see a state or federal permit and check with your county agricultural extension agent before buying large plants. Cacti require good drainage at all times. On desert flats, they need some watering. If the stems turn brown at the base, it is a sure sign of too much water—the most common killer of cacti.

The flowers are a source of nectar for Costa's hummingbirds, Scott's Orioles, and butterflies. Songbirds, White-winged Doves, and many species of desert mammal, eat the fruits.

FIELD NOTES

- Zone 9
- Adapted to southern WC
- Evergreen
- Less than 1' (30 cm)
- Full sun to a little shade
- Low

Costa's
Hummingbird

367

Teddybear cactus (Opuntia bigelovii)

Prickly Pear, Cholla

Opuntia spp.

The stems of prickly pear are round or elliptical flattened pads. The silhouette is dense. Chollas' stems have tubular joints and are much taller and airier in structure. Flowers for both are large and gaudy—usually yellow, orange, hot pink, or magenta, but occasionally a pale yellow-green. These appear in spring or summer. The fruits ripen in late summer or fall. They are juicy, sometimes spiny, and most turn red, mauve, or yellow.

| J | F | M | A | M | J | J | A | S | O | N | D |

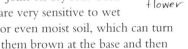

prickly pear flower

Propagation is simple: remove a pad or joint, allow the wound to harden and dry, and then place the pad or joint on dry soil. Cacti are very sensitive to wet or even moist soil, which can turn them brown at the base and then cause them to rot. A cactus needs water only if it shrivels and wrinkles. Place these cacti away from paths and patios to avoid contact with the painful spines. Chollas must be planted with great care, as the joints readily detach.

Bees visit the pollen-rich flowers, and desert mammals and birds eat the fruit. The prickly branches are used for nesting by Cactus Wrens and Roadrunners. In drought, many animals eat the pads for their water and food content.

Cactus Wren

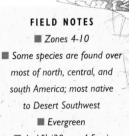

FIELD NOTES

■ Zones 4-10

■ Some species are found over most of north, central, and south America; most native to Desert Southwest

■ Evergreen

■ 1–15' (30 cm–4.5 m)

☀ Full sun to a little shade

💧 Low

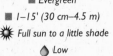

Desert Marigold

Baileya multiradiata

The low-growing, pale blue-green foliage of desert marigold looks handsome in all seasons. The daisies, which top slender, leafless stems, appear year-round, except when heat or cold are at their fiercest. The yellow flowers are multilayered with matching yellow centers.

The tiny seeds ripen and scatter over a period of several months. Although desert marigold lives only one to two years, you can maintain a colony by allowing it to self-sow. Let these flowers weave themselves in and out of your other plantings: the garden will look a little different each year, but it will always be attractive. Good drainage is essential.

J F M A M J J A S O N D

A mulch of decomposed granite or a natural desert covering of rocks hides enough of the seed from predators to ensure a continuing crop of plants. The nectar-rich flowers attract butterflies, such as the Leanira checkerspot and the desert and pima orangetips. Birds, insects, and small mammals eat the seeds. Rabbits are fond of the foliage, so protect young plants with wire cages until you have enough desert marigold to share. The desert grassland whiptail lizard may be found sheltering beneath the foliage. Horses also like the foliage, but it seems to be poisonous to other domestic animals.

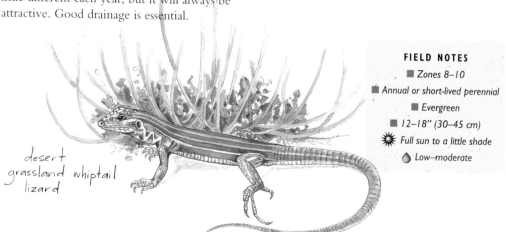

desert grassland whiptail lizard

FIELD NOTES
- ■ Zones 8–10
- ■ Annual or short-lived perennial
- ■ Evergreen
- ■ 12–18" (30–45 cm)
- ✺ Full sun to a little shade
- ◌ Low–moderate

369

Parry's Penstemon

Penstemon parryi

Every spring, several stems emerge from a single rosette to bear clusters of tubular, rosy pink flowers. Small, round capsules within the flower head quickly ripen to tan and release tiny, black seeds. The stems then die back, and only the rosette remains green all year. There are many attractive species of penstemon, ranging in color from blue and lavender to white.

J F M A M J J A S O N D

Propagation is easy from seed, and most gardeners let their penstemons self-sow. Start with at least three penstemons of one species to assure good cross-pollination. Mulch them with decomposed granite: the granite hides the tiny seeds from birds and insects, and they can wait for rain to trigger germination. Ensure there is constant good drainage and water sparingly—the result should be a bumper crop every spring.

Large clumps of penstemon several years old will have an almost constant stream of hummingbirds darting in and hovering while probing the flowers for nectar with their beaks. The leaves host butterfly larvae and are browsed by deer.

FIELD NOTES

- ■ Zones 8–10
- ■ Perennial
- ■ Evergreen rosette
- ■ 3–4' (1–1.2 m)
- ☀ Full sun to a little shade
- 💧 High

Blue-throated Hummingbird

370

New Mexico Agave

Agave neomexicana

New Mexico agave looks like a large, blue-green artichoke with beautiful but dangerous black-tipped spines. It is much smaller than the giant maguey (*A. americana*), making it a more suitable size for home landscapes. The flower stalks look like a candelabrum of golden yellow scrub brushes. These plants flower once only, in spring, when 8–20 years old. After setting seed, the original plant dies, but baby agaves, called offsets or pups, then appear at the base.

These pups will form a colony, or they can be cut free with a clean knife, allowed to air-dry, and then planted in a new spot. Soil should be open and gravelly with low organic content, and always well drained.

J F M A M J J A S O N D

Agaves are very easy to grow, but they rot if they are overwatered. The flowers are a source of nectar for butterflies, hummingbirds, lesser long-nosed bats, and long-tongued bats. The leaves serve as food for the larvae of the agave borer butterfly. The Lucifer Hummingbird nests in the rosettes, and the Agave Woodpecker nests on the dead flower stalks.

rosette base

long-tongued bat

FIELD NOTES
- Zones 7–10
- Evergreen
- 2' (60 cm) with much taller bloom stalk
- ☀ Full sun to a little shade
- ◊ Moderate

Ajamete

Asclepias subulata

Ajamete, or rush milkweed, is one of the most drought tolerant of the milkweeds. It has a grassy texture composed of a dense cluster of very pale green stems. The flowers are small and creamy white, usually appearing in March. The seedpods, like other milkweeds, are large and filled with fluffs of silvery silk.

JFMAMJJASOND

Propagation is easiest by root cuttings or division, but seed may be sown any time there might be at least two months without either frost or scorching drought. Ajamete grows in deep soil along washes, and stays green in summer only when moisture is always present. Although it likes water, it must always be well drained. Ajamete is important for monarch butterflies. They lay their eggs on the stems and their larvae feed on the plant.

milkweed seedpod

The butterflies return to sip nectar from the flowers, where they are often seen alongside the tarantula hawk wasp.

monarch butterfly

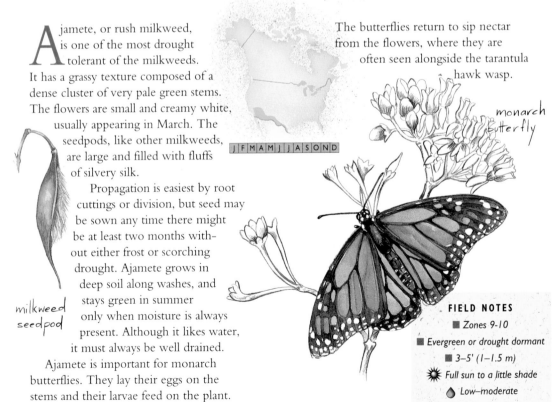

FIELD NOTES

■ Zones 9-10

■ Evergreen or drought dormant

■ 3–5' (1–1.5 m)

☀ Full sun to a little shade

◐ Low–moderate

Red Barberry

Berberis haematocarpa (Mahonia haematocarpa)

R ed barberry is a large shrub with tiny, dark gray-green leaves that are as prickly as holly. In very early spring, red barberry is fragrant with a profusion of small, golden yellow flowers. These are followed in early summer by red berries. Frosts turn the foliage purple, the color lasting throughout winter.

Collect the fruit when ripe, clean and air-dry the seed, and store the seed in a tightly sealed container in the refrigerator. In fall, or after the last frost in spring, plant the seed ¼" (5 mm) deep directly in the ground where you want it to grow;

| J | F | M | A | M | J | J | A | S | O | N | D |

transplanting is hard, because the root system develops extensively before top growth begins. Cuttings are difficult without professional equipment, such as a mist bench. Once established, red barberry is long-lived if its soil is well drained and more dry than moist.

Nectar-seeking butterflies and bees visit the flowers, and mammals and birds, such as White-winged Doves, Verdins, and Desert Sparrows, eat the sweet fruits. The spiny, dense branches provide cover for many small desert creatures. The roots and bark have medicinal properties and the stem yields a yellow dye.

Black-throated Sparrow ♂

FIELD NOTES
■ Zones 7–9
■ Native to Pinyon/Juniper belt of Desert Southwest
■ Evergreen
■ 6–12' (2–4 m)
☀ Full sun to a little shade
💧 High

373

Ocotillo

Fouquieria splendens

It is useful for the desert landscape designer to think of ocotillo as a tree because it is so tall. Instead of a trunk or spreading branches, however, it has a vase-shaped cluster of spiny stems, tapering inward toward their roots. The stems remain green with occasional irrigation. After every warm-season rain, the ends of the stems become bright with magnificent, large, red to orange flowers.

The easiest way to propagate ocotillo is from cuttings taken any time of year, but it is also easy to propagate from seed. Collect the seed in summer as the capsules turn brown, but before they split. Dry the seed thoroughly and store it in the refrigerator. Sow the seed in fall or spring, barely covering it with soil, and water very lightly. Too much moisture for cuttings, seedlings, or the mature plants, causes rotting and fungal diseases. Good drainage is essential.

The flowers are a source of nectar for hummingbirds, orioles, butterflies, and bees. Small songbirds build nests on the spiny stems.

J F M A M J J A S O N D

ocotillo flower

Hooded Oriole ♂ ↗

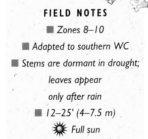

FIELD NOTES

■ Zones 8–10

■ Adapted to southern WC

■ Stems are dormant in drought; leaves appear only after rain

■ 12–25' (4–7.5 m)

☀ Full sun

💧 Low

374

Chuparosa

Justicia californica (Beloperone californica)

Chuparosa is a sprawling shrub with evergreen stems so dense that the absence of leaves most of the year is hardly noticeable. Leaves actually do appear, but only for a short time after heavy rain. Chuparosa has no spines, making it safe to plant by paths and doorways. It is covered with hundreds of small, red flowers in March to May, and scattered blooms continue to appear throughout summer and fall.

Propagation is best from softwood cuttings. Seeds are rarely used because they are so hard to collect at the right time; they pop as soon as they are ripe. Growing chuparosa in a garden is easy if drainage is excellent and irrigation is sparse. It is commonly used as a flower or evergreen shrub (not hedged, of course, because of the leafless green stems), but it can also climb up a palo verde tree or a trellis, and it drapes itself becomingly over a wall or the sides of a large patio pot.

Several species of hummingbird, and butterflies, orioles, warblers, and goldfinches visit the flowers. Quail and House Finches eat the tiny seeds. Chuparosa is also a larval plant for the Chara checkerspot butterfly.

J F M A M J J A S O N D

Calliope
Hummingbird

FIELD NOTES

■ Zones 9–10

■ Adapted to southern WC

■ Evergreen stems

■ 5–8' (1.5–2.4 m)

☀ Full sun to dappled shade

◗ Moderate

375

Texas Ranger

Leucophyllum frutescens

Texas ranger and the other cenizos are all attractive, low-growing, silver-leaved, velvet-textured shrubs native to the Chihuahuan Desert. Texas ranger has the most cold tolerance, but boquillas silverleaf (*L. candidum*) and Sierra cenizo (*L. revolutum*) have the palest, showiest leaves.

J F M A M J J A S O N D

The blossoms come in colors ranging from deep purple-blue to pink or pure white. These flowers appear after rain in spring, summer, and fall and are sometimes so numerous that the silvery leaves are almost hidden. The fruits are tiny and tan-colored. Propagation is easy by seed or cuttings, but there are so many pretty selections for sale that most people buy their cenizos. In the garden, give cenizos plenty of sun and good drainage. Pruning keeps them small, but old specimens with twisting silver trunks are also attractive.

Several species of butterfly and bee visit the flowers. Theona checkerspot, a pretty orange-and-black butterfly, uses cenizos as its larval plants as well as for nectar. The larvae are velvety, very dark brown, dotted and banded with cream, and decorated with many branching spines.

FIELD NOTES
- ■ Zones 8–10
- ■ Native to Texas (Chihuahuan Desert)
- ■ Evergreen
- ■ 4–8' (1.2–2.4 m)
- ☀ Full sun
- ◖ Moderate

Theona checkerspot butterfly

376

Littleleaf Sumac

Rhus microphylla

Littleleaf sumac is a large shrub with small, dark, shiny green leaves. Occasionally, it forms a multitrunked tree. The clusters of white flowers are quite profuse in early spring. The bright orange-red fruits appear in early summer and last for several weeks. Littleleaf sumac is evergreen during mild winters, but whenever frosts make fall color possible, it turns beautiful shades of red, orange, and purple.

Littleleaf sumac can be challenging to grow from seed. The best way is to pick seed that is almost ripe but still soft, and to plant it immediately ½" (1 cm) deep exactly where the plant is to grow. Place a wire cage around the spot and keep checking it for several months. If it doesn't germinate in fall, it is most likely to appear in early spring after all danger of frost is past. Good drainage is necessary, but any soil is acceptable, even gypsum.

Summer fruit

J F M A M J J A S O N D

Butterflies and lots of bees visit the flowers. Gambel's Quail, chipmunks, and other creatures eat the fruits. Mule and other deer browse on the leaves.

Gambel's Quail

FIELD NOTES

- Zones 8–9
- Evergreen, drought deciduous, or cold deciduous
- 8–25' (2.4–7.5 m)
- Full sun to a little shade
- Moderate–high

377

Roemer Acacia

Acacia roemeriana

R oemer acacia is a small tree with feathery leaves and white, fluffy balls of extremely fragrant flowers. Unlike most acacias, its stems and branches are not very prickly. An old tree might have a trunk 12–16" (30–40 cm) in diameter, but multitrunks of 3–4" (8–10 cm) in diameter are more common. The flowers appear in spring, except in drought years, when they occur following the first good rain. Seedpods are broad and flat and turn a warm pink-tan when ripe.

Plant seed in spring. If germination is not rapid, scarify the seed and try again. Softwood cuttings may be taken in late spring. Roemer acacia prefers deep soil with good drainage. It grows quickly but rarely lives more than 50 years.

| J | F | M | A | M | J | J | A | S | O | N | D |

There are many Southwestern acacias and they all provide nectar for butterflies, such as the marine blue, and pollen for bees. Birds, such as the Broad-billed Hummingbird and the Black-tailed Gnatcatcher, nest in the branches. Quail eat the seeds, which can be ground into an edible meal called pinole. Deer browse on the leaves and pods.

seedpod

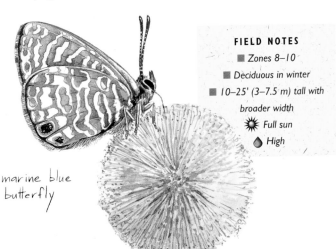

marine blue butterfly

FIELD NOTES
- Zones 8–10
- *Deciduous in winter*
- *10–25' (3–7.5 m) tall with broader width*
- ☀ *Full sun*
- 💧 *High*

378

Blue Palo Verde

Cercidium floridum

Blue palo verde and the more cold-tolerant foothill palo verde (*C. microphyllum*) are two of the best-loved desert trees. Whether covered with yellow flowers, as they are in April, or with delicate lime-green leaves, as in the spring and fall rainy seasons, these multitrunked trees always look elegant because of their smooth, light green trunks. Blue palo verdes have pale, blue-green trunks and fragrant golden flowers. Foothill palo verdes have lime-green trunks and creamy flowers that bloom two weeks later than blue palo verde. The fruits are very short beanpods that ripen in midsummer.

Propagation is easy from fresh, untreated seed planted in October. Germination should occur in two to three weeks. Blue palo verde grows in the hottest deserts along washes, so it is tolerant of extra watering. It must always be well drained, but it loves to be planted in a fast-draining swale with lots of irrigation heads.

Bees use the nectar from flowers to make honey and the flowers also attract butterflies and the tarantula hawk wasp. Doves, pack rats, and other desert wildlife eat the seeds.

J F M A M J J A S O N D

tarantula
hawk wasp

FIELD NOTES

■ Zones 9–10

■ Adapted to southern WC

■ Drought deciduous and
cold deciduous

■ 15–30' (4.5–9 m)

☀ Full sun

💧 Moderate

Desert Willow

Chilopsis linearis

Desert willow is a graceful, multitrunked tree. Though not a true willow, it has slender, willow-like, dark green leaves and very showy flowers. These blooms are tubular with flaring mouths and come in white, pink, rose, and burgundy, as well as two-tone combinations—sometimes with ruffles. Desert willow flowers from spring until fall, after rain, and flowering is almost continuous with irrigation. The fruits are string bean-sized and last through winter.

Germination is easy from fresh seed. If you want a particular color, try dormant cuttings or semihardwood cuttings taken in late summer. There are many pretty selections available in nurseries. Desert

J F M A M J J A S O N D

willow is fast growing and quickly grows into a tree, but benefits from careful pruning. In desert gardens, place it in a swale and channel rain runoff from your roof or driveway to it.

The flowers are a summer boon to hummingbirds, butterflies, and bees. The leaves are sometimes eaten by the Texan crescentspot butterfly in late spring and early summer. Pigeons and doves eat the flaky seeds.

Texan crescentspot butterfly

FIELD NOTES

- Zones 7–10
- Winter deciduous, sometimes drought deciduous
- 15–40' (4.5–12 m)
- Full sun
- High

380

Golden Ball Lead Tree

Leucaena retusa

Golden ball lead tree is a small, multitrunked tree. After rain, but especially in spring or fall, it is covered with golden globes of sweetly scented flowers. The leaves, divided into lime-green leaflets, cast light shade and appear to dance in even the slightest breeze. By late summer, the long, flat, pale green beanpods have ripened to tan, twisting open to release the seeds.

Gather the fresh seed just before the pods split open. Air-dry for two days, and dust with a natural insecticide, such as Sevin, before storing them in a jar at room temperature. Sow the untreated seed in fall as soon as the weather starts to cool down or in spring after all danger of frost is past. Any well-drained soil is acceptable, but rich, moist soil encourages too-rapid growth and weak branches. This is an excellent courtyard tree.

The fragrant flowers are a source of nectar for butterflies and bees. Insects and songbirds eat the seed.

The Broad-billed Hummingbird and the Varied Bunting like to nest in its branches. The foliage and pods are a favorite browse of deer.

J F M A M J J A S O N D

FIELD NOTES
- Zones 8–10
- Winter deciduous
- 15–25' (4.5–7.5 m)
- Full sun to a little shade
- High

bordered patch butterfly

381

Honey Mesquite

Prosopis glandulosa var. glandulosa

A mesquite tree in winter is a sculpture of dark, twisting trunks and knobby, thorny, black branches. Good pruning is important to make this phase as beautiful as possible. In late spring, delicate, feathery leaves are soon joined by fuzzy fingers of yellow to cream flowers that are fragrant close up. Beanpods follow in late summer. Usually mottled purple and cream, the pods are occasionally a brilliant ornamental red.

J F M A M J J A S O N D

Honey mesquite is native to the Chihuahuan Desert. Torrey mesquite (*P. glandulosa* var. *torreyana*) is its native equivalent in the Sonoran, Mojave, and Lower Colorado deserts. Both have light green leaves. Propagation is by fresh or scarified seed or by root cuttings. Drainage must be good, but extra moisture is appreciated; in a desert garden a swale is ideal.

The flower nectar attracts bees and butterflies, including the great purple hairstreak. Birds and mammals eat the beans, which are sweet-tasting and rich in protein. The roots provide shelter for burrowing animals. Many birds use mesquite for nesting.

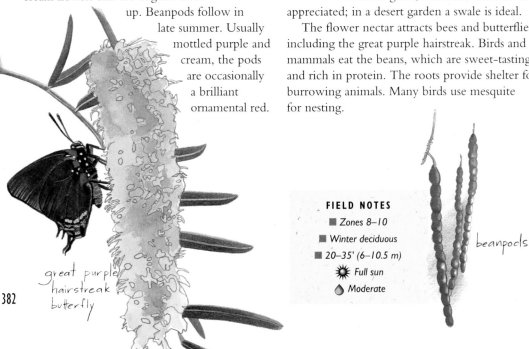

great purple hairstreak butterfly

FIELD NOTES
- Zones 8–10
- Winter deciduous
- 20–35' (6–10.5 m)
- ☀ Full sun
- ◌ Moderate

beanpods

382

Joshua Tree

Yucca brevifolia

J F M A M J J A S O N D

All the shrub yuccas and tree yuccas native to the Desert Southwest are important to wildlife. Joshua tree, the tree yucca of the Mojave Desert, has numerous branches and short leaves. Every few years, clusters of white flowers appear in the late spring followed by hard, tan, seed capsules.

Yuccas can be grown from fresh seed harvested before the capsules split open. Press the seed into sand so that the tops are barely showing, and then lightly dust them with more sand. If you can't plant the seed immediately, store it in moist sand in the refrigerator. Yuccas germinate best in temperatures ranging from 60–70°F (16–21°C). Good drainage is essential, and it is very important not to overwater.

Seedlings are eaten by mule deer, rabbits, wood rats, and ground squirrels. The branches of the Joshua tree provide nesting for songbirds, doves, and lizards. Desert night lizards climb the tree looking for insects. Woodpeckers and flickers carve homes in dead trunks. As with the other yuccas, the flowers are pollinated by a small, white yucca moth that deposits eggs in the flower. The larvae eat some of the seeds but leave enough to ensure a continuing supply of yuccas. Giant skipper butterfly larvae feed on the stems and leaves.

FIELD NOTES

- Zone 8
- Adapted to southern WC
- Evergreen
- 20–30' (6–9 m)
- ☀ Full sun
- 💧 Low

desert night lizard

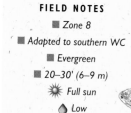

Yellow columbine (left); Mexican redbud (right)

Additional species

Plant name/flower color	Zone	Height	Visitors/attraction/season
CACTI Fishhook barrel cactus (orange) *Ferocactus wislizenii*	8–10	2–11' (60–330 cm)	bees/flowers/summer mammals/fruits/fall
HERBACEOUS FLOWERS Yellow columbine (yellow) *Aquilegia chrysantha*	8–10	1–3' (30–90 cm)	hummingbirds/flowers/spring
Blackfoot daisy (white) *Melampodium leucanthum*	7–10	1' (30 cm)	butterflies/flowers/all year
Bush muhly (pink) *Muhlenbergia porteri*	4–10	1–3' (30–90 cm)	birds/seeds/fall mammals/browse/summer
Mexican plumbago (white, blue) *Plumbago scandens*	9–10	2–3' (60–90 cm)	butterflies/flowers/spring, fall
Skeletonleaf goldeneye (yellow) *Viguiera stenoloba*	8–10	2–4' (60–120 cm)	butterflies/flowers/after rain caterpillars/leaves/spring
Dwarf white zinnia (white) *Zinnia acerosa*	9–10	3–6" (8–15 cm)	butterflies/flowers/spring–fall
SHRUBS Flame acanthus (orange) *Anisacanthus quadrifidus* var. *wrightii*	8–10	2–6' (60–180 cm)	hummingbirds/flowers/summer–fall
Littleleaf cordia (white) *Cordia parviflora*	9–10	6–12' (1.8–3.7 m)	butterflies/flowers/spring birds, mammals/fruits/summer
Mormon tea (yellow) *Ephedra trifurca*	8–10	4–15' (1.2–4.5 m)	birds/cones/fall bighorn sheep/stems/all year
Apache plume (white) *Fallugia paradoxa*	8–10	4–6' (1.2–1.8 m)	butterflies/flowers/spring–fall
Red yucca (coral) *Hesperaloe parviflora*	8–10	2–5' (60–150 cm)	hummingbirds/flowers/spring–fall
Desert lavender (lavender) *Hyptis emoryi*	9–10	8–12' (2.4–3.7 m)	birds, butterflies/flowers/spring birds/seeds/summer
Creosote bush (yellow) *Larrea tridentata*	8–10	6–10' (1.8–3 m)	quail/cover/all year birds, mammals/seeds/fall–winter
Texas sacahuista (white) *Nolina texana*	8–10	2' (60 cm)	bees/flowers/spring mammals/seeds/fall
TREES Netleaf hackberry (n/a) *Celtis reticulata*	8–10	15–75' (4.5–23 m)	caterpillars/leaves/spring birds/seeds/winter
Mexican redbud (pink) *Cercis canadensis* var. *mexicana*	8–10	20' (6 m)	bees/flowers; caterpillars/leaves/spring birds/seeds/fall–winter
Ironwood (pink) *Olneya tesota*	9–10	15–30' (4.5–9 m)	bees/flowers/summer mammals/beans/fall
VINES Thicket creeper (n/a) *Parthenocissus inserta*	4–10	10' (3 m)	birds/fruits/fall mammals/fruits/fall
Canyon grape (n/a) *Vitis arizonica*	8–10	50' (15 m)	birds/mammals/fruits/fall sphinx moth caterpillars/leaves/spring

The Prairies

THE PRAIRIES
The Prairie Garden

The Prairie region forms the heart of North America. The Prairies were once a vast grassland, with taller grasses to the east, and progressively shorter grasses to the west. In spite of the low annual rainfall, the rich soil proved conducive to farming on a scale never before seen. The resulting devastation of the prairie grasslands in the interests of agriculture was no less significant and thorough than the current destruction of the great rainforests of the world. Today, only tiny remnants of true prairie grassland remain, mostly in preserves and parklands. Fortunately, renewed interest in the plants of the prairie now influences the development of gardens in this region.

The prairie garden recalls the wide open aspect of the plains. Even in the small garden, the effect of distance can be achieved by leaving the margins of the garden open to the far-off views. Reflecting the importance of water in the prairies, the gardener may place a small pond near the patio, within view of the house. One or two riparian trees shade the house, and provide excellent habitat for a broad range of birds who prefer the shelter of trees to the open plains. The bur oak (*Quercus macrocarpa*) or the common hackberry (*Celtis occidentalis*) offer food also for squirrels and Cedar Waxwings. The downy hawthorn (*Crataegus mollis*) and chokecherry (*Prunus virginiana*) provide a dense screen for privacy and to hide the nearby highway. Their flowers attract butterflies in late spring, their fruits bring birds, particularly during the fall migration, their fall foliage brightens the landscape, and their dense growth helps buffer cold, winter winds.

A small lawn surrounding the patio serves the needs of a children's playground, as well as a foreground to the simulated prairie beyond. Here, a mass of native grasses, mostly sideoats grama (*Bouteloua curtipendula*) and little bluestem (*Schizachyrium scoparium*), provide a fabric of delightful texture, color, and movement, with drifts of native perennials offering additional color and textural variety. Monarchs and other butterflies are attracted to purple coneflower (*Echinacea purpurea*) and Maximilian's sunflower (*Helianthus maximiliani*), interspersed with butterfly weed (*Asclepias tuberosa*) on drier ground, or wild bergamot (*Monarda fistulosa*) where there is more moisture. In fall, American goldfinches flock to feed on the golden seed heads of the grasses, ripening alongside the late flowers of goldenrods (*Solidago* spp.).

Big Bluestem

Andropogon gerardii

Big bluestem is a tall, long-lived bunchgrass of the eastern Great Plains and wet areas farther west. It is one of the dominant grasses of the tallgrass prairies, once found in almost pure stands over vast areas. In midsummer, big bluestem rapidly develops a tall, reddish stem, topped with three-pronged flower heads. These flower heads look surprisingly like a turkey's foot, and from this comes another common name, turkeyfoot bluestem. Native American names usually referred to the beautiful, burgundy-red fall color of this grass.

J F M A M J J A S O N D

grass head

Big bluestem is widely adapted to a range of soils. Propagate it from seed, which won't germinate until the soil is warm in spring. You can plant it at other times if the effects of wind and water erosion can be controlled.

Songbirds and hoofed browsers, including white-tailed deer, are the main wildlife users of this grass. Sparrows and juncos will perch on the stalks to pluck and eat the seeds. Big bluestem is an important host of butterflies, including the regal fritillary. Adult regal fritillaries feed on the nectar of milkweeds and thistles within the tallgrass ecosystem.

white-tailed deer

FIELD NOTES

- Zones 3–8
- Perennial
- 3–9' (1–3 m)
- Full sun
- Moderate–high

388

Blue Grama

Bouteloua gracilis

Extremely drought-tolerant, blue grama is a long-lived, warm-season bunchgrass. The seed heads are very distinctive, resembling eyebrows on stalks. The blue–green color inspires the name blue grama, a common color of plants of hot, sunny, dry conditions. This lighter color reflects some of the sun's heat, allowing photosynthesis to occur for longer periods.

Blue grama is widely adapted to a variety of soils. Propagate it from seed, which requires warm soil to germinate—wait until catalpa trees are about to bloom. It is best not to plant blue grama after mid-July at latitude 40°N to allow the plants time to become established before winter.

You can use blue grama as a wonderful, informal lawn. You can either mow it, or leave it unmowed and plant a large number of short-grass prairie wildflowers such as chocolate flower (*Berlandiera lyrata*), gayfeather (*Liatris punctata*), and poppy mallow (*Callirhoe involucrata*).

J F M A M J J A S O N D

Wild Turkeys, Brown-capped Rosy Finches, and Chestnut-collared Longspurs are reported to eat blue grama seeds. Mice and voles gather the seeds for their winter storehouse.

FIELD NOTES
- Zones 3–9
- Seed heads, generally, 6–12" (15–30 cm); leaves, generally 3–6" (7.5–15 cm)
- Full sun essential
- Low

Chestnut-collared Longspur

389

Little Bluestem

Schizachyrium scoparium

Little bluestem is a warm-season, long-lived bunchgrass. The fall color is an attractive reddish brown, and the plant is topped with decorative, fuzzy seed heads. It is especially beautiful when backlit by the sun. Plant it as a single specimen or as a meadow planting.

| J | F | M | A | M | J | J | A | S | O | N | D |

To survive the severe dry conditions so common in midgrass prairies, little bluestem develops extensive roots that reach deep below the surface. Little bluestem is widely adapted to a range of soils. Propagate it from seed, which won't germinate until the soil is warm. You can plant it at other times of the year if the effects of wind and water erosion can be controlled.

Rosy Finches and juncos, as well as Chipping, Field, and Tree Sparrows, eat the seeds of little bluestem. Meadowlarks nest in the midgrass prairies, where little bluestem grows, and dusky skipper butterfly caterpillars overwinter in tube tents above the base of little bluestem clumps.

Eastern Meadowlark

♂

grass head

FIELD NOTES

- Zones 3–10
- Perennial
- 1–4' (30–120 cm)
- ☀ Full sun
- ◊ Low–moderate

Pearly Everlasting

Anaphalis margaritacea

Pearly everlasting produces masses of small, white flowers beginning in midsummer. The seed heads that form later extend the showy period considerably. The silvery white leaves are attractive throughout the season. The species name *margaritacea* is from the Greek for pearl-like. The flowers dry well for bouquets—thus, the name everlasting. Cut the flowers when the centers begin to show, and then put them in water briefly before hanging them upside down for drying.

J F M A M J J A S O N D

Pearly everlasting is adapted to a wide range of moisture conditions, from quite dry to quite damp, so long as the drainage is good. It is an unusual example of a plant with silvery leaves that tolerates moist conditions. Propagate it from seed or division. Butterflies, bees, and hover flies relish the nectar of pearly everlastings. American painted lady butterflies lay their yellowish-green eggs on pearly everlastings, and later, the colorful caterpillars form nests of silk and leaves on these same plants. American painted ladies may overwinter as adults.

FIELD NOTES

■ *Zones 3–9*

■ *Perennial*

■ *To 4' (1.2 m)*

☀ *Best in full sun, but adapted to some shade*

◐ *Low–moderate*

hover fly

391

Butterfly Weed

Asclepias tuberosa

milkweed bug

Butterfly weed is widely adapted to a range of soils, from very dry to very moist. You can try propagating it from seed, but results are often poor; otherwise, propagate it from root division. You can transplant nursery-grown plants at any time, but unfortunately, the plants' success is often uncertain. The flowers do well in bouquets. Unpicked flowers will develop showy seedpods with silky seeds. Be patient when weeding in spring, because butterfly weed is slow to emerge.

Butterfly weed is well named, for it is very attractive to many butterflies, as well as bees. The broad, flat flower heads provide generous landing platforms for butterflies, with lots of individual flowers offering tiny "pots" of sweet nectar. After their caterpillars feed on various milkweed plants, monarch and other milkweed butterflies, including the queen, develop a bitter taste that helps protect the adults from predators. The chrysalises are beautiful, jade-green, and studded with gold dots.

J F M A M J J A S O N D

queen butterfly caterpillar

FIELD NOTES
- Zones 4–9
- Perennial
- 2–3' (60-90 cm)
- ☀ Full sun
- ◊ Low–moderate

Purple Coneflower

Echinacea purpurea

Purple coneflower is an easy-to-grow, showy, long-lived flower that is native in the tallgrass prairie region.

It is adapted to a wide range of soils. Propagate it from seed: sow seed in spring or fall; no special treatment is required. The plant was named after the Greek word *echinos*, for hedgehog—a reference to the prickly, showy, flower centers. Purple coneflower makes attractive bouquets, either with fresh flowers or by using the dried, prickly seed heads in dry arrangements.

J F M A M J J A S O N D

The flowering of this plant almost epitomizes midsummer, and it seems as if all the butterflies of midsummer, such as the red admiral, like it. Fritillaries are especially frequent visitors. Birds such as the American Goldfinch will feed on the seeds in late summer and fall. A big plus is that deer do not eat this plant.

The plant contains a compound toxic to mosquitoes and houseflies, and efforts are under way to use another insect-inhibiting compound as a natural insecticide on sunflower crops.

red admiral butterfly

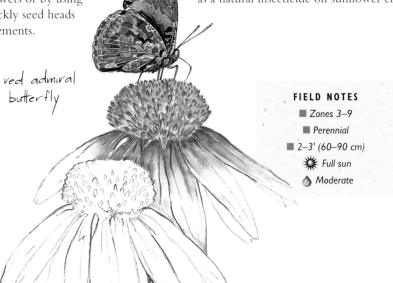

FIELD NOTES
- Zones 3–9
- Perennial
- 2–3' (60–90 cm)
- ☀ Full sun
- ◍ Moderate

Maximilian's Sunflower

Helianthus maximiliani

Maximilian's sunflower makes a real show in the fall landscape. It blooms late, often into October, and the numerous stems lined with many bright yellow flowers create quite a display. It is named after Maximilian Alexander Philipp of Wied-Neuwied, who collected many plants on an expedition up the Missouri River in 1833 and 1834. This is a long-lived perennial that is considered native throughout the Great Plains, but it is most associated with the tallgrass prairies, where there is relatively ample moisture. In dry locations, this sunflower is much smaller than on moist sites. It has become a significant part of northern New Mexico landscaping, where it adds to the dramatic,

J F M A M J J A S O N D

yellow fall flowers of rabbitbrush (*Chrysothamnus* spp.), various senecios, and the wonderful blue of Bigelow's asters (*Machaeranthera bigelovii*).

Maximilian's sunflower is adapted to a wide range of soils. Propagation is usually by seed.

The flowers attract numerous butterflies. Colorful Lazuli Buntings and White-crowned Sparrows feed on the seeds, which have been grown as a source of excellent birdseed.

FIELD NOTES
- Zones 2–8
- Perennial
- 5–10' (1.5–3 m)
- ☀ Full sun
- ◊ Moderate

White-crowned Sparrow

394

Bush Morning-glory

Ipomoea leptophylla

Bush morning-glory is a shrub-like perennial with fine, narrow leaves and extremely showy, pink, funnel-shaped flowers from late May to August.

Bush morning-glory prefers sandy, well-drained soil. Propagate it from seed or from root-crown division. It prefers dry conditions—no more than 12–14" (300–350 mm) average annual rainfall. Bush morning-glory will grow in most zones, provided the preferred soil and dry climate are present.

The deep, tubular flowers of this plant are pollinated mostly by bees, but ants seem fond of the plant, too. The ants are likely acting as guards, warding off some other insect that would "waste" valuable pollen or nectar. Ants themselves are considered pollination scoundrels, because their slippery bodies don't carry pollen well. They like nectar so much, however, that many plants have developed external nectaries to attract them to areas outside the pollen-bearing parts of the flowers, where they can fend off other would-be robbers. Butterflies, including the cloudless sulfur, are also attracted to the flowers of bush morning-glory.

J F M A M J J A S O N D

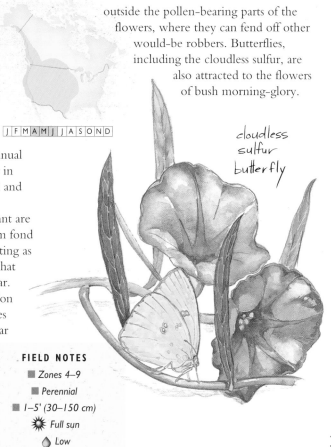

cloudless sulfur butterfly

FIELD NOTES
- Zones 4–9
- Perennial
- 1–5' (30–150 cm)
- Full sun
- Low

395

Dotted Gayfeather

Liatris punctata

This is a very ornamental flowering plant, useful in dry gardens or in shortgrass meadows. It has a moisture-storing rootstock from which it develops erect stems covered with pretty, pink flowers from late summer well into fall. Individual plants probably bloom for no more than two weeks, but other plants keep the show going for nearly three months. Gayfeathers are unusual in that flowering begins at the top of the flower spike, then progresses downward (most plants with flowers in vertical spikes bloom from bottom to top). Dotted gayfeather makes an attractive cut flower for bouquets.

Gayfeather prefers well-drained soil and will grow in most zones provided it has dry conditions—more than 12–14" (300–350 mm) average annual rainfall may cause problems. Propagate it from seed or root division; sow seed in very early spring or in late fall (stratify seed for spring planting); plant root divisions in the same periods.

When dotted gayfeather is in bloom, its nectar attracts bees and numerous butterflies, including the regal fritillary.

mason bee

J F M A M J J A S O N D

regal fritillary butterfly

FIELD NOTES
- Zones 3–10
- 6–24" (15–60 cm)
- Full sun
- Low

Wild Bergamot

Monarda fistulosa

Wild bergamot is an upright plant with fragrant foliage on square stems, topped by clusters of pretty, tubular summer flowers. It is common in the Rocky Mountain foothills and in the relatively wet, eastern tallgrass prairies. Wild bergamot, wild monarda, bee balm, horsemint, Oswego tea, purple bergamot, oregano, plains bee balm, and fern mint—this plant has many names! The most interesting, however, may be the Pawnee name *tsakus tawirat* (shot-many-times-and-still-fighting), which no doubt refers to the medicinal properties of this plant, such as its antibacterial and antifungal properties.

Like so many of the mints, wild bergamot is likely to spread rapidly with fertile soil and plenty of water. It is adapted to a wide range of soils but does not like dry conditions.

J F M A M J J A S O N D

Propagate it from seed, or from plant division in early spring, or in fall after flowering.

A range of butterflies, hummingbirds, bees, and diurnal moths, such as the hummingbird moth, will be attracted to wild bergamot flowers.

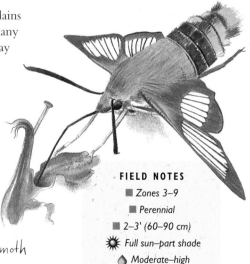

hummingbird moth

FIELD NOTES
- Zones 3–9
- Perennial
- 2–3' (60–90 cm)
- ☀ Full sun–part shade
- ◊ Moderate–high

Ozark Sundrop

Oenothera missouriensis

Ozark sundrop is a long-lived perennial with large, fragrant, lemon-yellow flowers that tend to open near sunset and close before noon the following day. The blooming season is from spring to fall. Although the genus *Oenothera* is often referred to as evening primrose, in reality, some species open in the evening; and others, in the morning. Oil of evening primrose is said to be the richest natural source of unsaturated fatty acids and is widely mentioned in natural-food publications. Scientific research has also shown it to be useful in cholesterol reduction.

J F M A M J J A S O N D

Ozark sundrop is adapted to a wide range of soils. Propagation is usually from seed, although you can propagate it from root division. All species of *Oenothera* are pollinated primarily by various night-flying moths, or, for those flowering during the day, by hummingbirds and butterflies, all attracted by the nectar. Tree crickets are attracted to caterpillars that feed on the plants.

FIELD NOTES
- Zones 4–8
- Perennial
- 6–12" (15–30 cm)
- ☀ Full sun
- 💧 Moderate–high

American tree cricket

398

Foxglove Penstemon

Penstemon cobaea

Penstemons make up the largest genus of wildflowers in North America, and they are native only to North America. There are tall ones, short ones, and some for dry as well as wet locations. The spring flowers can be white, red, blue, or yellow.

| J | F | M | A | M | J | J | A | S | O | N | D |

The genus name *Penstemon* refers to the five stamens they possess, but the fifth stamen has no anther. Instead, it serves as a barrier to crawling insects that might rob nectar without distributing pollen to flowers on distant plants. Foxglove penstemon is among the showiest penstemons, and is one of the longest-lived in gardens. The flowers are white and very large, with pretty, reddish lines.

bumblebee on
P. cardinalis

Plant foxglove penstemon in well-drained soil. Propagate it from seed (which will probably need stratification). Sow seed in fall, winter, or early spring.

Foxglove penstemon is pollinated mostly by bumblebees, which "muscle" their way into the large, tubular flowers. Hummingbirds will also be attracted to the flowers.

bumblebee on
P. cobaea

FIELD NOTES
- Zones 4–9
- Perennial
- 3' (1 m) when in bloom.
- ☀ Full sun
- ◊ Moderate

399

Salvia azurea var. grandiflora

Blue Sage

Salvia azurea

hover fly

eastern
box turtle

Blue sage is a tall, long-lived plant with appealing, light blue flowers in spike-like clusters. Flowers typically bloom from late August to early October. It is generally associated with tallgrass prairie plant communities, where it is particularly showy amidst the various grasses and yellow-flowered Maximilian's sunflower (*Helianthus maximiliani*).

In gardens, blue sage usually stands upright better when grown in dry conditions, but it is adapted to a wide range of soils. Propagate it from seed; you can also propagate it from root divisions and cuttings. It will self-sow and naturalize in garden areas. Pinching back the stems several times before early July results in more stems and, therefore, more flowers. *S. azurea* var. *grandiflora* is a natural variety with larger, lighter blue flowers.

A variety of insects, including bees, hover flies, and butterflies, will visit blue sage. Adult monarch butterflies have shown considerable interest in the flowers, which bloom from late summer to early fall. Hummingbirds in the area will also discover the nectar in the blue flowers.

| J | F | M | A | M | J | J | A | S | O | N | D |

FIELD NOTES

- Zones 4–10
- Perennial
- 3–4' (90–120 cm)
- ☀ Full sun
- ⬡ Low–moderate

400

Goldenrods

Solidago spp.

There are many species of goldenrod in Europe, Asia, and North America. They are widely adapted to a range of soils and grow in hot, cold, dry, and wet areas. They have a generally similar appearance and can be quite showy, with numerous stems topped by clusters of yellow flowers.

Despite their showiness, some are very invasive, while others remain compact. European gardeners have developed some of the best new garden cultivars from the North American *S. canadensis*. 'Baby Gold' is one of these.

Propagate goldenrods from seed, division, or stem cuttings. Sow seed or plant young specimens in spring. Some seed may need stratification.

Goldenrods tend to bloom from midsummer into fall, and are good butterfly-attracting plants. While the tiny tubes of goldenrods' flowers contain only minuscule amounts of nectar, the large number of flowers in each cluster compensates for this. Monarch, orange sulfur, and red admiral butterflies will all be attracted to goldenrod flowers.

J F M A M J J A S O N D

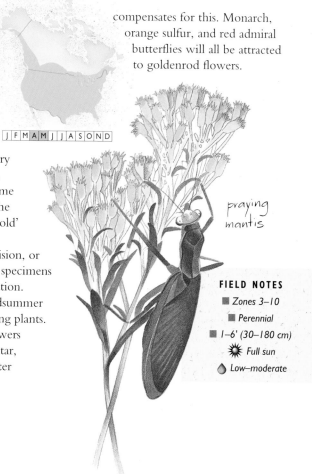

praying mantis

FIELD NOTES
- Zones 3–10
- Perennial
- 1–6' (30–180 cm)
- ☀ Full sun
- ◐ Low–moderate

401

Verbena canadensis 'Homestead Purple'

Rose Verbena

Verbena canadensis

Rose verbena is a low-growing, short-lived perennial generally associated with the eastern tallgrass prairies. The variable bloom time ranges from spring to fall, with flowers that are usually more pink than blue. Various verbenas have been used for many medicinal purposes, including stomach troubles, respiratory inflammations, fevers, and, perhaps best of all, "a feeling of relaxed well-being".

In the garden, rose verbena will self-sow and naturalize if the ground is open and there is little competition from other plants. It prefers a well-drained soil. Propagate it from seed or from cuttings.

J F M A M J J A S O N D

This verbena is a typical butterfly-pollinated flower. Its flat-topped flowers make landing easy for butterflies, and butterflies have the long tongues needed to reach deep into the flowers for nectar. Bees generally do not have mouthparts long enough for verbena flowers, but some bees have special forelegs that allow them to collect pollen by inserting them into the tubes. Verbenas support all phases (egg, caterpillar, chrysalis, and adult) of the attractive Theona checkerspot butterfly.

FIELD NOTES

■ Zones 5–10

■ Perennial

■ 6" (15 cm)

☀ Full sun

◗ Low–moderate

great spangled fritillary butterfly

Chokecherry

Prunus virginiana

Chokecherries are tall, thicket-forming shrubs with attractive, spring flower clusters and very useful, midsummer fruits. Native Americans used the bark to treat coughs, fevers, and arthritis. In mainstream modern medicine, chokecherry is used mainly in cough medicine for its mild, sedative properties and pleasant taste. The name chokecherry is well deserved: the berries are very astringent when eaten raw. They are, however, delicious as a syrup topping.

Chokecherry tolerates a range of soils but prefers well-drained soil. Propagate it from seed sown in fall, or stratify seeds till spring.

Tiger swallowtail, two-tailed swallowtail, and Lorquin's admiral butterflies use chokecherries for their chrysalis phases. The chrysalises of the swallowtails are usually green or brown and mimic pieces of leaf or wood.

J F M A M J J A S O N D

A favorite fruit of raccoons, chokecherries are also popular with fruit-eating birds, such as the Eastern Kingbird and, particularly, the robin. Even a single plant can become the center of a very conspicuous feeding frenzy.

Eastern Kingbird ♂

tiger swallowtail cocoon

FIELD NOTES
- Zones: 2–8
- Deciduous
- 10–25' (3–8 m)
- ☀ Full sun
- ◊ Moderate–high

403

Smooth Sumac

Rhus glabra

Smooth sumac is a medium-sized, thicket-forming shrub. Despite a dense and leafy appearance in summer, when smooth sumac drops its compound leaves in fall, the result is a shrub with few branches, which creates a distinctive branching pattern in the winter landscape, but limits its use as a year-round screen. Before dropping, the large, divided leaves turn brilliant shades of red, orange, and purple, lighting the fall landscape.

Smooth sumac is widely adapted to a range of soils. Propagate it from scarified seed, cuttings, or root pieces collected in midwinter. Scarify the seeds in sulfuric acid for 50–80 minutes.

Thirty-two species of bird eat the reddish sumac berries, which last from fall into winter, including Wild Turkeys, pheasants, robins, Steller's Jays, flickers, quails, and Downy Woodpeckers. The thicket-forming habit

creates very good cover for both birds and mammals, including chipmunks and rabbits. Rufous-sided Towhees seem to be especially fond of foraging beneath these sumacs.

J F M A M J J A S O N D

FIELD NOTES

- Zones 2–9
- Deciduous
- 9–15' (2.7–4.5 m)
- Full sun or light shade
- Low–moderate

Downy Woodpecker ♂

Wood's Rose

Rosa woodsii

Wood's rose is a low-growing shrub that forms patches in grassland areas. The rosy red to orange fall color can be quite attractive. The pink flowers are pretty, and the fall fruits (hips) are both attractive and useful, being high in vitamin C.

Wood's rose is widely adapted to a range of soils. Propagate it from fresh seed, which may not germinate until the second year after planting. You can also use root divisions and cuttings of green wood.

Deer are especially fond of rose buds and twigs, so be aware that after browsing on them, they may move on to other plants in the garden.

J F M A M J J A S O N D

Rose hips remain on the plants for a long time, sometimes until spring, and are an important source of food when other sources are gone. Birds are attracted to the hips. Pollination of Wood's rose is usually by native bumblebees rather than European honeybees. So many interesting insects are attracted to wild roses for the nectar, pollen, and foliage that full appreciation of these roses might require an insect field guide!

black-and-yellow argiope

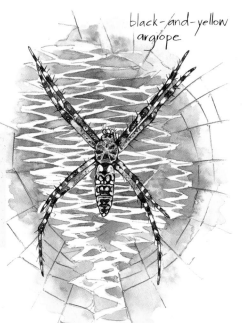

fall fruit (hip)

FIELD NOTES
- Zones 3–8
- Deciduous
- Usually less than 3' (1 m)
- ☀ Full sun or light shade
- ◊ Moderate

405

Downy Hawthorn

Crataegus mollis

Hawthorns have a long history in legends. Most famous is that Christ's crown of thorns was made of hawthorn. Downy hawthorn is an attractive, small tree with pretty bark, spring flowers, attractive, red fall fruits, and beautiful red or yellow fall color. The name hawthorn refers to the plant's thorns and haws (fruits).

Downy hawthorn is adapted to a range of soils. Propagation is difficult, so buy nursery-grown specimens to plant.

The thorniness of hawthorns, and the tendency to grow in thickets, create excellent cover for wildlife. Rufous-sided Towhees can be heard more often than seen, as they scratch around on the ground foraging for food in hawthorn thickets. Fox Sparrows and Cedar Waxwings are among the surprisingly few wildlife species that eat hawthorn fruits, which is one reason the fruits are ornamental for so long. Striped hairstreak, northern hairstreak, white admiral, and red-spotted purple butterflies use hawthorns as hosts for their egg, caterpillar, and chrysalis phases.

J F M A M J J A S O N D

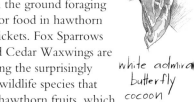

white admiral butterfly cocoon

FIELD NOTES
- Zones 3–8
- Deciduous
- 20–30' (6–9 m)
- ☀ Full sun
- ◊ Moderate

Eastern Rufous-sided Towhee

406

Eastern Cottonwood

Populus deltoides

Found throughout the eastern two-thirds of the continent, the eastern cottonwood is a huge tree that visually marks stream corridors, especially on the western high plains. The brilliant yellow fall color of this easy-to-grow tree heralds the end of the fall color season.

| J | F | M | A | M | J | J | A | S | O | N | D |

Northern Orioles in nest

♀

Eastern cottonwood will tolerate a range of soils. Propagate it from seed, without stratification, or from twigs before spring leaves appear.

The buds, catkins (flowers), seeds, twigs, foliage, bark, and the numerous insects that inhabit the tree, are very important to a wide array of wildlife for shelter and food. Both Orchard and Northern Orioles are especially closely associated with cottonwoods. These colorful, noisy birds often build their intriguing, hanging nests in the topmost branches. Beautiful Black-headed Grosbeaks frequently project their nonstop, robin-like song from the highest branches. Mourning cloaks, Compton tortoise-shells, white admirals, and red-spotted purples are among the butterflies that use cottonwoods in various phases of their development.

FIELD NOTES
- Zones 3–9
- Deciduous
- 75–100' (23–30 m)
- ☀ Full sun
- ◐ High

Bur Oak

Quercus macrocarpa

Bur, or mossy cup, oaks are massive, spreading trees with conspicuous, large, dark branches and rounded leaf lobes. The acorns have a distinctive, large cap with "burs", hence, the names bur oak and mossy cup oak. This is a relatively slow-growing tree (compared with cottonwoods, for example), but a long-lived tree—to 300 years or more. It develops just two leaves from stored reserves in the acorn, then grows a taproot up to 3' (1 m) long, before producing any more leaves. The thick bark is fire-resistant.

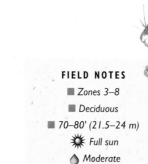

acorn

J F M A M J J A S O N D

Bur oak is adapted to a range of soils and grows well in clay. Propagate it from seed; stratification for 30–60 days at 41°F (5°C) is suggested.

Bur oak acorns are an important food source for many wildlife species—particularly in the Prairies, where there are few trees—including Wild Turkeys, eastern fox squirrels, and chipmunks. In all, possibly 500 wildlife species use acorns in North America, including most of the larger seed-eating birds. The greatest value of acorns is in winter, when other food sources are scarce.

eastern fox squirrel

FIELD NOTES

■ Zones 3–8

■ Deciduous

■ 70–80' (21.5–24 m)

☀ Full sun

◊ Moderate

408

Trumpet Creeper

Campsis radicans

Trumpet creeper is an extensive, rambling vine with clusters of spectacular, red to orange, trumpet-shaped flowers. The lush, compound leaves appear rather late compared to those of other deciduous plants. The flowers occur in midsummer, in most areas, and continue into fall. Trumpet creeper can cover huge areas—it is not a vine for small spaces. In the wild, it climbs by tangling itself among branches as it rambles through trees and larger shrubs. It also has aerial, root-like holdfasts that help attach the vine to flat surfaces by secreting adhesive substances. In gardens, it climbs best on some sort of natural or artificial support, such as a trellis, fence, or arbor.

Trumpet creeper is widely adapted to a range of soils. Propagate it from seed (stratified for two months at 41°F [5°C] or sown in fall) or from softwood cuttings.

| J | F | M | A | M | J | J | A | S | O | N | D |

The flower nectar is very attractive to hummingbirds, such as the Ruby-throated Hummingbird, which are lured into gardens where they otherwise would rarely be seen. The tangled vines provide shelter for many species of bird.

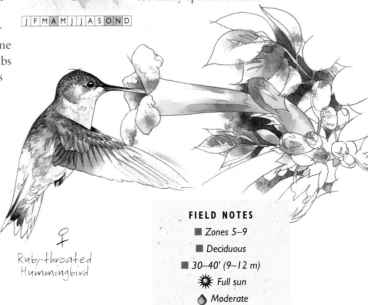

♀
Ruby-throated Hummingbird

FIELD NOTES

■ Zones 5–9

■ Deciduous

■ 30–40' (9–12 m)

☀ Full sun

💧 Moderate

Showy milkweed (left); smooth penstemon (right)

Additional species

Plant name/flower color	Zone	Height	Visitors/attraction/season
CACTI Pincushion cactus (pink) *Coryphantha vivipara*	4–9	4" (10 cm)	bees/flowers/spring
HERBACEOUS FLOWERS Showy milkweed (pink, purple) *Asclepias speciosa*	3–10	3–5' (90–150 cm)	butterflies, bees/flowers/summer monarch caterpillar/leaves/end summer
Day flower (blue) *Commelina dianthifolia*	7–9	6–12" (15–30 cm)	bees/flowers/summer, fall
Sacred datura (white) *Datura meteloides*	6–10	1–3' (30–90 cm)	sphinx moths/flowers/spring–fall
Cutleaf iron plant (yellow) *Haplopappus spinulosus*	3–8	1–2' (30–60 cm)	bees/flowers/fall
Great blue lobelia (blue) *Lobelia siphilitica*	4–9	1–3' (30–90 cm)	bees/flowers/summer, fall
Showy evening primrose (white) *Oenothera speciosa*	5–10	15–24" (38–60 cm)	moths/flowers/spring–fall
Buckley's penstemon (pale pink) *Penstemon buckleyi*	5–8	1½–3' (45–90 cm)	bees/flowers/spring
Smooth penstemon (white) *Penstemon digitalis*	4–9	2–3' (60–90 cm)	bees/flowers/spring
Sidebells penstemon (pink) *Penstemon secundiflorus*	4–7	1–2' (30–60 cm)	bees/flowers/spring
Broom groundsel (yellow) *Senecio spartioides*	4–9	3' (90 cm)	butterflies, bees/flowers/fall
Prairie zinnia (yellow) *Zinnia grandiflora*	5–9	12–18" (30–45 cm)	bees/flowers/spring–fall
SHRUBS Chocolate flower (yellow) *Berlandiera lyrata*	6–9	12–20" (30–50 cm)	bees, butterflies/flowers/summer
Coyote willow (n/a) *Salix exigua*	3–9	3–25' (1–7.5 m)	birds/insects/all year
Silver buffaloberry (n/a) *Shepherdia argentea* (exotic)	2–6	15' (4.5 m)	birds, bears, ground squirrels/ berries/fall, winter
TREES Green ash (n/a) *Fraxinus pennsylvanica*	3–9	66' (20 m)	squirrels/seeds/fall
Hop tree (green) *Ptelea trifoliata*	4–8	25' (7.5 m)	carrion flies/flowers/spring birds/cover/spring–fall
Peach-leaf willow (n/a) *Salix amydaloides*	5–8	50–65' (15–20 m)	birds/insects/all year
Soapberry tree (white) *Sapindus drummondii*	8–10	50' (15 m)	birds/cover/spring–fall
VINES Western virgin's bower (light yellow) *Clematis ligusticifolia*	3–10	3–50' (1–15 m)	bees/flowers/summer

The Northeast

THE NORTHEAST
The Backyard Meadow Garden

The Northeast region stretches north to the Canadian maritime provinces, west to the Great Lakes, and south to northern Tennessee and Virginia. Eastern North America is essentially a vast plain, bisected down the middle by the ancient Appalachian mountain range. To the west of the mountains is a more or less level plateau that extends across to the Mississippi River. East, the land falls away gradually through the hilly piedmont ("foot of the mountain") to the coastal plain—a level stretch of land, only a few feet above sea level, that runs from northern New Jersey to tidewater Virginia. The maritime provinces and New England have no coastal plain; there, the hills descend directly to the rocky coastline.

The backyard meadow garden of the Northeast has trees and shrubs around the perimeter to provide nesting sites and food for wildlife. A large tree in the background may be the majestic white oak (*Quercus alba*), a favorite of migrating warblers, as well as Wood Ducks, Blue Jays, deer, and squirrels. Canadian hemlock (*Tsuga canadensis*) is the evergreen accent that provides winter cover for many birds and animals, as well as nesting sites for veeries and juncos.

In front of these trees may be some graceful paper birch trees (*Betula papyrifera*) and sassafras (*Sassafras albidum*). The shrub spicebush (*Lindera benzoin*) is planted for its wash of yellow flowers in spring. All these plants host butterfly larvae: the birch attracts the mourning cloak butterfly, and the spicebush and sassafras attract the spicebush swallowtail butterfly.

Allegheny serviceberry (*Amelanchier laevis*) grows near streams. Its early summer fruits feed red foxes, bluebirds, and orioles. The versatile high-bush blueberry (*Vaccinium corymbosum*) has pink, bell-like flowers in spring and edible, blue berries in summer, which are a favorite of Scarlet Tanagers. American hornbeam (*Carpinus caroliniana*) attracts Myrtle Warblers. Its twisted, black trunk will combine with red-osier dogwood (*Cornus sericea*) and winterberry (*Ilex verticillata*) to provide winter interest in the garden.

Meadowlarks nest in grassy meadows among sweeps of black-eyed Susans (*Rudbeckia hirta*) and New England asters (*Aster novae-angliae*). Both these flowers attract monarchs, painted ladies, swallowtails, and other butterflies. So does bee balm (*Monarda didyma*), which grows in the moist soil where the meadow meets the stream.

Wild Columbine

Aquilegia canadensis

I n spring, the sprightly red and yellow flowers of wild columbine nod in the breeze on wiry stems. The flower is distinctive for its delicate, spurred or tubular petals that alternate with spreading, colored sepals.

In nature, wild columbine is found nestled in tight crevices on rocky, wooded slopes in dappled shade. It is very adaptable in the garden, however, combining equally well with ferns or other woodland wildflowers in the shade, or with

J F M A M J J A S O N D

early field flowers in a meadow. In hot climates, it needs protection from the afternoon sun.

Wild columbine propagates readily from seed, which should be planted in spring, although it will take two years for the young plants to reach flowering size. It prefers a well-drained, dry, slightly acid soil.

Long-tongued moths, hummingbirds, and checkerspot butterflies are attracted to the nectar contained in wild columbine's tubular petals, while the columbine duskywing butterfly lays its eggs on the foliage.

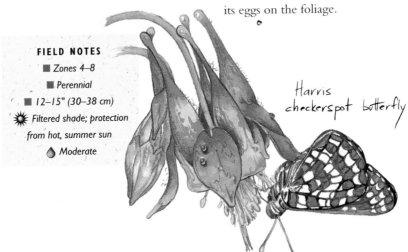

FIELD NOTES
- ■ Zones 4–8
- ■ Perennial
- ■ 12–15" (30–38 cm)
- ☀ Filtered shade; protection from hot, summer sun
- 💧 Moderate

Harris checkerspot butterfly

414

New England Aster

Aster novae-angliae

The New England aster grows in moist soil, and is often found along streams and roadsides, where its rich purple or red–violet ray flowers accent the tawny reds and yellows of the fall landscape. The plant may reach 6' (1.8 m) in the wild but it can be kept to a more compact size by shearing or mowing in early summer. While it prefers a moist position in the garden, it will also do well in an average perennial bed.

A stately plant, its narrow, downy, light green leaves clasp the stem at the base, and showy, daisy-like flowers appear in late summer to fall. It is adaptable, easy to divide and move, and grows readily from seed.

J F M A M J J A S O N D

common sulfur butterfly

All asters attract butterflies, as they are among the few nectar sources available so late in the season. Among those that visit New England aster are painted ladies, tiger swallowtails, common sulfurs, and monarchs. American toads are common throughout the Northeast, particularly in moist areas where asters grow.

FIELD NOTES
- Zones 4–9
- Perennial
- 6' (1.8 m)
- ☀ Full sun
- ◊ Moderate

American toad

Bee Balm

Monarda didyma

In midsummer, bee balm's ragged, scarlet pompoms bloom in low meadows and along the sunny banks of streams. It is a plant that grows well in any garden bed but really comes into its own in a moist meadow. It spreads readily in rich, moist soil and is, therefore, both easier to control and far more effective when given plenty of room.

honeybee

Bee balm is a plant for full sun—it tends to flop in the shade. If you remove the spent flowers, the plant will go on blooming for several weeks. Easily divided, bee balm is also readily grown from seed, although there may be considerable color variation in the resulting plants. In areas of poor air circulation, it may be susceptible to mildew, especially where the summers are hot and humid, but there are mildew-resistant plants among the many available selections.

A blooming patch of bee balm will attract bees and clouds of colorful butterflies, including monarchs, viceroys, painted ladies, and fritillaries. Quick, darting, Ruby-throated Hummingbirds also probe the tubular flowers for their sweet nectar.

J F M A M J J A S O N D

Ruby-throated Hummingbird ♂

FIELD NOTES

- Zones 4–9
- Perennial
- Deciduous
- 3–4' (1–1.2 m)
- ☀ Full sun
- ◊ Moderate–high

Black-eyed Susan

Rudbeckia hirta

Swaths of black-eyed Susans, that familiar yellow daisy with the dark brown center, color our eastern meadows bright gold every summer. Yet, like many of our meadow flowers, the fast-growing black-eyed Susan originated elsewhere: it is a mid-western Prairie flower that spread eastward when the forest was cleared.

Rudbeckia needs full sun but will grow in any ordinary soil. It is grown from seed. A short-lived perennial, it must continually reseed itself or eventually die out. There are many cultivars on the market; the widely advertised gloriosa daisies are nothing more than tetraploid black-eyed Susans.

J F M A M J J A S O N D

The black-eyed Susan, like all members of the daisy family, is a composite flower. What we see as a single yellow and brown blossom is actually a ring of tubular ray flowers surrounding a tight cluster of flowers. All composites attract butterflies; they provide ample room for landing and perching as well as numerous sources of nectar. In addition, the black-eyed Susan is a food plant for the larvae of a small orange-and-black butterfly called the silvery checkerspot.

FIELD NOTES
- Zones 5–8
- Annual/biennial/perennial
- 3' (1 m)
- Full sun
- Low–moderate

monarch butterfly

417

Red-osier Dogwood

Cornus sericea (stolonifera)

Red-osier dogwood is a common shrub in New England, where it typically grows along the banks of streams. In winter, its bright red stems appear to glow against the snow. Readily adaptable to the garden, it is particularly attractive in late winter and early spring, when the color of the stems seems to intensify.

Clusters of small, creamy white flowers appear in late spring, and the white fruits ripen during July and August. The plant sends up shoots along the roots, eventually forming a sizeable clump. The twigs root readily, making it easy to propagate. Red-osier dogwood prefers a moist, acid soil. A water source or mulch can help to retain moisture. Combine it with paper birch against a background of evergreens to make an attractive winter planting for a northern garden.

All dogwoods are good wildlife-attracting plants. Among the many kinds of animal and bird that feed on the fruit of red-osier dogwood are rabbits, Wood Ducks, Evening Grosbeaks, robins, Wood Thrushes, and Cedar Waxwings. The larvae of the small, blue spring azure butterfly also feed on its leaves.

J F M A M J J A S O N D

American Robin ♂

FIELD NOTES
- Zones 4–9
- Deciduous
- 10' (3 m)
- ☀ Full sun or partial shade
- ⬦ Moderate–high

Winterberry

Ilex verticillata

Winterberry is a deciduous holly and, like all members of that group, it bears male and female flowers on separate plants. Bees readily pollinate the flowers, but there must be a male plant nearby for the female plant to set fruit. Winterberry is primarily a plant of the coastal plain, growing naturally on stream banks, in swamps, and at the edge of salt marshes. It is the perfect choice for low, poorly drained areas, but is adaptable to drier conditions. Propagation is by stem cuttings or layering.

In the wild, winterberry is a tall, upright shrub but smaller cultivars are available. It is a shrub that is inconspicuous in spring and summer, but comes into its own in fall and winter, when the medium green foliage turns yellow and the pea-sized, scarlet berries begin to ripen. They will cover the bare, black branches until January to February, enlivening the winter garden and feeding a wide range of songbirds, including mockingbirds, robins, and Cedar Waxwings. The woolly bear caterpillar feeds on winterberry leaves.

summer foliage

J F M A M J J A S O N D

FIELD NOTES
- Zones 4–8
- Deciduous
- 10' (3 m) tall
- ☀ Half sun–full sun
- ◊ Moderate–high

woolly bear caterpillar

419

Spicebush

Lindera benzoin

In very early spring, the fragrant flowers of the spicebush appear as a haze of soft yellow in the still leafless woods and are immediately visited by the first bees of the season. The spicebush bears male and female flowers on separate plants. The bark is a rich, reddish brown, dotted on the branches with conspicuous white spots; both twigs and foliage emit a spicy, aromatic odor when broken.

J F M A M J J A S O N D

In the wild, this shrub is commonly found on the flood plains of woodland streams. In the garden, it is a tidy plant, always attractive yet never intrusive, easily grown and transplanted. Propagation is by cuttings. Spicebush prefers a moist, acid soil but does not require a wet location in the garden.

In fall, the smooth, green eaves turn a bright golden yellow and shiny red fruits appear on the female plants. These fruits are valuable food for Wood Thrushes and veeries before their long fall migration. They are also relished by quail, Ruffed Grouse, and pheasants. Rabbits and white-tailed deer browse on spicebush twigs in the winter, and the shrub is also one of only two known hosts of the beautiful spicebush swallowtail butterfly (the other is sassafras, *Sassafras albidum*).

spring flower

FIELD NOTES

- Zones 4–8
- Deciduous
- 3–10' (1–3 m) tall
- ☀ Filtered sun or partial shade
- ◊ Moderate–high

spicebush swallowtail butterfly

Bayberry
Myrica pensylvanica

ayberry's glossy, olive-green leaves and graceful, mounded shape are attractive all summer and especially so in fall and winter, when the foliage turns bronze and the angular, twiggy branches of the female plants are covered with thick clusters of metallic-gray berries.

Bayberry thrives in the dry, sandy soil of coastal dunes and lake shores. In the garden, it combines well with red cedar (*Juniperus virginiana*) for an attractive winter grouping. Because bayberry bears male and female flowers on separate plants, however, you will have to include at least one male plant for every 10 females. Since nurseries rarely differentiate between the two, it is best to select plants in fall when the female plants bear fruit. Propagation is from root cuttings.

The Tree Swallow, after eating insects all summer, consumes quantities of bayberries along its fall coastal migration route to Florida and Central America. The uneaten fruit remains on the plant until early spring, when it is stripped off by returning orioles, bluebirds, and Yellow-rumped Warblers.

J F M A M J J A S O N D

Tree Swallow

FIELD NOTES
- Zones 2–7
- Deciduous
- 4' (1.2 m) tall
- Full sun
- Low

421

■ Sow-teat blackberry (*Rubus allegheniensis*)

Blackberry, Raspberry

Rubus spp.

The genus *Rubus* contains many species that interbreed freely, but there are two general types: the blackberry and the raspberry. Raspberries can be black or red and usually ripen in July. When picked the berry is hollow, like a small cup, leaving its white core on the shrub. A blackberry is not hollow. It keeps its core when

J F M A M J J A S O N D

picked and ripens in August. Both groups have white, five-petaled flowers, three-part leaves, and prickly stems, with one exception: the purple-flowering raspberry (*R. odoratus*).

blackberry flower

The woody stems, called "canes", are short-lived, but the roots go on indefinitely. First-year stems are unbranched; they develop side branches which bloom and set fruit during the second summer, after which they die and can be removed. The canes can arch over, sometimes rooting where they touch the ground. For easier handling, keep them about 6" (15 cm) apart and cut back to 4' (1.2 m) high. Propagation is by stem or root cuttings.

Rubus berries are well loved by birds as well as foxes, bears, raccoons, and squirrels. The canes also provide birds with valuable nesting cover.

Blue-winged Warbler ♂

FIELD NOTES

■ Zones 4–8

■ Deciduous

■ 5–6' (1.5–1.8 m)

☀ Full sun

◊ Moderate

422

Highbush Blueberry

Vaccinium corymbosum

Highbush blueberry is the common, tall blueberry of swamps, bogs, and low wet ground, but it also invades old fields and pasture lands where the soil is considerably drier. In spring, the shrub is festooned with small, white or pink, bell-shaped flowers, followed in summer by the sweet, blue-black berries that we all love. The new twigs are yellow-green in summer, turning pale red in winter, and in fall, the smooth, green leaves turn a deep, brilliant red. While any of these attributes would be reason enough to grow highbush blueberry in the garden, older shrubs also acquire a twisted, gnarled trunk, reminiscent of ancient Japanese gardens. Highbush blueberry prefers a rich, moist, acid soil and can be propagated by cuttings or layering.

J F M A M J J A S O N D

Another attractive species is the lowbush blueberry (*V. angustifolium*). It is a northern shrub of open, rocky hillsides that produces quantities of sweet berries.

Blueberry flowers are pollinated by a variety of native bees. In the north, black bears are well-known for their fondness for the fruit, as are chipmunks and other small mammals. Scarlet Tanagers, bluebirds, catbirds, and mockingbirds are but a few of the many songbirds that feast on them.

FIELD NOTES
- Zones 4–9
- Deciduous
- 10' (3 m)
- ☀ Full sun or partial shade
- ◊ Moderate–high

eastern chipmunk

423

Highbush Cranberry

Viburnum trilobum

Highbush cranberry is one of a large clan of native viburnums that make attractive garden plants. A tall, arching shrub, it is found growing at or near the edge of woodlands and swamps, and prefers a moist, rich soil. In May, highbush cranberry is laden with lacy, white flower clusters, each surrounded by a ring of large, sterile flowers. The maple-shaped leaves are opposite, like all members of the honeysuckle family, and turn red in fall. The shiny, red, translucent fruits ripen in fall and hang

J F M A M J J A S O N D

on for most of winter. Propagation is by seed or cuttings.

Highbush cranberry is a plant of the northern woods and may not thrive in hot, humid summers. Other viburnums enjoy those conditions, however, including black haw (*V. prunifolium*), withe-rod (*V. cassinoides*), and possum haw (*V. nudum*). These viburnums' fruits are spectacular; starting in late August, they change gradually from green to white to pink and finally to blue-black. The show may be brief, however, if red foxes, chipmunks, Cedar Waxwings, and white-tailed deer get to them first! Viburnums also host the larvae of two butterflies, the spring azure and Henry's elfin, and provide nectar for a broad range of others.

Baltimore butterfly

FIELD NOTES
- ■ Zones 4–6
- ■ 10' (3 m)
- ■ Deciduous
- ☀ Full sun; partial shade
- ◊ Moderate–high

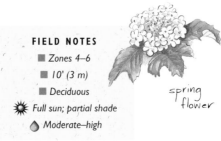

spring flower

424

Allegheny Serviceberry

Amelanchier laevis

Loose clusters of white Allegheny serviceberry blossoms appear in early spring, just as the shad swim up the cleaner eastern rivers to spawn. Each flower has five slender petals and numerous stamens. It is pollinated by bees. In fall, the foliage turns red or yellow and the light gray bark is attractive all winter.

The many eastern species of serviceberry tend to hybridize freely, making identification difficult. Most, however, are shrubs. Allegheny serviceberry is a small tree, one of only two to reach such a height. The other is downy serviceberry (*A. canadensis*). Allegheny serviceberry thrives in moist, acid soil. Propagation is difficult but plants are readily available from nurseries. A member of the rose family, it may be susceptible to insect damage in some areas.

J F M A M J J A S O N D

The red fruits ripen in June, providing food for wildlife at a time when few other fruits are ripe. In the wild, these early summer fruits are relished by everything from bears to Wild Turkeys, and they will attract many songbirds, including bluebirds, cardinals, Evening Grosbeaks, orioles, and tanagers, to the garden.

Scarlet Tanager ♂

FIELD NOTES
- ■ Zones 3–8
- ■ Deciduous
- ■ 25' (7.6 m)
- ☀ Partial shade preferred
- 💧 Moderate–high

Paper Birch

Betula papyrifera

A graceful, often multitrunked tree from the far north, paper birch's distinctive, white, peeling bark once covered canoes and wigwams of Native Americans. The bark is a smooth, reddish brown on young trees, but it turns creamy white with age and peels readily. In the garden, the clean, white bark shows to best advantage against a background of evergreens.

J F M A M J J A S O N D

gray comma anglewing butterfly

The pointed, dark green leaves turn a clear yellow in fall.

Although widely planted throughout the East, paper birch is less susceptible to insects and disease where summers are cool. Even in the North, it usually occurs on north- or east-facing slopes, and farther south, is found only in the mountains. It is relatively fast-growing and prefers a well-drained, sandy loam. Paper birch is readily available from nurseries.

Paper birch seeds provide valuable food for birds such as the redpoll and pine siskin. The larvae of the gray comma, an anglewing butterfly, feed on the foliage. So do the Compton tortoiseshell, the mourning cloak, and the Canadian tiger swallowtail.

FIELD NOTES
- Zones 2–5
- Deciduous
- 80' (24 m)
- ☀ Full sun (north); partial shade (south)
- 💧 Moderate

426

Eastern Redbud

Cercis canadensis

Clusters of bright, purple-pink, pea-like blossoms appear along the bare branches of the eastern redbud in May. It looks lovely planted in combination with flowering dogwood (*Cornus florida*).

fall leaves

Eastern redbud occurs naturally inland as far north as southern Michigan. Farther east, it is confined to the piedmont, south of Pennsylvania, yet it will succeed in gardens north to southern New Hampshire and Vermont.

A compact tree, it has a short trunk and smooth, gray bark that develops scaly plates as the tree ages. The usual flower color is a bright purple-pink, but there are selected slight variations. The leaves are heart-shaped and have a papery texture. Bright green in summer, they turn yellow in fall. The seeds are borne in pods.

J F M A M J J A S O N D

Eastern redbud blooms well in filtered shade. In full sun it prefers soil which is rich and moist. Propagation is slow.

It is valued more as a garden ornamental than a wildlife tree, but it does provide larval food for the small, brown Henry's elfin butterfly, and provides good nesting branches for Blue Jays and other birds.

FIELD NOTES

- Zones 5–10
- Deciduous
- 25' (7.6 m)
- ☀ Full sun or partial shade
- ◊ Moderate

Blue Jay

427

American Beech

Fagus grandifolia

A mature American beech is a majestic sight. In the woods, it grows straight toward the light, forming a broad crown in the forest canopy. When grown in the open, however, its broad, welcoming branches frequently sweep the ground.

The bark is a smooth, light gray, often with horizontal folds at the base, giving the trunk the look of an elephant's foot. Long, pointed buds unfold in early spring, and the leaves often remain through winter, in fall turning the light brown of old parchment and rustling softly in the breeze. Both male and female flowers appear on the same tree.

fall foliage

J F M A M J J A S O N D

The American beech grows best in rich, moist loam. It is found in moist forests throughout the East, reaching its greatest size in the Mississippi and Ohio river valleys. Though easily grown from seed, the tree's slow growth suggests planting from nursery stock is preferable.

Triangular nuts, contained in a spiny husk, ripen by the first frost. Black bears and porcupines particularly depend on them; chipmunks, squirrels, chickadees, and Tufted Titmice all love them. The larvae of the early hairstreak butterfly also feed on the leaves.

fall husk and beech nuts

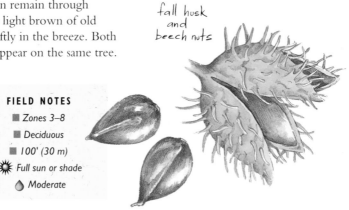

FIELD NOTES
- Zones 3–8
- Deciduous
- 100' (30 m)
- Full sun or shade
- Moderate

Eastern White Pine

Pinus strobus

Widely planted throughout the East, eastern white pine has soft, dense, feathery, blue-green needles in bundles of five, and an attractive pyramidal shape when young. As the tree ages, it tends to drop some of its branches, eventually acquiring an irregular silhouette and sweeping, horizontal crown.

When considering an eastern white pine for the garden, remember that this is a fast-growing tree eventually reaching a great size and needing ample room to do so. You will need to be watchful for white pine blister rust and white pine weevil. It prefers a well-drained soil. Propagation is by seed, but it is readily available from nurseries.

A mature eastern white pine is not only one of the most conspicuous and beautiful components of the eastern landscape, but also a good food source for wildlife. Red-breasted Nuthatches, Black-capped Chickadees, red Crossbills, squirrels, chipmunks, and mice, feed on the seeds in the pendulous cones which take two years to mature. Beavers, porcupines, and white-tailed deer browse on the foliage and twigs.

J F M A M J J A S O N D

Black-capped Chickadee ♂

FIELD NOTES

- ■ Zones 3–6
- ■ Evergreen
- ■ 150' (45 m)
- ☀ Full sun
- ◊ Moderate

429

Pin Cherry

Prunus pensylvanica

In much of the East, pin cherry is a small, early-blooming tree of fields and pastures. Farther north, it is known as fire cherry, because of its propensity to move into a forest after a fire, providing shade for the seedlings of the trees that will eventually replace it. It also grows plentifully along the banks of prairie rivers.

J F M A M J J A S O N D

white admiral butterfly

In the garden, pin cherry is a medium-sized tree with a rounded crown. It is beautiful in early spring when clusters of small, white flowers cover the branches, and again in late summer when the red fruits are ripe. Green summer foliage turns reddish, then bright yellow, in fall. Like other wild cherries, it may be susceptible to disfiguring attacks by the tent caterpillar in early summer. Propagation is by seed or cuttings, but it is faster to purchase plants from the nursery. Pin cherry is adaptable to a variety of soils.

Over 30 birds in the Northeast eat the cherries. They are relished by grouse and pheasant, as well as Evening and Rose-breasted Grosbeaks, bluebirds, and thrushes. Flocks of robins fly back and forth to cherry trees, picking off the fruit. Chipmunks, squirrels, and foxes feed on fallen fruit, and the bark and twigs attract browsing deer. Pin cherry also serves as a host plant for the larvae of coral hairstreak, spring azure, and white admiral butterflies.

FIELD NOTES

- Zones 3–6
- Deciduous
- 40' (12 m)
- Full sun
- Moderate

430

White Oak

Quercus alba

The regal white oak is truly the king of the eastern forest; it is a tree that grows tall and straight in the woods, but spreads its mighty branches in more open situations. The leaves are smaller than those of many oaks, with deeply cut, rounded lobes, and the acorns ripen in a single season.

The white oak's majestic size and spreading crown bring a sense of maturity and permanence to any garden. In spring, the unfolding leaves are a velvety pink, and in fall, the whole tree turns burnt orange, deep rich carmine red, or rich brown. Oaks are always among the last to turn, and often retain their leaves into early

November. Young trees may keep them all winter, providing cover for birds and other animals. White oak grows best in rich, moist, well-drained loam. Propagation is from seed but is very slow.

new spring leaf

White oak acorns, like those of all oaks, provide regular food for Wood Ducks, Wild Turkeys, Blue Jays, nuthatches, titmice, chickadees, woodpeckers, bears, raccoons, mice, and white-tailed deer. Squirrels often bury the acorns for later use, inadvertently planting more oaks in the process. Returning migrants, such as warblers, vireos, and tanagers, also flock to oak trees for the insects the trees harbor in spring.

J F M A M J J A S O N D

gray squirrel

FIELD NOTES

- Zones 4–8
- Deciduous
- 115' (35 m)
- Filtered sun
- Low–moderate

431

Sassafras

Sassafras albidum

Sassafras is truly a tree for all seasons. It has bright, greenish-yellow flowers in early spring, brilliant red-orange leaves in fall, green twigs in winter, and an attractive, horizontal branching pattern. It is one of the first trees to move into old fields and is also common in hedgerows throughout the East, where it grows from seeds dropped by birds that eat the fruit.

As a garden tree, sassafras is both underused and underappreciated. Difficult to propagate, it is rarely seen in nurseries, possibly because large specimens can be difficult to transplant. Sassafras spreads by underground runners. In the wild, a single sassafras tree will soon sprout a ring of satellite trees from its roots. This habit of growth can also be used attractively in the garden. Sassafras prefers a sandy, well-drained loam.

The deep blue fruit is never plentiful, but is eaten by a number of birds, including two that normally eat only insects: the Eastern Kingbird and the Phoebe. Catbirds and Pileated Woodpeckers also love sassafras fruit and the tree is one of only two known hosts of the larvae of the spicebush swallowtail butterfly (the other is spicebush, Lindera benzoin).

J F M A M J J A S O N D

FIELD NOTES

■ Zones 5–8

■ Deciduous

■ 60' (18 m)

☀ Full sun

💧 Moderate

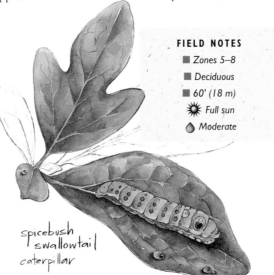

spicebush
swallowtail
caterpillar

432

Canadian Hemlock

Tsuga canadensis

I n the wild, Canadian hemlock grows on cool slopes, rocky ridges and ravines, often in pure stands. It is a dark, dense evergreen with small, flat needles and slightly pendulous branches that sway gracefully in the wind. Each stalked needle is a lustrous dark green above and silvery white beneath. Perfect miniature cones hang from the tips of the branches. Canadian hemlock is both slow-growing and very long-lived; an individual tree may live to be several hundred years old. In the garden, hemlocks make good background plants and can be maintained at almost any height. For this reason, they make excellent informal hedges. They prefer a

J F M A M J J A S O N D

moist, acid soil. Canadian hemlock is widely available from nurseries.

Hemlocks in the East are presently under attack by a prolific insect pest called the woolly adelgid. Insecticidal soap or oil (applied in July–September) is effective in treating infested garden trees.

Hemlocks are good wildlife trees. The dense, low foliage of young trees provides good winter cover for a number of birds and animals. Birds that seek out hemlocks for nesting sites are veeries, Black-throated Blue Warblers, and Northern Juncos. The small, winged seeds feed Pine Siskins, crossbills, chickadees, and red squirrels.

hemlock cones

FIELD NOTES
- ■ Zones 4–6
- ■ Evergreen
- ■ 80' (24 m)
- ☀ Full sun–deep shade
- ◖ Moderate

red squirrel

433

Virginia Creeper

Parthenocissus quinquefolia

Virginia creeper is an easily grown vine which is among the first plants to change color in fall. As early as midsummer, the leaf petioles turn a brilliant red, contrasting dramatically with the dark green leaves and ripening blue-black fruit. The foliage gradually turns a deep red, eventually fading to a translucent pink.

The most conspicuous feature of Virginia creeper is its five-part leaf, which immediately distinguishes it from that other well-known eastern vine: poison ivy (*Rhus radicans*)! The vine climbs by means of adhesive disks. It can be grown up tree trunks without damaging them, and looks particularly attractive draped over stone walls.

J F M A M J J A S O N D

A vigorous grower, yet easily kept in check by judicious pruning, Virginia creeper thrives in any kind of soil and does equally well in sun or shade. It will bloom and set fruit far more plentifully, however, if given a few hours per day of bright sunlight. Propagation is by seed or layering.

Bluebirds, mockingbirds, and woodpeckers, including the handsome Pileated Woodpecker, relish the fruit of this vine. Virginia creeper is the main food plant for the three eastern species of sphinx moth: the myron, Pandora, and white-lined sphinx moths.

FIELD NOTES
- Zones 4–10
- Deciduous
- 30' (9 m)
- Sun or shade but prefers some direct sunlight
- Low–moderate

Northern Mockingbird ♂

Concord grape (*Vitis labrusca* 'Concord')

Wild Grape

Vitis spp.

Grapes are large-scale vines that cling by means of tendrils to the slender branches of trees. They have large, flat leaves which can smother young plants by blocking out light. The flowers of all grapes are inconspicuous, but intensely fragrant. The heart-shaped leaves often have white or tan felt on the underside. Their fruits range from tart to musky sweet.

J F M A M J J A S O N D

There are about 30 species of grapevine native to North America, many of which interbreed freely. Grapevines are fast-growing and can be readily trained on an arbor to shade a terrace. They prefer a rich, well-drained loam and can be propagated from cuttings. For best production of fruit, prune them back in early spring to a few buds on the previous year's wood. One native species that adapts well to the garden is the fox grape (*V. labrusca*).

A common pest of wild and cultivated grapes, found throughout the East, is the grapevine beetle.

Gold- and Purple Finches, catbirds, mockingbirds, Brown Thrashers, and cardinals commonly use strips of peeling grapevine bark in constructing their nests. Most also eat the fruit, as do robins, Fox Sparrows, Cedar Waxwings, Pileated and Red-bellied Woodpeckers, foxes, black bears, and skunks. The larvae of various moths and butterflies feed on the leaves.

grapevine beetle

white-lined sphinx moth caterpillar

FIELD NOTES

- Zones vary with species; most 4–10
- Deciduous
- 20' (6 m)
- ☀ Sun or partial shade
- ◊ Moderate

435

Turk's-cap lily (left); chokeberry (right)

Additional species

Plant name/flower color	Zone	Height	Visitors/attraction/season
HERBACEOUS FLOWERS			
Rock cress (white) *Arabis caucasica* (exotic)	4–9	9" (22 cm)	butterflies/flowers/spring
False spiraea (various) *Astilbe* spp. (exotic)	4–8	2–4' (60–120 cm)	butterflies/flowers/spring–summer
Turtlehead (pink, white) *Chelone glabra*	4–9	1–3' (30–90 cm)	caterpillars/leaves/summer
Bunchberry (white) *Cornus canadensis*	2–5	3–8" (7.5–20 cm)	birds/fruits/fall
Coralbells (red) *Heuchera sanguinea*	3–10	2–3' (60–90 cm)	hummingbirds/flowers/spring–summer
Rose mallow (pink) *Hibiscus moscheutos palustris*	6–9	4–5' (120–150 cm)	butterflies/flowers/summer
Turk's-cap lily (orange) *Lilium superbum*	4–8	3–6' (90–180 cm)	hummingbirds/flowers/summer
Summer phlox (pink, white, lavender) *Phlox paniculata* (exotic)	4–8	3' (90 cm)	hummingbirds, moths, butterflies/flowers/summer
SHRUBS			
Chokeberry (white) *Aronia arbutifolia*	4–9	3–8' (90–240 cm)	caterpillars/leaves/spring birds, foxes/fruits/fall–winter
Buttonbush (white) *Cephalanthus occidentalis*	4–8	3–10' (90–300 cm)	butterflies, bees/flowers/summer ducks, deer/seedheads/fall
Flowering quince (red, pink, white) *Chaenomeles japonica* (exotic)	4–8	6–10' (1.8–3 m)	hummingbirds/flowers/spring birds/nesting/spring–summer
Witch hazel (yellow) *Hamamelis virginiana*	4–8	12' (3.6 m)	grouse, squirrels/seeds/fall–winter
Mountain laurel (pink, white) *Kalmia latifolia*	4–8	3–12' (90–360 cm)	Ruffed grouse, deer/leaves/all year
Sargent crab apple (pink, white) *Malus sargentii* (exotic)	4–8	6' (1.8 m)	birds/fruits/fall butterflies, bees/flowers/spring
Shining sumac (yellow) *Rhus coppallina*	5–9	2–8' (60–240 cm)	rabbits, deer, birds/fruits/fall
Elderberry (white) *Sambucus canadensis*	4–9	5–8' (1.5–2.4 m)	birds/fruits/summer
TREES			
Sugar maple (red-orange foliage) *Acer saccharum*	3–8	90' (27.5 m)	birds, chipmunks, squirrels/ seeds/summer
American hornbeam (green) *Carpinus caroliniana*	3–9	20–30' (6–9 m)	birds/nuts/fall birds/nesting/spring–summer
Willows (yellow, white) *Salix* spp.	2–10	10–40' (3–12 m)	caterpillars/leaves/spring–summer birds: nest/spring–summer; buds/spring
American mountain ash (white) *Sorbus americana*	3–8	10–30' (3–9 m)	birds/fruits/fall

The Southeast

THE SOUTHEAST
The Woodland Garden

In the Southeast region, from Florida to eastern Texas and north to Tennessee and Virginia, gardeners must deal with extreme heat and humidity for much of the year. They are fortunate, however, to have a large and diverse group of native trees and shrubs to choose from in creating a cool, shady woodland garden that is a haven not only for mammals, butterflies, and birds, but for people, too. Plants such as the deciduous fringe tree (*Chionanthus virginicus*) with its fleecy, fragrant, white flowers, the lemon-scented sweet bay (*Magnolia virginiana*) with waxy, white flowers amidst evergreen leaves, and the red maple (*Acer rubrum*) with its brilliant fall foliage all help to render the natural woodland garden a place of year-round beauty.

Trees form the framework for the garden and absorb the sun's heat. Lower evergreen trees and large shrubs work well as screening for privacy and help to channel any cooling breezes through the garden. A woodland garden with both evergreen and deciduous trees—eastern red cedar (*Juniperus virginiana*) on the sunny margin, American holly (*Ilex opaca*) and flowering dogwood (*Cornus florida*) within the shelter of the woods—combines attractive and colorful flowers, fruit, and foliage. These same plants are a source of food and shelter for gray squirrels, bluebirds, catbirds, flickers, and many other birds.

Shrubs in the woodland garden include those grown for their fragrant flowers, varied foliage, and colorful and edible fruits. The hoary azalea (*Rhododendron canescens*), is just one of many species of rhododendron native to the area that provide a nectar source for butterflies, such as gulf fritillaries and swallowtails. Hoary azalea flowers best along the sunnier margins of the woodland. Cardinals, robins, and Cedar Waxwings dine on the dark fruits of inkberry (*Ilex glabra*) and sour gum (*Nyssa sylvatica*), both found in moist woodland areas.

The sunlight enters the garden through an opening in the woodland canopy, encouraging a meadow-like planting of herbaceous flowers, most notably the bright yellow tickseed (*Coreopsis lanceolata*), and the thick-leaved phlox (*Phlox carolina*).

A quiet pond or gurgling stream provides water for wildlife as well as dependably moist soil for dramatic clumps of cardinal flower (*Lobelia cardinalis*), whose brilliant red flowers are irresistible to hummingbirds. On the edge of the woodland, the flowering stems of trumpet honeysuckle (*Lonicera sempervirens*) reach up toward the sunlight and are a food source for butterflies and hummingbirds.

Tickseed

Coreopsis lanceolata

Tickseed is an ideal perennial for hot, dry situations. A tall plant, it produces bright yellow with some orange, 2" (5 cm), daisy-like flowers from mid-spring until July. Cultivars are available in pale yellow and other shades of yellow-orange. This species has been used in hybridizing many of the double-flowering *Coreopsis* common in nurseries.

Propagation is by seed or division. Tickseed prefers a sandy, moist, well-drained soil. It tolerates drought well. The flowering season will be extended if early flowers are deadheaded; later flowers will still produce seed in late summer.

Plant several varieties of *Coreopsis* and you will have blooms in the garden from early spring until the first frost. For a bright combination, combine tickseed with bee balm (*Monarda didyma*) and summer phlox (*Phlox paniculata*), both of which attract butterflies.

A colorful addition for a naturalized meadow planting or by itself, the seeds of this easy-care plant attract birds such as juncos, buntings, sparrows, and finches.

J F M A M J J A S O N D

American Goldfinch

♂

FIELD NOTES
- Zones 6–9
- Perennial
- 2–3' +
  (60–90 cm) +
- ☀ Full sun
- 💧 Low–moderate

Joe-pye Weed

Eupatorium purpureum

Joe-pye weed is a large, impressive perennial that brings a welcome splash of color to the late summer and fall garden. There may be from five to as many as nine of the late summer, purple flower heads (sometimes with some pink) packed together, the overall diameter of these flower heads together measuring 12–18" (30–45 cm). The coarse-textured, 8–12" (20–30 cm), dark green leaves are in whorls of three to five leaves each; if crushed, they give off a vanilla-like scent. Joe-pye weed is a bold plant for the back of a border, along a stream, or by a pond, where it will get the moisture and full sun it prefers.

Propagation is by seed, division, or cuttings. Under most conditions, Joe-pye weed will become a massive clump, best suited to a large garden.

Late season butterflies that seek out its nectar include the large wood nymph, spicebush swallowtail, and zebra swallowtail.

| J | F | M | A | M | J | J | A | S | O | N | D |

FIELD NOTES

- Zones 4–9
- Perennial
- 4–7'
  (1.2–2 m)
- ☀ Full sun–part shade
- ◊ High

large
wood nymph
butterfly

441

Cardinal Flower

Lobelia cardinalis

Cardinal flower is a beacon in the late summer (August) garden, with its tall spikes of bright red flowers and dark green leaves. It is ideal for a flower border with other perennials, in a woodland shade garden with ferns and other plants, or for a spot of color along a stream, as it might be found in the wild.

Propagation is by seed, offshoots, or stem cuttings. Cardinal flower prefers a moist, rich soil and tolerates both light shade and full sun, especially if kept moist. It resents extreme dry conditions. Blooming for several weeks, this plant is sure to attract the

J F M A M J J A S O N D

Ruby-throated Hummingbird if it's in the neighborhood, as well as the spicebush, two-tailed, and pipevine swallowtail butterflies. The green tree frog feeds on insects attracted to cardinal flower's blooms.

green tree frog

FIELD NOTES
- Zones 2–9
- Perennial
- 2–4' (60–120 cm)
- ☀ Shade–part sun
- ◌ High

two-tailed swallowtail butterfly

442

Thick-leaved Phlox

Phlox carolina

Thick-leaved phlox is found growing in and along the edges of deciduous woodlands. The pink-purple flowers appear in big clusters on 3' (1 m)-tall stems, set off by thick, shiny green leaves in May to July. By pinching back plants in early spring, before they set flower buds, plants will be bushier and produce more flowers. Easy to grow, thick-leaved phlox does best with some shade but will take full sun. Feature it in flower borders, or place drifts at the edge of a shrub border or woodland garden.

Goldenrods (*Solidago* spp.) and asters (*Aster* spp.) are good companion plants for thick-leaved phlox.

J F M A M J J A S O N D

Propagation is by seed or cuttings, and thick-leaved phlox prefers a moist, well-drained soil.

Butterflies that are attracted to the flowers include the eastern black swallowtail, the gray hairstreak, and the palamedes swallowtail.

gray hairstreak butterfly

FIELD NOTES

- Zones 7–9
- Perennial
- 2–3' (60–90 cm)
- Shade–part sun
- Moderate

443

Red Buckeye

Aesculus pavia

Red buckeye grows as a large, clump-forming shrub or a small tree. Its showy flowers, a blend of red and yellow, brighten the woodland or shrub border in spring, especially when planted in masses. Red buckeye is also a good understory plant. The handsome, lustrous, dark green foliage has five to seven leaflets, and provides visual interest even when the plants are not flowering.

fall fruits

spring flower

J F M A M J J A S O N D

Propagation is by seed. The moist, fertile soils of woodland conditions are ideal for growing red buckeye; in such shaded conditions, red buckeye will be taller and more open than in full sun. Under stressful conditions, it should be mulched to reduce moisture loss.

The shiny seeds, which ripen in October, are thought to be a good luck charm by people who carry them, but are poisonous to cattle and to people if ingested. Ruby-throated Humming-birds are attracted to the flower nectar in spring.

FIELD NOTES
- Zones 4–8
- Deciduous
- 10–20' (3–6 m)
- ☀ Full sun best, but can take dense shade
- ◊ Moderate

Fringe Tree

Chionanthus virginicus

Fringe tree is an old-fashioned favorite, also called grancy gray-beard for its fleecy, beard-like, white flowers that perfume the air in spring. The dark green, leathery leaves turn a clear yellow in fall. A slow-growing, graceful shrub or small tree, it is ideal for gardens with only limited space, as a substitute for the flowering dogwood (*Cornus florida*). Plant fringe tree as a small specimen, or stand-alone, tree or as part of a shrub border along a woodland edge or stream.

Propagation is by seed. Fringe tree likes a moist, rich, acid soil, but it adapts to a range of conditions. It should be watered during dry periods.

J F M A M J J A S O N D

The dark blue, egg-shaped fruits that appear in late summer are favored by many birds, including bobwhites, Gray Catbirds, mockingbirds, robins, and starlings. Many birds also find suitable nesting sites among the fringe tree's branches.

FIELD NOTES

- Zones 3–9
- Deciduous
- 12–20' (3.6–6 m) or taller in the wild
- Full sun–part shade
- Moderate

Northern Bobwhite ♂

445

Ilex glabra 'Compacta'

Inkberry

Ilex glabra

Inkberry is a spineless, evergreen holly that is effective for hedges, screening, or in combination with deciduous shrubs and trees. The ink-colored, berry-like fruits last from September through to the following May. The small leaves, ¾–2" (2–5 cm) long and ⅓–⅝" (8–15 mm) wide, are a lustrous dark green, providing year-round color, as well as shelter and food for birds. Creamy flowers appear in late spring but are not showy; male and female flowers are produced on different plants. This adaptable shrub can grow to 8' (2.4 m) or more depending on the conditions.

J F M A M J J A S O N D

Easy to grow, it tolerates shade or sun and wet or dry soil, although moist, fertile soil is best. Propagation is by cuttings. Inkberry sometimes suckers and forms colonies. Be sure to plant at least one male and one female to be assured of some fruit production.

Birds that are attracted to the fruit of inkberry and other hollies include bluebirds, bobwhites, Northern Cardinals, Gray Catbirds, Cedar Waxwings, Yellow-shafted Flickers, Blue Jays, robins, and Woodpeckers.

spring flowers

Gray Catbird

FIELD NOTES
■ *Zones 4–9*
■ *Evergreen*
■ *6–8' by 8–10' (1.8–2.4 m by 2.4–3 m)*
☀ *Full sun–part shade*
◊ *Moderate–high*

446

Hoary Azalea

Rhododendron canescens

Hoary azalea, also called piedmont or Florida pinxter, is a large, upright shrub. Its fragrant, funnel-shaped flowers vary from white to pink to rose and appear from March to mid–April, often before the light green leaves have developed. Native along streams, hoary azalea is a wonderful addition to the sunny edge of a woodland planting. Easy to grow, it spreads readily by underground stems.

J F M A M J J A S O N D

Hoary azalea prefers a moist, well-drained soil, but it will tolerate less than perfect conditions, including poor soils. Water it during drought conditions. Propagation is by seed or from cuttings.

Butterflies that love the sweet nectar of this native include the tiger and spicebush swallowtails and the American painted lady. The leaves of the hoary azalea are also a source of larval food for the gray comma and the striped hairstreak butterflies.

gray comma
butterfly

FIELD NOTES

■ Zones 5–9

■ Deciduous

■ 10–15' (3–4.5 m)

☀ Full sun–part shade

◌ Moderate–high

447

Pignut Hickory

Carya glabra

Extensive oak–hickory woodlands still cover much of the eastern states; a major element of this woodland community is the pignut hickory, a large tree with compound leaves that turn a beautiful gold in fall. Early European settlers called it broom hickory, for the brooms they made from narrow strips of wood split from the tree. Flowers appear with the leaves in early spring, male flowers on catkins and female flowers on short, upright spikes; the fruits (pignuts) ripen in fall. As the tree matures, the smooth bark develops ridges, and the silhouette provides interest in the winter landscape.

J F M A M J J A S O N D

fall fruits (pignuts)

Its long taproot makes the pignut hickory difficult to transplant, so start it from seed planted where the tree is to be grown. Be prepared to wait, as it may take 25 years or more to begin fruiting. Tolerant of a wide range of soil types and moisture levels, pignut hickory can be used by itself as a specimen, or stand-alone, tree or as part of a woodland planting.

In spite of their bitter taste, the nuts are popular with squirrels. The large trees provide nesting sites for Blue Grosbeaks, Ruby-throated Hummingbirds, Blue Jays, White-breasted Nuthatches, and mockingbirds. The banded hairstreak butterfly larvae feed on the leaves.

White-breasted Nuthatch

FIELD NOTES

- Zones 4–9
- Deciduous
- 50–60' (15–18 m), may grow as tall as 100' (30 m)
- Full sun–part shade
- Low

♂

448

Sugarberry

Celtis laevigata

Sugarberry is a large, broad, rounded tree, sometimes with graceful, pendulous branches, that grows 60–80' (18–24 m) in height, with a similar spread. This adaptable tree tolerates compact, wet, clay soils. The overall effect of the simple, egg-shaped leaves—light green above, pale green below—is delicate. Tiny fall fruits change color from orange-red to dark purple.

Propagation is by seed, grafts, or cuttings. Plant sugarberry by itself in a large, open area or with smaller trees underneath it. Sugarberry is resistant to the witches' broom that commonly disfigures other hackberries.

It is named sugarberry because of its sweet, juicy fruit, which is a favorite of many birds, including bluebirds, Blue Jays, Northern Cardinals, mockingbirds, orioles, and robins. The sugarberry sap is a nectar source for the hackberry butterfly, and the young leaves provide important larval food for the snout, question mark, hackberry, tawny emperor, mourning cloak, and other species of butterfly.

J F M A M J J A S O N D

hackberry butterfly

FIELD NOTES
- ■ *Zones 5–9*
- ■ *Deciduous*
- ■ *60–80' (18–24 m)*
- ☀ *Full sun–part shade*
- ◐ *Moderate–high*

449

Flowering Dogwood

Cornus florida

The flowering dogwood is an elegant native. A tree of year-round interest, it is perhaps best loved in spring, when its branches are covered with white flowers (bracts) blooming in the woods as well as in sunnier locations. A small to medium-sized tree, it grows wider than its height, with horizontal branches giving a layered effect that makes the tree stand out in the winter landscape. In fall, the dark green summer leaves turn red and purplish red.

Eastern Bluebird ♂

Glossy, red fruits ripen in September to October, until birds or other wildlife, such as the eastern gray squirrel, devour them.

spring flower

Propagation is from seed and softwood cuttings. Flowering dogwood prefers acid, moist, and well-drained soil. Plant it in the garden as a single specimen, or stand-alone, tree or in groups with other dogwoods and native shrubs.

Flowering dogwood attracts a whole range of birds; who use the tree for cover, nesting, and as a source of food; including bobwhites, bluebirds, Gray Catbirds, mockingbirds, robins, sapsuckers, starlings, grackles, Red-bellied Woodpeckers, and quail. Young leaves are larval food for the spring azure butterfly.

FIELD NOTES

- Zones 5–9
- Deciduous
- 20' (6 m), can grow 30–40' (9–12 m), wider than tall
- Full sun–part shade
- Moderate

American Holly

Ilex opaca

Amerian holly is a slow-growing, broadleaf evergreen associated with Christmas, when its red berries and dark green leaves are popular for use in wreaths and other decorations. Dense and pyramidal as a young tree, it becomes more open with age. Fruits mature in October, and often persist well into winter. To ensure that your holly will produce fruit, it is a good idea to plant both female and male of the same type; however, only the female will bear fruits.

Propagation is from cuttings, and American holly prefers an acid, well-drained soil. It does not tolerate heavy, wet soil or extreme, dry conditions. This tree is ideal for screening, hedging, as a specimen, or stand-alone, tree, or as a background for deciduous trees. It is easily pruned to control its size.

Birds that eat the fruit, or use the tree for shelter, include bluebirds, bobwhites, Northern Cardinals, Gray Catbirds, Cedar Waxwings, Yellow-shafted Flickers, Blue Jays, robins, and woodpeckers. Henry's elfin butterfly relies on American holly leaves for larval food.

| J | F | M | A | M | J | J | A | S | O | N | D |

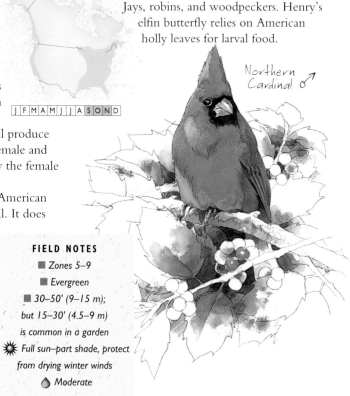

Northern Cardinal ♂

FIELD NOTES
- Zones 5–9
- Evergreen
- 30–50' (9–15 m); but 15–30' (4.5–9 m) is common in a garden
- ☀ Full sun–part shade, protect from drying winter winds
- 💧 Moderate

451

Eastern Red Cedar

Juniperus virginiana

Eastern red cedar is a large, tough, adaptable tree that grows across North America in a wide range of soils, in sunny, open places. It is perfect for hedgerows, screening, mass plantings, or mixed with deciduous trees. The habit varies from narrow, upright, and pyramidal to broad, open, and spreading. The cut wood and bruised leaves are intensely aromatic and the wood has long been popular for lining chests and closets.

J F M A M J J A S O N D

Flowering occurs in late winter with male and female flowers on separate trees. Female cones are greenish blue or violet; males are insignificant. Propagation is by seed or from cuttings and grafting. Eastern red cedar tolerates poor soils and high pH, but it prefers a moist, well-drained soil.

Avoid using red cedar if there are apple trees nearby, as the two are alternate hosts of the cedar-apple rust, a serious disease of apples.

The sweet berries are the favorite of many birds, especially the Cedar Waxwing, which gets its name from this tree. Other birds that like red cedar fruits include bluebirds, Gray Catbirds, Purple Finches, Yellow-bellied Sapsuckers, mockingbirds, robins, flickers, starlings, grackles, and Pileated Woodpeckers.

Cedar
Waxwing

FIELD NOTES
- Zones 2–9
- Evergreen
- 40–50' (12–15 m) by 8–20' (2.4–6 m) wide
- ☀ Full sun
- 💧 Low

452

Tulip Tree

Liriodendron tulipifera

A stately tree, this member of the magnolia family is the tallest hardwood in North America, reaching heights of 150' (45 m). A large tree, it starts out pyramidal in form and develops an oval, rounded crown. The beautiful flowers, for which the tree is named, have six greenish-yellow petals with orange at the base. From April to early June they sit up above the leaves at the top of each branch. The foliage starts out as a glossy light green, turns deep green and then a golden yellow in fall.

Propagation is by seed or from cuttings, and it prefers a deep, moist, well-drained loam. Ensure that you water tulip

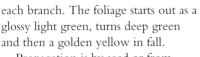

spring flower

J F M A M J J A S O N D

trees during periods of drought. This is a choice species for use as a large specimen, or stand-alone, tree or in a large property; it is not suitable for the small garden.

Tulip tree is home to the eastern gray squirrel and birds such as Purple Finches and Northern Cardinals. Its leaves are a source of larval food for the tiger swallowtail and spicebush swallowtail butterflies. An excellent honey is produced by bees collecting the nectar.

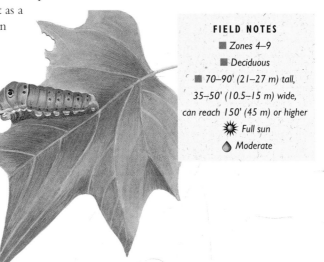

tiger swallowtail caterpillar

FIELD NOTES

- Zones 4–9
- Deciduous
- 70–90' (21–27 m) tall, 35–50' (10.5–15 m) wide, can reach 150' (45 m) or higher
- ☀ Full sun
- ◉ Moderate

453

Sweet Bay

Magnolia virginiana

A small, evergreen to semi-evergreen tree, the dark green leaves with silver on the underside shimmer in the breeze, and the lemon-scented, creamy white flowers perfume the air from May to June, and then on and off until early fall. With its fragrant flowers, silvery leaves, and bright red, late summer to fall fruits, this small magnolia provides interest in the garden throughout the year, and makes a lovely specimen tree. It is often pruned as a shrub.

J F M A M J J A S O N D

This slow-growing, adaptable native can tolerate wet soils, making it ideal to plant along a stream bank or in a flood plain, by itself or in a mixed planting. It also tolerates acid, dry soil; propagation is by seed or from softwood cuttings.

Tiger swallowtail and spicebush swallowtail butterfly larvae eat the new leaves, and Gray Catbirds eat the seeds of the fruit.

seed head

spring–summer flower

FIELD NOTES

- Zones 5–9
- Evergreen
- 60' (18 m)
- ☀ Full sun–shade
- ◗ Moderate–high

Red Mulberry

Morus rubra

Red mulberry is an adaptable, fast-growing tree, best planted as part of a mixed planting of deciduous and evergreen trees. A large tree, it may be as wide as it is tall. It is not particularly ornamental, but many consider it more attractive than white mulberry (*M. alba*), which was used to feed silk worms to make silk. Red mulberry has darker green leaves that turn yellow in fall. Yellowish-green flowers appear in March to April. The approximately 2" (5 cm)-long fruits occur in June to July.

Propagation is by seed or cuttings, and red mulberry prefers a rich, moist soil. Red mulberry is not drought tolerant like white mulberry.

Birds and squirrels love the sweet, juicy fruits that resemble blackberries. Birds attracted to the red mulberry include bluebirds, bobwhites, Purple Finches, Indigo Buntings, doves, orioles, Eastern Kingbirds, mockingbirds, and robins.

| J | F | M | A | M | J | J | A | S | O | N | D |

Indigo Bunting

♂

FIELD NOTES

- Zones 5–9
- Deciduous
- 40–70' (12–21.5 m)
- Full sun–light shade
- Moderate

455

Sour Gum

Nyssa sylvatica

fall fruit & leaves

Sour gum, or black gum, is an excellent native specimen, or stand-alone, tree or can be used as part of a woodland planting. Pyramidal as a young tree, its branches spread horizontally and it acquires a more rounded habit as it matures. It has beautiful, thick, shiny green foliage all summer, and in fall, it turns shades of brilliant red, orange, and gold. It is often one of the first trees to exhibit its fall color before other leaves have started to turn. A tree for all seasons, in winter, the checkered or scaly bark is picturesque in the landscape. Winter buds turn a brilliant red in spring.

J F M A M J J A S O N D

Propagation is by seed. Because of its taproot, sour gum is difficult to transplant. It is best to transplant balled and burlapped plants in early spring (March or April). Container-grown plants are also best planted in spring. Sour gum prefers moist, well-drained soil, but it is found in swamps and also in very dry conditions.

The dark blue fruits ripen in fall and are eaten by birds, such as bobwhites, Painted Buntings, crows, Purple Finches, Yellow-shafted Flickers, Blue Grosbeaks, and robins.

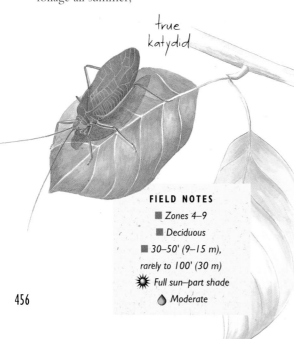

true katydid

FIELD NOTES
■ Zones 4–9
■ Deciduous
■ 30–50' (9–15 m), rarely to 100' (30 m)
☀ Full sun–part shade
💧 Moderate

456

Southern Live Oak

Quercus virginiana

Southern live oak is a large, majestic, oval-crowned tree. It is perfect as a specimen, or stand-alone, tree in a large garden. With a large, short trunk and massive horizontal and arching branches, often covered with Spanish moss, it is usually wider than it is tall with a spread of 60–100' (18–30 m). Sometimes, the branches reach down and touch the ground. Southern live oak's thick, narrow leaves, which start out olive green and turn a dark green, provide a fine-textured canopy. Inconspicuous, yellowish flowers appear in clusters in early spring.

Southern live oak is adaptable to most soil types, including sandy, moist, and compact soils. This slow-growing tree will grow well in dry conditions and also tolerates salt spray. Propagation is by seed.

Squirrels and birds favor this oak for shelter and for its acorns.

Birds that find southern live oak appealing include both common and colorful species, such as bobwhites, Indigo Buntings, crows, grackles, Ruffed Grouse, Ruby-throated Hummingbirds, and Blue Jays.

J F M A M J J A S O N D

Common Grackle

♂

FIELD NOTES
■ Zones 7–10
■ Evergreen
■ 40–80' (12–24 m)
☀ Full sun
💧 Moderate

457

Cabbage Palm

Sabal palmetto

For a tropical effect, the cabbage, or sabal, palm is the perfect tree. Its foliage resembles giant fans, each 3–5' (1–1.5 m) long by 2–3' (60–90 cm) wide. Growing in a wide range of soil types, from swampy to sandy, this palm looks good in groves, clumps, or as a single specimen, or stand-alone, tree.

J F M A M J J A S O N D

Large, drooping clusters of the flowers hang down below the leaves and the fruits are black and shiny. Young seedlings start out by growing downward into the soil before they turn upward permanently. A slow grower, it can reach 20–80' (6–24 m) by 6–10' (1.8–3 m) wide. Full sun or partial shade is best, and when transplanting, older plants do better because of the water they have stored for use during drought times. Propagation is by seed.

Birds that are attracted to the late summer fruits of cabbage palm include mockingbirds, robins, sapsuckers, warblers, Fish Crows, Pileated Woodpeckers, and Red-bellied Woodpeckers.

Red-bellied Woodpecker ♂

FIELD NOTES
- Zones 8–10
- Evergreen
- 20–80' (6–24 m)
- Full sun–part shade
- Low–moderate

Dutchman's Pipe

Aristolochia durior

Dutchman's pipe is an old-fashioned, vigorous, climbing, twining vine. Its huge, heart-shaped leaves, 4–8" (10–20 cm) across or larger, and its 3" (7.5 cm)-long flowers shaped like a pipe, make this curious vine a conversation piece. The spring flowers are yellow-green on the outside and brownish purple at the opening of the pipe. It needs support for climbing and does well when trained up a trellis, fence, or tree. The curious pollination strategy of this plant involves the flowers releasing a faint, unpleasant fragrance which draws flies and other minute insects into the pipe, where they become trapped. In their struggle to find an exit, they are pressed into contact with male and female parts, and pollination occurs.

spring flower

Propagation is by division or cuttings. Dutchman's pipe tolerates most soil types, as long as they are moist and well drained. It requires water during drought conditions.

The leaves of Dutchman's pipe are a source of larval food for the pipevine swallowtail butterfly.

J F M A M J J A S O N D

FIELD NOTES
- Zones 4–8
- Deciduous
- 20–30' (6–9 m) in a single season
- Full sun–part shade
- Moderate

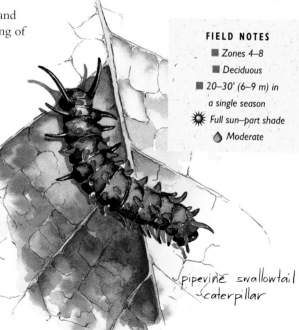

pipevine swallowtail caterpillar

459

Trumpet Honeysuckle

Lonicera sempervirens

Trumpet honeysuckle is a twining, climbing vine that is easily trained on a trellis, arbor, or through a garden shrub. It is deciduous in mild winters except it will hold on to its leaves. Its early spring flowers, although not fragrant, are a beautiful combination of red or coral on the outside with yellow-orange inside. Red fruits follow in summer. The leaves turn a dark, bluish green as they mature.

Propagation is by cuttings or seed, and trumpet honeysuckle prefers a moist, well-drained soil, although it will tolerate some drought.

Trumpet honeysuckle's colorful flowers attract swallowtail butterflies and Ruby-throated Hummingbirds, while Northern Cardinals and Gray Catbirds feed on the fruits.

summer fruit

FIELD NOTES

- ■ Zones 6–9
- ■ Deciduous
- ■ 10–20' (3–6 m) or higher
- ☀ Full sun–part shade
- 💧 Moderate

tiger swallowtail butterfly

Jackson Vine

Smilax smallii

Jackson vine is a tough vine with handsome, glaucous foliage and, when they are ripe in fall, dark, almost black, berries. A fast grower, it is also easy to control. It is a choice vine for an evergreen screen on a trellis or fence, or as an accent in the garden. Jackson vine grows in various habitats, including sandy woodlands. Leaves are used in the florist trade because they hold their color and shape long after cutting.

Propagation is by division and cuttings, and Jackson vine prefers a rich, moist, well-drained soil, although it will tolerate some drought.

| J | F | M | A | M | J | J | A | S | O | N | D |

A number of birds are attracted to the fruit of this vine, including Gray Catbirds, mockingbirds, robins, flickers, Brown Thrashers, thrushes, Pileated Woodpeckers, Northern Cardinals, sparrows, grouse, turkeys, Cedar Waxwings, and waterfowl. Lizards, such as the agile green anole, can be found climbing among the vines.

green anole

FIELD NOTES
- Zones 7–9
- Evergreen
- 20–30' (6–9 m) in a season
- ☀ Full sun–part shade
- ◐ Moderate

461

Daylily (left); sourwood (right)

Additional species

Plant name/flower color	Zone	Height	Visitors/attraction/season
HERBACEOUS FLOWERS			
Swamp sunflower (yellow) *Helianthus angustifolius*	6–9	6–8' (1.8–2.4 m)	butterflies/flowers/summer–fall birds/seeds/late summer–fall
Daylily (many) *Hemerocallis* spp. (exotic)	3–10	1–3' (30–90 cm)	butterflies/flowers/summer
Dame's rocket (white, purple) *Hesperis matronalis* (exotic)	3–9	3–4' (90–120 cm)	butterflies/flowers/spring, summer
Virginia bluebells (blue/pink) *Mertensia virginica*	3–10	2' (60 cm)	hummingbirds/flowers/spring
Flowering tobacco (white) *Nicotiana alata* (exotic)	all (annual)	2–4' (60-120 cm)	moths/flowers/summer–fall
Showy stonecrop (pink, red, white) *Sedum spectabile* (exotic)	3–10	24' (7.3 m)	butterflies/flowers/summer
SHRUBS			
Glossy abelia (white/pink) *Abelia* x *grandiflora* (exotic)	5–10	6' (1.8 m)	butterflies/flowers/summer, fall
Butterfly bush (purple, yellow, white) *Buddleia davidii* (exotic)	5–10	10' (3 m)	butterflies/flowers/summer, fall
Summersweet clethra (white) *Clethra alnifolia*	3–9	3–8' (90–240 cm)	butterflies/flowers/summer
Climbing hydrangea (white) *Decumaria barbara*	6–9	30' (9 m)	squirrels/shelter/spring
Heliotrope (violet/purple) *Heliotropium arborescens* (exotic)	9–10	6–8' (1.8–2.4 m)	butterflies/flowers/summer
Black haw (white) *Viburnum prunifolium*	3–9	15' (4.5 m)	birds/fruits/fall
TREES			
Devil's walking stick (white) *Aralia spinosa*	4–9	20' (6 m)	birds/fruits/fall
Common persimmon (white) *Diospyros virginiana*	4–9	35' (10.5 m)	opossum, deer/fruits/fall
Sweetgum (green) *Liquidambar styraciflua*	5–10	60–100' (18–30 m)	birds/seeds/fall–winter birds/nesting/spring–summer
Sourwood (white) *Oxydendrum arboreum*	5–9	30' (9 m)	bees/flowers/summer
Longleaf pine (n/a) *Pinus palustris*	5–10	100–130' (30–39 m)	birds, mammals/seeds/fall birds/nesting/spring–summer
Chaste tree (white, purple, pink, blue) *Vitex agnus-castus* (exotic)	7–10	8–10' (2.4–3 m)	butterflies/flowers/summer–fall
VINES			
Moonflower (white) *Ipomoea alba* (exotic)	9–10	10' ± (3 m) ±	moths/flowers/summer
Passion flower (lavender/white) *Passiflora incarnata*	5–10	20' (6 m)	butterflies/flowers/summer caterpillars/leaves/summer

INDEX and GLOSSARY

INDEX *and* GLOSSARY

In this combined index and glossary, **bold** page numbers indicate the main reference, and *italics* indicate illustrations and photographs. Plants are listed under both their common and scientific names.

CAPTIONS

Page 1: The Anna's Hummingbird is one of the most common and familiar hummers on the west coast.

Page 2: A native wildflower garden will attract a variety of wildlife, particularly butterflies.

Page 3: Birdwatchers look out across the marsh.

Pages 4–5: Quaking aspen (*Populus tremuloides*) forms beautiful groves, particularly in fall.

Pages 6–7: A tree hollow provides an excellent nesting site for the nocturnal screech owl.

Pages 8–9: Atlantic Puffins nest on grassy, cliff-top slopes along the northeastern coast.

Pages 10–11: The delicate beauty of frost.

Pages 12–13: After decades of scarcity, the Brown Pelican is gradually recovering its numbers.

Pages 44–45: A Northern Cardinal with Common Goldfinches at a winter birdfeeder.

Pages 58–59: Every natural garden should contain a quiet spot for people to sit and enjoy nature, and watch the wildlife their garden attracts.

Pages 70–71: Small mammals, such as the eastern chipmunk, are delightful garden visitors, particularly in fall when collecting nuts.

Pages 92–93: Flowering grass-like sedges—such as the star sedge (*Dichromena latifolia*)—provide convenient landing places for insects, such as this grasshopper.

Pages 108–109: The beautiful Roseate Spoonbill occurs only in coastal wetlands in Florida and westward along the Gulf Coast.

Pages 134–135: The Green Heron is common in the wetlands of the eastern US, but less so in the west.

Page 145: A group of starlings (*top inset*) perched on powerlines. A Blue Jay (*bottom inset*) sits on a birdfeeder.

Page 169: A Virginia's Warbler (*top inset*) foraging deep in deciduous forest. A Blue-gray Gnatcatcher (*bottom inset*) in the Everglades National Park, Florida.

Page 207: A Horned Lark (*top inset*) perches on a rock beside some California poppies. Two male prairie-chickens (*bottom inset*) compete at a lek.

Page 235: A male Barrow's Goldeneye duck (*top inset*) paddles with ducklings in Grand Teton National Park, Wyoming. A flock of Roseate Spoonbills (*bottom inset*) feed in mangroves on Sanibel Island, Florida.

Page 267: A flock of white ibises (*top inset*) fly above coastal waters. A lone Avocet (*bottom inset*) feeds at the water's edge as the sun sets.

Page 289: A tiny Rock Wren (*top inset*) sits on a desert ledge. A pair of Turkey Vultures (*bottom inset*) perch imposingly on top of a cactus.

Pages 304–305: Red-breasted Robins light up a bare, wintry garden.

Page 309: Rustic bench in a Californian dry summer garden.

Page 335: Wild buckwheats (*Eriogonum* spp.) and penstemons (*Penstemon* spp.) are colorful flowers for a wildflower garden in a mountainous region.

Page 363: The yellow flowers of desert marigold (*Baileya multiradiata*) light up the landscape.

Page 385: Even in an open prairie garden a few trees can provide useful shade and habitat for birds who prefer shelter to the wide open spaces of the plains.

Page 411: Sweeps of black-eyed Susans (*Rudbeckia hirta*) grow in the meadow gardens of the Northeast region. All plants appreciate a constant water source, such as a pond or stream.

Page 437: A woodland garden is a place to escape from the heat and enjoy a walk along a path through the glades.

Page 463: The two-spotted ladybug beetle is a common garden visitor and is found throughout North America.

PICTURE CREDITS

(t=top, b=bottom, l=left, r=right, c=center, bkgr=background)
A=Auscape International Pty Ltd; AA/ES=Animals Animals/Earth Scenes; APL=Australian Picture Library; BAL=Bridgeman Art Library, London; BCI=Bruce Coleman Inc, NY; BCL=Bruce Coleman Limited; BPL=Boltin Picture Library; BP=Biological Photo Service; Cornell=Cornell Laboratory of Ornithology; Culver=Culver Pictures, Inc.; DJC=DJC & Associates; DRK= DRK Photo; GH=Grant Heilman Photography, Inc.; IB=The Image Bank; J=Jacana; MEPL=Mary Evans Picture Library; MP= Minden Pictures; NHPA=Natural History Photographic Agency; NS=Natural Selection; NW=North Wind Picture Archives; OSF= Oxford Scientific Films Ltd; PA=Peter Arnold, Inc.; PE=Planet Earth Pictures; PI=Positive Images; PN=Photo/Nats, Inc.; PR= Photo Researchers, Inc.; S=Scala; SB=Stock Boston; TPL=The Photographic Library of Australia; TS=Tom Stack & Associates; V= Vireo; VU=Visuals Unlimited; WC=Woodfin Camp & Associates.

1 John Cancalosi/A. **2** Gay Bumgarner/PN. **3** Thomas Buchholz/BCL. **4–5** Rod Planck/NHPA. **6–7** Karen Bussolini/PI. **8–9** Frans Lanting/MP. **10–11** John Shaw/NHPA. **12–13** Alan Briere. **16** t NW; bl Jean Vertut; bkgr NW. **17** tl C M Dixon; tr David Woo/SB; c by permission of the Linnean Society of London; b Lawrence Migdale. **18** t Louvre, Paris/BAL; b William E Ferguson. **19** b Gunter Ziesler/BCL. **20** tl Giraudon/BAL; tr B Henry/V; bl John Gerlach/AA/ES; bc Wayne Lankinen/DRK; bkgr NW. **21** t MEPL; c Steven Holt/V; b Will & Deni McIntyre/PR. **22** t Frans Lanting/BCL; **23** cl Jim Zipp/PR; cr Thomas Kitchin/TS; br Lee Boltin/BPL. **24** tl Art Resource, NY/S; c Geoff Avern/Australian Museum; bl Michael Melford/IB; **26** tl John Shaw/A; cr A Morris/V; bl Stephen J Krasemann/DRK. **27** tl Stephen J Krasemann/DRK; tr Wayne Lankinen/DRK; b J Carmichael, Jr/IB. **28** tl Joe McDonald/TS; tr R J Erwin/NHPA; cl Jordan Coonrad; b Andrew J Purcell/BCL. **29** cr Palazzo Vecchio, Firenze/S; b NW; bkgr MEPL. **30** t J White/ET Archive; c Jim Brandenburg/MP; b Maslowski Productions/PR. **31** tl NW; tr Mary Clay/PE; c1 Mary Clay/TS; c2 Gary Milburn/TS; b Brian Kenney/PE. **32** tr S J Lang/V; bl Dieter & Mary Plage/BCL; **33** t J Johann Schumacher/V; tr S J Lang/V; **34** t C M Dixon; b Dr Scott Nielsen/BCL. **35** tl Diana L Stratton/TS; tr Priscilla Connell/PN; cl Phil Dotson/PR; br Thomas Kitchin/TS. **36** t A & E Morris/V; b Erich Hartmann/Magnum. **37** tl Jim Brandenburg/MP; tr Wayne Lankinen/BCL; cl Cornell. **38** t C M Dixon; bkgr Steve Maslowski/VU; br Steve Kaufman/DRK. **39** tl Don Enger/AA/ES; tr Roger Tidman/NHPA; b Wide World Photos/AP. **40** tl Michael Melford/IB; c 1, 2 & 3 Breck P Kent/AA/ES; bl Diana L Stratton/TS; bkgr Stephen J Krasemann/DRK. **41** t Life Magazine ©Time Warner/Nina Leen; c Tom J Ulrich; b Wayne Lankinen/DRK; **42** t Jonathan Blair/WC; c D Robert Franz/PE; b John Eastcott/PE. **44–45** Tom Vander-schmidt/AA/ES. **46** tl J H Robinson/PR; tr Harry Haralambou/PI; cr Daniel J Cox/DJC; bl Culver. **47** t Casa del Bracciale d'Oro, Pompeii/S; b John Cancalosi/BCL. **48** t Colin McRae Photography; tl George H Harrison/Grant Heilman Photography; bl Ron Austing. **49** br Daniel J Cox/DJC. **50** Colin McRae Photography; tl Sam Fried/V; bl Stephen J Krasemann/DRK; **51** Colin McRae Photography; cl George H Harrison/Grant Heilman Photography; br Robert A Tyrrell/OSF. **52** tr Phillips, The International Fine Art Auction/BAL; bl Gay Bumgarner/PN; br Mary Clay/PE. **53** tr Jane Burton/BCL; cl C M Dixon; br Jim Brandenburg/MP; bkgr Joe McDonald/TS. **54** Colin McRae Photography; tl Jerry Howard/PI; bl Stephen J Krasemann/NHPA. **55** tr Jack Dermid/OSF; cr Ron Austing; bl Lang Elliott/Cornell. **56** tr Casa del Bracciale d'Oro, Pompeii/S; bkgr NW; br Grace Davies/Envision. **57** t C C Lockwood/AA/ES; c Patti Murray/AA/ES. **58–59** Saxon Holt. **60** t The Granger Collection, NY; b D Cavagnaro/DRK. **61** tl Sonja Bullaty & Angelo Lomeo; tr Stephen J Krasemann/DRK; b Jerry Howard/PI. **62** t Archive Photos/APL; b Sonja Bullaty & Angelo Lomeo. **63** tl John Gerlach/DRK; tr Mike Read/PI; b Richard Shiell/AA/ES. **64** t Courtesy of Hunt Institute for Botanical Documentation, Carnegie Mellon University, Pittsburgh, PA. **64–65** Renee Lynn/PR. **65** t Pamela J Harper; b D Cavagnaro/VU. **66** t R & D Aitkenhead/PI; b Tim Firzharris/Masterfile/Stock Photos. **67** Sonja Bullaty & Angelo Lomeo. **68** t Lee Lock-wood/PI; b Jerry Howard/PI. **69** l Robert A Lubeck/AA/ES; tr Margaret Hensel/PI; c & b Jerry Howard/PI. **70** t Pat O'Hara; ic Tom Bean/DRK; r Stephen G Maka/PN. **70–71** Daniel J Cox/DJC. **72–73** t Dan Griggs/NHPA; b Jerry Howard/PI. **73** Saxon Holt. **74** t Patti Murray/AA/ES; b Charlie Palek/AA/ES. **75** l Les Campbell/PI; tr Sonja Bullaty and Angelo Lomeo; b Saxon Holt. **76** t Martin Mills/PI; r Dick Canby/PI; b Elvan Habicht/AA/ES. **77** t Saxon Holt; b John Gerlach/DRK. **78** t Tom & Pat Leeson/PR; b Jerry Howard/PI. **79** t Charles Mann; c Doug Wechsler/AA/ES; b Daniel J Cox/DJC. **80** Pamela J Harper. **81** tl Rich Kirchner/NHPA; tr Leonard Lee Rue IV/BCI; cr Ken Cole/AA/ES; bl S Nielsen/DRK; br Doug Wechsler/AA/ES. **82** t Wayne Lankinen/DRK; r Link/VU. **83** tl Mary Clay/PE; tr David McDonald; bl Carole Ottesen; br Jon Mark Stewart/BPS. **84** t Jerry Howard/PI; r John Neubauer; b Margaret Hensel/PI. **85** t Kathy Merrifield/PR; l W J Weber/VU; bl D Cavagnaro. **86** t Stephen Dalton/NHPA; r Charles Mann; b Dennis Frates/PI. **87** t Virginia Twinam-Smith/PN; l Jerry Howard/PI; b Wayne Lankinen/PI. **88** bl John Neubauer; r D Cavagnaro. **88–89** Saxon Holt. **89** John Shaw/NHPA. **90** t The Granger Collection, NY; r Jerry Howard/Positive Images. **91** tl Patti Murray/AA/ES; tr Priscilla Connell/Envision; br & l Jerry Howard/PI. **92–93** Leo Meier. **94** t S Dalton/NHPA; b Jacob Mosser III/PI. **95** t Margaret Hensel/PI; c John Shaw/NHPA; b John Shaw/A. **96** t George Sanker/DRK; bl Milton Rand/TS; br John Gerlach/DRK. **97** t Dwight R Kuhn/BCI; b S Nielsen/DRK. **98** tl The Granger Collection, NY; tr D Cavagnaro/DRK; b W Greene/V. **99** Robert A Tyrrell/OSF/AA/ES. **100** bl Robert A Tyrrell/OSF; br C H Greenwalt/AA/ES. **101** tl Humm-Zinger by Aspects/photo C Fogle; tr Robert A Tyrrell/OSF/AA/ES; b The Granger Collection, NY. **102** t John Gerlach/DRK; b Les Campbell/PI. **103** tl Stephen J Krasemann/DRK; tr John Parker/PI; bl Bob & Clara Calhoun/BCL; br Stephen J Krasemann/DRK. **104** t Dogwood and Mockingbird by Mark Catesby from the National History of Carolina (1730-48)/Lindley Library, RHS, London/BAL; c Paul Rezendes/PI; bl John Cancalosi/DRK; br Barbara Gerlach/DRK. **105** t John Gerlach/DRK; c John Shaw/NHPA; b Hal H Harrison/DRK. **106** t Steven M Rollman/NS; r E R Degginger/BCI; b James R Fisher/DRK. **107** t Merlin D Tuttle/Bat Conservation International Inc; b Brian Kenney/PE. **108–109** John Hall/AA/ES. **110** tl, r, & cl Colin McRae Photography; cr Jiri Lochman; bl Susan Day. **111** t Hellio-Van Ingen/J/A; b Colin McRae Photography. **112** tl Paul Resendez/PI; tr Colin McRae Photography; b Dennis Frates/PI; inset Brock May/PR. **113** t & c Stephen J Krasemann/DRK; **114** tl Tom Bean/DRK; cr William H Mullins/PR; cc Colin McRae Photography; b Jim Brandenburg/MP. **115** tl William M Smithey, Jr/PE; tr Jack Wilburn/AA/ES; bl Richard Day; br Stephen J Krasemann/DRK. **116** t Culver; c Ron Austing; b Stephen J Krasemann/PR. **117** tl Jerry Howard/PI; tr Leonard Lee Rue/PR; cl John Cancalosi/DRK; bl J H Robinson/PR. **118** t Marie Read/BCL; c Jon Mark Stewart/Biological Photo Service; b Frans Lanting/MP. **119** b George Holton/PR. **120** tl Steve Maslowski/PR; cl A Morris/V; bl Charlie Ott/BCL. **121** tr Dr Scott Nielsen/DRK; cr Jean-Paul Ferrero/A; b John Cancalosi/BCL. **122** t Colin McRae Photography; cr John Shaw/TS; br Cynthia Berger/Cornell; bkgr NW. **123** tl Haroldo Castro; bl Colin McRae Photography; tr Rod Planck/TS; bl Steve Pantle. **124** tl Art Resource, NY/S; bl Colin McRae Photography. **125** bl Candice Cochrane/PI; tr Colin McRae Photography; cr Mark Catesby/BPL; bl Cornell; bc Culver; br NW. **126** tl & r Colin McRae Photography; bl & r Joe McDonald/AA/ES. **127** t Courtesy R Gunz & Co Pty Ltd & Cannon Australia; bl Alan Briere; br Daniel J Cox/DJC. **128** tl Julie O'Neil/PN; cl Ron Austing; bl Alan Briere. **129** tr NW; tl Richard Day; bl Jim Kahnweiler/PI; bc William H Mullins/PR; br Frans Lanting/MP. **130** tl Daniel J Cox/DJC; bl Culver; br NW. **131** tr Ron Austing; bl Annie Griffiths Belt/DRK; br Tom McHugh/PR. **132** tr John Shaw/NHPA; cl Kenneth W Fink/PR; cc Mary Clay/PN; cr Anthony Mercieca/NS; br John Cancalosi/DRK. **133** tl Tom McHugh/PR; tc Stephen J Krasemann/DRK; tr Liz Ball/PN; cr Jeff Lepore/PR; br M P Kahl/DRK; **134–135** John Shaw/NHPA. **136** tl John Shaw/A; b Frank Huber/OSF; **136–143** bkgr Frans Lanting/MP. **137** tl A & E Morris/V; tr Peter Gasson/PE. **138** t Peter Gasson/PE. **139** t John Shaw/A; cl Gil Lopez-Espina/NS; c2 John Cancalosi/A; b Frank Schneidermeyer/OSF. **140** tl Gordon Langsbury/BCL; tr Joseph Van Wormer/BCL; bl Francois Gohier/A. **141** tl Francois Gohier/A; tr Bob & Clara Calhoun/BCL; bl Wayne Lankinen/BCL; br John Cancalosi/A. **142** bl Mark Schumann/PE; bc Wayne Lankinen/BCL; br Glenn Jahnke/Root Resources. **143** tl Stan Osolinski/OSF; tr Stephen J Krasemann/NHPA. **145** bkgr Jerry Howard/PI; t Frans Lanting/MP; Richard Hutchings/PR. **146** t Daniel J Cox/OSF; cl D Newman/VU; br G Dremeaux/V; bl Daniel J Cox/VU. **147** tl Bullaty-Lomeo Photo; tc Galen Rowell/Mountain Light; tr John Cancalosi/A; b Julie O'Neil/PN. **148** Manfred Danegger/A. **149** Ron Austing. **150** Nick

Bergkessel/TPL. **151** F K Schleicher/V. **152** Tom Ulrich/OSF. **153** Hans Reinhard/BCL. **154** Wayne Lankinen/BCL. **155** John Shaw/BCL. **156–7** Robert P Carr/BCL. **158** S J Lang/V. **159** John Shaw/A. **160** Wayne Lankinen/BCL. **161** A Morris/V. **162** J Cancalosi/A. **163** P La Tourette/V. **164–5** A & E Morris/V. **166** Dr Scott Nielsen/BCL. **167** A & E Morris/V. **168** R Villani/V. **169** bkgr Catherine Ursillo/PR; t D & M Zimmerman/V; b Eric A Soder/NHPA. **170** J Krasemann/DRK; cr C R Sams II & J F Stoik/V; br Michael Leach/OSF; bl Roger Tidman/NHPA. **171** Tom Ulrich/OSF; c1 Dick Scott/A; c2 Roger Tidman/NHPA; b Francis Lepine/AA/ES. **172** Leonard Lee Rue/BCL. **173** Brian Hawks/A. **174** John Cancalosi/A. **175** Tom & Pat Leeson/DRK. **176** Stan Osolinski/OSF. **177** Dick Scott/A. **178** John Cancalosi/A. **179** R & N Bowers/V. **180** S J Lang/V. **181** Mary Clay/PE. **182** Ron Austing. **183** A & E Morris/V. **184** W Greene/V. **185** Marie Read/BCL. **186** Bob & Clara Calhoun/BCL. **187** P La Tourette/V. **188** B Schorre/V. **189** A & E Morris/V. **190–1** B Schorre/V. **192** A & E Morris/V. **193** Will Troyer/VU. **194** B Schorre/V. **195** A & E Morris/V. **196** Bob & Clara Calhoun/BCL. **197** Stephen J Krasemann/BCL. **198** Stephen J Krasemann/J/A. **199** Hector Rivarola/BCL. **200** Bob & Clara Calhoun/BCL. **201** Wayne Lankinen/BCL. **202** Jack Dermid/BCL. **203** Wayne Lankinen/BCL. **204** Marie Read/BCL. **205–6** B Schorre/V. **207** bkgr R J Erwin/DRK; t Franz J Camenzind/PE; b Richard Thom/VU. **208** t Leonard Lee Rue/BCL; bl Paul Rezendes/PI; cr Marie Read/BCL; Joe McDonald/TS. **209** t Lone E Lauber/OSF; bl Michael Sacca/AA/ES; br Rod Planck/NHPA. **210** Jean-Louis le Moigne/A. **211** Werner Layer/A. **212** Francois Gohier/BCL. **213–4** Bob & Clara Calhoun/BCL. **215** Francois Gohier/A. **216** Leonard Lee Rue/BCL. **217** Gens/J/A. **218** S J Lang/V. **219** George McCarthy/BCL. **220** Francois Gohier/A. **221** Robert P Carr/BCL. **222** Leonard Lee Rue/A. **223** C B Frith/BCL. **224** John Shaw/A. **225** Stephen J Krasemann/J/A. **226** A & E Morris/V. **227** Wayne Lankinen/BCL. **228** Tom Ulrich/OSF. **229** Bernd Thies/BCL. **230** W Greene/V. **231** A & E Morris/V. **232** Cyril de Klemm/A. **233** M P Kahl/BCL. **234** Wayne Lankinen/BCL. **235** bkgr Helen Cruickshank/V; t Scott McKinley/PE, b Jeff Foott/A. **236** t Wayne Lynch/DRK; bl R Glover/BCL; br Stephen J Krasemann/BCL. **237** Joe & Carol McDonald/TS; tr Helen Cruickshank/V; bl & r Stephen J Krasemann/PA. **238** Dr Scott Nielsen/BCL. **239** G Nuechterlein/V. **240** Erwin & Peggy Bauer/BCL. **241** Shaw/A. **242** John Shaw/BCL. **243** Jeff Foott/A. **244** John Shaw/A. **245** Rinie Van Meurs/BCL. **246** Erwin & Peggy Bauer/A. **247** Jack Dermid/BCL. **248** W Greene/V. **249** Tom Walker/A. **250** Gordon Langsbury/BCL. **251** Erwin & Peggy Bauer/A. **252** Dr Scott Nielsen/BCL. **253** J R Woodward/V. **254–5** Dr Scott Nielsen/BCL. **256** Erwin & Peggy Bauer/A. **257** Fritz Polking/A. **258** John Shaw/A. **259** Dr Scott Nielsen/BCL. **260** Dr Scott Nielsen/BCL. **261** A & E Morris/V. **262** Johann Schumacher/V. **263** F K Schleicher/V. **264–5** A & E Morris/V. **266** Stephen J Krasemann/J/A. **267** bkgr Brett Froomer/IB; t Brian Alker/PE; b Hermann Brehm/BCL. **268** t Francois Gohier/A; bl Francois Gohier/PR; John Shaw/TS; br A & E Morris/V. **269** tl Frans Lanting/MP; tr Stephen J Krasemann/DRK. **270** Erwin & Peggy Bauer/A. **271** T H Davis/V. **272–3** Francois Gohier/A. **274** Werner Layer/A. **275** H Clarke/V. **276** A & E Morris/V. **277** John Shaw/A. **278** Doug Wechsler/V. **279** A & E Morris/V. **280** A & E Morris/V. **281** Jean-Louis Dubois/A. **282** Gordon Langsbury/BCL. **283** John Shaw/A. **284** Francois Gohier/A. **285** Philippe Prigent/A. **286** Helen Cruickshank/V. **287** A & E Morris/V. **288** M & A Boet/A. **289** D & M Zimmerman/V; t Rob Curtis/V; b Francois Gohier/A. **290** t Tom Bean; bl Larry Ulrich/DRK; br C Allan Morgan/DRK. **291** t Doug Wechsler/V; cr Kennan Ward/DRK; bl John Cancalosi/DRK; br Pat O'Hara. **292** J Hoffman/V. **293** John Cancalosi/BCL. **294** Jeff Foott/BCL. **295** Bob & Clara Calhoun/BCL. **296** Francois Gohier/A. **297** P La Tourette/V. **298** John Cancalosi/A. **299** Bob & Clara Calhoun/BCL. **300** John Cancalosi/A. **301** Jeff Foott/BCL. **302** John Cancalosi/DRK. **303** Charlie Oti/BCL. **304–5** Daniel J Cox/DJC. **306–7** Ken Druse/The Natural Garden. **308–9** Saxon Holt. **312** Harry Smith Collection. **313** Ken Druse/The Natural Garden. **314** Harry Smith Collection. **315** Saxon Holt. **316** Charles Mann. **317** Dr Glenn Keator. **318** Eric Crichton/BCL. **319** Saxon Holt. **320** C. Colston Burrell. **321** Roger Raiche. **322** Carl May/BPS. **323** Saxon Holt. **324** Bruce A Macdonald/AA/ES. **325** Robert C. Perry. **326** David McDonald. **327** Carl May/BPS. **328** Jack Wilburn/AA/ES. **329** Saxon Holt. **330** D Cavagnaro. **331** David Middleton/NHPA. **332** John Shaw/TS. **333** Dr Glenn Keator. **334** l Hal Benzl/VU; r D Cavagnaro. **335** Saxon Holt. **338** Charles Mann. **339** George F Godfrey/AA/ES. **340** Charles Mann.

341 Stephen J Krasemann/DRK. **342** Saxon Holt. **343** Charles Mann. **344** David A Ponton/PE. **345** Tom Bean/DRK. **346** Barbara J. Miller/BPS. **347** Jim Knopf. **348** Charles Mann. **349** W D Bransford/National Wildflower Research Center. **350** Milton Rand/TS. **351** Valorie Hodgson/PN. **352** David A Ponton/PE. **353** Kahout Productions/Root Resources. **354** Larry Ulrich/DRK. **355** Charles Mann. **356** Andy Wasowski. **357** Patti Murray/AA/ES. **358** Breck P Kent/AA/ES. **359** Willard Luce/AA/ES. **360** David Middleton/NHPA. **361** Richard Shiell/AA/ES. **362** l Saxon Holt; r Robert E Heapes. **363** Charles Mann. **366** Larry Ulrich/DRK. **367** Rod Planck/NHPA. **368** Doug Sokell/TS. **369** Kahout Productions/Root Resources. **370** Patti Murray/AA/ES. **371** Leo Meier. **372–3** Andy Wasowski. **374** Ken Druse/The Natural Garden. **375** Mickey Gibson/AA/ES. **376** Jon Mark Stewart/BPS. **377** Charles Mann. **378** Scooter Cheatham. **379** Charles Mann. **380** Saxon Holt. **381** Andy Wasowski. **382** Gregory G Dimijian/PR. **383** Francois Gohier/A. **384** l Charles Mann; r W D Bransford/National Wildflower Research Center. **385** Saxon Holt. **388** Charles Mann. **389** Stephen Trimble/DRK. **390** Susan Gibler/TS. **391** Zig Leszczynski/AA/ES. **392** John Lemker/AA/ES. **393** Ken Druse/The Natural Garden. **394–5** Charles Mann. **396** Charles Mann. **397** Ken Druse/The Natural Garden. **398** Leo Meier. **399** Charles Mann. **400** Charles Mann. **401** Doug Wechsler/AA/ES. **402** Pam Spaulding/PI. **403** Robert E Heapes. **404** David Stone/PN. **405** Jeff March/PN. **406** E R Hasselkus/Arboretum, University of Wisconsin, Madison. **407** Wendy Shatil & Bob Rozinski/TS. **408** Pat Kennedy/NS. **409** Harry Smith Collection. **410** l D Cavagnaro; r Leo Meier. **411** Sonja Bullaty & Angelo Lomeo. **414** David Stone/PN. **415** Jerry Howard/PI. **416** E R Degginger/AA/ES. **417** Rod Planck/NHPA. **418** Ann Reilly/PN. **419** Ken Druse/The Natural Garden. **420** Jeff Lepore/PR. **421** Stephen G Maka/PN. **422** Michael P Gadomski/AA/ES. **423** Paul Rezendes/PI. **424–5** Ken Druse/The Natural Garden. **426** Les Campbell/PI. **427** Patti Murray/AA/ES. **428** Pam Spaulding/PI. **429** Walter H Hodge/PA. **430** Robert P Carr/BCI. **431** Jerry Howard/PI. **432** Larry Lefever/GH. **433** David McDonald. **434** Pamela J Harper. **435** Jerry Howard/PI. **436** l Jerry Howard/PI; r William J Weber/VU. **437** Saxon Holt. **440** Wendell Metzen/BCI. **441** Ken Druse/The Natural Garden. **442–3** Ken Druse/The Natural Garden. **444** Robert E Lyons/PN. **445** Pamela J Harper. **446–7** Pamela J Harper. **448** Stan Osolinski/OSF. **449** D Cavagnaro. **450** John Shaw/NHPA. **451** Larry Lefever/G H. **452** Michael P Gadomski/PR. **453** Eric Crichton/BCL. **454** David McDonald. **455** Andy Wasowski. **456** Lucy Jones/VU. **457** Jack Dermid/BCL. **458** Tyler Gearhardt/Envision. **459** Deni Brown/OSF. **460** Harry Smith Collection. **461** Dr Glenn Keator. **462** l Steve Solum/BCI; r Andy & Sally Wasowski. **463** S Neilsen/DRK.

ILLUSTRATION CREDITS

Anne Bowman 38, 43, 57. **Simon Darby** 62. **Helen Halliday** Bandings 146–271. **David Kirshner** 18, 19t, 22. **Frank Knight** 23, 29, 99, 120–121. **Terence Lindsey** 161, 165, 173, 198, 199, 222. **Angela Lober** 72, 314, 315, 317, 323, 325, 331, 333, 355, 376, 381, 441, 442, 443, 444, 447, 453, 454, 456. **Robert Mancini** 32, 33, 88, 113, 148, 149, 154, 155, 158, 159, 162, 163, 164, 167, 168, 174, 175, 178, 179, 182, 183, 186, 187, 190, 191, 196, 197, 200, 201, 203, 204, 205, 206, 212, 213, 216, 217, 220, 221, 224, 225, 228, 229, 232, 233, 240, 241, 244, 245, 248, 249, 250, 251, 252, 253, 256, 257, 259, 260, 262, 263, 264, 270, 271, 274, 275, 279, 280, 281, 283, 284, 285, 287 288, 292, 293, 296, 297, 298, 300, 301, 303, 316, 318, 319, 321, 324, 327, 329, 330, 332, 338, 340, 346, 348, 354, 358, 359, 360, 367, 368, 370, 373, 374, 375, 377, 389, 390, 394, 403, 404, 408, 407, 409, 416, 418, 421, 422, 425, 427, 429, 434, 440, 445, 446, 448, 450, 451, 452, 455, 457, 458. **Robert Morton** 14–15. **Nicola Oram** 312, 328, 339, 341, 342, 343, 344, 345, 347, 349, 351, 352, 353, 356, 366, 369, 372, 378, 379, 380, 383, 391, 392, 393, 395, 399, 400, 402, 405, 408, 414, 415, 417, 419, 423, 424, 428, 432, 435, 459. **Maurice Pledger** 112, 277, 294. **Ngaire Sales** 81, 310, 311, 334, 335, 364, 365, 386, 387, 412, 413, 438, 439. **Steve Travaskis** 133. **Genevieve Wallace** 313, 320, 322, 326, 350, 357, 361, 371, 382, 388, 396, 397, 398, 401, 420, 426, 430, 431, 449, 460, 461. **Trevor Weekes** 150, 151, 152, 153, 156, 157, 160, 161, 164, 165, 172, 173, 176, 177, 180, 181, 184, 185, 188, 189, 192, 193, 194, 195, 198, 199, 202, 203, 210, 211, 214, 215, 218, 219, 222, 223, 226, 227, 230, 230, 234, 238, 239, 242, 243, 246, 247, 250, 251, 254, 255, 258, 261, 265, 266, 272, 273, 276, 278, 279, 282, 283, 286, 295, 399, 402. **David Wood** 14–15, 67, 119.

Jefferson County Library
P.O. Box 990/620 Cedar Ave.
Port Hadlock, WA 98339
(360) 385-6544
www.jclibrary.info